CHILD WELFARE

*principles
and
methods*

CHILD
WELFARE

NEW YORK · JOHN WILEY & SONS, INC.

London · Chapman & Hall, Limited

principles
and
methods

DOROTHY ZIETZ
M.S.W., Ph.D.

Associate Professor of Social Welfare

Sacramento State College

Sacramento, California

*It is a frequent Saying in our Law-Books,
De Minimus non curat Lex; which is true if
it be understood of Things and minute
Circumstances, but if we apply it to Persons,
it is not so; for it is most certain, that our
Law hath a very great and tender consideration
for Persons naturally Disabled and especially
for Minors. The Law protects their Persons,
preserves their rights and Estates, Excuseth
their Laches, and assists them in their Pleadings.
. . . They are under the Special Aid and Protection
of his Equity, who is no less than Keeper of the
King's Conscience. . . .*

THE INFANT'S LAWYER, 1712

Preface

The twentieth century has been called the "Age of the Child." This characterization has some validity in the sense that modern medicine, psychiatry, psychology, sociology, and social work have opened doors to a new understanding of the needs of the child and of the services required to meet those needs. Conversely, however, our children still live in a world colored by traditional ways of thinking about their behavior, about the location of responsibility for their welfare, and about the type of services that can best meet their needs.

Professional persons and informed lay groups with deep concern about the lack of services for children in their communities are often frustrated by the tenacity with which the general citizenry clings to outmoded methods of child care or, at best, shows only apathetic interest in developing needed services. Too often those who would create a brave new world for children have not understood the strong influence of tradition upon our culture. Those who seek to equip children to cope with the complexities of modern living are often perplexed, too, by the widespread survival of negative attitudes which affect the welfare of the child—directly or through the social institutions which they preserve. Without an understanding of their historical roots, regional differences or geographic variations in the pattern of child care may seem equally puzzling.

The child's world is inherently related to those things that have meaning to him: his family, his school, his church, his community, and his contemporaries. It is through these that he learns to trust and to love the people and the ideals that create his universe. It is through these relationships, too, that he learns to think, to act, and to believe in himself and in his special destiny.

Many children still have limited opportunities for positive and constructive identifications, for economic and social well-being, or for the development of healthy personalities. Children become the unhappy victims of family pressures and breakdowns, death separates children from their parents, and often children with parents are caught in a stream of emotional upset from which neither the child nor the parent is able to extricate himself. Often children have physical or intellectual problems which set them aside and accentuate their "difference."

This book is written about the child with special needs and the programs and services that have been developed in his behalf. In general, it describes services available for the socially, physically, and intellectually handicapped child. The reader will learn, however, that his community has become a partner with the state and federal government in its earnest hope to preserve family living and to provide a more hopeful tomorrow for those children who must live away from their own homes.

The book is addressed to the college classroom. It provides a backdrop for an examination of current services and traces the origins and antecedents of the various methods through which our communities attempt to meet the needs of children today. It shows, too, the evolution of the principles on which contemporary services to children are based. The development of casework, social group work, and community organization as the three basic methods in social work is also described as well as the modern settings in which these methods are used for the benefit of children.

Although the material is presented from the social welfare, social action, and planning point of view, it indicates clearly the interrelationships of social work, medicine, nursing, education, psychiatry, psychology, and law. For the student who will enter any of these professions, it will provide a broad base of understanding upon which more specialized knowledge can be built. For others, the book presents a bird's eye view of existing services, which may have value to them as they take their place in the affairs of their community.

I am grateful to the many persons who helped in making this book a reality. It might never have been written had it not been for a group of teachers, interested lay people and social workers in Marion, Ohio, who suggested that I transpose my lecture notes into book form. It was this extension class which inspired my belief that the needs of children will be better served if the problems of child welfare can be discussed widely, frankly, and sensitively.

Writing this book has given new meanings to the past and a better basis for evaluating the services and programs available to the child of this century. Since this would have been impossible without the dedicated efforts of the men and women from whose work I have drawn so freely, I express my gratitude to them as well as to my contemporaries who have enriched my knowledge of the child's status and his welfare.

Special thanks are due many of my colleagues who read selected parts of the manuscript and offered helpful counsel, to the librarians at the California State Library, the California State Department of Social Welfare Library and the Sacramento State College Library. Miss Elizabeth Ann Fagunes, Mrs. Hazel Donat, and Mrs. Carol Larsen provided excellent assistance in editing and typing the manuscript.

My greatest debt, however, is to Mrs. Dorothy M. Kurtz, whose long and devoted experience in the child welfare field was invaluable and inspirational to me. Mrs. Kurtz read the manuscript in its entirety and suggested many of the ways by which the content was developed in perspective, scope, and meaning.

DOROTHY ZIETZ

Sacramento, California
February 1959

Contents

xi

Part Three
The Child in the Twentieth Century

Part Four
Children in Need of Special Protection

Part Five
Services for Children with Special Needs

CHILD *principles*
and
WELFARE *methods*

Part One · The Inheritance

Although more than three hundred years have passed

since the first communities in America were established,

many of our laws, our concepts of child care,

and our methods of financing needed services for children

have their roots in the social, economic,

and religious problems of pre-Colonial England

and in the legal and social institutions

which our ancestors developed to meet these problems.

# of a New Nation

Chapter 1   *Our English Heritage*

*A*merican public welfare policies and practices are often regarded as having their most significant identification with the Elizabethan Poor Law of 1601. However true this is, there can be little understanding of the quality of our English heritage without at least a telescopic observation of other influences which preceded, followed, or were concurrent with that legislation.

THE OLD ORDER CHANGES

Feudalism, with its economic and social cleavage and strong class consciousness, was rapidly disintegrating by the end of the fourteenth century. In this process, paternalism was repudiated and rejected by the serf, who now sought mobility and work for wages. Inexperienced in the use of his freedom, the newly emancipated servant quickly became aware of the devastating insecurities it afforded.

3

For many years the churches, guilds, and private philanthropy had been able to sustain the poor by offering food, shelter, clothing, and the essentials of existence. By the time feudalism weakened, however, the church had lost its power and its sources of amelioration were gone. As the number of freemen grew, problems increased not only for the man who no longer had recourse to his master, but for the king and Parliament as well.

THE STATUTE OF LABOURERS

The Statute of Labourers, England's first poor law, enacted in 1349, was premised on many years of domestic tragedy. England had suffered a severe famine which lasted for almost a decade. In 1348 the plague, or Black Death, ravaged the kingdom and a third of the population perished. The scarcity of labor became a critical problem since previously enslaved workmen were now free to offer their services to whomever they wished. The advantages of serfdom, and the master's reliance on enforced servitude, again became highly desirable and significant to the lawmakers. This situation produced an urgency to recapitulate one of the major characteristics of feudalism—the power to affix a man and his family to the community by law.

The Statute of Labourers attempted to control the scarce labor supply through rigid restrictions which approximated slavery. Not only was the laborer forbidden to travel, but he was compelled to work for those who demanded his services and he could not refuse work and accept alms. If the worker left his enforced employment, he could be recovered and reclaimed by the employer and, at the discretion of the justices, branded on the forehead with the letter F symbolizing his falsity.

OTHER STATUTES

By 1531, poverty and begging had increased and legislation was enacted when it appeared necessary to provide for those in real and desperate need. Parliament therefore empowered mayors, justices of the peace, and other local officials to locate all poor persons who were aged or impotent (incapacitated) and to certify their eligibility to engage in begging. The registered beggar was to be allowed to beg only within an assigned area, while the able-bodied and voluntarily unemployed were to be severely punished for their idleness. The enactment of this law is considered the first positive step taken by England in meeting economic deprivation.[1]

In spite of the institution of laws to control vagrancy and begging, the number of paupers continued to increase. By 1536, legislation was enacted to deter the "valiant beggar" or "sturdy vagabond" and idle wandering became punishable, first by whipping and then by the return of the beggar to his place of residence. If the vagrancy continued, the individual was subject to removal of the upper part of the gristle of the right ear or execution as a felon. More compassion was afforded those who were unable to provide for themselves, since the governors of all cities, towns, parishes and hamlets were directed to "find and keep every aged, poor and impotent person, who was born or dwelt three years within the same limit, by way of voluntary and charitable alms . . . so as none of them shall be compelled to go openly in begging."[2]

Children under fourteen and above five who were found to be living in idleness or begging were to be bound into industrial or agricultural service by the justices or other officials.

THE STATUTE OF ARTIFICERS

In 1563, under the Statute of Artificers, children could be compulsorily used for "the better advancement of husbandry and tillage," and any householder who was at least 24 years of age and "having and using half a plow land at least in tillage" was allowed to receive an indentured child above the age of 10 and under the age of 18. Children were to be indentured for at least seven years or until the age of 21 or 24. The sons of freemen who were not engaged in husbandry or in any other type of labor could also be bound out as apprentices to artisans for seven years. If indenture was refused, the justices of the peace, the mayor, or other governmental official had the authority to bind the child out.[3]

---

[1] Karl de Schweinitz, *England's Road to Social Security 1349–1947* (Philadelphia: University of Pennsylvania Press, third revised edition, 1947), pp. 20–21.

[2] 27 Henry VIII, c. 25 (1535) Great Britain, Statutes at Large, IV, in Grace Abbott, *The Child and the State* (Chicago: University of Chicago Press, 1938), I, p. 91.

[3] *Ibid.*, pp. 91–97.

Voluntary Support of the Poor

The parish had long been the unit of local administration and for many years the churchwarden and archdeacon had been empowered to solicit and collect voluntary contributions for the care of the sick, the aged, and orphaned children.

We are indebted to the historian Ware for an interesting insight into this ecclesiastical approach to government. Non-parishioners were highly suspect, and especially so if they had dealings with the parish. For them, wedding and funeral fees were doubled and settlement would never have been extended to "foreign" individuals if the local parishioners had had their way, even though these non-natives had lived within the parish for many years.[4]

Ware also reports the "organized hypocrisy" which characterized parish life, especially as it related to supposedly immoral single women. It was not a crusade for morality that stimulated these attitudes but rather the fear that the community would be burdened with the support of the child born out of wedlock.

They were apprehensive, they say, lest by this licentious life of hers not only God's wrath may be powered downe uppon us . . . but also hir evill example may so greatly corrupt others than great and extraordinary charge . . . may be imposed uppon us.[5]

The First General Tax
for the Support of the Poor

England first instituted legislation for the collection of taxes for relief purposes in 1572. The law decreed that "aged poor, impotent and decayed persons" who were born within the county or who had resided there for three years be located, "registered, and assigned to meet and convenient places . . . for their habitations and abidings." The justices were authorized to tax and assess the inhabitants for the recipients' care at a weekly rate and to appoint collectors who, along with the Overseers of the Poor, would administer the program. There was also a beginning recognition of the need to extend help to the able-bodied poor, in that surplus funds not needed for the care of

---

[4] Sedley Lynch Ware, *The Elizabethan Parish in its Ecclesiastical and Financial Aspects* (The Johns Hopkins University Studies in Historical and Political Science, Series XXXVI, Nos. 7 and 8. Baltimore: Johns Hopkins University Press, 1908), p. 91.

[5] *Ibid.*, p. 92.

the impotent poor were to be used to "place and settle to work the rogues and vagabonds"[6] who were born within the county or who had been in residence there for three years.

Children fared little better in this legislation than before, since indenture and apprenticeship remained the principal methods of child care.

The Poor Laws of 1597 and 1601

Since the poor law legislation of 1597 provided the blueprint for the 1601 law, these acts have equal importance. Their provisions served as the nucleus for more than two centuries of poor law legislation and administration, and reflected a final acknowledgment of the transition from the tyranny of feudalistic paternalism to the ultimate responsibility of government in matters of categorical indigency.

The 1597 legislation was based on the urgency of the times and the perils induced by domestic tragedy. The Webbs point out that the years 1594–98 were critical periods of high prices, starvation, and internal rebellion. The prolonged cold rains affected the growing crops and grain rose to famine prices. Unemployment was widespread; the towns were populated by beggars; and men, women, and children died of hunger in the streets.

The 1597 Poor Law is significant because it required that Overseers of the Poor be appointed in every parish to share responsibility with the churchwarden in relief matters relating to the destitution of the impotent, the able-bodied, the infirm, the aged, and the dependent child. The overseers were to levy a direct tax on every inhabitant within the parish and to administer the program under the supervision of the justices of the peace.

The specific content of the 1597 statute is interesting not only in terms of its clearly delineated categories of recipients but also in the way in which it translates into law the policies and character of Elizabethan life and thinking. Although assistance was no longer restricted to those belonging to the parish, the justices were authorized to commit any able-bodied person who would not work to the House of Correction. There was strong emphasis on support by relatives; parents were to maintain their own children and the children of their par-

---

[6] Sidney and Beatrice Webb, *English Local Government: English Poor Law History* (London and New York: Longmans, Green and Company, 1927), Part I, p. 52.

ents and grandparents if they were able to do so. The aged and impotent poor were to receive relief, either by alms or by employment provided for them, and the parish was empowered to build an almshouse for their care. Poor children were to be indentured or apprenticed by the Overseers of the Poor.[7]

At the time, the national experiment of 1597 proved workable and fulfilled its objectives. The Elizabethan Poor Law of 1601 merely reinforced, in more definite terms, the intent of the earlier legislation to charge each local community with the care of its dependent adults and children. The administration of the 1601 law demonstrates, however, that local autonomy, with all of its diverse and peculiar uniqueness, soon formulates patterns of its own, interprets laws to its own liking, or rejects these laws completely if it so chooses. It indicates, too, that provincialism tends to separate the local community from centralized government in the area of finance, in social and political policy, and even in matters relating to individual behavior and morality. This premise is borne out by the fact that the English parishes had a myriad of approaches to the interpretation and enforcement of the 1601 legislation. The Webbs, in their exhaustive study of poor law administration, felt certain that throughout the entire seventeenth century there were a great many parishes in which no overseers were appointed and many more in which provision for the poor amounted only to a casual dole.

OTHER ATTEMPTS
TO SOLVE THE PROBLEM OF DEPENDENCY

The diversity of proposals how best to handle the continuing pauper problem was most evident in the matter of dependent children.

Thomas Firmin, a successful Little Britain businessman, saw the possibility of creating profits from the employment of poor children. To achieve this, he established a combination school, factory, wholesale warehouse, and retail shop where children were admitted from the age of three and were taught to read and spin. So convinced was Mr. Firmin regarding the wisdom of employing children in this manner that he suggested that homework be furnished to the indigent mothers of small children in every parish.

In a pamphlet entitled "A Letter to a Friend," Firmin wrote of his own experience with the useful employment of children. He ex-

---

[7] *Ibid.*, pp. 64–65.

plained that, with the help of a friend, ready-dressed flax had been purchased, a building erected at Aldersgate, and arrangements made for people to go there for the flax, work on knitting and spinning at home, and bring back the finished work. Children were taught to work rather than to beg and homework was found advantageous both to the child and to his parents. Children of seven and eight could earn twopence a day, or two shillings a week if they were older. Firmin stated that by knitting fine jersey stockings the children of Norwich who were six to eight years old gained 12,000 pounds more than was spent on materials.[8]

John Locke, the political philosopher, proposed that any boy or girl under the age of fourteen who was found begging be soundly whipped and that all children and their mothers living at home be given partial employment to reimburse the community for their care. Locke further recommended the establishment of "working schools" in which parents and children could be put to work and the children given free meals as an incentive for attendance.[9]

John Cary, the Bristol merchant, alarmed at the growing indigency in the city of Bristol, proposed that a large workhouse be established for the purpose of sheltering the aged, those unable to work, and those who could be employed there. Persons unable to support their children would place them in the workhouse at any age "so that these children may be bred up to labour, principles of virtue implanted in them at an early age, and laziness be discouraged . . . and that their children will be settled in a way serviceable to the public good, and not bred up in all manner of vice as they now are."[10] The governor would be authorized to place out the boys in navigation and the girls in domestic service and to bind them out for a certain number of years.

Cary's proposals were carried out when Parliament incorporated them into a bill which, when passed in January, 1696, divested Overseers of the Poor of their authority and established a new Corporation of the Poor.[11] It was in this legislation that the "workhouse test" and "farming out" of the poor to the lowest bidder were also initiated.

The workhouse philosophy and program advocated by Cary were enthusiastically adopted by many parishes. Whether labeled the "spinning school," "house of industry," "house of instruction," or

---

[8] *Social Service Review* (Vol. V, No. 4 December 1931), pp. 633–634.

[9] Sidney and Beatrice Webb, *op. cit.*, pp. 109–112.

[10] *Ibid.*, p. 117.

[11] *Ibid.*, pp. 118–119.

"college of instruction," these facilities were designed to put dependent children and adults to work and thus avoid idleness, which was considered tantamount to crime, to spare the community the cost of maintaining the able-bodied poor, and to use the labor of the pauper to enhance the national economy. This form of family and child care continued to be prevalent in England for many years.

Later Legislation

Thomas Gilbert, a member of the House of Commons and long opposed to repressive poor law measures, sought to correct some of the abuses of the 1696 legislation. Gilbert's Act of 1782, entitled "Plan for Better Relief and Employment of the Poor," embraced a new concept in poor law philosophy and administration by classifying and aiding indigent persons according to their needs. It forbade contracting for the care of the poor and was the first proposal to break with tradition and to move toward a pattern of outdoor relief.

The Gilbert Act decreed that all poor, aged, sick, and those too infirm to work were to be placed in the poorhouse, as well as "such children as shall necessarily go with their mothers." Poor infants were not to be placed in the poorhouse but with "proper persons," presumably in family settings. Persons wanting to work were to be given gainful employment by the guardian of the poor and to receive lodging and maintenance until employment was available.

The act proposed that the parishes be combined into unions, and that the overseers of the poor be succeeded by "guardians of the poor."[12]

Significant Religious Developments

In tracing the evolution of the English methods of dealing with the problem of dependency, mention has been made of the early role of the church and of its decreasing ability to cope with the widespread poverty which developed after the breakdown of feudalism. In the tapestry of our English heritage, however, religion and its manifestations in contemporary political, economic, and social life continued to play a significant role.

Before the fourteenth century, the medieval church supplied the intellectual leadership of the country, but the same period which produced the emancipation of the serf also created extensive rebellion

---

[12] de Schweinitz, *op. cit.*, pp. 67–68.

against the religious and intellectual domination of the papal church. This rebellion had many forms and received impetus from many directions. Within England, a furtive evangelical movement developed after the first complete English translation of the Bible was produced at Oxford in 1374. Trevelyan reports that, although violently suppressed, this movement survived underground in English villages and towns and subsequently "became merged in the return wave of Protestanism from Luther's Germany" in the sixteenth century.[13]

During the Elizabethan period, "Puritanism" encompassed a variety of beliefs. All Puritans desired "a ministry of learned and godly men preaching in every village the gospel of conversion and repentance."[14] Notestein observed:

The Puritan believed in the careful use of time. At his back he heard always time's winged chariot. Much time ought to be reserved to the use of God and the remainder should be devoted to one's calling. In that calling it was his duty to earn a good living and support his family. The more earnest Puritans frowned upon such pastimes and wordly pleasures as interfered with their occupation. Much casual evidence could be adduced to indicate that they were the best of workers. . . . Whether their activity was the result of their form of faith, or whether the more active of the artisan and trading classes took up with a religion of zeal and effort, would be a question deserving consideration.[15]

During the Elizabethan era, the influence of Puritanism grew. When James I became king in 1603, Puritan leaders attempted to obtain permission for some variation in ritual and in parish work within the framework of the Church of England. James, believing that the Calvinist concepts of church structure were in conflict with his firm belief in the "Divine Right of Kings," angrily refused to grant any toleration and swore that he would make them conform or "harry them out of the land."[16] Subsequently, three hundred English clergy were ejected from their livings. Severe laws against the Catholics were also passed and the laws against all Nonconformists enforced with greater diligence.[17]

---

[13] George M. Trevelyan, *History of England* (London and New York: Longmans, Green and Company, 1926), p. 250.

[14] Wallace Notestein, *The English People on the Eve of Colonization—1603–1630* (New York: Harper and Brothers, 1954), p. 150.

[15] *Ibid.*, p. 153.

[16] *Ibid.*, p. 156.

[17] Herbert Eugene Bolton and Thomas Maitland Marshall, *The Colonization of North America—1492–1783* (New York: The Macmillan Company, 1921), p. 136.

In this environment of fear, Puritans were meeting secretly in small groups and, when discovered, their members were imprisoned and some of the leaders hanged. To avoid persecution, the families in one congregation moved to Amsterdam in 1608 and later to Leyden. Their hopes for religious freedom were fulfilled in Holland but it was necessary for their children to work so hard that their bodies were becoming deformed and, as they grew older, many were slipping away to become soldiers or sailors, intermarrying with the Dutch, or having their behavior contaminated "by the gay city life."[18] In 1617, the leaders decided to seek new lands and within three years these families were numbered among our "Pilgrim fathers" at Plymouth.

During the reign of Charles I (1625–1649), the influence of his Catholic wife, Henrietta Maria of France, temporarily stopped the persecution of Catholics. It was in this era that George Calvert, or Lord Baltimore, a recent Catholic convert (and former secretary of state under James I), procured a charter giving him the right to establish the colony of Maryland (named for the queen).

OTHER IMPORTANT DEVELOPMENTS

No real understanding of the early scene is possible without a review of other social and economic factors which precipitated the English migration to America.

Plans to establish plantations in America were discussed as early as 1570 and two unsuccessful attempts were made to establish a colony within three years after Sir Walter Raleigh had given the name "Virginia" (in honor of Queen Elizabeth) to the territory between Newfoundland and the Spanish settlement in Florida.

About 1585, Richard Hakluyt, a Bristol clergyman, prepared for the queen a manuscript which "was destined to become the classic statement of the case for English colonization."[19] Hakluyt envisioned colonization as a means of securing needed products, setting up in business again the bankrupt merchants then in debtors' prison, converting the natives to the Christian faith, and "shunting the large vagrant population of England to the new world to learn new ways of living."[20] This document was widely circulated and aroused the interest of many men.

---

[18] *Ibid.*, p. 137.

[19] Notestein, *op. cit.*, p. 255.

[20] *Ibid.*, p. 256.

In 1606 the Virginia Company was organized by a group of businessmen and two patents obtained. Two subsidiary stock companies were formed to operate under the control of the Central Council appointed by the Crown. One company, known as the London Company, was authorized to establish a settlement in southern Virginia, while the Plymouth Company was to plant colonies in northern Virginia.

The first efforts to establish a colony were made by the London Company. In May, 1607, three vessels landed in Chesapeake Bay and their passengers began the hard struggle for existence recorded in every American history book. When anticipated financial returns were not forthcoming, the English stockholders reorganized the company. The colonists continued to suffer many vicissitudes, however, and the stockholders still received no return from their investment.

In 1619 the management of the company was changed and a system of "landed proprietorship" inaugurated. Under this plan the company retained 12,000 acres for itself, and granted 500 to 1,500 acres to each of its officers and 50 acres to any person who would transport another to the colony. Large grants were also awarded to groups of capitalists who agreed to bring colonists from England. In later years a large number of waifs and vagabonds from the streets of London were sent and those who could not pay their transportation were indentured.

Between 1606 and 1619, the Plymouth Company made several unsuccessful attempts to establish a colony along the New England coast but the first colony in its territory was not established through these efforts.

As the Puritan congregation at Leyden was searching about for a new and more satisfactory location, news of the inducements offered to colonists by the London Company reached their leaders. After many negotiations, a patent was finally granted by the Royal Council although the king and the archbishop did not look with favor upon their request for religious liberty or the articles they had drawn up stating their religious beliefs. With land in Virginia assured, 35 of the Leyden congregation sailed for Southampton, England, where they were joined by others from London and Southampton. The Mayflower sailed for Virginia in September, 1620, but the storms encountered resulted in the establishment for a settlement at Plymouth, far removed from the territory covered by the patent issued by the London Company.

For the colonists, this situation was solved by drawing up "The Mayflower Compact" establishing a government based upon "the will of the colonists rather than that of the sovereign."[21]   Their position as squatters on the land held by the Plymouth Company was finally terminated in 1621 when they received a separate patent.

The failure of the Plymouth Company to establish a colony in its allotted territory led some of its influential stockholders to petition for a new charter and on November 13, 1620, the "Council for New England" was incorporated.   With the assistance of English merchants, the Council succeeded in establishing small settlements at several points within the present states of New Hampshire and Maine.   One group of colonists sent out by the Council also settled at Cape Anne (near Boston) where the Plymouth colony also held a tract of land.   Subsequent difficulties between the two colonies over fishing rights were not settled until troops were sent by the Plymouth colony.   In 1625, another settlement was broken up by the Plymouth colony after the leader established an Episcopalian service and set up a Maypole which became a center of gaiety.

The Puritans' desire to escape persecution by Charles I, and the great depression of the 1620's in England, combined to produce still another settlement under a patent granted by the Council for New England.   With the help of influential Puritans and London merchants, a charter for the "Massachusetts Bay Company" was finally obtained in 1629 despite the Crown's opposition to Puritan leaders.   The first fleet of colonists arrived in 1629 and by 1634 it was estimated that 4,000 colonists had settled near Salem.

In 1632, Charles I granted to George Calvert (Lord Baltimore), a stockholder in the London Company, a charter with authority to establish a colony in Maryland.   Lord Baltimore died in the same month, however, leaving his son, Cecilius, the charter and the responsibility for its implementation.[22]

The government of the colony authorized by the charter was similar to that of the Palatinate of Durham, a feudatory in which the bishop had almost absolute powers.   The lord proprietor of Maryland, however, was restricted by a provision that the laws which he proclaimed must be approved by a majority of freemen in the province or by their delegates.   Despite this limitation, the proprietor was given extensive powers, including the right to "create manors, over which the

---

[21] Bolton and Marshall, *op. cit.*, p. 138.

[22] *Ibid.*, p. 126.

Lord of the manor would have the rights of a feudal baron."[23]   The proprietor was also given authority to found churches "consecrated according to the Ecclesiastical Laws of our Kingdom of England." Since the establishment of other churches was not prohibited, Lord Baltimore used this omission for the benefit of Catholicism.   When the "Ark" and the "Dove" arrived at the mouth of the Potomac in March, 1634, most of the 20 gentlemen aboard were Catholics and 3 Jesuit priests accompanied the expedition.   The 200 laborers and servants who completed the passenger list were predominantly Protestant, however.[24]

In keeping with the charter, manors of 1,000 to 5,000 acres were established, with the lord of the manor being granted lands in proportion to the number of colonists he provided.   Thousands of indentured servants were later brought from England to provide labor for the tobacco plantations and slavery was also introduced to augment the labor supply.

It is not the intent to trace here the economic and social forces which resulted in the establishment of each American colony.   For our purposes it is sufficient to state that Maryland became the pattern for other proprietary charters (North Carolina, Pennsylvania, etc.) and that other stock companies established many small settlements throughout New England.

THE SIGNIFICANCE OF THESE EVENTS

This information has primary value in establishing an economic, religious, and social background for many of the developments in child welfare to be examined in subsequent chapters.   It also serves to place in proper perspective, perhaps, the English poor laws which provided the legal precedent for many of the attempts to solve social problems in the American colonies.   More specifically, it provides an explanation of the reasons why the principles of local autonomy and local responsibility became an intrinsic part of the thinking and behavior of the separate and competitive communities of New England. It is evident that these settlements were established by different companies and that the residents of each settlement were intent on protecting their own religious beliefs, their own financial interests, their own concepts of government, and their own way of life.

---

[23] *Ibid.*, p. 127.

[24] *Ibid.*

Selected Bibliography

Abbott, Grace. *The Child and the State*, Vol. I. Chicago: University of Chicago Press, 1938.

de Schweinitz, Karl. *England's Road to Social Security, 1349–1947*. Third revised edition. Philadelphia: University of Pennsylvania Press, 1947.

Nicholls, Sir George. *A History of English Poor Law*. London: John Murray, 1854.

Rodgers, Betsy. *Cloak of Charity*. London: Methuen and Company, 1949.

Webb, Sidney, and Beatrice Webb. *English Local Government: English Poor Law History*, Part I. London and New York: Longmans, Green and Company, 1927.

Chapter 2   *Our Colonial Heritage*

$\mathcal{J}$n the preceding chapter, the colonization of America was described
within a framework of pertinent English history. It is now
necessary to trace some of the subsequent legal and social developments which affected the welfare of children, to indicate other influences on our social institutions, and to examine the role of the
dependent child and the methods of care available to him in colonial
America.

MARYLAND AND VIRGINIA

It was understandably difficult for the proprietary colonies to
disavow themselves of the opportunity to establish feudalism in the
new land. Workmen were needed and, by 1641, 75 per cent of the
Virginia colony was made up of involuntarily imported freemen,
Negro slaves, and indentured adults and children from the cities and

17

towns of England. Immigration from England later decreased as the flourishing business of slavery began to take root.[1] By 1760 it was estimated that approximately 30 per cent of the population of Maryland and 40 per cent of the Virginia settlers were slaves.[2]

Under these circumstances it is natural that the early social problems of these colonies were somewhat different from those which caused the northern colonies to establish the legislative pattern so frequently repeated in other states. As we shall see in subsequent sections, however, the methods of caring for children in the proprietary colonies were similar to those used elsewhere in the new world.

MASSACHUSETTS

The group of men and women who came into the harbor of Plymouth on the Mayflower had no such aristocratic inclinations as had Lord Baltimore. These hard working and religiously devout people had a stake in building and developing a new country which would be strongly communal in nature. Each person worked for and participated in the community's economy, not for individual gains or prestige, but for the common good. Land was worked by all with equal sharing of its benefits and the colony dealt swiftly with those who attempted to share without effort. Consequently, there was no room for the stranger whose ambitions and contributions were in contradiction to these aims.

With this strong inclination toward joint enterprise, it is understandable that these communities would use the concept of legal settlement to control indigency. By 1637, regulations for the newcomer had been instituted and the matter of settlement had assumed great importance. "Warning out" and certificates indicating freedom from pauperism gave the colonists a feeling of security that strangers would not come to the territory without adequate funds to insure solvency, and would not be allowed to stay should poverty occur.[3]

Legitimate children followed and had the settlement of their father if the father had such settlement. If he had none, the children followed the settlement of their mother. Illegitimate children fol-

---

[1] Charles M. Andrews, *The Colonial Period of American History* (New Haven: Yale University Press, 1934), pp. 207–208.

[2] Bolton and Marshall, *op. cit.*, p. 336.

[3] Robert W. Kelso, *The History of Public Poor Relief in Massachusetts, 1620–1920* (Boston: Houghton Mifflin Company, 1922), p. 39.

lowed the mother's settlement at the time of their birth and no child gained settlement by birth if neither parent had settlement in the place of birth. A person who served a four-year apprenticeship and continued in his trade for five years gained settlement, provided he was 21 years of age.[4]

The New England town was the center of local government and its policies were administered through a committee known as selectmen. Overseers of the Poor usually cared for dependent children by indenturing them. Poor children, as well as adults, were also bid off at public auction, either singly or as a family unit, to a contractor who operated a privately owned almshouse.

Massachusetts instituted a state aid program for the unsettled poor as early as 1767, but in other respects its provision for children followed the traditional lines of the English poor law. Long-time indentures were common for the "proper objects of charity." Ill-behaved and idle children were sent to the house of correction and later bound out. The stubborn child, sixteen years or over, who was found living in crime could be severely punished and even put to death. The child who was parentally neglected, if not indentured, was institutionalized.

THE DUTCH INFLUENCE IN NEW YORK

New Netherland was founded in 1623 by the Dutch East India Company. Early in its history the social pattern in the colony deeply resembled feudalism. Instead of the traditional master or landowner, a similar class known as the "patroons" was established. The colonists were bound to the service of the patroons and were threatened with termination of their contract if they did not cooperatively continue their service. The Dutch government seemingly considered more than man's material needs, however, since the New Netherland charter required that the patroons and the colonists find a means of supporting a minister, a schoolmaster, and a Comforter of the Sick.

To the Dutch, the community poor "belonged to the family next door."[5] Implicit in this mutual aid concept was the fact that the church continued to be the center of charitable activity and the repository of the community's conscience. The patroon instituted

---

[4] *Ibid.*, pp. 66–67.

[5] David M. Schneider, *The History of Public Welfare in New York State, 1609–1866* (Chicago: The University of Chicago Press, 1938), p. 10.

rigid demands upon the indentured colonists, but the civic and political structure was sufficiently humane and flexible to provide for those who were "worthy" but pauperized.

Although the practice of neighborliness and Christian compassion was inculcated in Dutch thinking, it was not carried on in lieu of community responsibility for the needs of the poor. Outdoor relief was granted and children of widowed mothers with property were given protection by the "orphan master," whose main function was to keep vigil over the family's estate. The orphan master also bound out children when this was deemed necessary. There was little thought and scanty legislation on behalf of the child without an estate, however, until 1654. At this time the Amsterdam director sent a shipload of orphaned children to New Netherland to increase the population and aid in the agricultural progress of the colony. This importation of children necessitated the creation of the first public orphanage in New Netherland, from which children were bound out as apprentices and servants from two to four years.

Ten years later the Dutch lost New Netherland to the English and English poor law was instituted. The parish became the unit of administration and overseers were designated to provide for the poor in cooperation with two churchwardens.[6]

RHODE ISLAND

In 1662 the Rhode Island Assembly made provision for the sick, the impotent, and dependent children. The Overseers of the Poor, elected annually, were made responsible to the Town Council for the administration of the poor law in each town. They were also authorized to collect money to support the poor and to enforce regulations regarding residence. All requests for public relief were to be made at the regular town meeting.[7]

Colonial movement and settlement were as important to the Rhode Island colonists as to the other early settlers. Penalties were imposed for harboring a stranger more than a week without informing the justices of the peace. These penalties included whippings, imprisonment in the house of correction, or fines of five pounds to be used for the care of the poor. Should the stranger in question become

---

[6] *Ibid.*, p. 30.

[7] Margaret D. Creech, *Three Centuries of Poor Law Administration in Rhode Island* (Chicago: University of Chicago Press, 1936), p. 21.

indigent, the harboring inhabitant would also be held liable for his poverty.[8]

The Dependent Child
in Colonial America

During the early years of American settlement, three types of child care prevailed. The indigent child lived in his own home supported by outdoor relief, he was apprenticed or indentured, or he lived in an almshouse. These patterns were of English origin, but involuntary servitude of a child by indenture was also in harmony with the feudalistic ambitions of the aristocratic founders of some colonies. In other settlements, indenture and other methods of child care represented an economic expedient of another nature.

CHILD INDENTURE IN MARYLAND

There were two specific indenture laws passed in Maryland, the first in 1638 and the second in 1793. Both laws defined the responsibilities of the servant and master but the reason for their enactment differed. The early law arose from the landlord's need for child servants for his own convenience and profit. The 1793 law was enacted because of the growing destitution among children that was leading them to become "useless and depraved members of society."[9]

The 1638 legislation outlined the rights and obligations of the mistress or master, as well as the apprentice transported to Maryland for the purpose of indenture. All male persons under the age of 18 were to serve until the age of 24, unless stated otherwise in the covenant. Every "maid servant," 12 years old or younger was to serve the party transporting her for seven years and, if over the age of 12, she was to serve for four years. When the terms of servitude had expired, the mistress or master was to give the man or maid servant the following:

. . . three barrels of corn, a hilling hoe and a weeding hoe and a felling axe and to a man Servant one new Cloth sute one new Shirt and one pair of new Shews one pair of new Stockins . . . and to a maid servant one

---

[8] *Ibid.*, p. 48.
[9] *Laws of Maryland*, 1793, Chapter 45.

new petty coat and a wast coat one new smock one pair of new shews one pair of new stockins. . . . [10]

Under the 1793 statute, the justices of the Orphan's Court were to bind out, as apprentices, every orphan child (boys until 21, girls until 16) without proper care and education to some manufacturer, mariner, mechanic, handicraftsman, or other person. The child was to be assured of clothing, food, and shelter. A knowledge of reading, writing, and arithmetic was to be provided if possible and male children taught a trade.[11]

Justices were also authorized to bind out children of extremely indigent parents, illegitimate children, and children of persons from out of the state. Parents were to be allowed to choose the person to whom the child was to be bound. The Trustees of the Poor of any county were also empowered to bind out any poor child placed in the almshouse. A bound apprentice who ran away from his master was subject to punishment but the justice of the peace had the power to remove any indentured child who was maltreated.[12]

A typical indenture petition was signed in 1718 when a Somerset County citizen brought a twelve-year-old orphan boy to the court asking for legal indenture of the child. The document read:

. . . If this (name of master) shall sustain the (name of child) in sufficient meat, drink, and clothes and shall learn him to read and write and give him a heifer not under three years old, when he shall come to the age of 18 years, then this recognizance is to be void else to stand in full force of the law.[13]

On August 12, 1777, the Court Record of Montgomery County reported:

An orphan aged eleven was bound to two townsmen until his majority during which apprenticeship his masters were to learn him the cooper's trade, to read, to write and to cypher as far as the rule of three, and when free to give him a set of cooper's tools and a decent set of apparel.[14]

INDENTURE IN MASSACHUSETTS

The indenture method of child care had somewhat different antecedents in Massachusetts. In the closely knit Plymouth colony, no

---

[10] Archives of Maryland, *Proceedings and Acts of the Assembly*, I, 80.

[11] *Laws of Maryland*, 1793, Chapter 45.

[12] *Ibid.*

[13] *Judicial Record of Somerset County, Maryland*, March 7, 1718.

[14] *Montgomery County, Maryland, Court Record*, 1777.

person remained unattached to a family or without an occupation, and the dependent child was required to have a guardian to act in his behalf. Other Massachusetts settlements soon adopted similar measures to insure that no child would become dependent upon the community.

In 1642, the Massachusetts Bay colony enacted a compulsory requirement that each dependent child be affixed to a family where he would be engaged in an occupation by which he would be assured of self-support. By 1672, parents were ordered to indenture their children or the town would assume that responsibility for them. Although the stated objectives of these requirements were to provide the child with an adequate family home and preparation for work, there is strong reason to believe that the authorities also wanted to impress upon the citizenry its accountability for the child's care. Kelso states:

Cleaning off the account on the treasurer's book by a long-term indenture, which for practical purposes amounted to a sale of the child with no guarantee of protection, save public indignation, against enslavement and abuse, was the constant effort of the early town authorities.[15]

The meaning that involuntary indenture had for the parents of these children is poignantly outlined in a letter to the Massachusetts governor general in 1756.

To His Excellency:
We have taken the liberty of presenting you this request, as we are in sorrow on account of our children. The loss which we have suffered . . . and our separations from one another is nothing compared with . . . that of taking away our children by force before our eyes. Nature herself cannot endure that. If it were in our power to have our choice we should choose rather the taking away of our bodies and our souls than to be separated from them. Wherefore we pray in pity and to your honors that you would have the goodness to mitigate this cruelty. We have not refused from the first to work for our support of our children, provided it were permitted in our own families.[16]

INDENTURE IN OTHER STATES

New York legalized the indenture of children in 1788. In New York City, Albany, and Hudson, a dependent child found begging could be bound out by the mayor, recorder, or alderman, or any two

---

[15] Kelso, *op. cit.*, p. 168.

[16] Eleanor Parkhurst, "Poor Relief in a Massachusetts Village in the Eighteenth Century," *Social Service Review*, Vol. XI, No. 3 (September 1937), p. 455.

of them, without the consent of the parents. The maximum age of indenture was 21 for a male and 18 for a female. Recalcitrant apprentices or indentured servants were sent to jail or to the house of correction. The master or mistress of the indentured child was obliged to teach the child to read and write.

The Rhode Island General Assembly of 1662 defined its philosophy of child indenture by stating that it would endeavor legally to "Employ or put out to Service, all such Young and Able Persons as are not of sufficient Estate to maintain themselves or which in Idlenes, may be likely to become a charge or damage to such Town."[17]

In Rhode Island, children whose parents were "chargeable to the town" were apprenticed as well as orphan children, children of state-supported parents, and children whose parents were for any reason unable to care for them properly. Boys were apprenticed to "Citizens of the State" until the age of 21 and girls until eighteen or until marriage.[18] Although the first almshouse was established in Newport in 1723, children were not apprenticed from the almshouse until 1765.[19]

OUTDOOR RELIEF

Outdoor relief, or "home relief," was the method by which the larger number of pauper children and adults received care. The provincial methods of handling the direct relief problem were vulnerable to attack on many fronts, however, because of the expenditure they imposed upon the taxpaying public and the prevalent attitudes toward indigency.

In all colonies there was a continuing tendency to relate poverty to the integrity and morality of the individual rather than to see the indigent person as a product of the social and economic environment in which he lived. Thus, affixing responsibility for poverty to the individual eliminated any need to examine pertinent societal influences.

Outdoor relief, although often extended in an arbitrary manner, did keep children in their own homes. There was little assurance, however, that many of these children were any better off than those cared for in the almshouses. The attitude toward the indigent parent was projected to his children and, since there was strong belief in the

---

[17] *The Charter and the Acts and Laws of His Majesties Colony of Rhode Island and Providence Plantations in America* (1719), cited in Creech, *op cit.*, p. 9.

[18] Creech, *Ibid.*, p. 114.

[19] *Ibid.*, p. 79.

inherent nature of poverty, the child on outdoor relief was considered to be genetically oriented to producing still another generation of indigents.

THE MIXED ALMSHOUSE

The mixed almshouse, or "poorhouse," served many purposes. It was used as an institution for the mentally ill and the mentally deficient, and it served as a hospital for those who were physically ill. It acted as an orphanage for parentless children and as a receiving home for children until indenture was arranged. It was used as a place of residence for the aged and as a penal institution for the vagrant and the criminal. In short, it was the reservoir of all persons dependent upon the community, regardless of the reasons for their need or the basis on which the community assumed responsibility for their support.

The first almshouse was established at Rensselaerswyck, New York, in 1657 and similar facilities honeycombed America during the next two hundred years. With the growing numbers of dependent adults and children and the increasing cost of outdoor relief to the taxpayers, legislators looked to congregate group care as an economical way of supporting the poor, and as a means of controlling their activities and forcing them to work. The effects that a conglomerate human environment would have upon a child, his feelings, and general welfare, seemingly had little meaning. Instead, the lawmakers were prone to be concerned about public expenditures and not about the lives of children.

The almshouse was generally a local facility. As a result, each community housed its inmates according to its own mandate. Boston, for example, established its first almshouse in 1660 and in 1739 added, for the able-bodied poor, a workhouse from which children were bound out.

The earliest almshouse legislation in Maryland was passed in 1768. Three counties established almshouses in 1773 and many similar institutions were created before the Revolution. Funds were raised by taxing the citizenry. "Trustees of the Poor" supervised the almshouse and were responsible for the admission of new inmates. A badge bearing the letter P, indicating "Poor," together with the first letter of the county name, was affixed to the right shoulder of the inmate. All able-bodied poor were put to work, and refusal to work earned for the inmate a whipping of 39 lashes.

While early America continued to struggle with increased mass dependency caused by wars, epidemics, and tragic economic occurrences, and as almshouses continued to be filled to overflowing, the states began to re-evaluate this method of care. Because of the high rate of infant mortality in almshouses, some states prohibited the use of these facilities for the very young. With respect to the less obvious consequences to children, however, the public conscience was not fully aroused until the nineteenth century.

The Historical Significance of the Colonial Period

Contemporary child welfare philosophy and practice still reflect much that was brought to these shores. Although history often mirrors only oblique images of the beliefs and values of the English immigrant, these factors can usually be found when the substance of his laws, and of his political, religious, and social institutions is examined. Many of the harsh and punitive practices from which these men fled were re-created in the new world to which they came. While they repudiated English repression, they developed a kind of their own which was tenaciously reflected in their values and sentiments.

As America strode along its pioneering pathways, ancient rigidities remained implanted in the hard earth of custom. It was only when new national experiences changed the social and economic perimeter that new insights were born and nurtured. In this regard the nineteenth century had a very special destiny.

Selected Bibliography

Creech, Margaret D. *Three Centuries of Poor Law Administration in Rhode Island*. Chicago: University of Chicago Press, 1936.

Earle, Alice M. *Child Life in Colonial Days*. New York: The Macmillan Company, 1927.

Kelso, Robert W. *The History of Poor Relief in Massachusetts, 1620–1920*. Boston: Houghton Mifflin Company, 1922.

Schneider, David M. *The History of Public Welfare in New York State, 1609–1866*. Chicago: University of Chicago Press, 1938.

Part Two · Significant Events

For America,

the nineteenth century was an era of pioneering effort.

Out of this period of growth and travail came many

of the present methods of meeting the needs of children and

a beginning recognition

of some of the problems yet to be solved.

in the Nineteenth Century

Chapter 3

Important Developments

in England

In most instances, the social institutional structure established during the nineteenth century was a direct result of our colonial heritage or an indigenous effort to meet the exigency of the moment. As will be seen in subsequent chapters, however, contemporary developments in England provided the pattern for several important movements which affected the welfare of children in this country. It is pertinent to note some of the bench marks that were subsequently reflected on the American scene.

CHILDREN AND THE LAW

During the nineteenth century the rights and status of English children remained a confused and contradictory patchwork of law, legal

29

theory, and judicial practice. Despite this fact, the conceptual framework upon which practice was based forms an important part of our modern judicial process.

When William the Conqueror established a special court to accept jurisdiction over all matters involving the proprietary rights of the Crown, a new judicial instrument was created in England. In the twelfth century this court was made available to those who could not obtain justice in the local or feudal courts, and by the fifteenth century the king's secretary or chancellor had begun to exercise extensive jurisdiction over situations not covered by common law, that is, law based on statute and earlier court decisions. As the common law became more rigid, the equitable powers of the Court of Chancery were increasingly used to protect the welfare of those who had no other legal redress.[1]

Under the common law of England, the father's right to the services, custody, and control of his children was almost unlimited. In 1722, however, a historic principle was enunciated by the lord chancellor in limiting the father's right to custody in the case of Eyre versus Shaftsbury, when he stated:

. . . The care of all infants is lodged in the King as *pater patriae* and by the King this care is delegated to his Court of Chancery. . . . the King is bound, of common right, and by the laws to defend his subjects . . . and by the law of this realm, every loyal subject is taken to be within the King's protection, for which reason it is, that idiots and lunatics, who are uncapable to take care of themselves, are provided for by the King as *pater patriae*, and there is the same reason to extend this care to infants.[2]

This concept proved of no immediate value in the protection of children, since the Chancery Court continued to accept jurisdiction only when property was involved. As the chancellor explained in his decision in the Wellesley case in 1827:

. . . this Court has not the means of acting, except where it has property to act upon. It is not, however, for any want of jurisdiction that it does not act, but from want of means to exercise its jurisdiction; because the Court cannot take on itself the maintenance of all children in the kingdom.[3]

In 1892, this opinion was reversed by another chancellor who wrote:

---

[1] Helen I. Clarke, *Social Legislation* (New York: Copyright, 1940, D. Appleton-Century Company), p. 16. Reprinted by permission of Appleton-Century-Crofts, Inc.

[2] *Ibid.*, p. 206.

[3] *Ibid.*, p. 207.

. . . The cases in which the court interferes on behalf of the infants are not confined to those in which there is property. This court interferes for the protection of infants, *qua* infants, by virtue of the prerogative which belongs to the Crown as *parens patriae*. . . . [4]

Through this process the concept of the court's responsibility for the welfare of children was finally established, but the Chancery Court remained primarily a resource for children with property.

Despite its rigidities in sustaining the rights of parents, the English common law did recognize that children should not be held criminally responsible for their acts. No child less than seven years of age could be held responsible for a criminal act and for children between the ages of seven and fourteen there was no presumption of guilt. Children over fourteen and those whom the evidence showed to be capable of criminal intent were subject to the same punishment as adults.

These concepts were not reflected in the rigid laws enacted by the American colonies, but they began to be evident in the laws enacted in this country during the latter part of the nineteenth century.

CHILD LABOR LEGISLATION

By the beginning of the nineteenth century the negative aspects of child indenture and apprenticeship had become apparent in England. Once heralded as ideal methods of preventing the vices of idleness and laziness while relieving the taxpayers of the cost of caring for dependent children, public attention was now directed to the tragic conditions engendered by this system.

As the Industrial Revolution brought new techniques in the manufacture of textiles, the value of child labor was quickly recognized. As the Webbs explained:

High up in the lonely valleys of Lancashire and Yorkshire, mills were built by the side of rushing streams, where the new machines could be driven by water power, and needed only "tending" by docile fingers, and bodies small enough to creep under the frames. The necessary operatives had to be brought from somewhere, and the cheapest source was the workhouse . . . Parish officers accordingly found themselves importuned by the agents . . . to recruit their staffs, who without asking any premium, carried off the children literally by cartloads, taking even infants three or

---

[4] Julian W. Mack, "Legal Problems Involved in the Establishment of the Juvenile Court," Appendix I, in Sophonisba B. Breckinridge and Edith Abbott, *The Delinquent Child and the Home* (New York: Russell Sage Foundation, 1912) p. 181.

four years old . . . (In one such) contract between a London parish and a Lancashire manufacturer, the manufacturer undertook to receive one idiot with every twenty sound children.[5]

By 1795, the plight of children employed in the cotton mills of London and Manchester raised the question as to whether the community "does not receive detriment from the manner in which children are thus employed during their early years."[6] Similar concern was expressed by a subcommittee which visited a mining operation in which girls 7 to 21 years of age worked naked to the waist beside adult colliers who were completely naked. This committee was equally horrified to find a 12-year old girl in the coal pit carrying one hundred pounds of coal and making 25 to 30 trips each day with this load.[7]

In 1802, the thinking of humanitarian citizens was reflected in the Health and Morals of Apprentices Act which prohibited night work by pauper apprentices in cotton and woolen mills, limited their daily hours of work to twelve, and required mills to be adequately ventilated, apprentices properly clothed, and a part of each day devoted to instruction. Although this act also required that justices of the peace appoint a clergyman and a magistrate to inspect the mills, the law was not enforced. Many mill operators also succeeded in evading its provisions by employing "free children" who were not covered by the act.

The law was amended in 1819 to cover the employment of children hired directly from their parents, but this act related to cotton mills only. It prohibited the employment of children under nine years of age and, with certain exceptions, limited to twelve the hours of employment for children between the ages of nine and thirteen. This act proved equally ineffective and many children continued to work fifteen and sixteen hours each day.[8]

In 1833, a new law was made applicable to all textile mills except those "deemed worthy of a subsidy of cheap child labor" because of their manufacture of silk.[9] Employment of children under nine years was again prohibited and children between nine and thirteen were per-

---

[5] Sidney and Beatrice Webb, *op. cit.*, pp. 201–202.

[6] Grace Abbott, *op. cit.*, p. 107.

[7] *Ibid.*, p. 164.

[8] Harry A. Millis and Royal E. Montgomery, *Labor's Progress and Some Basic Labor Problems* (New York: Mc-Graw-Hill Book Company, 1938), p. 420.

[9] *Ibid.*

mitted to work only nine hours and children between thirteen and eighteen years, only twelve hours. Work between the hours of 8:30 P.M. and 5:30 A.M. was prohibited for all children under eighteen years. Provision was also made for the enforcement of the law by a staff of national inspectors.

In 1842, the Mines' Regulation Act was passed, forbidding the employment of women and girls underground and the employment of boys under ten in the pits. This legislation represented an attempt to correct conditions reported by the Children's Employment Commission, which found children as young as four years in the mines and learned that eight to nine years was the customary age of initial employment. It is possible that legislative action was also hastened by the publication of Elizabeth Barrett Browning's deeply moving poem, "The Cry of the Children," during the same year. ("For all day we drag our burden tiring through the cold dark underground . . . .")

In these early decades of the nineteenth century the exploitation of children employed as chimney sweeps and in street trades was also immortalized by Dickens, Kingsley, Goldsmith, and others. As England came to recognize the social costs of child labor, legislation was more effectively enforced and the amount of child labor gradually reduced after 1850.

In 1876, elementary education was made compulsory up to the age of ten and, in 1899, school attendance to the age of twelve was required. These laws, together with those which made free education available after 1891, served to limit further the incidence of child labor. As a result, the employment of children did not constitute a serious social problem in Great Britain after the nineteenth century.

Perhaps it was fortunate that when factories first came into existence they immediately made full use of child labor. If the obvious physical effects of early employment, long hours, and hazardous working conditions had not created national alarm over the evils of child labor in England, it is possible that protective legislation would have been delayed for another century.[10]

REVISION OF THE POOR LAWS

The basic concepts of the Elizabethan Poor Law of 1601 continued to provide the legal framework for the relief of destitution until the

---

[10] Frank J. Bruno, *The Theory of Social Work* (Boston: D. C. Heath, 1936), p. 461.

Industrial Revolution created an ever-increasing number of indigent adults and children. By 1832 the problem had reached such serious proportions that a royal commission was appointed to make recommendations for new legislation.

The resulting Act of 1834 required "that the relief afforded to each class of paupers should be uniform throughout the kingdom . . . ; that the conditions of existence afforded by the relief should be less eligible [that is, less attractive] to the applicant than those of the lowest grade of independent labourers . . . ." and that a system of workhouses be the established method of providing care for the able-bodied and their families.[11]

In itself this legislation had little significance in America since national regulation of poor relief was not adopted in this country, and the other principles enunciated merely made compulsory the concepts and methods previously used by local authorities to implement the Poor Law of 1601. England's subsequent concern about the plight of children damaged by this repressive legislation, and concurrent efforts to develop more effective methods of meeting the problems of dependency, were reflected, however, in the changing pattern of child care and other services provided for families on this side of the Atlantic.

The London Charity Organization Society

The London Society for Organizing Charitable Relief and Repressing Mendicancy was established in London in 1869. This organization, which later changed its name to the London Charity Organization Society (COS), owed its philosophy and administrative pattern to a clergyman, Thomas Chalmers, who had introduced the casework method to charitable enterprise in Scotland fifty years before.

As a parish minister, Chalmers learned to know the urgent problems of the poor. He was impressed by the fact that relief without personal interest in the welfare of the recipient was both wasteful and degrading. He believed strongly that the best approach to deterring chronic poverty was the rehabilitation of the client and that rehabilitation could only be accomplished by personal contact. Opposed to public taxation for the care of the poor, he was equally opposed to any other type of giving which provided no insight into the lives of those

---

[11] Sidney and Beatrice Webb, *English Poor Law Policy* (New York and London: Longmans, Green and Company, 1910), p. 11.

receiving help and which underestimated the client's potentiality for self-support.

In accepting a new parish at St. John's in 1819, Chalmers had an opportunity to implement his concepts about assistance. He divided the parish into 25 districts, giving deacons the responsibility for administering the relief program. Under his direction, needs were investigated and homes visited. Names of recipients were registered to avoid possible duplication of grants and each case was treated on an individual basis. The districting of the parish, he believed, assured personal contact with the recipient as well as the equal distribution of assistance.

The London Charity Organization Society was established in the aftermath of a serious economic depression. As dissatisfaction with the administration of the 1834 poor law grew, philanthropic activity also increased, but there was little cooperation between the work of the poor law officials and that of private charities. Another paradoxical situation had also arisen; while questions were being raised as to the efficacy of "too much help to people," there was simultaneous interest and concern about the personal problems of the poor.

Chalmers' counterparts in England were Edward Denison, the son of a bishop, who had elected to teach the poor in London's East End, and Octavia Hill, granddaughter of a physician active in the public health movement, who had long been interested in the housing conditions of the poor.

Although Denison had little to do with the actual formation of the society, his knowledge and enthusiasm greatly influenced its philosophy. He believed that relief had a proper function, but that it was given too routinely and without plan and that it demoralized the poor and impaired their sense of self-respect. More importantly, Denison believed that relief, when given indiscriminately, deprived the recipient of the acceptance and understanding of his fellow men.[12]

Following Chalmers' concepts, the London Charity Organization Society used district committees to mobilize volunteers who would visit clients and undertake their rehabilitation. Its unique contribution to the history of social work, however, was the establishment of district offices. These offices were used as a center for the district committees and a means of promoting the cooperation of other agencies and individuals serving a given area. Each district office had at

---

[12] Mary E. Richmond, *The Long View* (New York: Russell Sage Foundation, 1930), p. 134.

least one paid official responsible for organizing and coordinating all volunteer effort and neighborhood activity.[13]

The Settlement Movement

Edward Denison's educational efforts in the slums of London and Octavia Hill's belief that the health and habits of tenement dwellers could be greatly improved by alleviation of the social distance between the rich and the poor played an even more important part in the development of the settlement movement. Queen describes this movement as an effort "to bridge the gulf that separated social classes."[14] Wayne McMillen, in a more recent analysis, termed it "a philosophy and a method" designed to supplement political democracy with a cultural democracy.[15]

Inspired by such intellectual idealists as Ruskin, Carlyle, and Kingsley, many students at Oxford and Cambridge became interested in studying conditions in the slum areas of London and in assuming an active role in the missions maintained there by the Anglican Church. Edward Denison, Arnold Toynbee, and Samuel Augustus Barnett were among this group of students. Barnett later became the vicar of St. Jude's Church in a slum section of East London, and Arnold Toynbee, while a lecturer and tutor at Oxford, assisted him with his parish work.

In 1883, Barnett received a letter from two Cambridge students asking what they could do for the poor that would allow them to give of themselves rather than of their money. His advice was to rent a house in a poor section of the city and go there to live. After he had elaborated on this idea in a subsequent lecture at Oxford, a group of students formed a committee to study the possibility of founding a University Colony in East London. Toynbee, who had been an enthusiastic member of the sponsoring group, died before this plan could be implemented. As a result, Toynbee Hall, the first settlement house in the world, was named in his honor when built by his friends in 1884.

Barnett became the first warden of Toynbee Hall and, as the program developed, classes, clubs, and discussion groups were initiated

---

[13] Karl de Schweinitz, *op. cit.*, p. 150.

[14] Stuart A. Queen, *Social Work in the Light of History* (Philadelphia: Lippincott, 1922), p. 131.

[15] Wayne McMillen, *Community Organization for Social Welfare* (Chicago: University of Chicago Press, 1945), p. 528.

for the underprivileged to promote the study of music, art, and various handicrafts.

By the end of the nineteenth century, 32 other settlement houses had been opened in Great Britain. Their usual purpose, like that of Toynbee Hall, was to provide a residence in a slum area for a group of educated "settlers." The settlers could thus learn from personal observation about the conditions under which the poor lived and the need for social reform, while they in turn, invested time and effort in providing education and cultural advantages for other residents of the neighborhood.

NEW RELIGIOUS ORGANIZATIONS

During the middle decades of this century, the revival of religious interest and missionary zeal in England resulted in the founding of three organizations which were to play significant roles in the history of child welfare.

In 1841, George Williams, a young draper's assistant, came to London and, in keeping with the customary "living in" system, was assigned to a dormitory in his employer's establishment. None of his roommates shared his interest in religion but he soon found a fellow Christian in an adjoining room. Together they prayed and studied contemporary religious books. Others soon joined in these activities and finally the firm provided a chaplain to conduct daily prayers. On June 6, 1844, twelve young men with four different church connections formed the first Young Men's Christian Association. Before long, the organization rented rooms for religious and social use and, with the support of leading clergymen and laymen, employed an organizing secretary and a missionary to administer and extend the work to other areas.

Before 1850, Williams also formulated a plan for a Young Ladies' Christian Association but apparently failed to gain support for this movement. In the following decade, however, the Crimean War "set in motion waves which permanently affected the thought and the work of British womankind—girls, young women, ladies and ladies of title in country and in city, down in the provinces and up in London."[16] In this process, ladies as well as employed nurses went out to Crimean hospitals under the leadership of Florence Nightingale.

---

[16] Elizabeth Wilson, *Fifty Years of Association Work Among Young Women, 1866–1916* (New York: National Board, Young Women's Christian Association of the U.S.A., 1916), p. 9.

One of the London institutions used as recruiting places for nurses also became a facility where they might live and prepare for sailing. In 1855, Lady Mary Jane Kinnaird, a sponsor of this "home," decided to enlarge its function. In addition to supervised living accommodations for young women, the home established an employment bureau and a lending library and provided social and religious activities. In 1858, the sponsoring group organized a Young Women's Christian Improvement Association for business girls "who needed a 'Sunday Home' and opportunities for recreation, instruction and Christian companionship."[17]

During the Crimean War the gentry also became involved in other social and religious projects. In 1855, Miss Emma Robarts "asked some of her friends to pray on Saturday evenings for young women, either for those in their own circle or for young women as a class."[18] By 1859, Prayer Unions had been established in various parts of England. The name Young Women's Christian Association was adopted "as the feminine of Young Men's,"[19] but the local groups continued to be known as Prayer Union branches.

In January, 1877, Miss Robarts and Lady Kinnaird met for the first time and agreed upon a union of the two associations. By that time many Prayer Unions, homes, and institutes had been established in England, Scotland, and Ireland. In 1892, plans for a World's Young Women's Christian Association were discussed and this organization came into being in 1894.

The third organization which originated in this period developed a very different program. In 1865, William Booth, a former Methodist minister, began an evangelistic street-corner crusade in the slums of London and "when his converts could not be successfully linked up with established church groups, he banded them together in an organization of his own" which in 1878, became the Salvation Army.[20] It was soon evident to Booth that "acute physical need among the poor had to be dealt with before their minds and hearts could be opened to understand and accept the Army's spiritual message."[21] In 1880, an international program was initiated and, as the organization grew, re-

---

[17] *Ibid.*, p. 17.

[18] *Ibid.*, pp. 9–10.

[19] *Ibid.*

[20] *Handbook of Information: Homes and Hospitals for Unmarried Mothers* (New York: The Salvation Army, 1952), p. 11.

[21] *Ibid.*

habilitative services and shelter facilities accompanied its religious activities.

From the date of founding, women members of the Salvation Army went into the slum districts of London seeking "fallen women"— prostitutes, drunkards, narcotic addicts, and other outcasts—begging them to reform and begin a new life. In 1884, the "Refuge" on Hanbury Street became the first Salvation Army Rescue Home and "the seed-bed from which sprang the beginnings" of the organization's subsequent social services for women.[22] In 1895, a home "for young girls who had been betrayed" was also opened in London, and thus began the Salvation Army's specialized services for unmarried mothers, some of whom were no more than eleven years of age.

THE INFLUENCE OF THESE EVENTS

As the next two chapters trace the development of a variety of methods of protecting and promoting the welfare of children in the United States, it will become evident that the counterparts of the events described in this chapter were repeated in the United States.

In some instances a direct transplantation occurred because American visitors to London were impressed with the success of a movement in England. In others, English citizens came to the United States for the specific purpose of expanding an English program, or for reasons which afforded an opportunity to introduce in a new setting, a familiar method of achieving the same objectives. The influence of the English experience is less tangible in some areas, and it can only be assumed that communication between the two countries led to a similar recognition of problems and to similar attempts to remedy existing conditions.

Selected Bibliography

Bruno, Frank J. *The Theory of Social Work.* Boston: D. C. Heath, 1936.
Queen, Stuart A. *Social Work in the Light of History.* Philadelphia: Lippincott, 1922.
Richmond, Mary E. *The Long View.* New York: Russell Sage Foundation, 1930.
Webb, Sidney and Beatrice Webb. *English Poor Law Policy.* New York and London: Longmans, Green and Company, 1910.

---

[22] *Ibid.,* p. 13.

Chapter 4   *The Development*

of Institutional Care in America

One of the most important developments in the nineteenth century was the rapid increase in the number of institutions for children. This movement stemmed in part from an increased recognition that mixed almshouse care was harmful to children, but other factors also played a significant role.

In Europe, many religious orders, guilds, and philanthropic groups had long provided institutional care for children. As wars, economic conditions, and pestilence increased the number of homeless needy children in America, it was inevitable that similar institutions would be established and that the pattern would be reproduced as new territories and states became populated. Slingerland stated:

These eastern people were reared where orphanages were already established, and the institutional care of dependents was accepted without question as the proper method. In facing similar needs in their new home region, they naturally began to rear congregate institutions.[1]

Since public responsibility for the care of needy children was an established pattern in England, it was only natural too that this concept would be reflected in various efforts to rescue children from the almshouses. Realization that neither towns, counties, nor charitable groups could be expected to provide the care required by certain groups of children led to an early assumption of state responsibility for the care of handicapped children. The availability of private institutions also caused many states and local units of government to feel that a financial subsidy to these facilities would be the least expensive method of meeting their responsibility for the care of children.

PRIVATE ORPHANAGES FOR HOMELESS CHILDREN

Although the nineteenth century is unique in the number of institutions established, four private orphanages had been founded prior to 1800.[2] For historical interest, it is appropriate to note briefly these "firsts" before returning to an examination of the movement characteristic of this later century.

The first institution for dependent children was established in New Orleans. Through the Jesuits who had come to engage in missionary work, the Order of Ursuline Sisters was induced to send ten sisters to establish a school in the French territory of Louisiana in 1727. Selected from ten different convents in France, these sisters are believed to have been "the first professional elementary school teachers to set foot on American soil."[3] Within two years, the Indian massacre at Natchez caused their convent to become both a boarding school and an orphanage. Their new convent, built in 1734, served the orphans of New Orleans until 1834, when the children were removed to the Poydras Female Orphan Asylum.

The first institution in an English colony was the Bethesda Orphanage in Savannah, Georgia, founded in 1738 by two prominent church-

---

[1] William H. Slingerland, *Child Welfare Work in California* (New York: Russell Sage Foundation, 1916), p. 28.

[2] Homer Folks, *Destitute, Neglected, and Delinquent Children* (New York: The Macmillan Company, 1902), pp. 9–10.

[3] John O'Grady, *Catholic Charities in the United States* (Washington, D.C.: National Conference of Catholic Charities, 1931), p. 18.

men with the encouragement of Governor Oglethorpe. Funds for the support of this facility were raised in England.

In 1797, members of the Catholic congregation in Philadelphia decided to accept responsibility for the care of Catholic children deprived of their parents by a yellow fever epidemic. A house was soon secured and the children placed in the care of a matron. This project was taken over by the Society of St. Joseph in 1807, and in 1814 the trustees of the society asked the Sisters of Charity to operate the institution.[4]

An institution "for the care and education of destitute girls" established in Baltimore by St. Paul's Church in 1799 was the only other facility founded before the nineteenth century. After 1800, orphanages were founded under a wide variety of religious and nonsectarian auspices and it was estimated that by 1850, 116 private institutions for children had been established.[5]

The first orphanage on the Pacific Coast was founded in 1851 by the San Francisco Protestant Orphan Asylum Society to care for orphans, half-orphans, and needy friendless children of the Protestant faith. Founded by a group of church people who recognized the need for a home for dependent children during the aftermath of the gold rush, the facility's first arrivals were five children who had lost their parents because of cholera aboard a ship that had turned Cape Horn.

In 1852, the Roman Catholic Orphan Asylum was established in San Francisco and by 1900 at least 49 institutions for dependent children had been established in California. Seventeen were conducted under Catholic auspices and the remainder by Protestant churches, fraternal orders, and nonsectarian groups.[6]

Some of the impetus for institutional care in California was undoubtedly supplied by the availability of state funds to help defray the cost of care. In 1855, the legislature authorized lump sum subsidies to the first two institutions in San Francisco and in 1879 all institutions were granted annual per capita amounts for the care of orphans and half-orphans.

In Maryland, a similar pattern of state subsidy developed and by 1900 there were 25 private institutions incorporated to serve children.

---

[4] *Ibid.*, pp. 20–21.

[5] Spencer H. Crookes, *Child Welfare: Social Work Year Book, 1954* (New York: American Association of Social Workers, 1954), p. 82.

[6] Slingerland, *op. cit.*, pp. 90–119.

In New York, where public funds were also made available, the number of private institutions increased from 2 in 1825 to more than 60 in 1866. Schneider explains that the loss of life during the Civil War was reflected in a marked increase both in the number of orphans and in the private institutions established for their care.[7] State subsidies initiated in 1811 were terminated by law in 1874, but local governmental units continued the practice of financial subsidy.

Although the provision of public subsidies to private institutions was also a common practice in many other states (for example, Delaware, Maine, North Carolina, Oregon, Pennsylvania) and in the District of Columbia, it has been observed that the generosity of appropriating bodies in California, Maryland, and New York resulted in a greater proportion of institutional care in these states than in states such as Massachusetts, Michigan, Washington, and Wisconsin, in which a more varied pattern of child care developed.

With the gradual western movement of population, the number of institutions in all states continued to increase. Exact figures are not available for an earlier date but a special Report on Benevolent Institutions issued by the United States Census Bureau in 1904 listed more than 1,000 such facilities.[8]

INSTITUTIONS FOR HANDICAPPED CHILDREN

Concurrent with the development of private institutions for the dependent child with normal physical and intellectual endowment, other institutions were founded to meet the special needs of handicapped children. These facilities were established under private, quasi-private, and state auspices.

INSTITUTIONS FOR THE DEAF. The American Asylum for the Deaf and Dumb, the first such institution in this country, was established in Hartford, Connecticut, in 1817 by Dr. Thomas Gallaudet after he had observed the training methods used in France. Supported at first by private funds, this facility later derived additional income from a federal land grant.

The New York Institution for the Instruction of the Deaf and Dumb, which opened on May 12, 1818, under private auspices, soon

---

[7] Schneider, *op. cit.*, p. 339.

[8] Hastings H. Hart, *Preventive Treatment of Neglected Children* (New York: Russell Sage Foundation, 1910), p. 65.

received a subsidy from local public funds, and state appropriations were provided for a similar institution founded in Philadelphia in 1820.

Kentucky established the first state residential school for the deaf in 1823 and subsequently received a federal land grant to aid in its support. Similar facilities were created in Ohio in 1829, in Virginia in 1838, and in Indiana in 1841. By 1850, state schools had been established in five additional states.

INSTITUTIONS FOR THE BLIND. Massachusetts enacted legislation to create the New England Asylum for the Blind at Boston in 1829. Dr. Samuel Gridley Howe was appointed as its director in 1831. This institution, later named the Perkins Institution for the Blind, became nationally famous under Howe's leadership.[9]

The New York Institution for the Blind, opened in 1832, was inspired by the work being done in the education of the blind in Scotland and England and by the founding of the institution in Boston. The first pupils were three pauper children who had been blinded during one of the ophthalmia epidemics in the city almshouse.[10]

Illinois, Kentucky, Mississippi, Ohio, Tennessee, and Wisconsin established state schools for the blind before 1850, and by 1870 there were 23 such institutions in the country.

INSTITUTIONS FOR THE MENTALLY RETARDED. The work of the noted French educator-physician-psychologist, Édouard Séguin, influenced American interest in the education of the mentally handicapped. After his arrival in America in 1848, Séguin assisted in the organization of institutions in five states, and later became the superintendent of the Pennsylvania Training School for Idiots.[11]

Massachusetts established the first state-supported educational program for the mentally deficient at the Perkins Institution for the Blind in 1848. Two years later, under Samuel Gridley Howe's direction, a separate institution was incorporated as the Massachusetts School for the Idiotic and Feebleminded Youth. Similar state-supported institutions were founded in New York, Pennsylvania, Ohio, and Connecticut within the next ten years.

---

[9] Gabriel Farrell, *The Story of Blindness* (Cambridge: Harvard University Press, 1956), p. 46.

[10] Schneider, *op. cit.*, pp. 371–372.

[11] J. E. Wallace Wallin, *Education of Mentally Handicapped Children* (New York: Harper and Brothers, 1955), p. 9.

INSTITUTIONS FOR JUVENILE DELINQUENTS. Interest in the plight of children coming to the attention of the police gained impetus from the growing child population in city jails and lockups. Widespread concern developed because child offenders were sentenced to prisons or jails and because these facilities were also used for the detention of children for long periods of time prior to a court hearing. Public protest about the association of child offenders and dependent children with adult criminals eventually stimulated a movement for separate facilities for children.

The first such institution, the New York House of Refuge, was established in New York City in 1825. It was hailed as an innovation since it represented a departure from penal care, introduced the concept of differential treatment of children, and was directed toward rehabilitation.

In 1823, the Society for the Reformation of Juvenile Delinquents in the City of New York was incorporated by an act of the legislature, and authorized to establish a House of Refuge which would admit vagrant children or those convicted of criminal offenses. The managers were also empowered to place children committed to their care in employment suitable to their age and capacities and, with their consent, to bind them out as apprentices or servants. Binding out for the period of the child's minority was intended to prepare the child for a trade and to make his reformation possible.[12]

The first annual report of the New York House of Refuge describes the emotional climate which prevailed on the day this historical institution opened:

The ceremony was interesting in the highest degree. Nine of those poor outcasts from society, three boys and six girls, clothed in rags with squalid countenances, were brought in from the Police Office, and placed before the audience. An address appropriate to so novel an occasion was made by a member of the board, and not an individual, it may safely be affirmed, was present, whose warmest feelings did not vibrate in unison with the philanthropic views which led to the foundation of this Home of Refuge.[13]

The founding of the New York House of Refuge stimulated interest in establishing this type of facility in other localities. In 1826, Boston followed with a municipally owned House of Reformation and the Philadelphia House of Refuge was founded in 1828 as a private cor-

---

[12] *First Annual Report, The Home of Refuge*, 1825, cited in Grace Abbott, *op. cit.*, II, p. 349.

[13] *Ibid.*, p. 352.

poration. The fourth juvenile reformatory was the New Orleans House of Refuge. Established as a municipal institution in 1847, it added a girls' section in 1852. Ohio pioneered a new type of school in 1856 by inaugurating the cottage plan whereby a family home was simulated and boys were housed in small units.

This pattern of care for child offenders flourished during the remainder of the century. From 1824 until 1900, seventy such institutions were established in many parts of the country. Originally called "houses of refuge," they were later known as "reform schools." The latter name placed a stigma on the released child, however, and proved a handicap to him. The establishment of "industrial schools" followed in the hope that this name would not be disadvantageous to the discharged child. It soon developed the same flavor as the reform school and, in addition, caused confusion with nonreformatory industrial schools.

Employment was considered the best means of treatment in early institutions of this kind. At first, inmates were "farmed out" to contractors through a special wage agreement but this practice eventually led to a plan whereby industries were operated within the institution. Emphasis shifted from work as a source of revenue to work as a means of learning, after it was seen that the industries which produced the most revenue were the least useful to the boy after discharge.[14]

PUBLIC INSTITUTIONS FOR DEPENDENT CHILDREN

The Charleston Orphan Home, in Charleston, South Carolina, is believed to have been the first public institution for children in the United States. Since the city charter required an assumption of responsibility for the care of destitute children, a building was rented for this purpose for a period of four years after the initial plan of boarding children with families was abandoned. A new structure was built in 1794 to receive the 115 orphans then dependent upon the city for support.[15]

Separate provisions for the institutional care of children were made by several large cities after 1816, but in most instances these facilities were administered by the officials responsible for the maintenance of the almshouse and were located on the same grounds. Education was provided and some of the disadvantages of mixed almshouses avoided,

---

[14] Folks, *op. cit.*, pp. 226–227.

[15] *Ibid.*, p. 7.

but contemporary reports deplored the high incidence of ophthalmia among the children, the high mortality rate caused by this disease and by cholera, and the practice of assigning adult paupers, vagrants, and even criminals from city institutions to care for the children.

In Philadelphia, a separate children's asylum was maintained under the direction of the almshouse managers between 1820 and 1831. When a new almshouse was constructed in 1831, children were returned to this facility and detached buildings resigned for their care. In describing this institution, Alfred Stille, a resident physician, wrote:

A hundred or more children were sheltered there on their way to an early grave to which most of them were destined. Illegitimate and other outcasts formed the majority, and ophthalmia, that curse of children's asylums, made of them a sore-eyed, puny group most pitiable to see. . . . I pointed out to the committee of the board how the disease was disseminated by the children washing in the same basins and using the same towels, . . . and also by the insufficient food permitted them. . . . But, of course the committee . . . knew better than I, and, . . . nothing was done to correct this wrong.[16]

In Massachusetts three state almshouses were built for the "unsettled poor" in 1851–52. When the Board of Charities was established in 1863, one of its first acts was to transfer all children who were state charges to the almshouse at Monson. In 1866, this institution was renamed the Monson State Primary School and became the first state institution for destitute children in the United States.

The Monson facility was also unique for another reason. As in all almshouses, it had been current practice to bind out the children who could be placed with families. Since no investigation of the applicants for destitute children was made, many children had been placed with wholly unsuitable persons. In 1869, Massachusetts created a separate agency whose staff was to visit all children who had been indentured from the state institution, and to investigate the homes of applicants for children receiving care in these facilities. In addition, staff members were to attend the trial of each juvenile offender, to make an investigation of each case, and to advise the magistrates as to whether the child should be committed to a reform school or to the custody of the Board of State Charities for the development of a suitable plan.[17]

---

[16] *Ibid.*, pp. 28–29.

[17] *Ibid.*, pp. 34–35.

As new centers of population were established, however, additional mixed almshouses were founded in many smaller cities, towns, and counties throughout the nation. In 1824, New York enacted a law which provided for the establishment of county poorhouses in eighteen counties and initiated in that state the principle of county responsibility for the poor. By 1856, a Senate committee reported on conditions in the almshouses that "if known would disgrace the State and shock humanity" and recommended that all children be placed either in institutions devoted to their special use or in private orphanages to be maintained at public expense. The proposed legislation was not adopted, but the laws of 1857 did authorize county and town overseers of the poor, in countries where there were no private orphanages, to place children in private orphan asylums in any part of the state at public expense. Some counties adopted this practice, but the number of children under sixteen years of age in New York almshouses increased from about 3,000 in 1847 to 26,251 in 1886. By the same act, child caring institutions authorized to bind out children were also required to maintain a register showing each child received and discharged and to record the address and occupation of the person with whom the child was placed.[18]

In 1866, the Ohio General Assembly authorized counties to establish children's homes to be administered at county expense under a board of trustees appointed by the Board of County Commissioners. In 1889, legislation authorized each county home to employ an agent to act as a home-finder and placement worker. Few such agents were appointed, but by 1899 fifty county homes had been established.

Indiana adopted similar legislation in 1881 and in 1897 inaugurated supervision of the county children's homes by the State Board of Charities. Children were placed in family homes at the discretion of these authorities.

In 1871, another pattern of care was initiated when Michigan enacted legislation to establish a "State Public School." In 1874, a cottage-plan facility was opened at Coldwater which admitted dependent and neglected children from four to sixteen years of age and gave preference to those previously maintained in county poorhouses.[19] By law, the child's stay in the state school was to be for only a temporary period of time, pending foster home placement by state and county agents. Children were committed to the institution

---

[18] Schneider, *op. cit.*, p. 342.

[19] *Laws of Michigan, 1871*, I, No. 172, p. 280.

by the probate court upon application of the superintendent of the poor. All children so placed were made wards of the state but could be returned to their own homes by official action of the institution's board of control. Although this facility was emulated by other states, Governor John J. Bagley, in describing the institution at the Second Conference of the State Boards of Charities held in Detroit in May, 1875, made this skeptical observation:

This "home," as we call it, is after all only a purgatory; a half-way house between Hell or the county poor-house, and heaven or a happy home. These children are absolutely worse than convicts' children. They are nobody's children. . . . What on earth is there so demoralizing, so degrading, so low down as our county poor houses?[20]

Minnesota, Wisconsin, and Rhode Island also established state schools in 1886. Wisconsin followed the Michigan plan and required that children be placed in family homes within sixty days. Minnesota adopted a similar plan but used employees of the facility for placement. Rhode Island also followed the Michigan plan, but placed responsibility for the administration and control of the institution with the State Board of Education. The Board of Education was authorized to place children in families and was made the legal guardian of all children admitted to the institution. Before 1900, additional state schools were founded in Colorado, Kansas, Montana, Nebraska, Nevada, and Texas.

At the close of the Civil War the number of orphans of soldiers requiring care resulted in the founding of institutions for this purpose in Illinois, Iowa, Kansas, Minnesota, Ohio, Pennsylvania, and Wisconsin. In Iowa and Kansas these facilities were later converted to state schools for dependent children.

INSTITUTIONS FOR
UNMARRIED MOTHERS AND THEIR CHILDREN

The first reported effort to provide specialized institutional care for unmarried mothers and their infants occurred before the middle of the nineteenth century. The Talitha Cumi Maternity Home and Hospital, established in Boston in 1836, appears to have been one of the first facilities of this type. It is believed that similar institutions were

---

[20] *Proceedings of the Conference of Charities, 1875* (Boston: Tolman and White, 1875), pp. 10–11.

organized under Protestant or nonsectarian auspices during the same decade but their history is not recorded.[21]

About the same time, Catholic leaders came to realize that existing institutions for children were not suitable for the care of infants and small children. Bishop Tinon in Buffalo conceived the idea of providing an asylum for "homeless widows and forsaken infants,"[22] and land was donated for this purpose in 1852. After a small wooden cottage was moved to the premises, four sisters from St. Mary's Lying-In Hospital in Buffalo "began to provide shelter and care for pregnant unmarried women."[23]

In 1853, the St. Anne's Widows' Home, Lying-In Hospital, and Foundling Asylum of St. Louis was established. From the beginning, this facility provided care for unmarried mothers since it was recognized that "many infants were abandoned because the mothers did not have any place to go" and that offering shelter and protection to the mother was one of the best means of protecting the baby.[24]

With the example of these pioneering efforts, nineteen additional Catholic infant and maternity homes were founded before the end of the nineteenth century. The most famous of these was the New York Foundling Hospital established in 1869 to alleviate the prevalent practice of infanticide. At first, a reception crib was placed on the outside of the hospital "where the mother might leave her baby without revealing her own identity."[25] When it became apparent that this practice was encouraging mothers to abandon their children, the facility attempted to induce unmarried mothers to avail themselves of the shelter of the institution. In 1880, the New York Protectory was built to provide care for unmarried mothers before and after confinement.

In 1883, another national movement in the provision of maternity home care originated when Charles N. Crittenton, a wealthy businessman, became interested in establishing a rescue home for girls in New York City. After the sudden death of his four-year old daughter,

---

[21] Maud Morlock and Hilary Campbell, *Maternity Homes for Unmarried Mothers* (Washington, D. C.: U.S. Department of Labor, Children's Bureau Publication 309, 1946), p. 7.

[22] John O'Grady, *op. cit.*, p. 129.

[23] *Ibid.*, p. 130.

[24] *Ibid.*, pp. 131–132.

[25] *Ibid.*, p. 133.

Florence, Crittenton began frequenting the noon prayer meetings in a church near his office, and one afternoon accompanied a member of the church on a missionary tour to the saloons near the Bowery. After the men had prayed with two girls and were about to say, "Go and sin no more," Crittenton suddenly realized there was no place for them to go. Out of this incident was born his plan to salvage "this helpless class."[26]

On April 19, 1883, the Florence Night Mission was opened to accommodate girls who sought shelter, and by 1890 Crittenton had formulated a plan for a national organization "with one or more homes in each state, not only to serve the needs of their own section, but to make it possible to send girls from one to the other in order to get them out of their old environment."[27]

From the example set by the Florence Night Mission, a "Door of Hope" or "House of Refuge" was established in many communities. The Pacific Rescue Home in San Francisco, founded in 1889, was a facility of this type. When Crittenton found that the home was in financial difficulty in 1892, a reorganization was effected and the facility reincorporated as a Florence Crittenton Home. Shortly after this, the Los Angeles Florence Crittenton Home Association was organized and "the Florence Home" dedicated on August 25, 1892. During 1892, Crittenton also learned that the Women's Christian Temperance Union had previously established several rescue homes with the same objectives as those of the Crittenton Homes. He immediately agreed to establish five new Florence Crittenton Homes under WCTU auspices and these facilities were opened in Denver; Chicago; Portland, Oregon; Fargo, North Dakota; and Norfolk, Virginia, during the same year.

Entirely separate from this activity, Mrs. Kate Waller Barrett had developed an earlier interest in meeting the needs of unmarried mothers. As the young wife of an Episcopalian rector in the slum district of Richmond, Virginia, she had been deeply impressed by her first contact with an unmarried mother. Her first efforts were directed toward helping individual girls in her husband's parish in Richmond and then in Kentucky and in Atlanta, Georgia. Later, she

---

[26] Otto Wilson, in collaboration with Robert South Barrett, *Fifty Years' Work With Girls, 1883–1933: A Story of the Florence Crittenton Homes* (Alexandria, Virginia: National Florence Crittenton Mission, 1933), p. 30.

[27] *Ibid.*, p. 36.

began an attempt to set up a rescue home in Atlanta and in this effort learned of Crittenton's endeavors. As a result, the Atlanta facility became another Florence Crittenton Home.

In 1893 Crittenton met Mrs. Barrett for the first time and discussed with her his plan for a national organization. Mrs. Barrett soon began to assist him, first by visiting homes which had asked for his financial help and admission to the Crittenton chain, and later by organizing new homes. When the "Hope and Help Mission" in Washington, D.C., became a Crittenton Home in 1895, headquarters for the long-hoped-for national organization were established at this facility. Crittenton became the president of the national organization and Mrs. Barrett, vice president and general superintendent.

When the first national conference was held in Mountain Lake Park, Maryland, in 1897, 53 homes had become members of the Florence Crittenton chain. After the national organization was perfected, the board of trustees felt the need for a more uniform legal relationship with the member homes. Through a special act of Congress, the first national charter ever granted to a philanthropic organization was signed by President McKinley on April 9, 1898.[28]

The third step to provide specialized care for unmarried mothers was interwoven chronologically with that of the Florence Crittenton movement. In 1880, seven women officers of the Salvation Army were sent from London to New York City to inaugurate the religious program of that organization and in 1887 a "rescue home" was established in Brooklyn. During the same year, similar facilities were opened in Grand Rapids, Michigan, and Oakland, California, and, by 1900, eighteen Salvation Army facilities for women were in operation in the major cities of fourteen states.[29] In later years the term "rescue home" was gradually replaced by the designation, "Home and Hospital for Unmarried Mothers," and the publicized name of these facilities changed to Booth Memorial or Salvation Army Home and Hospital.

Thus, by the close of the nineteenth century, three major efforts to provide specialized institutional care for unmarried mothers and their children were rapidly expanding. Although religious motivation prompted each of these movements, their primary concern became an effort to insure a greater chance for survival for children born out of wedlock, and, for their mothers, an opportunity for rehabilitation.

---

[28] *Ibid.*, p. 45.

[29] *Handbook of Information: Homes and Hospitals for Unmarried Mothers,* p. 11.

DAY NURSERIES

In 1854 still another form of institutional care was inaugurated in New York City, when the Nursery and Child's Hospital opened a nursery in which former patients could leave their babies in the care of nurses during the day. Patterned after the crèches first established in Paris in 1844, day nurseries "came into existence in this country as the result of two major influences: the desire to prevent child neglect from lack of care during the mother's working hours; and the desire to prevent and counteract the excessive institutionalization of children of destitute parents."[30] Sponsored usually by a philanthropic women's group or a religious organization, the early facilities were designed to serve primarily the children of widowed mothers. However, their services were also made available to working mothers forced to supplement a father's meager earnings.

The New York City example was followed in Troy, New York, in 1858, and in Philadelphia in 1863. By 1892, a total of 90 day nurseries had been established throughout the country and by 1897 the number had grown to 175. In 1898, the National Federation of Day Nurseries was organized "to unite day nurseries in a common body and purpose."

THE SIGNIFICANCE OF THESE DEVELOPMENTS

From the preceding sections it is evident that attempts to solve a problem affecting children often resulted in the development of a new type of congregate care.

Tracing the origin of the various types of institutions established in the nineteenth century is of value since these facilities still form an important segment of the current pattern of child care. Presenting this material in one chapter, however, tends to create an erroneous impression of the history of child welfare during the last half of the nineteenth century. As we have seen, the number and variety of institutions for children continued to increase, but this fact in itself produced extensive efforts to meet the needs of children in other ways. Other developments also gave impetus to the initiation of new services to children and, after 1850, the founding of institutions became only one thread of the complex pattern which developed before the end of the century.

---

[30] Mary F. Bogue and Katherine F. Blake, *A Survey of Day Nurseries* (White House Conference on Child Health and Protection, 1931 copyright), p. 11.

Selected Bibliography

Abbott, Grace. *The Child and the State*, Vol. II. Chicago: University of Chicago Press, 1938.

Crookes, Spencer H. "Child Welfare," *Social Work Year Book, 1954.* New York: American Book-Stratford Press, 1954.

Farrell, Gabriel. *The Story of Blindness.* Cambridge: Harvard University Press, 1956.

Folks, Homer. *The Care of Destitute, Neglected, and Delinquent Children.* New York: The Macmillan Company, 1902.

Hart, Hastings H. *Preventive Treatment of Neglected Children.* New York: Russell Sage Foundation, 1910.

Slingerland, William H. *Child Welfare Work in California.* New York: Russell Sage Foundation, 1916.

Chapter 5

Other Developments in Nineteenth Century America

By the third decade of this century, the rapid growth and changing technology of the new nation were becoming economically and socially disturbing. There were recurrent epidemics and prolonged periods of economic depression and unemployment. The population continued to increase owing to heavy immigration, and there was an unprecedented movement of people within the country as families attempted to relocate during periods of unemployment. All of these factors affected family stability and the quality of child care.

During these momentous times private fortunes were also amassed and, as social problems became more evident, many philanthropic agencies were organized under a variety of auspices. Since the problem-solving efforts of these agencies provided the basis for many of our modern services for children, it is important to trace their development. It is also necessary however, to examine corollary attempts to meet the needs of children under governmental auspices.

NEW APPROACHES TO DEPENDENCY

The New York Association for Improving the Condition of the Poor (AICP) was founded by Robert Hartley in 1843 in response to the suffering brought about by a depression which lasted for six years. During this period serious question had been raised about the methods used by private and public agencies in attempting to cope with the relief problem. Many persons believed that help given to the needy in times of depression tended to inculcate chronic dependency which, in turn, caused an increasing number of persons to seek relief. That the causes of dependency were rooted in the economic system did not occur to this group. Instead, it was believed that the agencies were making "mistakes" in giving material aid.

The AICP endeavored to remedy the indiscriminate almsgiving procedures of some thirty private agencies in the New York area. This was done by dividing the city into districts. The work in each district was carried out by an advisory committee and a "visitor," and applicants were helped only by applying to the visitor in the area in which they lived.[1] The pioneer effort of the AICP in the use of these methods seems to have received little recognition, though it preceded by 26 years a similar plan made famous by the London Charity Organization Society.

The AICP did not confine its activities to the organization of relief giving, but attempted to combat the causes of dependency on all fronts. In 1851, the New York Juvenile Asylum was established and within two years, two free dispensaries (clinics) were founded to meet the medical needs of slum residents. In 1897, the AICP opened the Hartley House Social Settlement to provide work rooms for unskilled women as well as a neigborhood center for children and adults.[2] Another landmark was achieved in 1879 when paid "visitors" were substituted for volunteers in direct services to clients.

Throughout the nineteenth century the AICP also focused attention on needed legislation and on its efforts to demonstrate the value of public services. As early as 1853, its members were responsible for the enactment of a state law to provide care for idle and truant children and, in 1860, for the employment of the first truant officers in the schools of New York City.

In the field of child welfare the early program of the AICP repre-

---

[1] Schneider, *op. cit.*, pp. 265–267.

[2] *The 91st Annual Report of the AICP, 1933–34* (New York: Association for Improving the Condition of the Poor), pp. 44–45.

sented one of the first efforts to mobilize a broad attack on conditions inimical to the welfare of children and provided a pattern which was followed by similar organizations in many other cities. In Baltimore and some other localities these organizations adopted the same name, but others were known as "Associated Charities."

NEW RELIGIOUS ORGANIZATIONS

During the period in which the first general concern about existing social problems was developing, J. V. Sullivan, a Boston sea captain, set in motion a chain of events which ultimately led to the establishment of two national youth-serving organizations.[3] After reading an account of the activities of the London Young Men's Christian Association, Sullivan was so impressed that he visited the headquarters of this organization. On his return he elicited equal enthusiasm among the young men of Boston and in December, 1851, representatives of twenty churches met to organize the first YMCA in this country. Within a year the membership of the new organization had increased to 1,200 and, 22 similar associations were soon established in major cities of the United States and Canada.

To the YMCA in Washington, D.C., belongs the credit for founding a national and international organization. The first international convention of Young Men's Christian Associations was held in Buffalo in 1854 and the Alliance of Young Men's Christian Associations, the first world body, established in Paris in 1855.[4]

Permanent headquarters for the national organization were established in New York City in 1866 and in the same year Dr. Luther H. Gulick, "the philosopher of the Association," contributed the concept of the "triangle—body, mind, and spirit" which later became the symbol of the YMCA.

Out of this philosophy, a national physical program was developed, an educational program initiated, and two colleges founded to provide trained leadership for the local associations. In all associations, reading rooms, lecture courses, and educational classes became a part of the program and, in some urban Associations, the educational department soon assumed the dimensions of a university.

In 1885 the first organized Boys' Camp was establisheed by the

---

[3] George Sherwood Eddy, *A Century with Youth: A History of the YMCA From 1844 to 1944* (New York: Association Press, 1944), pp. 22–23.

[4] *Ibid.*, p. 36.

YMCA on Lake Champlain, New York, and in 1900 the international committee employed the first Secretary for Boys' Work. Despite these early beginnings, the YMCA remained primarily a religious organization for young men throughout the nineteenth century, though Gulick maintained that "manhood began with adolescence and that work with boys is more important than work with adults."[5]

Unlike that of the YMCA, the origin of the Young Women's Christian Association in the United States cannot be traced to a single event or to any direct influence of its predecessor in England. In New York City, one of the prayer circles organized during the great religious revival of 1857–58 formed the Ladies' Christian Association. In 1858, a constitution was adopted which required that members "seek out especially young women of the operative class, aid them in procuring employment and in obtaining suitable places, furnish them with proper reading matter, establish Bible classes and meetings for religious exercises . . . and use all practical means for the increase of true piety in themselves and others."[6] A home for young girls was established in June, 1860, and other properties were later acquired for this purpose.

In 1867, the Hartford Women's Christian Association was organized for the specific purpose of establishing a home for self-supporting girls, and almost simultaneously organizations with the same name and purpose were founded in five other cities.

At a meeting held in Hartford in 1871, officers of the twenty associations known to be in existence made plans for regular biennial sessions, and in 1875 a formal organization was established which adopted the title "International Conference of Women's Christian Associations."

Within the preceding decade another movement with somewhat similar objectives developed after the first YWCA was organized in Boston on March 3, 1866. Patterned on the YMCA, lodging for young women was provided, a restaurant and employment service made available to nonresident girls, and a Department of Instruction established. The Boston YWCA has importance, not only because it was the first association in this country to use the name of the modern organization but because its program was limited to activities that are now characteristic of the YWCA.

Meanwhile, a completely separate movement had developed under the same name in a group of coeducational colleges. Modeled after the Young Men's Christian Association, the first student association

---

[5] *Ibid.*, p. 62.

[6] Elizabeth Wilson, *op. cit.*, p. 23.

was established at the Illinois State Normal School in 1873. Similar organizations soon developed and in 1884 the first state Association was formed in Michigan. Other state Associations soon were established and in August, 1886, the National Association of the Young Women's Christian Associations of the United States was formed by representatives of these student associations.

In 1891, the International Conference of Women's Christian Associations recognized the value of a single national organization and changed its name to "The International Board of the Women's and Young Women's Association." This action, however, did not accomplish its objective and the two national organizations continued their separate ways for fifteen years.

During the nineteenth century neither association concerned itself to any great extent with girls who were not college students or self-supporting. The idea of a branch organization for junior activities was conceived during the last decade of the century, but the plan was not implemented during this period.

Child Saving Organizations

After 1850 a new movement developed as a means of rescuing children from the almshouse, preventing congregate care of any type, and providing more adequate care for children whose homes were considered unsuitable. As we have seen, all public institutions engaged in the placement of children for indenture and most private institutions were authorized to bind out children entrusted to their care. Other charitable organizations had also been authorized to place children, but the New York Children's Aid Society, founded in 1853, and its founder, Charles Loring Brace, a Protestant clergyman, are usually considered to have originated the modern foster care movement.

Strongly opposed to institutional care and impressed with the growing number of homeless children in the New York City streets, Brace sought homes for these children in other states. By developing home-finding committees in the farming communities of the East and Middle West, and by use of newspaper announcements in these areas, the New York Children's Aid Society transported trainloads of children who were chosen by foster families after they arrived at their destination.

In reply to charges made by the American Prison Congress that children sent West by the society were often found in jails, reformatories, or orphan homes, Brace presented a paper at the annual meeting of the Conference of Boards of Charities which met in Saratoga, New York, in September, 1876. In describing the philosophy and experience of the Society, he explained:

> . . . This great class of street children . . . are not at all a hopeless class. They are often of very good stock, coming from honest European peasantry who, in a foreign land have become unfortunate. They are not links in a chain of criminal inheritance.[7]

Elaborating on the value of the remote farm homes where many placements were made, he further described these children by stating:

> Under a patient and orderly mistress, they make the best kind of family help. . . . Their natures are open to religion, and under a pious lady of the house, they soon feel the inspiration and hope of Christian piety. . . . The poor little barbarian of the city streets becomes the honest and Christian farmer of the west, or even the teacher and preacher of the best truths to others.[8]

Brace informed the conference that in the 23 years of its service to children the New York Children's Aid Society had placed about 35,000 children.

The plan for placing children was relatively simple and, Brace felt, "generally successful." A resident agent of the society with headquarters at Chicago explored farming communities where children might be needed. When a locality was found, the agent sought the interest of prominent citizens who would assist in the recruitment of homes. The public was then informed that a company of orphans would arrive on a certain day. Children were temporarily housed with families in the community, fed and washed, and later appeared at the place designated for their meeting with the prospective foster parents. Brace explained that on these occasions "the farmers gather from the country for miles around." No payment was offered for the care of children since Brace felt it would tend to dishonor "a deep and fervent spirit of humanity toward these unfortunate children implanted by Christianity."[9]

Although the early methods used by the New York agency were subject to considerable criticism, similar agencies were established in Baltimore, Philadelphia, and Boston by 1864.

When Charles W. Birtwell became associated with the Boston

---

[7] Charles L. Brace, "The 'Placing Out' Plan for Homeless and Vagrant Children," in *Proceedings of the Conference of Charities*, (Albany: John Munsell, December 1876), pp. 135–136.

[8] *Ibid.* pp. 136–137.

[9] *Ibid.*, pp. 139–144.

Children's Aid Society at a later date, he also pioneered in the field of child welfare but with a vastly different effect upon child care philosophy and practice. His contribution to modern concepts of foster home placement stemmed from his vision in perceiving that service to a child is not merely a manipulation of the child's environment. In his thinking, the placement process revolved around the important question: "What is best for the child? What will meet his need?" This was a progressive departure from the traditional question: "Where shall we put the child?" The emphasis thus shifted from the familiar agreement that fresh air, country living, piety, industry, and rescue of the child from his own parents would be of maximum benefit, to a recognition of the unique and separate needs of each child.

Three highly important innovations in the child placing process were developed by Birtwell as attention was turned to the child himself. These included knowledge of the child, an adequate and comprehensive study of potential foster homes, and supervision of the child and the foster home after placement. The blending of these three processes, Birtwell believed, would insure a high order of cooperation between the child, the agency, and the foster family.[10]

It was in methods of working with the child in his own home, however, that Birtwell made his most creative contribution to contemporary child care practice. He strongly believed that no child could be separated from his own family without its having a distressing effect upon him and that every means should be afforded the child and his parents to strengthen and reinforce the quality of their relationship.[11] It can be assumed that it was Birtwell's conviction that the rehabilitation of the child's own home had priority over foster home placement. By modern standards it can be readily agreed that Birtwell was embarking upon one of the most valuable services to the child—that of preserving his home and consequently his most urgent "rights."

Recognizing that no one agency could meet all of these needs, the Boston Children's Aid Society also sought to establish itself as a coordinating agency to mobilize the services of other agencies. Thus the groundwork for casework services to children and community organization on behalf of children made substantial beginnings.

The movement to establish children's agencies continued throughout

---

[10] *Massachusetts State Board of Charities Annual Report, 1888*, pp. 13–16.

[11] *Ibid.*, p. 10.

the remainder of the nineteenth century. In 1883 the American Educational Aid Association was established in Chicago by the Rev. M. Van Buren Van Arsdale, another pioneer in the home-finding movement. This organization, whose original function combined child placing with assisting young women to acquire an education, later became the parent agency of a federation of 28 children's home societies which was renamed the National Children's Home Society.

The support received by agencies of this type was premised on the increasing conviction that congregate care did not meet the emotional needs of children. It also reflected a growing awareness of the advantages of the socialization and individual attention which could be afforded the child in a substitute parental home where he would be regarded as a member of the foster family. Financial advantages were also seen by comparing the cost of foster care and institutional placement. In many instances, foster home care was also more readily available than institutional care since the population in an institution was more permanent and vacancies did not occur with any degree of frequency. Perhaps, as Slingerland pointed out, it was the "universality" of the acceptance of "child placing" (in foster homes) that caused the rapid development of the child saving agency.[12]

STATE BOARDS OF CHARITIES

The schools for the deaf in Connecticut and Kentucky had received federal land grants on the premise that these facilities would have regional importance in view of their service to the deaf residents of other states. A bill authorizing a land grant for use in providing more adequate care for the insane was vetoed, however, by President Pierce on April 24, 1854. This event had great significance since the veto message enunciated the principles that the federal government does not have constitutional authority to provide "for the care and support of all those, among the people of the United States, who, by any form of calamity, become fit objects of public philanthropy," and that "all objects which have not been entrusted to the Federal government . . . therefore belong exclusively to the States."[13]

---

[12] William H. Slingerland, *Child Placing in Families* (New York: Russell Sage Foundation, 1918), pp. 185–189.

[13] *Congressional Globe* (33rd Congress, 1st. Session, May 3, 1854) pp. 1061–1063, in Sophonisba P. Breckinridge, *Public Welfare Administration: Select Documents* (Chicago: University of Chicago Press, 1927), p. 224.

This pronouncement effectively terminated any further attempt during the nineteenth century to secure federal participation in the extension of needed services for children. Breckinridge believes that it also impressed upon the various states their responsibility for the administration, regulation, and supervision of activities related to the general welfare of the people, and the need for "the establishment of a central state supervisory authority."[14]

In Massachusetts, a special commission appointed in 1858 expressed concern about the increased outlay for charity and the recent establishment of nine state institutions without any reference to each other. This group later recommended "the creation of a permanent State Board of Charities to be entrusted with the duty of constantly supervising the whole system of public charities, in order to secure the greatest usefulness, without unnecessary expense."[15] The board created in October, 1863, was an unpaid body empowered to investigate and supervise state and municipal institutions and to make recommendations regarding matters relating to administration and to the care of inmates in these institutions. Although it had the right of inspection and the power to transfer, admit, and discharge inmates, it did not have administrative control over the institutions.

During the next two decades, the Massachusetts State Board of Charities made several notable contributions to the child welfare field. As we have seen, it recommended separation of all children from contact with adults in the almshouses and the placement of child in family homes as soon as possible. By 1889, legislation for the protection of infants who were victimized by "baby farming" was adopted on recommendation of the board. Thus, it became a crime to abandon a child under two years of age and all persons placing or receiving children were required to notify the State Board of such action. Perhaps one of the most significant contributions of this legislation was the requirement that unrelated persons caring for more than two infants under the age of two years be licensed and supervised by the State Board.[16]

Ohio followed the Massachusetts pattern in establishing a Board of State Charities in 1867 and, although the board was abolished in 1872, it was reestablished in 1876. The reactivated board concerned itself immediately with the plight of more than 1,000 children under

---

[14] *Ibid.*, p. 237.

[15] Kelso, *op. cit.*, p. 142.

[16] *Acts of Massachusetts*, Chapter 416.

fifteen who were then housed in county infirmaries (almshouses) throughout the state.

The New York Board of Commissioners of Public Charities was also established in 1867, and by 1874 similar supervisory boards had been developed by Connecticut, Illinois, Kansas, Michigan, North Carolina, Pennsylvania, and Rhode Island. Other states, such as Minnesota and Wisconsin, established boards which subsequently became "boards of control" with administrative authority over public institutions and the funds allotted for the subsidy of private institutions. By 1897, fifteen states had established boards with various patterns of supervisory or administrative authority.

THE FIRST NATIONAL FORUM

Another important event in this period grew out of the decision that state boards might profitably share their experiences with each other. The first meeeting of the Conference of Boards of Public Charities was held in New York City in May, 1874. The plan to bring together members of the State Boards was inspired by Frank Sanborn, the first secretary of the Massachusetts Board of Charities, who was also associated with the American Social Science Association. As a result, the first four conferences were conducted under the auspices of the latter organization.

A separate organization was established in 1879, entitled the National Conference of Charities and Correction. This organization and its successor, the National Conference of Social Work (renamed in 1917) became a permanent annual forum for the exchange of social welfare information and the proceedings of its meetings have continued to tell the story of American life through the intervening years. An examination of these volumes reveals the broad sweep of public opinion, scientific knowledge, and concern for children and adults. It is generally agreed that no other source so vividly outlines, or so meaningfully portrays, the development of child welfare in this country.

SOCIETIES FOR THE PREVENTION OF CRUELTY
TO CHILDREN

After 1825 the statutes of many states began to reflect

. . . more recognition and practical application of the principle that it is the right and duty of the public authorities to intervene in cases of parental cruelty, or gross neglect seriously endangering the health, morals, or elementary education of children, and to remove the children by force if necessary, and place them under surroundings more favorable for their development."[17]

These laws were useful in providing a legal basis for the action taken when a dependent child was brought to the attention of an institution for children, a child saving agency, or the police. No agency or official, however, accepted responsibility for searching out the neglected child or taking any responsible action in protecting the welfare of children who were not currently a charge upon the taxpayers or a charitable group.

This picture changed in a unique manner. In 1866, the New York Society for the Prevention of Cruelty to Animals was organized and a number of societies with similar concerns were incorporated in other cities during the next five years. In 1874, a group of charitable people, interested in the plight of a child who was being cruelly treated, discovered that there apparently was no way of interesting the authorities in removing her from the care of a couple who had taken her from an institution several years before. In desperation, the group referred the situation to the New York Society for the Prevention of Cruelty to Animals. The case was accepted on the basis that the child was an animal; evidence necessary for legal action was secured by the society; and the child was removed from the custody of her guardians, who also received a prison sentence for their maltreatment of the child. This development stimulated interest in the establishment of a separate organization to rescue neglected children and to prosecute their offenders, and in 1875 the New York Society for the Prevention of Cruelty to Children was founded.[18]

Within five years, agencies of the same name and purpose were established in Baltimore, Boston, Brooklyn, Buffalo, Philadelphia, Portsmouth, Rochester, San Francisco, Wilmington, and Richmond County, New York. By 1900, 161 agencies were actively engaged in a program of child protection. Many of these agencies, previously established for the protection of animals, broadened their functions to serve children. Some new agencies adopted the name of "Humane Society" to include both purposes in their program. In 1887, the societies serving children were admitted to the American Humane

[17] Folks, *op. cit.*, pp. 168–169.

[18] Roswell C. McCrea, "Societies for the Prevention of Cruelty to Children," in Hart, *op. cit.*, p. 194.

Association, an organization established in 1877 by the societies for the protection of animals.[19]

The New York society, upon which the other agencies were patterned, saw as its primary function the investigation of complaints of neglect and the presentation of necessary evidence to the courts. To achieve this purpose, agents were assigned to all magistrate courts to learn of cases involving children. As the courts accepted this service, increasing responsibility and authority were granted to the society. Police powers were assigned to its agents, and children were placed in its care pending investigation. Folks states that by 1890 the society controlled the lives of about 15,000 children and administered approximately $1,500,000 annually in their behalf.[20]

In many cities the SPCC operated a temporary shelter for children and, in a number of states, private funds for their support were augmented by public subsidies or per capita payments. The early agencies did not establish child placement programs and the children in their care were therefore committed to institutions or child placing agencies if removed from the custody of their parents.

These societies also made important contributions to the history of child welfare through their active support of legislative measures designed to prevent various dangers to children. Perhaps the most significant achievement of the New York society was an amendment to the State Penal Code which paved the way for the subsequent establishment of a special court for children. This change in law, adopted in 1892, required that children brought to court be separated from adult criminals.[21]

THE CHARITY ORGANIZATION MOVEMENT

The charity organization movement in this country was introduced in Buffalo in 1877 by Rev. S. Humphreys Gurteen, an Episcopal rector who had served on one of the district committees of the London COS.[22] Like that of the London organization, the purpose of the Buffalo society was to coordinate the work of various charitable

---

[19] Folks, *op. cit.*, p. 173.

[20] *Ibid.*, pp. 173–175.

[21] Emma Octavia Lundberg, *Unto the Least of These* (New York: Copyright D. Appleton-Century Company, 1947), p. 104. Reprinted by permission of Appleton-Century-Crofts, Inc.

[22] Amos G. Warner, *American Charities* (New York: Thomas Y. Crowell and Company, 1894), p. 377.

agencies and to create a framework of communication and common practice. The movement soon spread to other cities and although there were variations in function the major goals were usually the same.

By creating working relations among all of the agencies in a given locality, each society hoped to effect coordination of services to clients. This was accomplished by comparison of case records, by "the mutual acquaintance of workers," and by the use of an alphabetical catalog of cases which was housed in a central office. This clearing house was designed to avoid duplication of service and to improve the quality of help extended to the client.[23]

Paid agents, assisted by volunteer visitors, assumed responsibility for the investigation of all cases. After verifying need, they sought to find prompt and adequate relief or employment for the recipient by bringing each case to the attention of the most appropriate agency. If there were no agency to meet a specific need, a "benevolent individual" was notified and the donor and recipient brought together under the society's supervision.[24]

The Charity Organization Societies also projected the beginnings of the casework method as well as the principles of contemporary community organization. Their belief that "scientific charity called for knowledge and skill, as well as good intentions,"[25] in effect marked the beginnings of social work in its professional sense. This is particularly true in the area of training for social work. As will be seen in the next chapter, the methods used to train workers during the last two decades of the nineteenth century played a significant role in the development of professional education. These agencies made important contributions, too, in securing needed legislation and in demonstrating the value of various projects. By 1892, agencies of this type existed in 84 Eastern and Midwestern cities.[26]

AMERICAN RED CROSS

During the nineteenth century the contribution of this organization in the field of child welfare was largely limited to disaster relief. Like

---

[23] *Ibid.*, p. 386.

[24] *Ibid.*, p. 384.

[25] Margaret E. Rich, *A Belief in People* (New York: Family Service Association of America, 1956), p. 37.

[26] *Ibid.*, p. 10.

many of the national programs originating during this period, its founding in 1881 followed an established European pattern.

In 1859, Henri Dunant, a young Swiss businessman, resolved to do something about the plight of wounded soldiers. In 1863, his efforts resulted in a Geneva Conference which recommended the formation of volunteer aid societies in all nations and "adopted as a symbol of these societies, a red cross on a white field, the Swiss flag reversed." At a second conference held in the following year, government representatives formed the International Red Cross and drew up the Geneva Convention—the first treaty "to assure protection to wounded soldiers and the personnel caring for them."[27] Because of its traditional avoidance of "entangling alliances," the United States did not participate in this treaty but many other nations soon established the societies recommended.

During the Civil War an organization known as the United States Sanitation Commission carried on a battlefield program similar to that envisioned by the Geneva Convention. Clara Barton established the American Red Cross in 1881 and in the following year the United States became a party to the Geneva Convention.[28]

In its first year of operation, the new organization aided the victims of forest fires in Michigan. A major relief operation was conducted during the Ohio-Mississippi flood in 1884 and the first program of mass feeding and shelter was initiated during the disastrous Johnstown flood in Pennsylvania in 1889.

During the Spanish-American War in 1898, the Red Cross provided its first assistance to the armed forces. This experience proved the value of the Red Cross in war time and led to the granting of a national charter in 1900 "by which the Red Cross became the nation's official agency for certain welfare services for members of the armed forces."[29]

THE SETTLEMENT MOVEMENT

As in England, a concern about the wide diversity in economic and social conditions led to the initiation of the settlement movement in this country. The need for some method of greater communication

---

[27] *This is the Red Cross* (Washington, D.C.: The American National Red Cross, revised, March 1955), p. 45.

[28] *Ibid.*, p. 46.

[29] *Ibid.*, p. 47.

between the social classes was intensified here by the tendency of immigrating nationality groups to settle in particular sections of a city and thus create veritable cultural islands, unrelated to other segments of the population.

As Bruno states, it is conceivable that the privileged might have found other ways of understanding the underprivileged and of "sharing the advantages of culture and wealth with their neighbors."[30]   It so happened, however, that the founders of the first five settlements in this country had had a brief residence in, or had visited, Toynbee Hall in London and were therefore motivated to establish similar resident centers in this country.

Neighborhood Guild, established by Dr. Stanton Coit in a tenement house on the lower east side of New York City in 1887, was the first settlement house in the United States.   When reorganized as the University Settlement Society in 1891, its constitution defined the objectives of the society as those of bringing men and women of education "into closer relations with the laboring classes of this city for their mutual benefit," and of maintaining in tenement house districts "places of residence for college men, and others . . . with rooms . . . where people may meet for social and educational purposes."[31]

Hull House in Chicago, the best known facility of this type, was founded in 1889 by Jane Addams and Ellen Gates Starr after Miss Addams' visit to Toynbee Hall.   Its purpose was "to provide a center for the higher civic and social life, to institute and maintain educational and philanthropic enterprises and to investigate and improve the conditions in the industrial district of Chicago."[32]

The Henry Street Settlement in New York City received its impetus from an entirely different source.   After Lillian D. Wald graduated from New York Hospital Training School, she became so concerned by the conditions in a tenement district that she and her classmate, Mary Brewster, moved into the neighborhood "to give our services as nurses, and . . . to contribute our sense of citizenship to what seems an alien group in a so-called democratic community."[33]

Within a brief period these nurses initiated a visiting nurse service

---

[30] Bruno, Frank J. *Trends in Social Work 1874–1956*, (New York: Columbia University Press, 1957), p. 116.

[31] Queen, *op. cit.*, p. 134.

[32] *Ibid.*

[33] R. L. Duffus, *Lillian Wald: Neighbor and Crusader* (New York: The Macmillan Company, 1938), p. 35.

which won support from many prominent persons and resulted in the acquisition of a house in 1893. Known first as the "Nurses' Settlement" and later as the "House on Henry Street," this facility acquired by 1900, a staff of fifteen trained public health nurses, a convalescent home on the Hudson, and a program which included, in addition to its health activities, the usual services of a social settlement. In subsequent years, Miss Wald's alert mind and imagination played an active part in the initiation of other services which became a part of our social scene, for example, the employment of school nurses, ungraded classes for mentally retarded children, and the United States Children's Bureau.

By 1900, more than one hundred settlement houses had been established throughout the country.[34] In most instances their programs included classes in English and civics for the foreign-born, classes in child care for mothers, and classes in home economics and manual training for youth. In addition, courses in art and music, clubs, and other opportunities for recreation were provided for children and adults. Other common characteristics were usually lacking, however, since each settlement attempted to fit its activities to the needs and interests of the local community. Hull House, for example, developed a free kindergarten and day nursery, operated a branch of the public library, established a boarding home for girls, secured the passage of a law governing sweat shops, and provided a meeting place for labor unions and other groups.

Probably the greatest contribution of these early settlement houses occurred through their demonstration of the value of services subsequently provided under other auspices, and the interest in social reforms which they stimulated in residents who later exerted great influence in achieving important gains in legislation and in developing other means of serving disadvantaged persons. Florence Kelley, Julia Lathrop, Edith Abbott, Grace Abbott, and many other leaders in the development of services for children during the twentieth century received their knowledge of existing conditions through residence in one of the early settlements.

The Visiting Nurse Movement

To a considerable degree the history of the visiting nurse movement bears a close relation to the development of the settlement movement,

---

[34] Edward T. Devine and Lilian Brandt, *American Social Work in the Twentieth Century* (New York: The Frontier Press, 1921), p. 14.

though its preprofessional antecedents originated in an earlier period of the nineteenth century.

In 1877, the Women's Branch of the New York City Mission inaugurated a program which is accredited as the first attempt to initiate in this country the type of visiting nurse service organized in England in 1859 by William Rathbone and Florence Nightingale. During the next ten years, nurses were employed by several groups to provide bedside nursing for the poor sick, but it was not until 1886 that it was recognized that a visiting nurse might also assume a teaching role in the health field. In that year, nursing associations organized in Philadelphia and Boston included among the duties of the nurses employed the utilization of the home visit as "an opportunity for giving health instruction to the patient and members of the family."[35]

As previously indicated, the founding of the Nurses' Settlement on Henry Street in 1893 resulted from a recognition of the need for a nursing service for the economically and socially deprived families in a New York tenement district. Welcome Hall, a settlement established by the First Presbyterian Church in New York in the following year, also employed a resident nurse who assumed duties outside the realm of nursing care and supervision (for example, working closely with probation and truant officers, explaining child labor laws to parents, etc.). Other settlements and private organizations soon provided a nursing service and, by 1900, it was estimated that forty to fifty "Visiting Nurse Associations" had been established.[36]

CHILD LABOR

Beginning efforts to control the evils of child labor were ineffective during the nineteenth century. This fact is understandable since the employment of children had been considered a proper practice throughout our national history. As indicated in an earlier chapter, child indenture and apprenticeship played an important role in the development of the economy of the Southern states and had received equal approval in colonial New England.

With the introduction of machinery, the employment of children was seen as a method of obtaining a plentiful supply of cheap labor for the new textile mills. Alexander Hamilton in fact approved the new industries because they would render children "more useful and more

---

[35] Katharine Tucker, "Public Health Nursing," *Social Work Year Book* (New York: Russell Sage Foundation, 1929), p. 362.

[36] Devine and Brandt, *op. cit.*, p. 8.

early useful than they would otherwise be."[37] As Edith Abbott
pointed out:

The introduction of children into our early factories was a natural consequence of the colonial attitude toward child labor, of the provisions of
the early poor laws and of philanthropic efforts to prevent children from
becoming a public charge, and, above all of the Puritan belief in the virtue
of industry and the sin of idleness.[38]

In the first cotton mill, established in Rhode Island in 1806, only
children between the ages of seven and twelve years were employed.
Later mills utilized a family system of employment so that the labor
of each member of the family would be available. The family system
was also prevalent in other states and employers made every effort to
attract families with the greatest numbers of children. By 1832 it
was estimated that children seven to sixteen years of age contributed
two-fifths of the factory labor supply in New England.[39]

The lack of educational opportunities for children employed in
factories produced the first efforts to control child labor by state law.
In 1813, the Connecticut legislature required mill owners to provide
instruction in reading, writing, and arithmetic for their child employees. In 1836, Massachusetts enacted a compulsory education law
which permitted the employment of children under fifteen in factories
only on condition that they had attended school during three of the
twelve preceding months. In 1842, both Connecticut and Massachusetts limited to ten the hours of employment for children in cotton
and woolen mills. In Massachusetts this law was applicable only to
children under twelve years, but in Connecticut the statute applied to
all children under fourteen years. By 1860 a number of states had enacted similar legislation forbidding the employment of children under
ten or twelve years in factories of any kind.

Although public opinion with respect to child labor began to change
at midcentury, the laws enacted were not enforced and child employment increased rapidly after the Civil War. As a result, children as
young as seven years went to work in textile mills at 4:00 A.M., worked
fourteen hours each day, performed household tasks, and then went to
evening school. The exact number of children employed could not

---

[37] Edith Abbott, "A Study of the Early History of Child Labor in America,"
The American Journal of Sociology, Vol. XIV, No. 1, July 1908, p. 15.

[38] *Ibid.*

[39] Millis and Montgomery, *op. cit.*, p. 422.

be ascertained, both because law-violating employers failed to submit reports and because many parents utilized their children as assistants and collected increased wages without the names of the children appearing on the payroll.

In addition to the children employed in factories, many young children worked long hours in tenement houses in the needle trades and in the home manufacture of cigars and artificial flowers. Others were employed as runners in glass bottle works, in domestic service as "little mothers," in retail and street trades, and as telegraph and messenger boys. In many areas the practical value of any existing legislation was nullified by failure to provide inspectors to enforce the legislation, by the unwillingness of parents to deprive themselves of income earned by their children, and by lack of sufficient schools to receive the children even if they were effectively barred from employment.[40]

In 1870, the United States census included for the first time statistics relative to the employment of children. Realization that more than three-quarters of a million children from ten to sixteen years of age were gainfully employed, in addition to an unknown number of children less than ten years old, appears to have had a salient effect upon many groups. Persons interested in social reform, as well as labor unions intent upon eliminating the wage depressing effect of child labor, joined forces in various ways to bring to public attention the evils of tenement house manufacture and the harmful effects of employment of children in factories. In 1881, the American Federation of Labor at its first convention urged the enactment of state laws completely prohibiting all employment of children under fourteen years, and other organizations sought various methods of control.[41] Despite these efforts, the number of children employed in Southern states continued to increase as textile mills were established in the absence of any protective legislation for children. As a result, the United States census of 1900 showed an increase of nearly one million children gainfully employed, in comparison with the figures for 1870. The total number of employed children (1,750,178) represented 18.2 per cent of all children in the United States.

In 1899, the National Consumers' League was organized to protect consumers from the dangers of products produced under unsanitary

---

[40] Florence Kelley, *Some Ethical Gains Through Legislation* (New York: The Macmillan Company, 1905), p. 36.

[41] United States Children's Bureau, *Why Child Labor Laws?*, Publication 313 (Washington, D.C.: Government Printing Office, 1946), p. 3.

conditions or fraudulently advertised.   Almost immediately this group took up the battle against child labor and became a potent force in the controversies which subsequently occurred.

THE FIRST JUVENILE COURT

As noted in the preceding chapter, public concern about the child offender resulted in the establishment of specialized institutions for his care and rehabilitation, in the founding of agencies which included him in their efforts to protect all disadvantaged children, and in the system of prehearing investigations and subsequent supervision inaugurated by the Massachusetts Board of State Charities.   Folks believes that the Massachusetts plan, established in 1869, marked the first use of the concept of probation for the child offender.   He explains that the practice of assigning a representative to each court created an opportunity to urge that juvenile offenders be placed on probation when appropriate, and that supervision be provided by agents of the state agency.   During the first year of this plan, probation was granted in 23 per cent of the juvenile trials.[42]

In 1869, Massachusetts also became the first state to require separate hearings for children under sixteen years of age.[43]   At first this legislation applied only to the county in which Boston is situated, but in 1877 separate hearings for children were required throughout the state, as well as separate records and dockets.[44]

Provision for special court sessions for children was made by New York in 1892 and by Rhode Island in 1898.   In 1899 the Rhode Island Board of State Charities and Corrections was also empowered to appoint probation officers throughout the state.

Despite earlier approaches to a differential legal treatment of children, credit for the establishment of the first juvenile court belongs to Illinois.   On April 21, 1899, the Illinois Juvenile Court Act was approved and the first juvenile court session held in Chicago on July 1, 1899.   For the first time in legal history, this law classified children who had violated laws or ordinances as delinquents rather than criminals.   Entitled an "Act to Regulate the Treatment and Control of Dependent, Neglected and Delinquent Children," this statute made spe-

---

[42] Folks, *op. cit.*, p. 231.

[43] *Massachusetts Acts and Resolves*, 1869, Chapter 453.

[44] *Massachusetts Acts and Resolves*, 1877, Chapter 210, Section 5.

cial provision for a juvenile court in Chicago, gave original jurisdiction to the circuit court in all cases involving children under sixteen years of age, and required that judges of the circuit court select one of their number to handle all cases covered by the act. A special juvenile courtroom was to be designated and the judges were given authority to appoint probation officers to:

> . . . make such investigation as may be required by the court; to be present in court in order to represent the interests of the child when the case is heard; to furnish to the court such information and assistance as the judge may require; and to take such charge of any child before or after the trial as may be directed by the court.[45]

This law specified that the probation officer should not receive any compensation. It is reported that this provision was made in fear that the bill might be defeated because of its cost and that, if passed, paid probation officers might be selected on a political basis. The first probation officers in the Chicago court were therefore persons whose salaries were paid by other agencies and later by public subscription.

The juvenile court movement quickly spread to other large cities and greatly influenced the development of other child welfare services.

THE MIXED ALMSHOUSE

In reviewing the development of other types of care for children, it must not be assumed that their care in mixed almshouses ceased immediately after the inception of specialized institutions and child placing programs—or at any point in the nineteenth century.

Even though Ohio authorized the establishment of county homes for children in 1866, the report of the Board of Public Charities for 1869 contained this statement:

> Nearly one thousand children in the poorhouses of Ohio! . . . Think of their surroundings. The raving of the maniac, the frightful contortions of the epileptic, the driveling and senseless sputtering of the idiot, the garrulous temper of the decrepit, neglected old age, the peevishness of the infirm, the accumulated filth of all these; then add the moral degeneracy of such as, from idleness or dissipation, seek a refuge from honest toil in the tithed industry of the county, and you have a faint outline of the surroundings of these little boys and girls. This is home to them. Here their first and most enduring impressions of life are formed.[46]

---

[45] *Illinois Session Laws*, 1899.

[46] Cited in Grace Abbott, *The Child and the State*, II, p. 52.

Similar efforts to arouse public and legislative interest in the plight of children living in almshouses were made by other newly established boards of state charities. In 1874 the Eighth Annual Report of the State Board of Charities of New York explained:

> It is sometimes thought that the injurious influences of poorhouses may be avoided by erecting separate establishments on the poorhouse grounds, for the care of children, and that within these they may be properly reared and educated with greater economy than could be secured elsewhere. But these well-designed establishments, call them nurseries, juvenile asylums or any other name, although regarded as independent in their functions are nevertheless a part of the poorhouse system, and bring children indirectly under its baneful influence, and into association with a greater or less number of the indolent, listless pauper inmates. These establishments are the more dangerous, because of the delusive idea that bad influences are removed . . . and because the greatest injury they do to society is not immediately demonstrated.[47]

In 1875, the New York legislature took action to correct this situation by adopting "An Act to Provide for the Better Care of Pauper and Destitute Children." This statute made it unlawful for any court to commit to the county poorhouse, and for any overseer of the poor to send to the poorhouse, any child between the ages of three and sixteen "unless such child be an unteachable idiot, an epileptic or paralytic, or be defective, deformed or diseased." A child not exempted was to be committed or sent "to an orphan asylum or another charitable or reformatory institution . . . that is governed or controlled . . . by persons of the same religious faith as the parents of such child, as far as is practicable." Superintendents of the Poor were also ordered to remove children from almshouses on or before January 1, 1876; to cause the removal of children born in the poorhouse or subsequently placed there, before they arrive at the age of three; and to provide for their support in families or appropriate institutions.[48]

Wisconsin also required the removal of children from almshouses in 1878 but made no other provision for their care until a state school was established in 1885.

In Massachusetts, the process of removing children from almshouses was accomplished in a more gradual manner. Although use of the facility at Monson for the exclusive care of children after 1872 pro-

---

[47] *Eighth Annual Report of the State Board of Charities of the State of New York*, 1875, in Abbott, *The Child and The State*, Vol. II, p. 68.

[48] *Laws of the State of New York*, 1875, Chapter 173.

vided specialized care for those who lacked legal settlement in a city or town, it did not protect children who were a proper charge on local communities. In 1879, however, "An Act Forbidding the Detention of Poor Children in Almshouses" was passed. This law required the overseers of the poor in any major city "to place all pauper children . . . over four years of age in some respectable family in the state, or in some asylum therein to be supported there, by said city . . . until they can be otherwise cared for." This act also made it "unlawful to retain in any almshouse" any child except one that has no legal settlement in the state or is "idiotic or otherwise so defective bodily or mentally as to make such child's retention in an almshouse desirable," or a child under eight years "whose mother is an inmate of the almshouse and a suitable person to aid in taking care of such child."[49] In 1893, this law was amended to include all towns and to authorize the State Board of Lunacy and Charity to place out at local expense any child who remained in an almshouse for more than two months.

By 1900, Pennsylvania, Connecticut, Ohio, Maryland, Indiana, New Hampshire, and New Jersey had enacted similar laws, but children in other states continued to receive care in almshouses. At a later date, Edward T. Devine wrote:

The removal of children from the almshouse to separate institutions, or to the care of placing-out agencies, is another step so obvious and so imperative that it is strange to find communities in which it has not yet been taken. . . . So great is the temptation to effect a petty economy, and so ignorant are so many local officials charged with the support of the poor, that statutory prohibition of the reception of children into almshouses is justified, and even the enactment of such statutes has accomplished the removal only with difficulty.[50]

THE NINETEENTH CENTURY IN RETROSPECT

During this century it was recognized that the earlier concepts of child care were incompatible with the domestic ferment of these times, but many of the colonial ideals and attitudes were carefully preserved and cherished. This was a period in which poverty and dependency were still regarded as personal evils and reformation was expected to occur by virtue of a change in environment. Men were

---

[49] *Massachusetts Acts and Resolves*, 1879, Chapter 103.

[50] Edward T. Devine, *The Principles of Relief* (New York: The Macmillan Company, 1904), p. 130.

not generally regarded as being victimized by circumstances over which they had little control. Instead, it was feared that to help them would contribute to their weaknesses. Poverty was accredited to gambling, to the rum shop, to vice, and to personal indolence, and seldom related to the defects of the social and economic structure in which indigency was spawned. The need to rescue children from damaging environments gained recognition but existing attitudes toward poverty frequently prevented the creation of appropriate services for them.

Despite impeding influences, this appears to have been an era of dynamic leadership in which many men and women strongly expressed their concern for children and made the current inadequacies of their care known throughout the country. Toward the end of the century an urgency developed in many areas to help dependent children to remain in their own homes. It was also considered important that children be removed from almshouses and placed in foster homes. These early steps were often crude and seemingly capricious, but they were symptomatic of the nation's beginning awareness of the special needs of children.

Selected Bibliography

Breckinridge, Sophonisba P. *Public Welfare Administration: Select Documents.* Chicago: The University of Chicago Press, 1927.

Devine, Edward T., and Lilian Brandt. *American Social Work in the Twentieth Century.* New York: The Frontier Press, 1920.

Duffus, R. L. *Lillian Wald: Neighbor and Crusader.* New York: The Macmillan Company, 1938.

Eddy, George Sherwood. *A Century With Youth: A History of the YMCA from 1844–1944.* New York: Association Press, 1944.

Kelley, Florence. *Some Ethical Gains Through Legislation.* New York: The Macmillan Company, 1905.

Lundberg, Emma O. *Unto The Least of These.* New York: The Appleton-Century Company, 1947.

Rich, Margaret E. *A Belief in People.* New York: Family Service Association of America, 1956.

Slingerland, William H. *Child Placing in Families.* New York: Russell Sage Foundation, 1919.

Thurston, Henry W. *The Dependent Child.* New York: Columbia University Press, 1930.

Warner, Amos G. *American Charities.* New York: Thomas Y. Crowell and Company, 1894.

Part Three · The Child

Like childhood itself, the twentieth century

has been a period of growth and change.

In some respects the development of services for children

is properly viewed as a continuum of the past,

but this process was punctuated and molded

by two world wars and a great economic depression.

With the impact of new knowledge,

new patterns also emerged from an increased understanding

of the child and of the importance of his childhood—to him

and to our democratic society.

in the Twentieth Century

Chapter 6   The First Two Decades

(1900-1920)

The initial years of this century represent an era in which prior achievements in diverse areas were consolidated, many modern concepts of child welfare articulated, and great effort expended in formulating principles and legal instruments through which the general welfare of children could be more universally protected and improved. In some instances, developments which proved most significant were not specifically directed toward the field of child welfare, but this fact does not alter their subsequent importance in the lives of children. To a unique degree, however, the special needs of children absorbed the interest and energies of many segments of our population during this period.

TRAINING FOR SOCIAL WORK

As we have seen in the preceding chapter, the last quarter of the nineteenth century witnessed the initiation of a national forum in which all persons engaged in the alleviation of human suffering and the protection of society could exchange their thinking and experience. As new organizations and agencies joined the National Conference of

Charities and Correction, it was recognized that a collective term had to be found which would include all persons identified with the fields of public relief, private charity, corrections, mental illness, and settlements; the prevention of child labor, tuberculosis, and infant mortality, and all other contemporary efforts to improve social conditions. After 1900, speakers at the National Conference gradually began to refer to its members as "social workers" and by 1905 the term "social work" was in comomn usage.[1]

Since social work had no identity in the nineteenth century, training for social work as a profession obviously did not exist. As private charitable agencies sought solutions to the many problems which beset their clients, however, a body of experience was accumulated, concepts formulated, and methods developed to effect desired changes in individuals and in their environment. To insure the use of accepted principles and techniques, many private agencies conducted in-service training programs based on the time-honored methods of apprenticeship and sometimes supplemented by more formalized methods of instruction.

In 1893, Anna Dawes presented to the International Congress of Charities, held in Chicago, a paper entitled, "The Need for Training Schools for a New Profession." At the National Conference of Charities and Correction, in 1897, Mary Richmond carried this theme further by presenting for the first time the concept that training for social work is an educational function which should be undertaken by a university. She believed, however, that the professional school should have a close relationship with public and private charitable agencies so that students could observe social work practice, and that classroom instruction should parallel experience in the field.

In 1896, the New York Charity Organization Society employed as its secretary Dr. Edward T. Devine, a former member of the faculty of the University of Pennsylvania. Devine soon realized that "staff conferences and supervision and oversight by committees were not sufficient to enable the society to keep pace with the demands which were developing from scientific progress and from practical experience."[2] In his thinking, "the real start toward the professional education of social workers as such, was made in 1898 when the

[1] Edward T. Devine, *Social Work* (New York: The Macmillan Company, 1922), pp. 15–16.

[2] Edward T. Devine, *When Social Work Was Young* (New York: The Macmillan Company, 1939), pp. 124–125. Material used with permission of The Macmillan Company.

society launched its summer school of philanthropy . . . ."[3] After five years, the summer sessions were supplemented by a late-afternoon course for employed social workers. The New York School of Philanthropy was founded in 1904, with Devine as its director.[4] By 1910, a two-year graduate course had been developed and in 1919 the name "New York School of Social Work" was adopted.

During the same period, similar schools were founded at Simmons College in 1904 and in Chicago. (The latter school later became the School of Social Service Administration of the University of Chicago.) By 1915, seven schools of social work were in operation and in the next four years this number had nearly tripled.

In 1919, the Association of Training Schools for Professional Social Work was organized to provide an opportunity for the exchange of views and experience among schools. Seventeen schools were charter members of this organization.

Thus, in a brief span of time, the need for special training for social work was recognized, a correlated pattern of internship and academic instruction formulated, and the base for professional education established.

Social Work in New Settings

As social work achieved an identifiable entity, its value was recognized by other professions and the services of social workers soon utilized in a variety of new settings.

MEDICAL SOCIAL WORK

The first full-time employment of a social worker in a hospital is believed to have occurred in England in 1895, when the London Charity Organization Society assigned a member of its staff to the Royal Free Hospital of London.[5] In this country, the development of medical social work appears to have been affected more directly by other events.

---

[3] *Ibid.*, p. 125.

[4] *Ibid.*, p. 128.

[5] Helen Beckley and Kate McMahon, "Hospital Social Work," *Social Work Year Book*, 1929, p. 202.

In 1902, Dr. Charles P. Emerson sought to develop a method through which medical students at Johns Hopkins University could acquire an understanding of the patient's way of life, his fears, his expectations, and his failures. Arrangements were made with the Charity Organization Society of Baltimore to allow students under his direction to serve as volunteer workers to learn the relation between the patient's illness and the economic and social environment in which he lived.[6] In New York City, the staff of the Nurses' Settlement had previously demonstrated to hospitals the fact that social and personal problems frequently affected the recovery of discharged patients.

Out of these two developments, social workers were employed in four hospitals in 1905. Massachusetts General Hospital in Boston is generally credited with being the first to employ social work staff, but Bellevue Hospital in New York City, Johns Hopkins Hospital, and the Berkeley Infirmary in Boston followed within the same year.

Following these examples, social service departments were established in more than one hundred hospitals in less than a decade. In 1918, the American Association of Hospital Social Workers was organized to facilitate communication among medical social workers and to safeguard professional standards.

PSYCHIATRIC SOCIAL WORK

The topics discussed in the early sessions of the National Conference of Charities and Correction indicate that problems stemming from mental illness had long been of concern to persons later identified with the field of social work. There appears to be no evidence, however, that social workers were employed in any hospital or clinic for mental or nervous diseases until 1905, when Dr. James P. Putnam added a social worker to the staff of the Neurological Clinic of the Massachusetts General Hospital. In 1906, a similar step was taken by Bellevue Hospital and by Cornell Clinic in New York City. In the same year, the State Charities Aid Association of New York appointed an "after-care agent" to assist patients discharged from state hospitals in reestablishing their relationships at home and in the community. By 1914, social workers were employed in eleven state hospitals in New York. In 1913, social service departments were established at Danvers State Hospital and Boston State Hospital in Massachusetts, in

---

[6] Ida M. Cannon, *Social Work in Hospitals* (New York: Survey Associates, Russell Sage Foundation, 1913), pp. 13–14.

the newly established Boston Psychopathic Hospital, and at Phipps Clinic at Johns Hopkins Hospital in Baltimore.[7]

The Social Service Department at Boston Psychopathic Hospital, established under the direction of Mary Jarrett, assumed particular importance since it originated the term "psychiatric social worker" and provided the first field work training in psychiatric social work. Miss Jarrett's book, *The Kingdom of Evils*, written with Dr. E. E. Southard, also presented the first detailed account of the activities of a psychiatric social service department.

After 1908, the employment of social workers in psychiatric settings received great impetus from the mental hygiene and juvenile court movements. Separate examination of these movements is indicated, however, in view of their wide significance in the field of child welfare.

SCHOOL SOCIAL WORK

The need for a closer relation between the home and the school was first recognized by the residents of two settlement houses in New York City. From her knowledge of the social and economic deprivation of the children served by Hartley House, Mary Marot, a teacher, saw the value that could result if a social worker could interpret to the school the home conditions which affect a child's school attendance, progress, and adjustment, and in turn could attempt to alleviate existing problems in the home environment. Because of Miss Marot's interest, Hartley House and Greenwich House assigned two staff members to provide this type of service for children in three slum districts in 1906.

In Boston, the Women's Education Association became concerned about the lack of cooperation between the home and the school. It also recognized that the size of classes prevented the teacher from knowing individual children and that parent-teacher conferences could not be easily arranged with employed and other busy mothers. In 1907, this group employed a "visiting teacher" to serve one school.[8]

Rochester and Mount Vernon, New York, inaugurated a visiting

---

[7] Lois Meredith French, *Psychiatric Social Work* (New York: Commonwealth Fund, 1945), pp. 35–45.

[8] Julius John Oppenheimer, *The Visiting Teacher Movement* (New York: Joint Committee on Preventing Delinquency, Commonwealth Fund, 1925), pp. 1–8.

teacher service in 1913, and in 1914 Rochester became the first city in which this program was financed directly by a board of education. New York City soon followed with the employment of six visiting teachers. In 1919, the Chicago Board of Education also employed three visiting teachers after a demonstration program had been financed by the Chicago Women's Club for a three-year period. In similar fashion the value of home and school visitation was demonstrated by other organizations, until by 1920 there were so-called "visiting teachers" in 28 cities in 15 states.

In 1919, the National Association of Home and School Visitors and Visiting Teachers was organized to unite the social workers employed in school systems throughout the country, to make recommendations concerning their qualifications and training, and to promote the development and extension of these services. The term "home and school visitor" or "school counselor" was used in many early programs, but the title "visiting teacher" was officially adopted by this organization to indicate the close connection with the teaching program. It also expressed the prevailing conviction that social workers employed as members of the school staff should have training as teachers as well as in social work. By 1945, however, the term "school social worker" had gained acceptance and the name of the professional organization was accordingly changed.

THE NURSE IN NEW SETTINGS

Lillian Wald's experience in the Nurses' Settlement in New York City and the initiation of the voluntary visiting nurse movement caused the employment of nurses in two new settings during the early years of the twentieth century.

New York City schools had provided routine medical examinations since 1897, but from her contacts with ill children of school age Miss Wald believed that these examinations were cursory in nature and usually resulted in sending a sick child home with little or no medical treatment. When she learned about a highly successful experimental project in public school nursing in England, she was inspired to stimulate interest in the employment of nurses in the schools of this country. During a trachoma epidemic in the schools in 1902 she was able to obtain permission from the board of education to assign a settlement nurse to one school to demonstrate the value of a nurse in a school setting. This service was so effective that 12 nurses were soon employed by the Department of Health to visit in 48 schools.

New York thus became the first American city to establish school nursing under municipal auspices.

In many communities a school nursing service was initiated by citizen groups. After the salaries of the first two school nurses in Boston had been paid by clubs, a bill was enacted by the legislature in 1907 providing for medical inspection in public schools and authorizing school boards to employ nurses. As the movement spread, 24 cities developed a school nursing service between 1903 and 1909.

The first decade of the twentieth century also witnessed the beginning of public health nursing. In 1903, the New York City Department of Health employed the first nurses to provide home nursing for tuberculosis patients under public auspices, and health departments in other cities soon added public health nurses to their staffs. After the first county health department was organized in Yakima, Washington, in 1911, steady progress was also made in the employment of public health nurses in rural areas throughout the nation.

During this period, too, nurses employed by voluntary nursing associations and benevolent agencies entered into other fields of service. In Cleveland, the Visiting Nurse Association and the Milk Fund Association established an infant clinic in 1906. Here the nurses gave instruction and assistance to mothers in the care of their babies. In 1908 the New York AICP, in cooperation with the New York Milk Committee, opened milk depots for infants in which instruction was provided by doctors and nurses and systematic records kept. The visiting nurse service, initiated by the AICP in 1904, was also expanded to supplement these services. By 1910, similar milk stations had been established in at least thirty cities.[9]

Gradually the milk stations changed their emphasis to preventive measures and became known as "Infant Welfare Stations." In this process the visiting nurse became recognized as the person best equipped to interpret good health practices and to provide preventive health instruction.[10]

In 1908, the New York AICP initiated, in cooperation with the New York Outdoor Medical Clinic, the first organized effort to provide prenatal care. In the following year, the Women's Municipal League of Boston also embarked upon a five-year project in which it demon-

---

[9] Blanche M. Haines, "Maternal and Infant Hygiene," *Social Work Year Book,* 1929, p. 252.

[10] Etta R. Gordon, *A Tabular Statement of Infant Welfare Work by Public and Private Agencies in the United States* (Washington, D.C., U.S. Children's Bureau, 1916), p. 28.

strated that prenatal care and confinement services given by a visiting nurse could greatly reduce infant mortality by preventing disease and relieving the mother's suffering.

Thus, throughout the nation, nurses found their services utilized in many ways to protect the welfare of children. In 1912, the alliance between the visiting nurse movement and the public health movement was symbolized by the establishment of the National Organization for Public Health Nursing, with membership composed of visiting nurses employed under public and private auspices. This organization sought to promote and develop public health nursing through co-operative relations with other national health and social agencies, and through the development of standards for the profession.[11]

FOUNDATIONS

The practice of donating or bequeathing sums of money to existing charitable organizations or for use in establishing a new institution or philanthropy was prevalent in preceding centuries. The word "foundation" did not come into common use, however, until the twentieth century and, with a few exceptions, the bequests or endowments established prior to 1900 did not have the distinguishing characteristics of a foundation.

A foundation is defined as "a non-profit, legal entity whose donor or donors have given or will give it a principal fund, whose management is under its own trustees or directors, and whose purpose is to conduct or aid activities which will serve the welfare of mankind."[12] Its essential difference from prior methods of channeling private wealth into activities designed for human betterment is found in the fact that its purpose is usually expressed in general terms (for example, to promote the advancement and diffusion of knowledge and understanding or to provide facilities for research) and its trustees are therefore free to expend funds for projects of current value. The development of foundations had particular importance in the field of child welfare since many previous grants were established with such limited statements of purpose that the funds could not be fully expended before the need ceased to exist. (Classic examples of this type

---

[11] Tucker, *op. cit.*, p. 362.

[12] Wilmer Shields Rich, "Foundations and Community Trusts," *Social Work Year Book*, 1954, p. 233.

of endowment are found in funds for institutions established to serve children whose parents died in a particular cholera epidemic or in a specific war.)

After 1901, the number of foundations increased rapidly. Of those established in the first decade, the Russell Sage Foundation was by far the most important in child welfare. Established in 1907 for "the improvement of social conditions in the United States," its early contributions resulted primarily from the studies made by its Child Helping and Charity Organization Departments and by the publication of various books and pamphlets describing the methods of social work. During this period the only foundation established to serve children specifically was the Elizabeth McCormick Memorial Fund, founded in 1908 "to promote and improve conditions of child life in the United States."

In 1913, the Rockefeller Foundation was endowed "to promote the well-being of mankind throughout the world." The interest of its directors was focused on the fields of physical and mental health, and many projects of direct and indirect value to children were made possible through funds allocated by this foundation. Perhaps the most significant contribution was the educational effort through which hookworm was eradicated from eleven Southern states.

The Judge Baker Foundation, established in 1917 as a memorial to the first judge of the juvenile court in Boston, sought "to study the personality, conduct and educational problems of childhood and youth." As constituted, its first duty was to serve children who came before the juvenile court, but children known to other agencies also benefited from the professional services made available.

Another foundation well known in the field of child welfare was the Commonwealth Fund, established by the Harkness family in 1918 "to do something for the welfare of mankind." Its most important activities occurred during a later period, however, and will be discussed in the next chapter. The White-Williams Foundation, originally founded in 1800 as the Magdalen Society of Philadelphia, also made a significant contribution in the prevention of juvenile delinquency after its reorganization in 1920.[13] By 1915, 23 foundations were in operation and before the end of this era the number had increased. Many of these supported research in the fields of health

---

[13] Harold Coe Coffman, *American Foundations: A Study of Their Role in the Child Welfare Movement* (New York: Young Men's Christian Association, 1936), p. 16.

and education and some provided scholarships to make higher education available to designated groups of children.

THE JUVENILE COURT MOVEMENT

The enactment of the Illinois Juvenile Court Act described in the preceding chapter was quickly followed by similar legislation in other states.

Juvenile court laws were passed in 1901 by New Jersey, Ohio, and Wisconsin, and in 1902 juvenile courts were established under existing or special legislation in New York City, Baltimore, and Cleveland. In 1903, Colorado, California, Indiana, Missouri, New York, and Pennsylvania enacted juvenile court legislation and by 1910, 34 states, the District of Columbia, and Hawaii had made some similar legal provision. The Illinois law and its subsequent modifications provided a model for the legislation of 22 states. As a result, the delinquent child in these states was regarded as "misguided and needing aid, encouragement, help and assistance; . . . kept entirely separate from the adult offender, and the probation system . . . used, whenever practicable."[14] Several states, including New York, Maryland, and New Jersey, "engrafted on the old criminal laws some of the conspicuous features of the new legislation, leaving however, the old system still unreformed in its fundamental principle."[15]

By 1919, all of the states except Connecticut, Maine, and Wyoming had enacted a juvenile court law of some type, and even these states had made some separate provision for children.

In the early years of the juvenile court movement, many problems of law and differences in philosophy were widely discussed. The belief that the juvenile court had inherited the parental powers of the Court of Chancery was gradually accepted after the supreme court of Pennsylvania held that no constitutional rights were violated because: "The act is but an exercise by the state of its supreme power over the welfare of its children, a power under which it can take a child from its father . . . if the welfare of the child . . . can be thus best protected. . . . "[16]

---

[14] Grace Abbott, "Abstract of Juvenile Court Laws," in Breckinridge and Edith Abbott, *op. cit.*, Appendix III, p. 247.

[15] *Ibid.*

[16] Commonwealth vs. Fisher, Appellant—213 Pennsylvania State Reports 48 (1905), in Grace Abbott, *The Child and the State*, II, p. 401.

It was generally agreed that it was the judicial function of the court to determine whether, in fact, a child comes within the legal definition of a child in need of the court's protection. Judge Julian W. Mack of the Chicago court, Homer Folks, and others believed, however, that the administrative function of providing necessary protection should be assumed by an independent probation department, and some objected to "a court having anything to do with the strictly dependent child whose parents must ask assistance merely because of poverty or misfortune."[17] Despite these objections, most juvenile court laws gave jurisdiction over dependent, neglected, and delinquent children to the juvenile court. Some laws avoided these designations, however, by simply defining the circumstances which would cause a child to fall within the jurisdiction of the court—for example, a child who violates a law, who is without proper care and guardianship, or is otherwise dependent or neglected.

In 1909, a new development in the juvenile court movement occurred when the Juvenile Psychopathic Institute, headed by Dr. William Healy, was established to serve the Cook County Juvenile Court in Illinois. Credit for securing the services of a psychiatrist and the routine use of psychological examinations is generally attributed to Julia C. Lathrop, a member of the Board of State Charities and one of the persons most active in advocating the establishment of the Juvenile Court. Private funds were provided for an initial five-year period but when the need for careful study and treatment had been demonstrated the clinic became a part of the juvenile court. The value of this experiment was made evident to other courts when Healy's book, *The Individual Delinquent: A Textbook of Diagnosis and Prognosis for All Concerned in Understanding Offenders,* was published in 1915.

Healy remained the director of the clinic until 1917, when he and his associate, Dr. Augusta F. Bronner, established a similar clinic in Boston under the auspices of the Judge Baker Foundation. In the interim, the Ohio Bureau of Juvenile Research, under the direction of Dr. Henry Goddard, had been established in 1914. This clinic was created by the Department of Public Welfare, but its initial purpose, like that of the Cook County Clinic, was the study of children who were adjudged to be delinquent.

By 1918 there were 2,034 courts dealing with children and it was estimated that 175,000 children were brought before the courts during

---

[17] Mack, *op. cit.,* p. 185.

that year. A study made at that time showed, however, that only 321 of these special courts could be classified as true juvenile courts and that only 43 per cent of the total population lived within the areas served by these courts.[18]

NEW YOUTH-SERVING ORGANIZATIONS

Unlike the juvenile court movement, the leisure-time organizations for children and youth cannot be traced to any single event or any precipitating cause. Frank J. Bruno points out that at the end of the nineteenth century America presented "the unique social phenomenon of a national culture which had had a vigorous and successful development over an unbroken period of nearly three centuries without any ingredients of folk or community play."[19]   This situation he attributes to the hostility toward play held by our Puritan forefathers and "the thoroughness with which Puritan New England discarded all recreational enjoyment"; the religious revivals which swept the country in the eighteenth and nineteenth centuries in which card playing, dancing, and theaters were condemned; and the stern economic conditions which caused our forefathers to consider play a "wicked waste of time."[20]

The first youth-serving organizations not founded for religious reasons were the clubs which in 1906 formed the Federated Boys' Clubs in Boston. The Boys' Club movement originated in New England, with the first club established in Hartford during the Civil War to make available to boys at all hours a reading room, a games room, and social activities. By 1900, at least twenty clubs had been founded in congested areas of various cities to provide a place where boys (usually between eight and sixteen years of age) could find hospitality, activities, and companionship. After the federation was formed, the movement achieved national scope and the number of clubs increased rapidly. Their most distinguishing characteristic was the fact that no club was eligible to membership in the federation if it included religious training as one of its activities. This requirement

---

[18] Grace Abbott, "History of the Juvenile Court Movement Throughout the World," in Edith Abbott, *The Child, the Clinic and the Court* (New York: New Republic, 1925), pp. 267–273.

[19] Bruno, *The Theory of Social Work*, p. 383.

[20] *Ibid.*, pp. 382–386.

reflected a belief that religious training is the function of the home and the church, and not that of an agency whose primary concern is the provision of leisure-time activities. Although the federation was formed to provide a clearing house for the activities of individual clubs, the principle of local autonomy was carefully preserved and the program of each club adapted to local needs.[21]

In 1900, a movement began in Illinois which resulted in the widespread establishment of 4-H clubs. When adult farmers did not respond to current efforts to develop Farmers' Institutes, it was decided to begin demonstration work in agriculture with young people. The first boys' and girls' clubs were actually founded in Ohio in 1902, however. In 1910, South Carolina inaugurated a girls' 4-H program and, as the movement spread, national interest in similar rural activities was aroused. In 1914, the Smith-Lever Act establishing the extension service in the United States Department of Agriculture gave the movement its greatest impetus. This act made provision for a cooperative program whereby the departments of agriculture in the land-grant colleges would accept as part of their function the promotion of 4-H clubs among all farm boys and girls. As the movement grew, these clubs provided rural youth between the ages of ten and twenty years with opportunities to develop their capacities for learning, to acquire skills in farming, homemaking, and community life, and to enjoy the companionship of others. In 1921, the National Committee on Boys' and Girls' Club Work was established "to encourage, aid and extend the 4-H clubs . . . throughout the United States."[22]

In 1910, the founding of the Boy Scouts of America initiated a rapidly developing movement which resulted in the establishment of a group of "character building" agencies. The Boy Scout movement was a direct outgrowth of the British Boy Scouts, which in turn reflected Lord Baden-Powell's concern about the health and character of British boys during the Boer War. In America, the aim of the movement became the development of character and the teaching of scout-craft, patriotism, self-reliance, and courage. By 1916 the movement had achieved such national recognition that a federal charter was granted by Congress.

---

[21] R. K. Atkinson, "Boys' Clubs," *Social Work Year Book*, 1929, pp. 46–47.

[22] "National Committee on Boys' and Girls' Club Work," *Social Work Year Book*, 1929, p. 550.

In the spring of 1911, Dr. and Mrs. Luther H. Gulick met with a group of educators and others interested in the leisure-time activities of girls to consider the advisability of forming an organization which would have the benefits of the Boy Scout troop. Later in the same year the Camp Fire Girls became a national organization.[23]

In the following year (1912), Mrs. Juliette Low, a friend of Lord Baden-Powell, established the first Girl Scout troop in Savannah, Georgia. After the National Council of Girls Scouts was formed in 1915, the movement spread rapidly through the nation.

By 1918, an interest in younger girls, twelve to eighteen, had developed in the YWCA and the Girl Reserves were organized in that year. A similar development in the YMCA resulted in the establishment of Hi-Y and Junior Hi-Y clubs. As the importance of work with boys and girls was recognized, activity programs of this type were also developed by the Young Men's Hebrew Association, the Young Women's Hebrew Association, and the Knights of Columbus. By 1920 every city and town in the United States provided a network of programs under a wide variety of religious, civic, and social auspices.

In addition to the organizations which relied primarily upon the use of group activities, another type of youth-serving agency originated during this period. In 1904, Ernest K. Coulter, clerk of the newly established Children's Court in New York City, enlisted the help of the Men's Club in the Central Presbyterian Church in providing friendly adult guidance to boys known to the court. Each man agreed to be "Big Brother" to a boy "whose physical, mental and moral development has been hindered or endangered because of bad environments or other conditions."[24] The results were so successful that headquarters were established for referral, assignment, and follow-up work and the organization became incorporated as the Big Brother Movement in 1909.

Before long, other Big Brother and Big Sister organizations were established throughout the nation under sectarian and nonsectarian auspices and the objectives of their programs broadened to include the prevention of juvenile delinquency. In 1917 the Big Brother and Big Sister Federation was established as a national agency to extend

---

[23] *The Book of the Camp Fire Girls* (New York: National Headquarters, fifth revised edition, 1914), p. 8.

[24] *The Art of Friendship* (Philadelphia: Big Brothers of America, Inc., 1954), p. 9.

the movement, provide advice and information to existing groups, conduct conferences and training courses, and publish educational papers in the field.[25]

THE FIRST WHITE HOUSE CONFERENCE

In 1908, James E. West, the secretary of the National Child Rescue League, conceived an idea which probably had more far-reaching effects in the development of child welfare than any other single episode in this era. From his own experience as a child in an institution in Washington, D.C., West had developed an abiding interest in the plight of dependent children and at this point envisioned the value that might occur if representatives of child caring institutions and agencies throughout the nation could meet with persons of similar concern to consider what might be done to solve existing problems. After enlisting the support of various leaders in the field, a letter signed by eight of these men was sent to President Theodore Roosevelt, asking that he call such a meeting.[26]

The Conference on the Care of Dependent Children, which convened at the White House on January 25–26, 1909, was attended by nearly two hundred delegates representing "every state in the Union and every kind of agency for dependent and neglected children," as well as "all forms of religious belief." Although it appeared that such wide variations in philosophy and practice would preclude the acceptance of any common platform, it was believed that "the conference ought to formulate some kind of a statement embodying those principles upon which these delegates could agree, which might contribute to a better understanding between them, pave the way for a greater degree of cooperation and serve as a point of departure for future progress and for the standardization of child welfare work."[27]

Many of the concepts expressed in the "Conclusions" adopted by this conference still form the nucleus of modern child welfare theory and method, and other propositions soon became the springboard for

---

[25] "Big Brother and Big Sister Federation, Inc.," *Social Work Year Book*, 1929, p. 514.

[26] *Proceedings of the Conference on the Care of Dependent Children* (Washington, D.C.: Government Printing Office, 1909), p. 18.

[27] Hastings H. Hart, "The Conclusions of the White House Conference Ten Years After," *Standards of Child Welfare*. A report of the Children's Bureau Conferences, May and June, 1919, Bureau Publication 60 (Washington, D.C.: Children's Bureau, 1919), p. 339.

more specific action. The most famous and enduring expression of
the philosophy of these delegates reads:

Home life is the highest and finest product of civilization. It is the great
molding force of mind and of character. Children should not be deprived
of it except for urgent and compelling reasons. Children . . . who are
without the support of the normal breadwinner, should, as a rule, be kept
with their parents, such aid being given as may be necessary to maintain
suitable homes for the rearing of the children. . . . Except in unusual
circumstances, the home should not be broken up for reasons of poverty.
. . . [28]

After stressing the importance of preventive work to eradicate the
causes of dependency, the conference urged upon "all friends of
children the promotion of effective measures, including legislation, . . .
to improve the conditions surrounding child life." It recognized, too,
that "children who for sufficient reason must be removed from their
own homes—should be cared for in families whenever practicable" and
that "the carefully selected foster home is for the normal child the
best substitute for the natural home." There was warning, however,
that foster homes "should be selected by a most careful process of
investigation, carried on by skilled agents through personal investigation" and that after placement "adequate visitation, with careful consideration of the physical, mental, moral and spiritual training and
development of each child . . . is essential." The use of boarding
homes was recommended, but it was recognized that "until such homes
are found, the use of institutions is necessary." It was also stated
that "these institutions should be conducted on the cottage plan, in
order that routine and impersonal care may not unduly suppress individuality and initiative" and that "effective personal relations between the adult caretaker . . . and each child" are essential. To
the members of the conference it was also evident that "cheap care
of children is ultimately enormously expensive, and is unworthy of a
strong community."[29]

Other sections of the report emphasized the belief that the care
of needy children is "a most serious responsibility" which should be
permitted only when proper safeguards are present. It was advocated
that child care be forbidden to all except duly incorporated agencies
which have "reasonable assurance of securing, the funds needed for

---

[28] *Proceedings of the Conference on the Care of Dependent Children*, pp. 9–10.
[29] *Ibid.*, pp. 10–11.

their support" and whose incorporation has been approved by a state board of charities or other body exercising similar powers. It was also stated to be "sound public policy that the State . . . should inspect the work of all agencies which care for dependent children, whether by institutional or by home-finding methods, and whether supported by public or private funds," and that thorough "inspection should be made by trained agents." The need for close cooperation between child caring agencies in each locality was stressed and "a joint bureau of investigation and information" recommended.[30]

In response to an address by Lillian Wald, the report also recommended the enactment of a bill pending in Congress "for the establishment of a federal children's bureau to collect and disseminate information affecting the welfare of children." In addition, the establishment of a permanent voluntary organization to undertake, in the field of child welfare, work comparable to that of other national organizations was proposed.[31]

Thus, in two days, a group of dedicated people who held in common only their concern for children had come together, contributed their differences, espoused the wisdom of their leadership, and presented to their contemporaries the first "permanent and authoritative declaration of the principles which should direct the treatment and care of dependent and neglected children."[32] For our purposes, the "Conclusions" of this conference had even greater significance since they provided a bench mark against which it is possible to measure all subsequent progress in the field of child welfare.

THE MOTHERS' PENSION MOVEMENT

The immediate impact of the first White House Conference was probably most evident in the enactment of laws making financial aid available to children living in their own homes without the support of the normal breadwinner. In one respect, however, the Mothers' Pension movement, as it was subsequently called, was not a true implementation of the principles enunciated by the White House Conference, since the conference recommended that aid necessary "to maintain suitable homes for the rearing of the children . . . be given . . .

---

[30] *Ibid.*, pp. 11–13.

[31] *Ibid.*, pp. 13–14.

[32] Hart, "The Conclusions of the White House Conference Ten Years After," *Standards of Child Welfare*, p. 343.

preferably in the form of private charity, rather than of public relief."[33]

The influence of the juvenile court movement was also apparent in the first two laws, enacted in 1911. Both the Missouri and Illinois statutes made provision for the administration of financial aid by juvenile courts and the Illinois law was in fact, proposed by Judge Merritt W. Pinckney of the Cook County Juvenile Court. His interest in legislation of this type stemmed from his own experience in being forced to commit children to institutions because mothers, unable to support their families from their meager earnings, could not obtain sufficient assistance from public relief or private charity. As a member of the White House Conference, Judge Pinckney had been greatly impressed by its recommendations, but as head of a public agency "he properly sought public funds" to implement the principles adopted.[34] The Missouri law was sponsored by a fraternal organization, but this group also believed the juvenile court to be the logical agency to administer the program.

One concept basic to all statutes of this type seemed to represent an unintended combination of the principles adopted by the White House Conference. The conference recommendation urging "legislation . . . to secure compensation or insurance so as to provide a family income in case of sickness, accident, death, or invalidism of the breadwinner; . . . and generally, to improve the conditions surrounding child life . . . ."[35] was intended to advocate support of the European systems of workmen's compensation and social insurance. The concept of compensation was subsequently reflected, however, in all mothers' pension laws. In some states the allowances were described as a method of compensating children for the loss of a father's income by providing assistance different from poor relief. In others, the statutory intent was declared to be the compensation of mothers for the care of their own children in a manner similar to that used in the payment of foster parents for the care of unrelated children.

The use of public funds for the support of children deprived of parental support was not wholly without precedent. As indicated in previous chapters, payment for care in institutions had long been an accepted practice and some states had made provision for the payment of board in foster family homes. In California, a court decision in

---

[33] *Proceedings of the Conference on the Care of Dependent Children*, pp. 9–10.

[34] Grace Abbott, *The Child and the State*, II, p. 231.

[35] *Proceedings of the Conference on the Care of Dependent Children*, p. 10.

1888 had also inaugurated the practice of granting state aid for orphans and half-orphans in their own homes or in the homes of relatives.[36] Oklahoma and Michigan had also authorized school authorities to provide funds to permit the children of indigent parents to attend school.[37] In general, however, out-of-home care, private charity, and public outdoor relief constituted the only resource for children deprived of parental support prior to 1911. In Philadelphia, Brooklyn, San Francisco, Baltimore, and Washington, D.C., even the last-named resource was nonexistent since public relief had been abolished as a result of maladministration or opposition by private agencies. In New York City, only coal orders and medical relief were provided, and in Cook County, Illinois, and many other communities, outdoor relief was limited to grocery and coal orders. Private agencies usually had some money for emergency assistance to widowed mothers, but in most instances work was found for the mother and she was either persuaded to give up one or two children she could not support or, at the end of a few years, she became so burdened by her dual role as housekeeper and wage earner that the children were neglected and finally became delinquent.[38]

The "Mothers' Pension Law" enacted by Missouri in 1911 was applicable only to Jackson County (Kansas City), and the "Funds to Parents Act" in Illinois, therefore, became the first state-wide law of this type. The Illinois act was in reality only an amendment to the Juvenile Court Law. The revised statute provided that if the parent or parents of any dependent or neglected "male child under the age of seventeen years or any female child under the age of eighteen . . . are poor and unable to properly care for the said child, but are otherwise proper guardians and it is for the welfare of such child to remain at home, the court may enter an order finding such facts and fixing the amount of money necessary to enable the parent or parents to properly care for such child, and thereupon it shall be the duty of the county board . . . to pay to such parent or parents, at such times as said order may designate the amount so specified . . . until the further order of the court."[39]

---

[36] County of Yolo vs. John P. Dunne (1888), 77 Cal. 133, cited in Frances Cahn and Valeska Bary, *Welfare Activities of Federal, State, and Local Governments in California, 1850–1934* (Berkeley: University of California Press, 1936), p. 4.

[37] Lundberg, *op. cit.*, p. 124.

[38] Abbott, *The Child and the State*, II, p. 230.

[39] *Laws of Illinois*, 1911, pp. 126–127.

Although Chicago social workers cooperated in testing the value of the Illinois law, a storm of protests immediately emanated from private agencies in the Eastern states, and particularly from those in cities where public relief had been abandoned. As explained by Grace Abbott:

The opinion was widespread at that time that public relief would never be well administered because adequate salaries would not be provided for administration, there would be political interference, relief from the public treasury would increase pauperism, and private charity could meet the need if it did not have to compete with public relief.[40]

Despite this controversy, legislation which produced some form of mother's allowance was enacted by 20 states within two years after the Illinois act became effective. Within ten years, similar legal provision had been made by 41 states. Under many early laws only the children of widows were eligible, though some states included children with incapacitated fathers. Even Illinois subsequently added restrictions of this type to its statute. Most of the laws were permissive in nature and, since they merely authorized the expenditure of county funds, many counties never made any actual grants. In Pennsylvania, California, and a few other states, state funds were made available, but most programs depended wholly upon the adequacy of local appropriations.

THE UNITED STATES CHILDREN'S BUREAU

The act creating the United States Children's Bureau, signed by President William Howard Taft on April 9, 1912, culminated a long series of efforts to establish an agency of this type.

Lillian Wald, founder of the Henry Street Settlement in New York City, is generally accredited with being the first person to suggest a Federal Children's Bureau.[41] Her idea, conceived in 1903, undoubtedly played an important role in mobilizing support for the measure but the basic concept seems to have had an earlier origin. In 1900, Florence Kelley, head of the National Consumers' League, gave a series of lectures in various parts of the country, in which she proposed a

---

[40] Grace Abbott, *The Child and the State*, II, p. 231.

[41] *Four Decades of Action for Children*, U.S. Department of Health, Education and Welfare, Children's Bureau Publication 358 (Washington, D.C.: Government Printing Office, 1956), p. 1.

"United States Commission for Children" which would collect and interpret facts about birth registration, infant mortality, child labor, illegitimacy, delinquency, orphanages, and other subjects "concerning the mental and moral conditions and prospects of the children of the United States."[42]

In 1904, the National Child Labor Committee was formed and Florence Kelley became its first executive. In 1905, her book, entitled *Some Ethical Gains Through Legislation*, presented many of the facts about child labor gleaned from her own experience as chief investigator of factories in Illinois, discussed "the right to childhood," summarized the status of current legislation to protect this right, and formally outlined her plan for a United States Commission for Children. At the annual meeting of the National Child Labor Committee held in Washington in December of that year, a proposed draft of legislation to establish a Federal Children's Bureau was approved and, with minor changes, incorporated in a bill introduced in Congress early in 1906. Until the bill was enacted into law, the National Child Labor Committee maintained a lobby in Washington and in cooperation with the settlement houses worked unceasingly to win support for this legislation.

During the next six years, eleven bills proposing the establishment of a Children's Bureau were introduced in Congress and prolonged hearings were held on each bill. President Roosevelt's special message to Congress reporting the recommendations of the White House Conference and urging favorable action on the bills currently pending, declared:

There are few things more vital to the welfare of the nation than accurate and dependable knowledge of the best methods of dealing with children, especially with those who are in one way or another handicapped by misfortune; and in the absence of such knowledge each community is left to work out its own problem without being able to learn of and profit by the success or failure of other communities along the same lines of endeavor.[43]

Lillian Wald and others also made strong pleas for approval of the bills during the Congressional hearings and in 1910 President Taft endorsed the proposal. As Grace Abbott later explained:

While scientific research in animal husbandry, foods, minerals, or fish was accepted without question as a function of the government, the proposal to

---

[42] *Ibid.*

[43] *Proceedings of the Conference on the Care of Dependent Children,* p. 7.

study the physical, mental, and social problems of childhood was opposed
as socialistic. Opposition, which delayed the enactment of the law . . .
was in part due, however, to the fact that the National Child Labor Committee urged its creation, and the issue of child labor was then highly
controversial.[44]

The bill sponsored by Senator William E. Borah and finally enacted
by Congress in 1912 established

. . . in the Department of Commerce and Labor, a bureau to be known as
the Children's Bureau (to be) under the direction of a chief to be appointed by the President, by and with the advice and consent of the Senate.
. . . The said Bureau shall investigate and report . . . upon all matters
pertaining to the welfare of children and child life among all classes of our
people and shall especially investigate the questions of infant mortality, the
birth rate, orphanage, juvenile courts, desertion, dangerous occupations,
accidents and diseases of children, employment, legislation affecting children
in the Several states and Territories.[45]

With a small staff and limited funds, Julia C. Lathrop, the first chief
of the Children's Bureau, found it necessary to select carefully the
projects which could be undertaken by the new agency. On recommendation of an advisory committee, a study of the incidence and
causes of infant mortality was selected as the project of most immediate importance.[46]

Efforts to determine the death rate and its causes soon disclosed that
birth records were not uniformly kept. With the help of committees
made up largely of members of the General Federation of Women's
Clubs, great improvements were soon made in the maintenance of
statistics. Early studies also disclosed that the death rate of babies
bore a close relation to the economic status of the family and the
consequent care received by the mothers before and after confinement.
To alleviate the problems identified, the Children's Bureau began a
series of publications and reports designed to provide instruction to
parents (*Prenatal Care*, published in 1913; *Infant Care*, first published
in 1914; etc.), to acquaint state and local governments with preventive
measures used in other states and nations, to stimulate cities and towns
to improve sanitary conditions and insure safe supplies of water and
milk, and to indicate the need for legislation which would assure bet-

---

[44] Grace Abbott, *The Child and the State*, II, p. 612–613.

[45] "Act Establishing the Children's Bureau" (37 Stat. 79), *Four Decades of Action for Children*, Appendixes, p. 87.

[46] *Ibid.*, p. 5.

ter maternal care and more adequate income for disadvantaged children, for example, mothers' pensions, minimum wage laws, and adequate provision for medical care.

To stimulate public interest in the protection of babies, the bureau, in cooperation with the General Federation of Women's Clubs, also inaugurated the national observance of "Baby Week" in March, 1916, and May, 1917. These events, in turn, culminated in President Wilson's proclamation of a "Children's Year" beginning in April, 1918. In this campaign, conducted to impress upon the nation the importance of preserving childhood during World War I, 11,000,000 women participated in the work of 17,000 committees.[47]

In view of the support given to the establishment of the Children's Bureau by those deeply concerned about child labor, it is not surprising that the second subject to receive consideration by bureau staff related to this field. Through the efforts of local committees working in cooperation with the National Child Labor Committee, forty states had enacted uniform child labor laws prior to 1914. After the United States Children's Bureau was transferred to the newly created Department of Labor in 1913, its staff began a compilation of these laws and an analysis of available statistics. A series of studies was also made of the conditions under which children worked and of existing systems of employment certification.

As a result of this activity, the first Federal Child Labor Law was enacted in 1917 and its administration assigned to the Children's Bureau. This law was declared unconstitutional within nine months, but the methods and procedures developed for its administration provided the basis for all subsequent federal legislation to regulate child labor. The enactment of this law had the further effect of bringing to the bureau as the head of the new Child Labor Division, Grace Abbott, who became the second chief of the bureau in 1921.

During this early period, the staff of the bureau also began to make studies of the needs of special groups of children. A series of studies of the administration of mothers' pensions and the care of dependent children in institutions and foster homes was initiated in 1914. Since the studies of infant mortality had shown that the mortality rate for children of unmarried mothers was approximately three times that of children of legitimate birth, a series of conferences with agencies serving unmarried mothers and their children was also held from 1913 to 1916. On completion of the study of illegitimacy laws in the various

---

[47] *Ibid.*, pp. 9–10.

states, two regional conferences were held in Chicago and New York in 1920 to discuss legal measures needed for the protection of these children. The principles adopted at these meetings later became the basis for legislation in a number of states.

In 1914, the bureau undertook its first study of juvenile courts and of juvenile delinquency. During World War I, its staff engaged in a survey of the nature and extent of the juvenile court movement, a study of the causes of juvenile delinquency during war time, and a field study of children under eighteen years of age who had violated federal laws.[48] The findings aroused the interest of juvenile court judges and social workers in the field of correction and provided the basis for future legislation and for the development of standards for juvenile courts.

STATE SUPERVISION AND CONTROL

At the first White House Conference private agencies unanimously lauded the value of state inspection and supervision,[49] and the conference recommendations paved the way for the enactment of laws requiring the annual licensing of boarding homes, child caring institutions, child placing agencies, and maternity homes.

The United States Children's Bureau also played an important role in encouraging states to adopt legislation which would improve the quality of care available to children through state supervision and control. To some extent, this was accomplished through efforts to direct national attention to existing defects in administration and to report developments in better methods of organization. The impact of the bureau in this area is not wholly distinguishable, however, from the effect of other developments which occurred during this period.

In a paper given at the National Conference of Charities and Correction in 1910, Judge George S. Addams of the Juvenile Court of Cleveland complained bitterly about the diverse aggregate of child caring institutions and agencies, and the morass of laws which affected the proper disposition of each case coming before the juvenile court. To remedy this condition, he urged that child welfare workers take responsibility for codifying the state laws affecting children. In response to this suggestion the Ohio legislature authorized the governor to appoint a commission to study the laws pertaining to children, and

---

[48] *Ibid.*, p. 16.

[49] *Proceedings of the Conference on the Care of Dependent Children*, p. 60.

in 1913 adopted the first "Children's Code" in the United States.[50] Within the next two years, similar commissions were appointed in Missouri, New Hampshire, and Oregon.

At the National Conference held in 1915, this movement was given further impetus by two papers stressing the need for comprehensive planning for children's services. The address given by C. C. Carstens, general agent of the Massachusetts Society for the Prevention of Cruelty to Children, was of particular importance since it outlined the role of the state in the supervision of local public and private child welfare agencies and suggested that a county board of public welfare be given responsibility for the care and protection of all dependent children.

The impact of these events is perhaps most evident in Minnesota's efforts to improve its program of child care. The Child Welfare Commission, appointed in 1916, drew heavily upon the material and advice provided by the United States Children's Bureau and presented to the governor a report recommending the enactment of 43 laws. Because of time limitations, the preparation of a Children's Code was not possible. The legal maze was clarified however, by the 35 statutes approved by the legislature in 1917.[51]

The Minnesota project had considerable significance in the total field of child welfare. The legislation centralized in the Board of Control broad responsibility for the administration of child welfare laws, authorized the creation of a special division in the Board of Control to be known as the "Children's Bureau," and permitted the establishment of county child welfare boards. The provisions relating to the county child welfare boards were of greatest import since they created a precedent for the delegation of state agency responsibility to a local unit, a close coordination of state-county effort, and a centralization of child welfare responsibility at the local level. In effect, the county child welfare boards were to act as agents of the State Board of Control in carrying out its responsibilities for the protection of children by securing court action for the support of children born out of wedlock, making licensing and adoption investigations, and supervising children committed to the state board. The local boards were also authorized to administer mothers' pensions and poor relief if requested by appropriate local officials.

---

[50] Bruno, *Trends in Social Work*, pp. 214–215.

[51] W. W. Hodson, "The Minnesota Child Welfare Commission," *Standards of Child Welfare*, 1919, p. 424.

A system of state-county administration was also established by North Carolina in 1917, but this plan differed from the Minnesota program in its inclusion of all public welfare functions. Within a short time, thirteen other states developed some type of county administration under the supervision of a state agency.[52]

As concern for children and a desire for better administration of the laws protecting their welfare developed, the number of state boards of charities or control also increased. Although only fifteen agencies of this type were reported to be in existence in 1904, the Bureau of the Census reported in 1913 that only ten states had no legally constituted central agency and that "there is not a single state that does not in some form recognize its duty to secure better care for those who cannot care for themselves."[53]

LOCAL COORDINATION OF EFFORT

As indicated in a previous chapter, the need for an exchange of information and coordination of effort among local agencies was first recognized by the New York AICP and later by the network of charity organization societies established throughout the nation. McMillen also attributes to the charity organization movement the credit for successfully implanting "the conviction that there is a community problem to be met and that the hope of success lies not in multiplying the number of agencies, but in achieving some kind of organization of group forces."[54]

The early societies were amazingly successful in mobilizing effective citizen support for needed legislation and social reforms. Like those of their London predecessor, however, their efforts to reform and coordinate the practice of other agencies met with less response, and the early goal of a city-wide organization of public and private philanthropic agencies was gradually abandoned in most cities.[55]

In 1908, Francis H. McLean recommended during the famous Pittsburgh study that a "central council of social agencies" be established

---

[52] Emma O. Lundberg, *The County As a Unit For An Organized Program of Child Caring and Protective Work*, Children's Bureau Publication 169. (Washington, D.C., 1926.) p. 1.

[53] United States Bureau of the Census, *Summary of State Laws Relating to the Dependent Classes* (Washington, D.C.: U.S. Government Printing Office, 1913), pp. 312–329.

[54] McMillen, *op. cit.*, p. 320.

[55] Bruno, *Trends in Social Work* p. 106.

as a separate organization. This plan was followed and an organization composed of representatives of various charitable and religious agencies was established "to promote cooperation among the individual societies and to pass upon the questions affecting the general welfare of the poor and the charitable activities of the city."[56] Pittsburgh's pattern is believed to have "served to set the example for council organization and function," although earlier plans to promote coordination of agency effort were developed in Elmira and Rochester, New York,[57] and the Milwaukee Council, organized in 1909, is sometimes cited as "the first council in the United States."[58] Regardless of its origin, the early council movement represented a cooperative attempt "to promote exchange of opinion and information among agency representatives and jointly to initiate and promote needed community improvements and reforms."[59] By 1917 this movement had spread to St. Louis (1911), Cleveland (1913), Cincinnati (1913), Minneapolis (1916), and Chicago (1917).[60]

This period also marked the beginning of the Community Chest movement. The first cooperative appeal for funds is reported to have occurred in Denver in 1887 when sixteen agencies developed a mutual fund-raising program. The Federation of Social Agencies in Elmira, New York, also initiated a plan of joint financing in 1910. The Cleveland Federation for Charity and Philanthropy, established in 1913, is considered to have been the first modern community chest, however, since its program included for the first time the concept of budgeting in accordance with agency needs. The Council of Social Agencies in Cincinnati developed a similar plan in 1915, and by 1917 fourteen cities had developed some form of joint financing.[61]

The American Association for Community Organization (now Community Chests and Councils, Inc.) was founded in 1918 "to assist in the improvement of joint finance and joint planning of social work through committee activities, research, correspondence, field visits, local studies of chests and councils, conferences, direction of financial

---

[56] McMillen, *op. cit.*, p. 416.

[57] Bruno, *Trends in Social Work*, p. 194.

[58] McMillen, *op. cit.*, p. 416.

[59] Rudolph T. Danstedt, "Councils in Social Work," *Social Work Year Book*, 1954, p. 142.

[60] Homer W. Borst, "Community Chests and Councils," *Social Work Year Book*, 1929, p. 96.

[61] *Ibid.*, p. 95.

campaigns and publications."[62]   In the field of child welfare, the leadership provided by this organization has played an important role in assisting local communities to assess the adequacy of their services to children, to arouse citizen interest in establishing new agencies, to provide needed services, and to secure necessary financial support for existing and proposed child serving agencies.   As local chests and councils have expanded their programs to include health and recreational resources as well as social services, their value to children has increased accordingly.   In subsequent chapters, the role played by these organizations in the formation of contemporary community patterns of services for children will become apparent.

The Mental Hygiene Movement

During the early years of the new century, Dr. G. Stanley Hall's interest in child study, the publication of several books on child psychology, the development of the Stanford-Binet Intelligence Tests (1905), Dr. Henry Goddard's research on the causes of feeblemindedness among New Jersey children, and Dr. William Healy's study of children brought before the juvenile court in Chicago, combined to create a new understanding of individual differences, a widespread interest in the measurement and classification of intellectual ability and mental abnormality, and a beginning realization of the importance of mental conflict as a causal factor in misconduct.

In the same period, other developments in the fields of psychiatry and mental hygiene were to have an even greater influence on the field of child welfare.   In June, 1900, a significant event occurred when Clifford Beers, a Yale graduate and a successful young businessman, began his three-year period of care in public and private mental hospitals in Connecticut.   His situation was unique in that he soon became sufficiently rational to resent the treatment received by inmates and, in his determination to do something to correct existing conditions, deliberately conducted himself in a violent manner so that he could experience "the worse phases of asylum care."[63]

Following his release, Beers portrayed his experiences in a vivid manner in his autobiography, *The Mind That Found Itself*.   Before its

---

[62] "Association of Community Chests and Councils," *Social Work Year Book*, 1929, pp. 512–513.

[63] *The Mental Hygiene Movement* (New York: The National Committee for Mental Hygiene, 1939), p. 34.

publication in 1908 he also sought the support of prominent psychiatrists for his plan to launch a "nationwide movement to advance the whole cause of mental health."[64] In May of that year he organized the Connecticut Society for Mental Hygiene and, in 1909, the National Committee for Mental Hygiene was formed, with a carefully selected membership of thirty men of national renown. This group selected Clifford Beers as the secretary of the new organization and in 1912 employed Thomas W. Salmon as the first medical director.[65]

State and local mental hygiene societies were later established and a broad educational program launched to help overcome "public apathy and misunderstanding, official inertia, archaic laws, parsimony toward mental institutions, the blight of political control."[66] In 1917 the quarterly publication, *Mental Hygiene,* became the voice of the national organization.

Other developments in psychiatry and psychoanalysis also contributed greatly to the total mental hygiene movement during the second decade of the century. In 1910, Hall brought Sigmund Freud to this country to speak. Translations of Freud's writings soon became available and within a period of six years numerous articles and books, written by such prominent American psychiatrists as William A. White, Adolph Meyer, and J. J. Putnam, appeared to explain Freud's theories or comment upon their application to behavior and personality.

During this period, too, the relationship between psychiatry, psychology, and social work became much closer than during any previous era. In 1911, Adolph Meyer, then the director of Phipps Psychiatric Clinic in Baltimore, addressed the National Conference of Charities and Correction on the subject, "Where Shall We Attack the Problem of Mental Defect and Mental Disease?" and after 1914 each program included the names of psychiatrists and psychologists actively engaged in research or other projects of interest to social workers.

OTHER NATIONAL PROGRAMS

Three national organizations which subsequently played an important role in the field of child welfare were founded in the decade which followed the initiation of the mental hygiene movement. Each

---

[64] *Ibid.,* p. 35.

[65] *Ibid.,* pp. 36–37.

[66] *Ibid.,* p. 38.

was established for the purpose of expanding and improving the services currently provided for families and children by their member agencies.

The National Conference of Catholic Charities, established in September, 1910, resulted from a variety of influences, but its inception was spearheaded by members of the Society of St. Vincent de Paul. This organization of Catholic laymen (first established in this country in St. Louis in 1845) had originally concerned itself primarily with the plight of immigrants. After 1870 the society had devoted considerable effort to finding homes "for children in the overcrowded Catholic institutions" to counteract the prevalent criticism of institutions and of "institutional methods of placing children."[67] Thomas M. Mulry and Edmond J. Butler, leaders of the society in New York City, were finally successful in establishing the Catholic Home Bureau, which in 1898 became the first Catholic child placing agency in the United States.

The Society of St. Vincent de Paul had attempted to organize a national conference of Catholic charities in 1898 and, after this effort failed, its own national conventions continued to discuss the problems of Catholic charities. In 1909, the Catholic group, meeting during the National Conference of Charities and Correction, agreed that Catholic University would be asked to sponsor a national organization.[68] In September, 1910, the National Conference of Catholic Charities was formally established, with Dr. William J. Kerby as its executive secretary.

The second organization founded during this period was the National Association of Societies for Organizing Charities, which became, after five name changes, the Family Service Association of America. Its founding was long delayed by other efforts to achieve its basic purposes, but in June, 1911, the long discussed plan finally became a reality.

In his *Handbook of Charity Organization* written in 1882, Rev. Stephen Humphreys Gurteen, founder of the first COS in Buffalo, had envisioned a national or international organization to facilitate an interchange of information among the societies in every city. The Committee on the Organization of Charity, appointed by the National Conference of Charities and Correction at its first meeting in 1879, continued to express the same idea intermittently, but the activities of

---

[67] O'Grady, *op. cit.*, pp. 250–252.

[68] *Ibid.*, p. 430.

this committee tended to reduce the need for such an organization. The long-awaited national association came into being as a result of a proposal made to representatives of the community organization societies meeting at the National Conference of Charities and Correction in 1909 by Francis H. McLean, former head of the Brooklyn Society. A constitution and program were developed during the next two years, and, shortly after their adoption, McLean became the first general secretary.

The constitution of the National Association stated that its primary purpose was "to promote the extension, cooperation and standardization of such societies for organizing charity in this country."[69] In carrying out his assigned responsibility, McLean made community studies at the request of member agencies and became a pioneer in the field which has since become known as "community organization." As we have seen, his recommendations in the Pittsburgh survey formed the pattern for the modern Council of Social Agencies. In his work with members of the new Association, McLean also developed further conviction about his belief that a charity organization society should devote its efforts to becoming a strong family agency rather than an organizer of community projects.

One of the most important functions of the association was the initiation of a process of accreditation, through which agencies could acquire membership in the national organization. To further the standardization of agencies, the constitution listed certain criteria for membership and, after 1916, each agency admitted was required to have a board elected by the membership of the society and a paid executive with at least one year's training in a charity organization society or similar agency with good standards of casework. As the years passed, other membership requirements were added to insure qualified staff, an acceptable quality of casework, and effective leadership in alleviating conditions harmful to family life. With these criteria, membership in the association did not increase rapidly, but by 1918 the number had risen to 170 societies and the association had become an effective body in the study of problems affecting member agencies.

During these years, Mary Richmond, former executive of the Philadelphia Charity Organization Society, contributed greatly to the development of social work as a profession and to the consequent emergence of an improved quality of service to families and their children.

---

[69] Margaret E. Rich, *op. cit.*, p. 85.

Beginning in 1910, Miss Richmond served as the leader of a "Charity Organization Institute" held in New York City each summer in cooperation with the New York School of Philanthropy. Her most significant contribution, however, was the book, *Social Diagnosis*, published by the Russell Sage Foundation in 1917. From material gathered from the institutes and from many agencies, Miss Richmond developed over a period of six years a text on the casework method which represented "the first rational and systematic approach to the analysis of individual social situations,"[70] and the first attempt "to make a scientific study of methods of diagnosing individual instances of trouble as these occurred in the practice of social work."[71]

In the same year, Miss Richmond played another important role in the extension of casework services when she prepared for the American Red Cross a *Home Service Manual* which became the basis for its war activities in this country. When the United States entered the war in 1917, the American Red Cross created a special department to serve the families of men in the armed forces, and in accordance with Miss Richmond's suggestion adopted the name "Home Service" for its program. The manual and case records which Miss Richmond prepared were used as the basis for training thousands of volunteer and professional workers throughout the nation. As a result, many communities which had been untouched by the charity organization movement began to feel the impact of casework concepts and methods. In discussing these activities, Bertha Reynolds later wrote:

For the first time in the history of organized philanthropy, it was *we* giving to *ours*, not one group handing down something to another which was outside its self-defined community. . . . This was not 'charity' but the due of those who had given their all. . . . Democracy was getting into philanthropy, and the latter could never be the same again.[72]

For the total field of family and child welfare, another important milestone occurred when the national association began publication of *The Family* in March, 1920. Although designed primarily for family social workers, neither the articles published nor its circulation were limited to that field. Much of the progress made in child welfare in subsequent years can be attributed to the ideas and examples of good

---

[70] Gordon Hamilton, *Theory and Practice of Social Casework* (New York: Columbia University Press, 1940), p. 19.

[71] Bertha C. Reynolds, *Rethinking Social Casework* (San Diego, California: Social Service Digest, 1946), p. 5.

[72] *Ibid.*, p. 12.

casework practice provided by this monthly publication. In later years its name was changed to the *Journal of Social Casework* and subsequently shortened to *Social Casework*, but its continuing emphasis on the importance of the family provided a steadfast beacon to which all specialized areas of child welfare practice eventually returned.

The establishment of the National Association of Travelers' Aid Societies in 1917 represented, in part, a realignment of functions previously performed by other agencies. The first organized effort to provide assistance for travelers in need of protection, counsel, or financial aid is believed to have occurred in St. Louis in 1851 as a result of a one million dollar bequest for the purpose of "assisting travelers to the West."[73] In 1866, the Boston YWCA had as one of its initial functions the assistance of young women taking up their residence in Boston and, as its program enlarged, a staff member was assigned to meet the boats on which immigrant girls were arriving from Europe. About the same time (1885–1890), workers were employed for a similar purpose by the Girls' Friendly Society in Boston and the Council of Jewish Women in New York City, and, for the protection of travelers, by the Society of Friends and the Women's Bible Society in New York City. The first true Travelers' Aid service was operated, however, by the YWCA at the Chicago World's Fair in 1893 and after that date a service of this type became an intermittent or continuing function of the YWCA in many cities. In 1905 Grace Hoadley Dodge, an active participant in the establishment of the National YWCA, also organized the first "all sectarian committee," which eventually became the Travelers' Aid Society of New York City.

Families who passed from one community to another because of lack of legal settlement or continuing problems of dependency were an early concern of the National Conference of Charities and Correction, and, after 1902, public and private agencies were urged to sign the Transportation Agreement developed by a special committee of the conference. Charity Organization Societies continued to abide by this agreement, but as separate Travelers' Aid Societies were established in an increasing number of cities, an agreement was usually reached whereby the new agency accepted for service persons traveling from one community to another and those who would need only temporary service in becoming established or reestablished in the community, or in implementing plans to leave the city. After the National Association of Travelers' Aid Societies was established, many

---

[73] Harriet E. Anderson, "Travelers' Aid," *Social Work Year Book*, 1929, p. 451.

charity organization societies and local YWCA's in areas not served
by a Travelers' Aid Society became "cooperating representatives" of
the new organization, and thus participated in the plan to provide a
national network of services to moving people.

The Second White House Conference

The Conference on Standards of Child Welfare held in 1919 was
unique in several ways. It differed from the first White House Conference in the fact that it was held under the auspices of the United
States Children's Bureau and not at the instigation of interested individuals. Unlike the earlier conference, too, its concern was not limited to the welfare of the dependent child. These differences served
to establish a precedent for similar conferences held in each successive
decade, but several other characteristics were peculiar to this conference.

In approving the plan to proclaim the second year of World War I
as Children's Year, as suggested by the United States Children's Bureau,
President Wilson wrote: "I trust that the work may so successfully
develop as to set up certain irreducible minimum standards for the
health, education, and work of the American child."[74]   A method of
developing such standards therefore became an inherent part of the
conference planned as a culmination of Children's Year.

At the first round-table discussion, held in Washington on May 5,
1919, three committees were appointed to prepare minimum standards
for children entering employment, for the protection of the health of
children and mothers, and for the protection of children in need of
special care. After discussion and amendment, the standards evolved
were adopted by the Conference and distributed for consideration at
large regional meetings subsequently held in New York, Cleveland,
Boston, Chicago, Denver, Minneapolis, San Francisco, and Seattle.

In many ways, these standards were epoch-making in the history of
child welfare since they established agreement on "the great essentials
of a child welfare policy for the nation";[75] defined a public responsibility for the welfare of children; provided an index of how far the
leadership of the nation had progressed in understanding the needs of
children; and presented guides for future effort to meet those needs.

"The Minimum Standards for Children Entering Employment" were

---

[74] *Standards of Child Welfare*, 1919, p. 7.

[75] *Ibid.*, p. 8.

expressed in mandatory terms. They prohibited the employment of all minors in hazardous occupations or any work which would retard proper physical development and required full-time school attendance for nine months of the year for all children between the ages of seven and sixteen years and for those between sixteen to eighteen years who had not completed the eighth grade. Conditions of eligibility for an employment certificate were also defined, together with requirements for the administration of the standards.

"The Minimum Standards for the Public Protection of the Health of Children and Mothers" described the needs of children in four different age groups. These included: (1) legislation requiring adequate training, licensing, and supervision of all midwives; immediate reporting of birth registration; and treatment of the eyes of every infant at birth; (2) a sufficient number of clinics and of prenatal and children's health centers; (3) the provision of one public health nurse for every two thousand persons in the population and one full-time school nurse for every one thousand children to make home visits; (4) adequate space and equipment for school medical work, necessary laboratory facilities, with a physician and two full-time nurses available for every four thousand students; (5) examination by a psychiatrist of all atypical and retarded children; (6) maternity and children's hospitals or beds in general hospitals, and provision for medical and nursing care at home; (7) special classes for children with physical or mental defects; (8) proper location, construction, space, hygiene, and sanitation in school buildings; (9) adequate playground and recreational facilities, physical training, and supervised recreation; and (10) general educational work in the prevention of infant mortality and communicable disease, health essentials, and hygiene.

The "Minimum Standards for the Protection of Children in Need of Special Care" recognized "the fundamental role of home, religion and education in the development of childhood," the ultimate responsibility of the state "for children who, on account of improper home conditions, physical handicap or delinquency are in need of special care," and the need for a correlation of state laws enacted for these purposes "as far as practicable in view of conditions in the several States, and, in line with national ideals."[76] The Conclusions of the First White House Conference were also reaffirmed, recommended for consideration by "all communities whose standards do not as yet conform to them," and amplified in some aspects. In addition, a number

---

[76] *Ibid.*, p. 440.

of new topics reflected the progress which had occurred in national thinking and state legislation during the intervening decade.

To insure for children the normal home life needed, the standards (1) urged that private and governmental agencies "supplement the resources of the family whenever the income is insufficient, in such measure that the family budget conforms to the average standard of the community"; (2) recommended that no child be removed from his home unless "it is impossible so to reconstruct family conditions or build and supplement family resources as to make the home safe for the child, or so to supervise the child as to make his continued presence safe for the community"; (3) emphasized the need for attention to the mental hygiene of the child and "for training teachers and social workers in mental hygiene principles"; (4) declared that "the desire for recreation and amusement is a normal expression of every child and an important avenue for moral education and for the prevention of delinquency"; (5) stressed state responsibility for the study of "the extent of feeblemindedness and subnormality"; for adequate provision of "special schools or classes with qualified teachers and adequate equipment for such defective children as may be properly cared for outside of institutions"; and for insuring that custodial care in institutions "not be resorted to until after due consideration of the possibility of adjustment within the community"; (6) recommended special safeguards for the protection of children of illegitimate birth, including the requirement that both parents be responsible for the child during its minority, that no parent "be permitted to surrender the child outside of its own family, save with the consent of a properly designated State department or a court of proper jurisdiction," and that the treatment and care of the unmarried mother and her child include "the best medical supervision and the widest opportunity for education under wholesome, normal conditions in the community"; and (7) advocated that the "essential principles of child welfare work . . . be applied to rural needs, and agencies for rural service encouraged."[77]

For children who must be removed from their own homes, the standards (1) urged a more extensive use of foster family care; (2) listed basic principles governing child placing; and (3) reaffirmed the conviction of the first White House Conference "that a State board of charities, or a similar supervisory body, should be held responsible for the regular inspection and licensing of every institution, agency or association, public or private, incorporated or otherwise, that re-

---

[77] *Ibid.*, pp. 440–443.

ceives or cares for children who suffer from physical handicaps, or who are delinquent, dependent, or without suitable parental care."[78]

In addition, a section on the "Juvenile Court" set forth the principles that (1) every locality should have "a court organization providing for separate hearings of children's cases, a special method of detention for children, adequate investigation for every case, provision for supervision or probation by trained officers, and a system for recording and filing social as well as legal information"; (2) "procedure should be under chancery jurisdiction, and juvenile records should not stand as criminal records against the children"; (3) jurisdiction "should be extended to deal with adult sex offenders against children, and all safeguards of that court be accorded to their victims"; (4) the court should make a full inquiry in all cases of adoption "through its own visitor or through some other unbiased agency"; and (5) "such administrative duties as child placing and relief should not be required of the juvenile court, but should be administered by existing agencies provided for that purpose, or in the absence of such agencies, special provision should be made therefore; nor should cases of dependency or destitution in which no questions of improper guardianship or final and conclusive surrender of guardianship are involved, be instituted in juvenile courts."[79]

These standards also included a statement of "the urgent need of a more adequate body of scientific literature dealing with principles and practices in the children's field of social work" and the responsibility of boards and directors to insure the participation of their staff "in the preparation of such a body of facts." In conclusion, it was recommended that in "States where children's laws have not had careful revision as a whole within recent years, the governor be requested to take necessary steps for the creation of a child welfare committee or commission" in order that "necessary revision and coordination may be made and that new provisions may be incorporated in harmony with the best experience of the day."[80]

THE CHILD WELFARE LEAGUE OF AMERICA

At the end of this era, one of the specific recommendations of the first White House Conference was finally achieved. In 1915 the

---

[78] *Ibid.*, p. 441.

[79] *Ibid.*, pp. 442–443.

[80] *Ibid.*, pp. 443–444.

stated purpose of a permanent voluntary organization of child caring agencies was partially fulfilled by the founding of the Bureau for the Exchange of Information Among Child-Helping Organizations.[81]   In 1920 this organization was incorporated as the Child Welfare League of America and, with funds provided by the Russell Sage Foundation, became a permanent "medium for nation-wide teamwork in conserving and developing America's resources for childhood and youth."[82]

Dr. C. C. Carstens, the executive of the Massachusetts Society for the Prevention of Cruelty to Children, was selected as the first director of the new organization, and under his leadership "the League accepted responsibility for promoting better understanding of child welfare problems; for formulating standards and improving methods in all forms of services to children; for providing information on sound child welfare practice and reporting currently on successful effort in any part of the field; and for developing interagency service."[83]

Because its major accomplishments belong to a more recent period, it is appropriate to note here only the fact that the Child Welfare League of America grew out of the impetus provided by two White House Conferences and that these conferences provided the mandate under which the new organization sought to carry forward the challenge and the ideals set forth in their "Conclusions" and "Standards."

THE SIGNIFICANCE OF THIS ERA

Important events during the first two decades of this century have been described to indicate the point in time in which many of our modern services to children were initiated and to provide a backdrop against which the further development of these services can be described. For some communities this material may have value in assessing how far they have progressed in meeting the standards established during the early years of this century.   For persons critical of current efforts to establish new services in a given community, these glimpses of the past may also furnish evidence that the initiation of such services will not represent a pioneer effort or a "socialistic" departure from tradition, since their value was demonstrated in decades long past.

---

[81] C. C. Carstens, "Dependent and Neglected Children," *Social Work Year Book*, 1929, p. 132.

[82] *Today . . . and Tomorrow* (New York: The Child Welfare League of America, May, 1955), p. 8.

[83] *Ibid.*

As more recent developments in the field of child welfare are traced in subsequent chapters, it will become apparent that these years of vision and action provided a blueprint for the future, whose goals have not been fully achieved in all parts of our nation.   In some areas, however, it will be seen that the building plans sketched by these early leaders provided only a framework, which their limited knowledge of human behavior and its causes could not convert into "working drawings" for the structure planned.   For many tasks, the tools developed by these dedicated groups needed only a multiplication in number and a process of refinement to achieve their stated purpose.   For other purposes, leaders in the first two decades recognized that "a more adequate body of scientific literature" and more extensive use of the scientific method were needed to define the methods through which their established goals could be reached.

Selected Bibliography

Barker, Lewellys F.   "The First Ten Years of the National Committee for Mental Hygiene," *Mental Hygiene*, Vol. II, No. 4, October 1918.

Cannon, Ida W.   *Social Work in Hospitals.*   New York: Survey Associates, Russell Sage Foundation, 1913.

Carstens, C. C.   "Dependent and Neglected Children," *Social Work Year Book*, 1929.

Coffman, Harold Coe.   *American Foundations: A Study of Their Role in the Child Welfare Movement.*   New York: Young Men's Christian Association, 1936.

Devine, Edward T.   *When Social Work Was Young.*   New York: The Macmillan Company, 1939.

Four Decades of Action for Children, U.S. Department of Health, Education and Welfare, Children's Bureau Publication No. 358.   Washington, D.C.: Government Printing Office, 1956.

French, Lois Meredith.   *Psychiatric Social Work.*   New York: Commonwealth Fund, 1945.

Hamilton, Gordon.   "Helping People—The Growth of a Profession," *Social Work as Human Relations.*   New York: Columbia University Press, 1949.

McMillen, Wayne.   *Community Organization for Social Welfare.*   Chicago: The University of Chicago Press, 1945.

Oppenheimer, Julius John.   *The Visiting Teacher Movement.*   New York: Joint Committee on Preventing Delinquency, Commonwealth Fund, 1925.

Richmond, Mary E.   "Motherhood and Pensions," *Survey*, Vol. 29, No. 22, March 1, 1913.

Chapter 7 *The Years of Progress*

(1920-1930)

*T*he decade which followed the establishment of the Child Welfare
League of America was an important period in the development
of contemporary services for children. Although this era began with
a brief period of postwar business recession and the "return to nor-
malcy" made famous by the Harding administration, it also included
a subsequent period of unprecedented industrial expansion and prosperity. Much progress was therefore possible in the development of
needed services, in experimentation to determine the most effective
method of solving existing social problems, and in the evolution of
new principles and practice.

These years are often described as "the roaring twenties," "the age
of the flapper and flaming youth," or the bizarre days of prohibition and
the "speakeasy." For those concerned with the welfare of children,
however, this was a period of quiet, dedicated effort to distill from the
application of the newly discovered scientific method a body of knowl-

120

edge and skill, through which children might be better served. For social workers it was also a period of analysis and appraisal in which their leaders, individually and collectively, attempted to assess progress, formalize areas of agreement, and determine the future direction which the new profession should take.

As the significant events in this period are traced, their role as a preparatory process in the development of a comprehensive pattern of services for children becomes evident.

DEMONSTRATION PROJECTS—COMMONWEALTH FUND

In 1921, the Commonwealth Fund initiated a program which was to have a far-reaching effect in all areas of child welfare. Originally conceived as a five-year project for the prevention of delinquency, its purpose was "to demonstrate and promote the wider application of modern psychiatric science and visiting teacher service to the study and guidance of children presenting problems of conduct and maladjustment in school and in society."[1] Its sponsors expressed recognition that although "problem children" do not all become delinquent in subsequent life, "the understanding and adjustment of children whose conduct suggests underlying mental or physical difficulties should . . . make for the prevention not only of juvenile delinquency but of later and more serious criminal tendencies. Even when delinquency is not involved, such study and treatment of problem children should remove the cause of much unhappiness both at the time and throughout life."[2] More specifically, the program was planned to develop sound methods of study and treatment for "problem children" in the schools and in the juvenile court, to provide a means of training psychiatric social workers, visiting teachers, and probation officers in these methods, and to disseminate information regarding the results of the projects.

Impetus for the project came from two sources. In 1917, the New York School of Social Work had organized a Department of Mental Hygiene under the direction of Dr. Bernard Glueck, and, in 1920, appealed to the Commonwealth Fund for the support of a clinic for the study and treatment of behavior problems, to be conducted under the auspices of the School. During the same year, Thomas W.

---

[1] "The Commonwealth Fund Program for the Prevention of Delinquency," *Three Problem Children* (Appendix), Joint Committee on Methods of Preventing Delinquency (New York: The Commonwealth Fund, 1926), p. 141.

[2] *Ibid.*

Salmon, medical director of the National Committee for Mental Hygiene, presented an appeal for the support of a program entitled "Work in Juvenile Delinquency that could be carried on by a Division of Delinquency in the National Committee for Mental Hygiene."[3]

The approved program included three projects to be conducted by cooperating agencies and established a Joint Committee on Methods of Preventing Delinquency "designed to promote the unity of the entire enterprise, to coordinate its various activities, to conduct related investigations and field studies, and to interpret the purpose, methods and results to various specially interested groups and to the public generally."[4]

The scope and function of Division I included the establishment "as a part of the New York School of Social Work and under its direction, a children's clinic . . . to be known as the Bureau of Children's Guidance";[5] an agreement that the Public Education Association of New York would provide, at the expense of the bureau, properly qualified visiting teachers in five schools to cooperate with the clinic in treatment of children, and the provision that fifteen annual scholarships of $1,200 each be made available "to enable properly qualified professional teachers, or visiting teachers, probation officers and social workers or persons preparing for these professions to take a year's course at the School of Social Work with special attention to psychiatric training."[6]

The five-year program of this division began operation on February 1, 1922, with Porter R. Lee, director of the school, acting as its director, and Marion E. Kenworthy as medical director.

Each child accepted for treatment was studied jointly by a psychiatrist, psychologist, and social worker whose efforts were closely correlated through regular conferences for discussion of his social history, physical, psychological, and psychiatric examination, and subsequent treatment. The children accepted were not limited to those referred by the five schools participating in the program, but a close relation

---

[3] George S. Stevenson, "Child Guidance and the National Committee for Mental Hygiene," in *Orthopsychiatry 1923–1948: Retrospect and Prospect,* editor, Lawson G. Lowrey, (New York: American Orthopsychiatry Association, 1948), p. 51.

[4] "The Commonwealth Fund Program for the Prevention of Delinquency," *op. cit.,* p. 142.

[5] Porter R. Lee and Marion E. Kenworthy, *Mental Hygiene and Social Work* (New York: Commonwealth Fund, 1931), p. 267.

[6] *Ibid.,* p. 268.

was maintained with the visiting teachers assigned to these schools. Case records from the bureau also provided material for *Three Problem Children*, published by the Joint Committee in 1924, and the *Problem Child in School* by Mary B. Sayles, published in 1927. *Mental Hygiene and Social Work*, by Porter R. Lee and Marion E. Kenworthy, later described the work and results of the project.

When this project ended on June 30, 1927, a new Institute for Child Guidance was established "to provide for a limited number of psychiatrists an opportunity to acquaint themselves with the techniques of child guidance, to practice these techniques under constant supervision . . . to learn how to collaborate with psychologists and social workers and to gain some familiarity with the administration and organization problems of the community clinic."[7]

Division II of the Commonwealth Program assigned to a Division on Prevention of Delinquency in the National Committee for Mental Hygiene a responsibility to establish demonstration psychiatric clinics in selected cities and to establish a department of psychiatric field service " . . . to supply to juvenile courts and probation officers a means of becoming acquainted at first hand with the value of psychiatric work, and to assist them in organizing such work on a permanent and scientific basis."[8]

One of the first field activities of the new division was the establishment of a child guidance clinic in Monmouth County, New Jersey, to conduct a mental hygiene survey and to treat children in need of help. This project had great significance since it formalized, for the first time, the child guidance clinic organization and techniques.

Early in 1922 the National Committee for Mental Hygiene announced that it would provide "a clinic team as a demonstration to communities whose juvenile court felt the need for such and which gave promise of continuance under local auspices."[9] The first clinic established under this plan began operation in St. Louis in April, 1922, and a second clinic was established in Norfolk, Virginia, in the same year. By 1925, similar clinics had been opened in Dallas, Minneapolis, St. Paul, Los Angeles, Cleveland, and Philadelphia, and a traveling clinic had been organized at the University of Minnesota. A demonstration team could not be made available to other communities, but

[7] Milton E. Kirkpatrick, "Fellowship Training in Orthopsychiatry," in *Orthopsychiatry 1923–1928: Retrospect and Prospect*, p. 86.

[8] Stevenson, *op. cit.*, p. 58.

[9] *Ibid.*, p. 65.

consulting field staff provided assistance in establishing or stabilizing clinics under local auspices in seven additional cities.

Division III of the Commonwealth Program authorized the Public Education Association of the City of New York to organize a National Committee on Visiting Teachers, which would cooperate with local school boards in thirty communities throughout the country in conducting "a series of three-year demonstrations of the value of such service in the study and adjustment of individual children whose behavior, environment or mental condition had prevented them from gaining full benefit from their school opportunities."[10]   Howard W. Nudd, director of the Public Education Association, and Jane F. Culbert, executive of its visiting teacher staff, were designated as director and secretary of the project.

The communities chosen were carefully selected to insure representation from a wide variety of geographical, education, and social situations.   Three centers were established under county auspices to demonstrate the value of a visiting teacher program in a rural area. Because the visiting teacher movement had not previously extended beyond the Midwestern states, the cities and towns selected included Berkeley and San Diego, California; Eugene, Oregon; Butte, Montana; Pocatello, Idaho; Rock Springs, Wyoming; Tulsa, Oklahoma; and Tucson, Arizona.[11]   Other participating communities were chosen for reasons not related to their geographical location.

The value of the demonstration projects is perhaps most evident in the fact that at their conclusion local boards of education continued a visiting teacher program in all but five of the thirty localities.   During this period, too, the total number of states with visiting teacher programs increased from 15 to 37.   The permanent contribution of the program was further extended by the Joint Committee's publication of *The Problem Child in School* by Mary B. Sayles, *The Visiting Teacher in Rochester* by Mabel Brown Ellis, and *The Visiting Teacher Movement* by Julius John Oppenheimer.

Thus the five-year program financed by the Commonwealth Fund greatly extended the nation's knowledge and appreciation of the principles of mental hygiene and of the value of the visiting teacher or school social work program; demonstrated the need for and the value of sound professional training in child psychiatry, in psychology, and in

---

[10] Mary Buell Sayles, *The Problem Child in School* (New York: Commonwealth Fund, 1927), p. 287.

[11] Howard W. Nudd, "The Purpose and Scope of Visiting Teacher Work," in Sayles, *The Problem Child in School*, p. 278.

psychiatric, school, and court social work; pioneered in the development of the "team approach" in the treatment of maladjusted children; and provided the impetus needed for the child guidance clinic movement.

THE CHILD GUIDANCE CLINIC MOVEMENT

Dr. William Healy, first director of the Juvenile Psychopathic Institute of Chicago, stated that the idea of a child guidance clinic was conceived in 1908 when he, Julia Lathrop, and Allen Burns of the Chicago Juvenile Court recognized the court's need for help in understanding the causes of behavior.[12] There is general agreement that the Institute founded in 1909 was "the first clinic for children in which the psychiatric, psychological and social approaches were combined."[13] The Institute did collaborate with probation officers and social workers in other agencies, but it did not use the team approach, and in fact did not have a social worker on its staff. It became, in name and in fact, a clinic of the juvenile court rather than a community child guidance clinic.

In the second decade of this century, six other clinics provided a similar service for juvenile courts, and psychiatric clinics for children were established at Bellevue Hospital in New York City and at Phipps Clinic in Johns Hopkins Hospital in Baltimore. Children as well as adults were also accepted for treatment at psychiatric clinics at Michigan State Psychopathic Hospital (1906) and the Boston Psychopathic Hospital (1912).[14] Social workers were employed in all of the hospital facilities but the team approach had not yet been developed.

The first clinic for children not attached to a juvenile court or a hospital appears to have been that established by the Department of Child Welfare in Westchester County, New York, in 1918. Here, under the direction of Dr. Bernard Glueck, the combined services of a psychiatrist, psychologist, and social worker were available.[15] By 1921, this staffing pattern had also been adopted by all of the clinics

---

[12] William Healy, and Augusta F. Bronner, "The Child Guidance Clinic: Birth and Growth of an Idea," in *Orthopsychiatry 1923–1948: Retrospect and Prospect*, p. 14.

[13] George S. Stevenson, and Geddes Smith, *Child Guidance Clinics—A Quarter Century of Development* (New York: The Commonwealth Fund, 1934), p. 17.

[14] Lawson G. Lowrey, "Clinical Facilities for the Study of Personality and Behavior Problems in Children," *The Annals of the American Academy of Political and Social Science*, Vol. 151 (September 1930), p. 138.

[15] French, *op. cit.*, p. 42.

serving juvenile courts but the term "child guidance clinic" was not coined until 1922.[16] Since its distinguishing characteristics were evolved from the experience of the demonstration clinics conducted under the Commonwealth Fund program, the initiation of that program in the same year is usually considered to mark the inception of the child guidance clinic movement.

In the original plan formulated by the Commonwealth Fund "the juvenile court was seen as a point of psychiatric attack on delinquency."[17] The experience of the clinic in St. Louis, however, emphasized the fact that "many of the children coming into court were past the stage of prevention and . . . pointed to social agencies, particularly children's agencies, and to schools, as affording a better medium of approach in preventing delinquency than the juvenile court."[18] When the Commonwealth demonstration ended in 1926, the child guidance clinic service available in the United States had increased approximately four times, the pattern of child guidance had been clarified, and a sufficient number of well-organized, permanent clinics had been established to serve as examples for any interested community.

The Commonwealth Fund later made provision for a continued consultation service to communities by making it financially possible for the Division on the Prevention of Delinquency in the National Committee for Mental Hygiene to become the "Division of Community Clinics" under the direction of Dr. George S. Stevenson. As a result, many community surveys were completed, existing clinics visited annually to learn of the advances made, consultation provided to communities interested in establishing a clinic, and the accumulation of experience documented in several publications. In writing about the child guidance movement in 1934, Stevenson described its current status in the following terms:

The child guidance clinic is an attempt to marshal the resources of the community in behalf of children who are in distress because of unsatisfied inner needs or are seriously at outs with their environment. . . . Its service is rendered through the direct study and treatment of selected children by a team consisting of a psychiatrist, a psychologist, and psychiatric social workers and also through focusing the attention of physicians, teachers, social workers, and parents on what is commonly called the mental hygiene approach to problems of child behavior. . . . The func-

---

[16] Lowrey, *op. cit.*, p. 138.

[17] Stevenson and Smith, *op. cit.*, p. 22.

[18] *Ibid.* pp. 24–25.

tions of the child guidance clinics are threefold: they study and treat patients; they seek to interest other community agencies in the prevention of behavior and personality disorders in children and in promising methods of dealing with them when they occur; and they attempt to reveal to the community, through the first-hand study of individual children, the unmet needs of groups of children. Some clinics also undertake the systematic analysis of case material in the hope of contributing to a more exact knowledge of child behavior and some provide training for students of various professions, chiefly psychiatry and social work.[19]

After the onset of the depression some clinics experienced serious financial difficulties but very few became inactive. Thus, by the end of this period the child guidance clinic had become an important part of the pattern of community services for children.

PUBLIC PROTECTION
OF MATERNITY AND INFANT HYGIENE

The early studies of the extent and causes of infant and maternal mortality conducted by the United States Children's Bureau, the public interest generated by the activities sponsored by the Bureau during the "Baby Weeks" of 1916 and 1917 and "Children's Year" (1918–1919), and the recommendations of the second White House Conference resulted in the enactment of legislation authorizing the first federal grant-in-aid program in the field of child welfare.

The statute enacted in 1921 bore the official title of "An Act for the Promotion of the Welfare and Hygiene of Maternity and Infancy," but was customarily known as the Sheppard-Towner Act. During the eight-year period in which its provisions remained in effect, the degree to which its purposes were fulfilled constituted an impressive record More importantly, however, the passage and subsequent administration of this law served to eliminate from the American tradition the concepts on which President Pierce had based his refusal to permit the expenditure of federal funds for welfare purposes in 1854. It also demonstrated the value of federal grants to the states for health and welfare programs and provided a precedent for the pattern later used in the Social Security Act and in subsequent health legislation.

The Sheppard-Towner Act did not represent a sudden congressional recognition of the need for federal participation in efforts to correct the alarming death rate among mothers and infants. Bills based upon

---

[19] *Ibid.*, pp. 1–2.

the principle of extending maternal and child health services to local communities through state health agencies, aided by matching grants from the federal government, were introduced in Congress in 1919, 1920, and 1921. Hearings on these bills caused bitter controversy over the expansion of the functions of the Children's Bureau:

The opponents of the Sheppard-Towner Bill argued that its adoption would be another step toward "socialized medicine"; it would provide the "entering wedge"; too much power would be centralized in Washington; States' rights would be violated. The proponents countered by pointing out that no state would be forced to accept grants-in-aid; no physician would be forced to participate; the actual administration of the program would be left entirely to the states, the Children's Bureau would serve only in a consultative and supervisory capacity; no medical services, as such, would be rendered by the agency; state and local initiative would be strengthened instead of weakened by grants-in-aid. The opponents appearing at the hearings were individual physicians, representatives of the American Medical Association. . . . The proponents appearing were from various women's organizations, child welfare organizations, the president of the American Public Health Association and representatives of other organizations.[20]

The act, signed by President Warren G. Harding on November 23, 1921, authorized for a period of five years an annual appropriation to be used for grants-in-aid to states, and administration of the program. It also (1) assigned to the U.S. Children's Bureau responsibility for formulating rules and regulations; (2) required that the program in each participating state be administered by an existing child hygiene or child welfare division of the state agency of health or by a state agency designated by the legislature; (3) created a Federal Board of Maternity and Infant Hygiene composed of the chief of the Children's Bureau, the surgeon general of the United States Public Health Service, and the commissioner of education; (4) vested in the states the authority to initiate and administer a state plan to reduce maternal and infant mortality and to protect the health of mothers and infants, subject to the approval of the Federal Board; and (5) stipulated that the board must approve the state plan "if reasonably appropriate and adequate to carry out its purposes."[21] The Federal Board was also authorized to withhold federal funds from any state whose program was not operated in accordance with the state plan approved by the board.

---

[20] Nathan Sinai and Oden W. Anderson, *EMIC* (*Emergency Maternity and Infant Care*), *A Study of Administrative Experience* (Ann Arbor: School of Public Health, University of Michigan, 1948), pp. 12–13.

[21] *Ibid.*, p. 14.

Throughout the duration of the program, the chief of the Children's Bureau acted as chairman of the board, and the state plans consisted largely of educational work designed to bring to small cities and rural areas the methods of preventive care previously in use in large cities. In 1929, a bill was introduced to extend the provisions of the act and, after vigorous debate, an extension of two years was finally approved by Congress. Efforts to secure a further extension in 1929 and to revive the act in 1931 and 1932 were not successful, however, since opponents of the original act assumed that the purpose of the legislation was to assist the states only until they could carry the full expense of their own programs.[22]

When the Sheppard-Towner bill was introduced, child hygiene divisions or bureaus existed in only 12 state health departments. Bureaus or divisions of this type were established in 25 states while the bill was pending and in 10 states and Hawaii after the law was enacted. Illinois, Massachusetts, and Connecticut operated their own programs and refused to accept federal funds. Before the expiration of the act on June 30, 1929, 45 states and Hawaii were cooperating in the program.[23]

Participating states reported that during the last five years (1924–1929) the act was in effect, nearly three thousand permanent prenatal and child health centers were established and approximately four million infants and preschool children were served in one way or another (for example, through visits by public health nurses). The United States Birth Registration area was also expanded from 27 states to 45 states and the District of Columbia.[24]

Figures compiled by the Children's Bureau showed that by 1929 the infant mortality rate had fallen to 67.6 in 1,000 live births, in comparison with 100.9 in 1918.[25] During this period the maternal mortality rate per 10,000 live births also decreased from 91.6 to 69.5.[26]

PARENT EDUCATION MOVEMENT

Several efforts to equip parents to deal with the problems of child development and child rearing reached maturity during the third

---

[22] *Ibid.*, pp. 15–17.

[23] Haines, *op. cit.*, p. 253.

[24] *Ibid.*, p. 254.

[25] "Perinatal, Infant, Childhood, and Maternal Mortality, 1954," *Children's Bureau Statistical Series*, No. 42, Table 6 (Washington, D.C.: Government Printing Office, 1957), p. 21.

[26] *Ibid.*, Table 10, p. 25.

decade of this century.   The emphasis for this movement came partly from parents who sought the help of specialists in meeting the problems with which they were confronted and partly from educators, psychologists, pediatricians, psychiatrists, home economists, nutritionists, and research workers who felt the need for more scientific knowledge of child development or recognized the importance of reaching the parent to secure for the child the advantages of a constructive experience during the early years of his life.

The first organization established for this purpose was the Society for the Study of Child Nature, founded in New York City in 1888 and incorporated as the Child Study Association of America in 1924.[27]

This association assumed an important role in the total parent education movement, not only through its own activities but through the stimulus provided for the development of other organizations and projects.   In 1917, its Summer Play School Committee founded the first play school for the group care of school-age children and began a program of work with their parents.   (In 1939 this group became the nucleus of a national organization later incorporated as the Play Schools Association.)[28]   Grants from the Laura Spellman Rockefeller Memorial were received in 1923 and 1924.   At this time, the organization employed Sidonie M. Gruenberg as its director, expanded its program to include the nation-wide organization and supervision of parent education groups, and cooperated with the Teachers' College of Columbia University in establishing the first course for graduate students in parent education.   In 1925, funds from the same foundation allowed the association to begin the publication of its magazine, *Child Study*.   In 1929, a new service was initiated when a full-time psychiatrist was employed to provide individual counseling to parents requesting help with a child's problems.[29]

By this time the membership of the association included 155 constituent organizations.   Its purpose was "to promote a better understanding between parent and child through a program of continuous

---

[27] Ralph P. Bridgman, "Ten Years' Progress in Parent Education," *The Annals of the American Academy of Political and Social Science*, Vol. 151 (September 1930), pp. 35–36.

[28] Jean Schick Grossman, "Parent Education," *Social Work Year Book*, 1949, p. 343.

[29] Aline B. Auerbach, Josette Frank and Anna W. M. Wolf, "Sidonie Matsner Gruenberg and the Child Study Association," *Child Study*, Vol. XXXIII, No. 4 (Fall 1956), pp. 18–22.

parental education."[30]   In addition to the traditional study groups and the new consultation service, its activities included lectures and conferences, a speaker's bureau, the training of leaders, publications, and summer play schools.

The early activities of two additional groups became so intermingled in the area of parent education that their contributions cannot be examined separately.   The nursery school movement, which originated in England in 1909 under the leadership of Margaret MacMillan and Grace Owen, appears to have attracted little attention in this country until it was seen as a potential laboratory for educational research, study of child development, and training in child care.   As a result, its early history is, in effect, the history of child development research.

The first nursery school in this country was organized by the Bureau of Educational Experiments of New York City in 1919 to study child development through observation and testing for the purpose of building an educational program based upon scientific findings.[31]   Although definitely influenced by the English experience, the nursery schools established at the Teachers' College at Columbia University and at the Merrill-Palmer School in Detroit in 1922 were founded for educational research and for the training of home economics students in the care of children, respectively.[32]

In 1924, the Laura Spellman Rockefeller Foundation furthered the interweaving of nursery education and research in child development by allotting grants-in-aid for the establishment of research centers at the following universities: Iowa, Minnesota, Columbia, California, Cornell, and Yale.   In all of these programs, a nursery school was established in which parent education assumed an important role, regardless of the particular type of research conducted.[33]   After that date the nursery school movement spread to other universities, colleges, and schools and was later embraced by many day nurseries, settlement houses, philanthropic agencies, and parent groups.   By 1930, a survey conducted by the United States Office of Education identified 157 nursery schools in 91 cities in 31 states.   In each of these facilities, parent education became "an integral part of their philosophy in order

---

[30] "Child Study Association of America," *Social Work Year Book*, 1929, p. 521.

[31] Helen T. Woolley, "Child Development Research," *Social Work Year Book*, 1929, p. 59.

[32] Lois Hayden Meek, "Nursery Schools," *Social Work Year Book*, 1929, p. 292.

[33] Woolley, *loc. cit.*

that children may have continuity of experience in home and in school."[34]

Although its purpose was not limited to the area of parent education, another early organization in this field was the National Congress of Parents and Teachers. Originally established in Washington under this name in 1897, the organization was later incorporated as the National Congress of Mothers and by 1908 had become the National Congress of Mothers and Parent-Teacher Associations.[35]

Programs in parent education were also developed in city, county, and state departments of education during this period. Oklahoma and Nebraska are reported to have pioneered in the establishment of "mother craft" and "mother training" courses as a part of their vocational education program, financed in part with federal appropriations under the Smith-Hughes Act. In 1926, California organized in the State Department of Education a Bureau of Child Study and Parent Education to provide leadership for parent study groups, and within three years similar plans were developed in New York and Ohio.[36]

Within a decade, the interest of many groups had converged to create a national movement which had as its purpose an intent to provide parents with the knowledge needed to understand their children and to promote their physical and emotional development.

ADOPTION

The first interest in adoption as a national concern occurred during this period. This emphasis appears to have developed from the spotlight turned upon the plight of the child of illegitimate birth by the earlier studies made by the United States Children's Bureau, by the safeguards recommended by the Second White House Conference, by later conferences on illegitimacy sponsored by the bureau in 1920, and from the activities of the Children's Code Commissions in reviewing existing state laws in the light of the recommendations made by these conferences.

The enactment of laws relating to adoption was not a phenomenon peculiar to this period. The Massachusetts Act of 1851 is generally cited as "the first state adoption act passed in the United States."[37]

---

[34] Meek, *op cit.*, p. 292.

[35] Anna Beach Pratt, "The Parent-Teacher Movement," *Social Work Year Book*, 1929, p. 311.

[36] Bridgman, *op. cit.*, p. 38.

[37] Correspondence with Dennis A. Dooley, State Librarian, Massachusetts State Library, September 28, 1953.

There is evidence, however, that Alabama and Texas had enacted adoption legislation during the preceding year, but their statutes were based on the concept of adoption as a means of acquiring an heir to property. The Massachusetts law is, therefore, properly considered the first statute designed to offer protection to the child by legalizing a new parental relationship. For this reason its provisions soon became a model for the statutes of other states, and by 1929 every state had enacted some type of adoption legislation.[38]

The first study of adoption laws published by the Children's Bureau in 1925 indicated wide variations in existing statutes. This report also stated:

To safeguard the interest of all of the parties concerned, the adoption law should provide for investigation of the fitness of the natural parents to care for the child, of his physical and mental condition and his heredity (as it bears on whether he is a proper subject for adoption), of the moral fitness and financial ability of the adopting parents, and in general of the suitability of the proposed home. . . . It should also provide for trial placement in the home either before the petition for adoption was filed or before a final decree was granted, and for supervision during this trial period.[39]

In the next ten years, 39 states enacted new adoption laws or amended existing legislation to reflect in whole or in part the recommendations made by the Children's Bureau. Twelve states provided for an investigation by the state welfare department, a licensed children's agency, a social worker of the court or some other competent person, and 19 states required that the final adoption decree be withheld until the child had lived in the proposed home for a minimum of six months. Additional safeguards were also provided in many states to insure the privacy of adoption records, to provide a new birth certificate for an adopted child, and to protect the child against undesirable placement. To prevent collusion in the disposition of children, several states prohibited maternity homes from advertising that they would place children for adoption, and at least 3 states prohibited any child placing by maternity homes.

Beginning in 1924, the study of adoption procedure and practice as a method of child care began to absorb the interest of public and private agencies on a local and state level. State-wide studies of practice in Pennsylvania, Massachusetts, Illinois, and Ohio were made between 1925 and 1929. The Child Welfare League of America,

---

[38] Clarke, *op. cit.*, pp. 296–297.
[39] United States Children's Bureau, *Adoption Laws of the United States*, Bulletin No. 148, 1925, cited in *Four Decades of Action for Children*, pp. 31–32.

through its studies of child caring agencies and institutions, its regional conferences, and its publications, also stimulated interest in the examination and improvement of practice.

EXTENSION OF OTHER PUBLIC SERVICES FOR CHILDREN

During this period, marked progress was made in the enactment, revision, and administration of laws designed to protect and promote the welfare of children. Like those relating to adoption and other safeguards for the child born out of wedlock, many of these changes reflected the recommendations of the White House Conferences and the more detailed objectives set forth in publications of the United States Children's Bureau and the Child Welfare League of America.

The greatest incidence of legislative change occurred in the requirement that child placing agencies, maternity homes, child caring institutions, and foster homes obtain a license from a designated state department. By 1935, 37 states had adopted some requirement of this type and 3 additional states had assigned this authority to a local official.[40] In 17 states it was also required that the state department of welfare approve the articles of incorporation of a child placing agency and a children's institution before a charter of incorporation could be issued.[41]

The laws of the various states showed considerable variation in the location of licensing responsibility, in the types of facilities subject to license, and in the requirements for license. In 31 states boarding homes were subject to license by a state department, but sole responsibility for this function was placed with the state welfare department in only 17 states. In 3 states, this function was assigned to the State Board of Health and in the remaining 11 states some cooperative procedure between these state departments was required. In 31 states maternity homes and child caring institutions were required to obtain a license and a similar requirement for child placing agencies existed in 33 states. In general, the pattern of licensing responsibility followed that established for boarding homes, except that the state welfare department held sole responsibility for the licensing of maternity homes in only 11 states.[42]

---

[40] Gladys Genevra Fraser, *The Licensing of Boarding Homes, Maternity Homes, and Child Welfare Agencies* (Chicago: University of Chicago Press, 1937), p. 5.

[41] *Ibid.* p. 13.

[42] *Ibid.*, pp. 14–19.

Great diversity was also evident in the ages of children protected by the licensing laws, the requirements relating to inspection, the records and reports which must be maintained or submitted by licensed facilities, the provision of penalty for violation of the licensing law, the method of administration, the standards and procedures used to determine eligibility to license, the number and qualifications of staff assigned to this function, and the extent to which supervision and consultation were provided by the licensing department. The study which produced these findings concluded that only a beginning had been made in protecting children through the licensing function.[43]

Considerable progress was also made in the development of other services for children during this era. In some instances the advances made resulted from the enactment of new laws. To a considerable degree, however, improvement in the administration of existing statutes produced more adequate services. This was particularly true in relation to the program of Mothers' Aid. By 1934, all states except Alabama, Georgia, and South Carolina had enacted legislation providing this type of assistance,[44] but a study made by the United States Children's Bureau in 1931 showed that grants were being paid in only 1,578 of the 2,723 counties in which state laws authorized the administration of the program.[45] Despite this fact, the standards of assistance and the quality of service had greatly improved in states in which there was state financial participation, state supervision, qualified staff, and an absence of legal restrictions on the maximum grant.[46]

As implied by the developments in licensing and in the administration of mothers' aid, this period showed marked extension in the degree of responsibility assumed for the protection of children by state departments of social welfare and an uneven development in the extent to which local communities moved from the traditional method of poor relief toward the provision of adequate services for children. As attention was focused on the revision of state laws, the United States Children's Bureau was repeatedly asked for recommendations with

---

[43] *Ibid.*, pp. 22–95.

[44] United States Children's Bureau, *A Tabular Summary of State Laws Relating to Public Aid to Children in Their Own Homes in Effect January 1, 1934*, Chart No. 3 (Washington, D.C.: Government Printing Office, 1934).

[45] *Four Decades of Action for Children*, p. 31.

[46] White House Conference on Child Health and Protection, *Dependent and Neglected Children* (New York: D. Appleton-Century Company, 1933), pp. 227–242.

respect to the most effective pattern of administration to insure "reasonable standards of service for children in smaller towns and communities."[47] From studies made in 1922 and 1925,[48] and from the conclusions reached by representatives of 32 state departments of public welfare in a conference on child dependency and protection held on February 5, 1929, Grace Abbott, chief of the Children's Bureau, concluded:

> The state can perform certain functions better than the local government, but in the performance of these duties, it has become increasingly clear that the functions . . . of the state and the local community must be made a correlated state and county responsibility. . . .
> Whether or not the cooperation between state and county should take the form of state subsidies for the local work is also being much discussed. . . . The collection of funds from the state as a whole and its redistribution to the counties can help to equalize . . . differences . . . and make possible an approximation of equality of treatment. State subsidies for education . . . are being generally adopted. . . . Why not then assistance in providing other kinds of social service? . . .
> To summarize, experience warrants the conclusion that the states should be completely responsible for certain social services and particularly for institutional treatment, provided that this is not allowed to interfere with the development of a local preventive program or discourage the choice of the best possible treatment of the individual child. For the proper functioning of a preventive program which requires early and direct contact with the individual, an efficient county organization is essential. The state departments of health or social welfare should assist in developing the necessary county services and should cooperate with the local units by loaning personnel and contributing to the cost of the local services.[49]

Three significant developments in relation to juvenile courts and the services provided for juvenile delinquents can be identified during this period. Perhaps the most far-reaching event occurred when the first set of *Standards for Juvenile Courts* was adopted at a conference sponsored jointly by the United States Children's Bureau and the National Probation Association in May, 1923.[50] These standards set forth the requirements of a well-organized court and provided the basis for

---

[47] *Four Decades of Action for Children*, p. 29.

[48] Lundberg, *The County As a Unit for An Organized Program of Child Caring and Protective Work*, p. 1.

[49] Grace Abbott, "The County vs. The Community As An Administrative Unit," *The Social Service Review*, Vol. IV, No. 1 (March 1930), pp. 12–16.

[50] Katharine F. Lenroot and Emma O. Lundberg, *Juvenile Courts at Work*, United States Children's Bureau, Publication No. 141 (Washington, D.C.: Government Printing Office, 1925), p. 3.

the standard juvenile court act, approved by the Annual Conference of the National Probation Association in 1924 to provide a model for state legislation.[51] By 1933 these standards had been "fully adopted in law or in administrative practice by only a small minority of courts,"[52] but a beginning had been made in establishing a yardstick by which future progress could be measured.

In 1927, the Children's Bureau created another milestone in the development of tools for the prevention and control of juvenile delinquency when it implemented a plan for uniform recording and reporting by juvenile courts and published the first report based upon the statistics collected. Courts were slow to cooperate in this project, however, and only fragmentary statistics were available for many years.

The services of local juvenile courts were also made available to children who had violated federal laws during this period. In 1931, a study made by the Wickersham Commission on Law Observance and Enforcement under the direction of Dr. Miriam Van Waters resulted in a recommendation that "the Federal Government recognize the concept of juvenile delinquency and withdraw the child offender from the ordinary operation of the Federal system of criminal justice" and permit the states "to assume responsibility for court hearings and subsequent treatment."[53] In accordance with this recommendation, a bill passed by Congress authorized the transfer of juvenile delinquents "to juvenile courts in their own communities provided that these juvenile courts were willing to accept them."[54] When he signed this bill on June 11, 1932, President Hoover stated:

This measure is an important step forward in that it sets an example through its recognition by the federal government of the principle that even the relatively small number of juveniles in the federal system should be handled on a modern scientific basis. It is also a recognition by the federal government of the juvenile court as the proper place for the handling of the cases of all the juveniles, and is an acceptance of the principle that juvenile offenders are the product of and the responsibility of their home community.[55]

---

[51] *Ibid.*

[52] Charles L. Chute, "Juvenile Courts," *Social Work Year Book*, 1933, p. 260.

[53] *Report of the Child Offender in the Federal System of Justice*, National Commission on Law Observance and Enforcement (Washington, D.C.: U.S. Government Printing Office, 1931), pp. 154–156.

[54] 47 U.S. Stats. 301 Chapter 243 (1932).

[55] *Child Welfare News Summary*, U.S. Children's Bureau, June 25, 1932.

CHILD LABOR LEGISLATION

Although each state in the union had some type of compulsory education law by 1918, the 1920 census showed that 1,400,000 children between seven and thirteen years of age were not attending school. In addition, more than one million children ten to fifteen years of age were reported to be employed, despite the fact that every state prohibited the employment of children under fourteen, at least during school hours.[56]   Considerable progress was made in alleviating this condition during the next two years, but in May, 1922, the United States Supreme Court declared unconstitutional the Revenue Act of 1919 which required payment of a tax of 10 per cent of the annual net profit of any industry which employed children in violation of the standards established by the act.[57]   This opinion was based on the court's belief that the legislation was designed to prevent child labor and therefore was not a valid revenue act.

This law, like the Child Labor Act of 1916 (declared unconstitutional in 1918), demonstrated the value of federal control of child labor in encouraging an improvement in the standards established by state laws and in protecting children in states which had failed to enact adequate provisions. Proponents of child labor legislation, spearheaded by the National Child Labor Committee, therefore began the active support of an amendment to the Constitution which would authorize Congress to enact needed legislation. In June, 1924, Congress passed a resolution proposing an amendment to the Constitution which read:

Section 1.   The Congress shall have the power to limit, regulate and prohibit the labor of persons under the age of eighteen years.
Section 2.   The power of the several states is unimpaired by this article except that the operation of state laws shall be suspended to the extent necessary to give effect to legislation enacted by the Congress.[58]

This bill met with little opposition in Congress, but a bitter controversy developed when the amendment was submitted to the various state legislatures.   The National Child Labor Committee, the National Consumers' League, labor groups, women's organizations, church

---

[56] Wylie H. Swift, "Child Labor," *Social Work Year Book*, 1929, p. 64.

[57] Elizabeth S. Magee, "Child Laborers' Gains and Losses Since the War," *The Annals of the American Academy of Political and Social Science*, Vol. 151 (September 1930), p. 57.

[58] 43 U.S. Stats., 670, Part I, H. J. Res. No. 184.

groups, and professional organizations worked continuously for ratification, but these efforts were actively opposed by the National Association of Manufacturers, many state manufacturers' associations, farmers, the State Rights League, and the "Committee for the Protection of Child, Family, School and Church."[59] These opponents of federal child labor legislation charged that the amendment" was framed in Soviet Russia; that it would nationalize the children; that it would give Congress new and unprecedented power to interfere between parent and child; that because of the upper limit of eighteen, it would prohibit all work under that age and keep the boy from milking the cows for his father and the girl from washing the dishes for her mother, and that it interfered with 'state's rights.' "[60] In addition, the Committee for the Protection of Child, Family, School and Church was successful in fostering the belief that the amendment would result in the closing of private schools maintained by the Catholic and Lutheran churches.[61]

As a result of these arguments, few advances were made in the improvement of state child labor laws after 1924 and only Arkansas, California, Colorado, Arizona, Wisconsin, and Montana ratified the amendment. In 1933, prevailing unemployment among adults produced a demand for a national control of child labor and 14 states ratified the amendment in that year.[62] By 1935, ratification had occurred in 24 Northern states but approval of 12 states was still needed.

After 1933, the codes developed under the National Industrial Recovery Act prohibited the employment of children under sixteen except in agricultural and domestic service. In 1935, this act was declared unconstitutional for other reasons, but its provisions had paved the way for the enactment of labor legislation. Ratification of the child labor amendment therefore ceased to be a national issue.

SOCIAL WORK AS A PROFESSION

In many ways the development of social services for children has been greatly influenced by the growth of social work as a profession.

---

[59] "The Child Labor Amendment," (Editorial) *The Social Service Review*, Vol. IX, No. 1 (March 1935), p. 107.

[60] Magee, *op. cit.*, 58.

[61] Editorial, *The Social Service Review*, March 1935, p. 108.

[62] *Ibid.*

It is, therefore, important to examine the process through which social work began to acquire professional characteristics and some of the bench marks which reflected its increased status during this period.

The first important step was taken when the American Association of Social Workers was established in June, 1921. As stated in the constitution, its purpose was "to bring together professional social workers for such cooperative effort as may enable the group more effectively to fulfill its function in service to society. To this end the Association may formulate and seek to establish preparation and training, disseminate information concerning social work as a profession and conduct research, investigations and such other activities as it may deem appropriate to this purpose."[63]

During the first five years of its existence the association studied, defined, and standardized positions in social work and their required qualifications; issued a monthly magazine to provide a channel of communication for its members; published a series of pamphlets describing family social work, psychiatric, medical, and child welfare work for students contemplating social work as a career; cooperated with the training schools in recruitment; and acted as a representative in the professional interest of its members when occasion arose.[64]

Although social workers employed in all settings were eligible for membership in the AASW, the establishment of this organization did not impede the trend toward the separate identification of those employed in specific settings. By 1926, social workers employed in child guidance clinics questioned their membership in the Section on Psychiatric Social Work of the American Association of Hospital Social Workers.[65] In the same year the American Association of Psychiatric Social Workers became the fourth professional organization to be established.

During this period the professional status of social work was advanced by a number of important additions to its literature. In 1922, Mary Richmond's *What Is Social Case Work?* provided for the profession a clarification of social casework, and in 1924 Karl de Schweinitz's *The Art of Helping People Out of Trouble* presented

---

[63] "American Association of Social Workers Constitution," adopted June 28, 1922, cited in Esther Lucile Brown, *Social Work As a Profession* (New York: Russell Sage Foundation, 1935), p. 48.

[64] Philip Klein, "The American Association of Social Workers," Appendix 2, cited in Alice S. Cheyney, *The Nature and Scope of Social Work* (New York: American Association of Social Workers, 1926), pp. 49–50.

[65] French, *op. cit.*, p. 46.

an interpretation of social work for a lay audience. In addition to the books published by the Commonwealth Fund as a part of its demonstration program, the first *Social Work Year Book* was published by the Russell Sage Foundation in 1929. This volume made available in encyclopedic form the history and current development of all activities within the field of social service and established a pattern for the publication of similar sources of reference in alternate years since 1933. *American Charities and Social Work*, by Amos G. Warner, Stuart A. Queen, and Ernest B. Harper, also joined Mary Richmond's *Social Diagnosis* as a standard reference for many schools of social work, and the *Proceedings of the National Conference of Social Work* continued to chronicle new ideas and experiences in the field. In addition, monographs issued by the United States Children's Bureau, the Child Welfare League of America, the Family Welfare Association of America, the National Committee for Mental Hygiene, and the American Association of Social Workers contributed greatly to the further development of the field of child welfare. The monthly journals published by these organizations and *The Jewish Social Service Quarterly*, a publication of the National Conference of Jewish Social Service, also provided a wealth of information. After March, 1937, these resources were augmented by the publication of *The Social Service Review*, a quarterly journal published by the School of Social Service Administration of the University of Chicago.

One of the most significant reports issued during this period was published by the American Association of Social Workers in 1929 under the title *Social Case Work: Generic and Specific, Studies in the Practice of Social Work*. This small volume described the process by which representatives of eight national organizations met in four annual meetings in Milford, Pennsylvania, and accepted the report prepared by a five-member committee chaired by Porter R. Lee, director of the New York School of Social Work. In summarizing its discussions over a three-year period, the committee concluded:

Social case work is a definite entity. It has a field increasingly well defined, it has all of the aspects of the beginnings of a science in its practice and it has conscious professional standards for its practitioners. The various separate designations (children's case worker, family case worker, probation officer, visiting teacher, psychiatric social worker, medical social worker, etc.) by which its practitioners are known tend to have no more than a descriptive significance in terms of the type of problem with which they respectively deal. . . . This report testifies to the importance of the specific fields of social case work and to the specific demands which each specific field makes upon case workers practicing within it. Nevertheless, the outstanding fact is that the problems of social case work and the equipment of the social case worker are fundamentally the same for all fields. In other words, in any discussion of problems, concepts, scientific knowledge or methods, generic social case work is the common field to which the specific forms of social case work are merely incidental.[66]

The report also expressed the belief that "social work is a unified profession and not an aggregate of specialties,"[67] and that "generic social work is as valid and important a conception as generic social case work."[68] The fundamental techniques of social work were listed as social case work, community organization, group work, social research, and administration, and emphasis was placed upon the need to include all of these techniques in the training of social workers.

This report had great influence on the development of social work as a profession and more specifically on the future pattern of training for social work. For a considerable period, many of its implications were not fully accepted by agencies intent upon assimilating the teachings of psychiatry and medicine or upon meeting the needs of individual children. This delay was perhaps accentuated by the 1930 publication of Virginia Robinson's *A Changing Psychology in Social Case Work*, another milestone in the development of professional thinking. Miss Robinson accepted fully the significance of the Milford Conference report in authoritatively establishing the belief in a common case work field.[69] Her emphasis on the individual and on the importance of the case worker's relationship with him as a tool in treatment, however, served to focus professional attention upon the need to refine this potential for change. For the children's agencies, this influence proved a mixed blessing, since it tended to prolong their belief in the value in removing a child from an unsuitable environment, without adequate appreciation of the importance of working with his family to prevent the need for foster care or to make possible an early return to his own home.

In other areas, the effects of the Milford Conference were more immediate. In 1930 the Association of Training Schools for Professional Social Work appointed its first curriculum committee. By 1935, courses in all of the five methods of social work were prevalent though

---

[66] *Social Case Work: Generic and Specific, Studies in the Practice of Social Work* (New York: American Association of Social Workers, 1935), p. 11.

[67] *Ibid.*, p. 66.

[68] *Ibid.*, p. 78.

[69] Virginia P. Robinson, *A Changing Psychology in Social Case Work* (Chapel Hill: University of North Carolina Press, 1934), pp. 79–80.

the varied content of the courses in group work and in community organization continued to indicate that the scope of these two fields had not yet been clearly demarcated or the differences between community organization and administration fully identified.[70]

Another significant event occurred in 1929 when plans were made for the organization of the American Association of Public Welfare Officials during the National Conference of Social Work. As established in 1930, the association was primarily concerned with the improvement of existing public welfare programs. By the time the first annual meeting of the association was held in June, 1931, however, the problems resulting from widespread unemployment absorbed the attention of its members and a committee was appointed "to work for increased public relief appropriations, especially in distressed rural areas and to promote better standards of administration."[71]

With the onset of the depression in 1930, social work received increasing recognition as its members assumed an active role in presenting the problems caused by existing economic conditions and in stimulating corrective legislation. During this period of crisis, the growth and development of social work as a profession was greatly influenced by the changing national scene. New alignments in the responsibilities of public and private agencies and new concepts about the role of government on a local, state, and federal level were of particular importance in this regard. As significant events in the depression years are described, their impact on the profession will be noted.

THE THIRD WHITE HOUSE CONFERENCE

The White House Conference on Child Health and Protection, called by President Hoover, assembled in Washington on November 19-22, 1930, with three thousand men and women in attendance.

The call for the conference announced that it was:

To study the present status of the health and well-being of the children of the United States and its possessions; to report what is being done; to recommend what ought to be done and how to do it.[72]

---

[70] Wayne McMillen, "The Content of Professional Courses in Community Organization," *The Social Service Review*, Vol. IX, No. 1 (March 1935), pp. 68–69.

[71] Josephine Chapin Brown, *Public Relief, 1929–1939* (New York: Henry Holt and Company, 1940), p. 85.

[72] Ray Lyman Wilbur, "Foreword," *White House Conference, 1930—Addresses and Abstracts of Committee Reports* (New York: Copyright The Century Company, 1931, p. v. (Reprinted by permission of Appleton-Century-Crofts, Inc).

Prior to the Conference, 1,200 experts working on nearly 150 different committees devoted sixteen months to study, research, and compilation of their findings on four major topics.[73] The results of this massive effort were subsequently published in 32 volumes, but the Conference is best known for its development of "The Children's Charter."

In his opening address, President Hoover defined the fundamental purpose of the conference to be that of providing an understanding of the "safeguards and services to children which can be provided by the community, the State or the Nation—all of which are beyond the reach of the individual parent."[74] He then identified three aspects of the problem: "first, the protection and stimulation of the normal child; second, aid to the physically defective and handicapped child; third, the problems of the delinquent child."[75] The Children's Charter followed a similar pattern. It pledged the conference to fourteen aims for every child; three additional goals for the child who is physically or mentally handicapped, the child who is in conflict with society, and the child who lives in a rural area; and two specific recommendations about the means by which "these minimum protections of the health and welfare of children" can be achieved.

Dr. Ray Lyman Wilbur, chairman of the conference, pin-pointed its essential difference from prior White House Conferences when he stated:

Within the past few decades there has been a growing consciousness of the significance of childhood. . . . We have seen what was once charity change its nature under the broader term welfare and now those activities looked upon as welfare are becoming to be viewed merely as good community housekeeping. In a word, parental responsibility is moving outward to include community responsibility. Every child is now *our* child. . . . [76]

Each of the committee reports reflected an effort to document current concepts about the assigned topic, the nature and extent of the problems noted, and the conclusions or recommendations believed essential to provide a sound basis for future action. Although the reports indicated a wider area of concern than that of previous White

---

[73] *Ibid.*, p. vii.

[74] "Address of President Hoover," *White House Conference, 1930—Addresses and Abstracts of Committee Reports*, p. 6.

[75] *Ibid.*, pp. 7–8.

[76] Ray Lyman Wilbur, "A Survey and A Challenge," *White House Conference, 1930—Addresses and Abstracts of Committee Reports*, p. 16.

House Conferences, the standards developed by the 1919 conference had included all of the general topics considered by this conference. Many of the principles stated, however, reflected the knowledge gained during the preceding decade and a new conviction about the methods through which desired objectives might be obtained.

The report of the Committee on the Prevention, Maintenance and Protection of the Handicapped provides an excellent example of the progress which had been made since the development of the "Standards for the Protection of Children in Need of Special Care." In the section on "State and Local Organizations for the Handicapped," it is boldly stated for the first time in a White House Conference report that (1) a child's opportunity for development should not be determined by the locality in which he was born; (2) grants-in-aid constitute the most effective basis for national and state cooperation in promoting child welfare; (3) there should be in every state a welfare department with special responsibilities for children; (4) the county is in most parts of the country the most practical unit for the general administration of child care; (5) when local administrative units of child care are organized, nonjudicial duties should, as speedily as possible, be transferred thereto from the juvenile courts; and (6) the treatment accorded each child must be determined solely by his needs, and not by reason of what tax unit should be made to pay the cost of his care.[77]

New content is also apparent in the section on the "Physically and Mentally Handicapped," which (1) set forth "A Bill of Rights for the Handicapped Child"; (2) listed the components necessary for a "comprehensive plan to prepare the physically and the mentally handicapped child for life's work"; (3) outlined a suggested program for children with each type of physical handicap, for example, the deaf and hard of hearing, the blind and the partially seeing, the crippled, and the child suffering from tuberculosis, heart disease, or intestinal parasites; and (4) discussed briefly the problems of mental health and mental deficiency with recommendations for programs of treatment and prevention.[78]

After reaffirming the principles established by preceding White

---

[77] Kate Burr Johnson, "State and Local Organizations for the Handicapped," *White House Conference, 1930—Addresses and Abstracts of Committee Reports,* pp. 275–285.

[78] William J. Ellis, "A Bill of Rights for the Handicapped Child," *White House Conference, 1930—Addresses and Abstracts of Committee Reports,* pp. 291–318.

House Conferences and measuring the interim progress made, the section on "Dependency and Neglect" likewise indicated new areas of concern by the identification of additional groups of children in special need—for example, the child of Negro, Mexican, Puerto Rican, or Indian parentage; emphasis on the value of skilled social case work in strengthening family life; and recognition of the need for an agency in each community equipped with personnel qualified for the specialized task of child protection.[79]

Other reports showed a similar introduction of new concepts about previously identified problems. This conference, therefore, preserved for posterity an extensive documentation of current opinion and practice and provided a detailed blueprint for future direction in the total field of child welfare.

Selected Bibliography

Lee, Porter R., and Marion E. Kenworthy. *Mental Hygiene and Social Work.* New York: Commonwealth Fund, 1931.

Lenroot, Katharine F. "Summing Up the Previous White House Conferences," *The Child,* Vol. 14, No. 4, October 1949.

Robinson, Virginia P. *A Changing Psychology in Social Case Work.* Chapel Hill: University of North Carolina Press, 1930.

Social Case Work: Generic and Specific, Studies in the Practice of Social Work. New York: American Association of Social Workers, 1935.

White House Conference, 1930—Addresses and Abstracts of Committee Reports. New York: The Century Company, 1931.

White House Conference on Child Health and Protection, *Dependent and Neglected Children.* New York: The Appleton-Century Company, 1930.

---

[79] Homer Folks, "Socially Handicapped—Dependency and Neglect," *White House Conference, 1930—Addresses and Abstracts of Committee Reports,* pp. 319–340.

Chapter 8   *The Years of Crisis*

(1930-1935)

In the lives of individual families and children, the traumatic period which followed the stock market crash on "Black Friday" in October, 1929, had little resemblance to the preceding decade. Similar contrast in the methods of meeting human need was also evident in every community, but the progress achieved during the past ten years made possible the emergency measures needed to cope with the problems created by widespread unemployment. The patterns evolved to meet the exigencies of the depression in turn contributed to the development of contemporary services for children since they provided guides for use in developing effective methods to prevent a recurrence of similar deprivation. In some instances, too, programs abandoned after the national emergency served as patterns for recent efforts to meet problems not created by unemployment.

147

THE ECONOMIC CRISIS

In the voluminous reports of the 1930 White House Conference many pages were devoted to the harmful effects of irregular and inadequate income on wholesome family life and child development. In this connection it was noted that the unemployment situation was currently receiving more attention than usual, but the reports gave no indication that unemployment was seen as a major problem. It must be remembered, however, that much of the research on which these reports were based was completed during the early months of 1929 and that in prior depressions private agencies had found it possible to mobilize the resources necessary during temporary periods of increased need. Despite these facts, the omission of any reference to the contemporary scene provides a significant clue to the attitudes characteristic of the early years of the depression. In reality, the United States Children's Bureau had become aware of the alarming rate of unemployment in the mining villages as early as 1927 and statistical reports received in the summer of 1929 indicated that the usual seasonal decrease in relief expenditures throughout the country had not occurred. By the end of 1930, the number of unemployed had increased to nearly 7,000,000 persons out of a potential working force of 48,000,000.[1]

During the early months of 1930 the general public expected that private agencies would meet the increased relief needs as usual, and they in turn attempted to carry the burden by securing additional funds from wealthy benefactors, by using reserve funds, or by incurring deficits. Government officials and industrial leaders tried to provide assurance that "prosperity is just around the corner" but severe droughts in several agricultural states during the summer added to the growing distress caused by ever-rising unemployment. President Hoover took the position, however, that voluntary contributions to community chests could take care of the situation.

In October, 1930, the "President's Emergency Committee for Employment" was organized under a name selected to indicate the emergency nature of the situation and its primary objective. The committee proceeded to carry out its assignment by (1) emphasizing to state and local governments the value of expediting public construction to provide employment; (2) encouraging industry to "spread the work";

---

[1] J. H. G. Pierson, *Full Employment* (New Haven: Yale University Press, 1941) p. 17.

(3) publicizing ways in which the individual citizen could help by giving jobs to unemployed men in his own neighborhood; (4) urging states and local communities to provide relief; and (5) giving publicity to the community chest drives and to Red Cross campaigns for drought relief.[2] The Family Welfare Association of America and the Association of Community Chests were also asked to secure information on local needs and methods of meeting these needs.[3]

A study made by the United States Bureau of the Census at the request of the President's Committee showed that 1,287,778 families received relief during the first three months of 1931 in comparison with 333,861 families during the same period in 1929. The U.S. Children's Bureau found, too, that in the 75 cities from which figures were obtained a major portion of the money spent for relief (72 per cent) came from public funds and not from private charities as was popularly believed.[4] By this time, however, tax delinquencies were rapidly decreasing available public funds and widespread bank failures were aggravating the total economic crisis. As it became increasingly evident that local governments could not cope with the mounting distress, many state legislatures met in special sessions during the spring of 1931 to consider unemployment problems. Four states appropriated funds for relief (Oklahoma, New Hampshire, Maryland, and California) and Ohio authorized local units to issue bonds for this purpose. Other legislatures took no effective action either because of a constitutional prohibition against the use of state funds for relief or because of a continued belief that existing problems must be solved by local units. When surveys made in mining communities by the United States Children's Bureau at the President's Committee's request showed that outside assistance was essential if slow starvation was to be interrupted, the Friends Service Society, which had administered American relief in Europe after World War I, was asked by the President's Committee to accept responsibility for feeding the children in poverty-stricken counties of West Virginia, Kentucky, southern Illinois, western Pennsylvania, and eastern Ohio.[5] The committee also requested the American Association of Public Welfare Officials

---

[2] E. P. Hayes, *Activities of the President's Emergency Committee for Employment* (Concord: The Rumford Press, 1936) pp. 3–4.

[3] *Ibid.* p. 99.

[4] *Ibid.*, pp. 36–37.

[5] *Ibid.*, p. 109.

to develop, in cooperation with the national organizations of private agencies, a program which would enable local and state organizations to meet the problems created by unemployment.[6]

On August 28, 1931, an event of far-reaching importance occurred when Gov. Franklin D. Roosevelt addressed a special session of the New York legislature. In this message he first articulated the philosophy which was to form the cornerstone of his administration for many years to come:

Our government is not the master but the creature of the people. The duty of the State toward the citizens is the duty of the servant to its master. The people have created it; the people by common consent, permit its continued existence.
One of these duties of the State is that of caring for those of its citizens who find themselves the victims of such adverse circumstances as makes them unable to obtain even the necessities for mere existence without the aid of others. . . .
In broad terms, I assert that modern society, acting through its government, owes the definite obligation to prevent the starvation or the dire want of any of its fellow men and women who try to maintain themselves but cannot. . . . To these unfortunate citizens aid must be extended by government—not as a matter of charity but as a matter of social duty.[7]

On September 23, 1931, the New York legislature appropriated twenty million dollars as state aid to local governments to supplement their relief work in the existing emergency. The act vested responsibility for the administration of these funds in the "Temporary Emergency Relief Administration," which was to "make and enforce rules which would best promote the efficiency and integrity of the relief which this Act is intended to furnish," and provided for a 40 per cent reimbursement to cities and towns for relief expenditures. In October, 1931, Harry L. Hopkins was appointed director of the new agency and operation began in the following month.

On a federal level the situation remained unchanged. In a message to Congress on December 8, 1931, President Hoover again expressed his approval of the mobilization of local efforts and stated:

I am opposed to any direct or indirect government dole. . . . Our people are providing against distress from unemployment in true American fashion by a magnificent response to public appeal and by action of the local governments.

---

[6] *Ibid.*, pp. 117–118.
[7] *New York Assembly Journal*, 1931, III, pp. 21–29.

Despite this statement, Senator Edward P. Costigan of Colorado immediately introduced a bill which provided for federal aid to the states to be administered by the Children's Bureau under a Federal Board of Unemployment Relief. At the first committee hearings, Senator Costigan stated in part:

. . . The hearing which is about to open is designed to be informative. . . . The facts if developed here, should establish that the hour has passed for reliance on incurable optimism and that our Nation must grapple with characteristic thoroughness with the realities of the present crisis.[8]

During the next two months, social workers and labor leaders from all sections of the country read into the Congressional Record a mass of first-hand information about relief loads, unmet needs, evictions, families separated and children handed around among neighbors, increasing disease, mental breakdowns and suicides, and "families of four trying to live on $5.50 a week, six families crowded into a six-room house."[9] In opposition to this record of actual suffering and inadequate resources to relieve the distress, appeared representatives of the President's Organization of Unemployment Relief, the United States Chamber of Commerce, the Detroit Board of Commerce, and other interested organizations. Their arguments included allegations that federal aid would seriously impair the credit of the federal government; make it impossible to balance the budget; retard the restoration of normal business; increase income, estate, and corporation taxes; violate American principles of local responsibility and state's rights; give citizens an excuse to shirk their responsibilities; demoralize recipients; increase demands for public handouts; and create waste and political interference. To no avail, members of the Senate traced the record of the federal government in 31 prior appropriations for emergency and disaster relief due to floods, cyclones, drought, earthquake, and fire; cited the precedent established by grants-in-aid for states for highways and agricultural purposes as well as President Hoover's own approval of continued federal support for county health work in 1929; and pointed out that Congress had already provided more than two billion dollars during the current depression for the relief of banks, railroads, industry, and insurance companies.[10]

---

[8] Josephine Brown, *op. cit.*, p. 105. Cited from hearings on S-174 and S-262, December, 1931.

[9] *Ibid.*, p. 106.

[10] *Ibid.*, pp. 109–114.

On January 15, 1932, Congressional hearings produced further evidence of distress indicating that practically every city of the nation was on the verge of bankruptcy. In February, 1932, a report of the United States Children's Bureau on the "Effects of the Depression on Child Health and Child Health Services" indicated clearly the results in terms of malnutrition and poor health.[11] The only action taken by Congress, however, was a joint resolution authorizing the distribution of government-owned wheat and cotton in distressed rural areas by the American Red Cross.

In July, 1932, the Emergency Relief and Construction Act was passed by Congress. It authorized the Reconstruction Finance Corporation to make three hundred million dollars available for advances to states and territories "to be used in furnishing relief and work relief to needy and distressed people and in relieving the hardship resulting from unemployment."[12] Through the governors, loans at 3 per cent interest could be made to states, cities, or counties on certificates of necessity and inadequate resources. This legislation did not solve existing problems, however, since many states refused to accept responsibility for relief and many cities had exhausted their borrowing power.

When Congress convened in December, 1932, another bill to "relieve the hardship and suffering caused by unemployment" was introduced. When Senator Costigan again addressed the subcommittee he declared:

Cold, hunger, malnutrition, illness and ever-menacing starvation from day to day are disastrously shattering self-respect. The most startling development of the nation-wide tragedy has been demonstrated unwillingness of a large part of our national leadership, both industrial and political, to face the facts; to admit national responsibility even where personal, local and state contributions have failed; and to organize with typical American thoroughness to combat and conquer our recognized crisis.[13]

Once again volumes of testimony chronicled the fact that the fourth winter of unemployment was proving more tragic than those which preceded it, despite the loans received from the RFC. In addition to the reports received from social workers and the United States Conference of Mayors, Harry L. Hopkins described his fourteen

---

[11] *Congressional Record*, Vol. 75, p. 3067.

[12] Emergency Relief and Construction Act of 1932, Chapter 520, 47. *U.S. Statutes at Large*, 79.

[13] Josephine Brown, *op. cit.*, p. 137.

months of experience with the New York TERA and advocated that a similar plan be established on a federal level. By the end of the Hoover administration, the relief bill had been referred to the floor of the Senate and to a House committee.

When President Roosevelt gave his inaugural address on March 4, 1933, approximately fifteen million people were unemployed and four million families, representing eighteen million persons, were receiving relief from public funds. In some states, 40 per cent of the population was on relief and in some counties this figure totaled 90 per cent of the population.[14] In addition, thousands of families were losing their homes, farms, deposits in banks, and life insurance policies. In many communities, schools had been closed, and throughout the nation the financial condition of cities, counties, and states was causing increasing alarm. After commenting upon the economic aspects of this critical situation, President Roosevelt uttered his oft-quoted assurance: " . . . the only thing we have to fear is fear itself—nameless, unreasoning, unjustified terror which paralyzes needed efforts to convert retreat into advance." For the unemployed, this fear was alleviated on May 12, 1933, when the President signed the Federal Emergency Relief Act passed by Congress during the preceding week and appointed Harry L. Hopkins as Federal Administrator of the program.

FEDERAL EMERGENCY RELIEF PROGRAMS

The diverse programs administered under the Federal Emergency Relief Act and related legislation made an immediate contribution to the physical and emotional welfare of children and their families during the worst years of the depression. Their permanent significance, however, stems from the new body of principles and practice established.

It is not appropriate to examine here in any detail the achievements or shortcomings of these massive emergency programs. It is important, however, to note their impact in areas which influenced the methods through which the needs of children are currently met and to trace the evolution of services initiated as a part of these programs.

The act of 1933 created for a two-year period a Federal Emergency Relief Administration and made available five hundred million dollars "to provide for cooperation by the Federal government with the several states and territories and the District of Columbia in relieving

---

[14] *FERA Monthly Report*, May 22nd–June 30th, 1933, p. 1.

the hardship and suffering caused by unemployment and for other purposes."[15]

Half of the appropriation was made available to states on a prescribed matching basis which acknowledged the joint responsibility of federal, state, and local governments for the welfare of people. The balance of the fund could be used at the discretion of the administrator for grants to states whose financial resources were so depleted that federal funds could not be matched to meet existing needs. The matching requirement was eliminated in January, 1934, but the principle of shared responsibility was not abandoned, since state and local units were still required to make funds available in accordance with their financial resources.

By the end of June, 1933, grants had been made to 45 states, the District of Columbia, and the Territory of Hawaii, and in a short period of time the program began operation in nearly 4,000 local units. This achievement was possible only through an unprecedented movement to establish a national network of public agencies. When the act became effective, no uniform or adequate method of making public funds available to families in need had been developed. Instead, unemployment relief was being administered by private agencies, poor relief offices, and special emergency relief commissions, as well as by city or county welfare departments. In approximately 2,000 rural counties, however, there were no social agencies, public or private.[16]

The movement to establish new public agencies resulted in part from the first rule issued by the FERA. Its provisions required that all grants of federal emergency relief funds be administered by public agencies after August 1, 1933. For many private agencies which had attempted to carry full responsibility for unemployment relief through public subsidies, this order necessitated a redefinition of function, a complete administrative reorganization, and, in many instances, a search for a new source of funds for the continuation of their family casework programs. For public agencies, the reduction of funds and case loads in the private agencies had another important effect. In many instances, the directors of private agencies were lent or released to head the new public agencies. In addition, large numbers of professional social workers formerly employed by private agencies now entered public employment. These developments, probably more than any others, served to make public relief "respectable,"

---

[15] Federal Relief Act, Chapter 30, 48. *U.S. Statutes at Large, 55.*

[16] Josephine Brown, *op. cit.,* p. 180.

and eventually made possible the development of skilled services for children as a part of a comprehensive public welfare program. More immediately, however, the order which produced this change established for all time the principle of governmental responsibility for the administration of public welfare funds.

The fact that public funds for unemployment relief were, to a large extent, administered by or under the direction of social workers was not wholly an accident resulting from this prohibition against payment of subsidies to private agencies. The Rules and Regulations issued by the FERA in July, 1933, stated that each local office administering relief should have "at least one trained and experienced investigator" on its staff and that larger units should have supervisors "trained and experienced in the essential elements of family case work and relief administration."[17] The degree to which it was possible to comply with these recommendations varied from county to county and many agencies in rural areas found it impossible to secure staff with the desired qualifications. These regulations, subsequent policy statements, and the interpretative efforts of the FERA field staff made clear, however, that the administration of relief was considered a social work function.

Perhaps the most significant contribution of the FERA to the total field of social welfare stemmed from the basic philosophy implicit in the instructions issued. The early regulations imposed "an obligation on the State emergency relief administration and on all the political subdivisions of the States administering relief . . . to see to it that all such needy unemployed persons and/or their dependents shall receive sufficient relief to prevent physical suffering and to maintain minimum living standards. . . . "[18] Subsequent sections defined in some detail a philosophy of adequate relief for those in need; emphasized that there "must be contact with each family through visits at least once a month, or oftener if necessary"; and admonished state administrations to "see to it that a sufficient number of workers are utilized . . . to insure reasonable investigation procedure.[19] The extent to which these rules were put into effect varied with the adequacy of funds, local and state tradition, and the qualifications of those in leadership positions. Despite this fact, the regulations expressed clearly the re-

---

[17] "Rules and Regulations," No. 3, in Edith Abbott, *Public Assistance: American Principles and Policies*, (Chicago: University of Chicago Press, 1940), I, p. 781.

[18] *Ibid.*, p. 780.

[19] *Ibid.*, p. 782.

sponsibility of government to provide adequate standards of assistance. Implicit, too, was a recognition of public relief as the right of all persons in need and a respect for their value as human beings. In this way the democratic philosophy was brought to the field of public welfare.

Many new methods of meeting the needs of children and their families were also pioneered by the programs developed by the FERA within its own structure or operated in conjunction with other federal departments. When the emergency programs were terminated, some of these services were continued under other auspices. Others have been revived in more recent years and some are still seen as desirable objectives not yet attained.

The first emergency program initiated by the Roosevelt administration preceded the FERA but its administration was closely integrated with that program. In March, 1933, the Emergency Conservation Act was passed by Congress at the request of the president, who envisioned a program which would simultaneously provide work relief for unemployed youth, preserve their morale and physical well-being, and conserve the national resources of the nation. In accordance with this act, the Civilian Conservation Corps was created by executive order on April 5, 1933. The first CCC camp was established at Luray, Virginia, during the same month, and by June of that year 1,300 camps were in operation with approximately 200 men in each.[20]

In December, 1933, the CCC camps added a more formal educational program to the instruction previously provided in conjunction with work assignments. By June, 1934, educational advisers functioning under the direction of the camp commanding officers were engaged in developing and administering eductional programs, providing educational counseling, and directing recreational activities. Separate camps were later established for veterans and, after the age limits for regular enrollees were extended to include youths from 17 to 28 years of age, the total enrollment in 2,652 camps reached 519,000.[21]

The first program initiated by the FERA conferred, for the first time in the history of the nation, equal rights upon persons whose need for assistance occurred in a place in which they had no claim to legal settlement. For three hundred years, each state had persisted in barring from continued assistance all "outsiders" and when the depres-

---

[20] Frank Ernest Hill, "Civilian Conservation Corps," *Social Work Year Book*, 1937, p. 84.

[21] *Ibid.*

sion caused thousands of families and older boys and girls to leave their homes in search of employment their plight became of increasing concern to the United States Children's Bureau and to all private social agencies. After this problem was discussed at the National Conference of Social Work in 1932, a Committee on Care of Transient and Homeless was appointed. On completion of a study showing the extent of the problem, the work of this committee was reflected in a provision of the Federal Emergency Relief Act authorizing the use of funds for "needy persons who have no legal settlement in any one state or community."[22]

In June, 1933, the Transient Bureau was created to assist the states in developing appropriate programs. Special funds were made available to each state relief administration for the employment of necessary staff, the organization of registration and treatment centers under the direction of trained social workers, the construction of more than two hundred shelters and camps, and the cost of meeting the needs of all persons who had not lived within the state twelve months prior to application. By September, 1934, a program had been developed in every state except Vermont.

Another new program was initiated by the FERA in September, 1933, when the Emergency Education Program was organized. Its basic purpose was to give employment to needy teachers, but children benefited greatly, particularly in the Southern states, where a shortage of funds had caused the closing of many schools. In addition to keeping elementary and secondary schools open in rural areas, the program made federal funds available to state departments of education for use in establishing nursery schools and in conducting various types of adult education, including parent education. By April, 1934, a total of 16,500 teachers were giving some type of instruction to a total of 1,500,000 students.[23] Through a student aid program, work relief was also made available to many college students who were thus enabled to continue their education.

In October, 1933, by arrangement with the Department of Agriculture, the Surplus Relief Corporation was established as an auxiliary to the FERA to purchase and distribute to states, a variety of surplus commodities. At first these supplies were made available only to

[22] "FER Act 1933," Section IV (C) in Edith Abbott, *Public Assistance: American Principles and Policies*, I, p. 747.

[23] Russell H. Kurtz, "Unemployment Relief," *Social Work Year Book*, 1935, p. 525.

families receiving relief, but before the end of the year surplus foods were also provided for clients of private agencies, employees on federal relief projects, members of self-help organizations, and inmates of public and private charitable and health institutions.[24]

In April, 1934, a new work relief program was initiated by the FERA. Its significance in the field of child welfare stems from the immediate attempt to identify the number of "unemployables" currently receiving benefits under the FERA program. Although the act indicated clearly that FERA funds had been provided to assist individuals and families suffering from unemployment, this provision had been interpreted broadly and the administration had made no prior effort to deny assistance to widows and dependent children or to any other ambulant person unable to accept employment on an available work project. As a result, many states had considered "employable" any individual or family in which one person conceivably might have accepted limited employment under optimum circumstances. The result of this survey indicated that 5 to 25 per cent of the relief loads was composed of such persons, with the largest proportion found in the Southern states, which had a few alternate resources for the care of needy persons. No immediate action was taken, but this information was later used in defining the role of the federal government in the welfare field.

Planning for the Future

When the Federal Emergency Relief Act was approved by Congress in May, 1933, its provisions and the widespread evidence of human misery existing in every state alerted the social work profession to the fact that a more permanent and comprehensive public welfare program would be needed to deal with the effects of the depression and to insure the machinery necessary to prevent any recurrence of a comparable period of national deprivation. Within a few weeks, the Great Lakes Institute conducted by the Community Chests and Councils adopted a report recognizing the need for an eventual combination of emergency relief administration and permanent welfare departments; for state departments with authority to set standards and equalize available funds through a grant-in-aid program; for a merit system in both local and state welfare departments to prevent political

---

[24] Joanna C. Colcord, "Report of the Committee on Current Relief Program," *Proceedings of the National Conference of Social Work* (Chicago: University of Chicago Press, 1934), p. 112.

interference; and for a federal department of public welfare which would complete the picture of federal, state, and local machinery by setting standards and providing assistance to states.[25]

In May, 1934, the American Public Welfare Association, at its annual meeting, adopted similar resolutions which subsequently formed the basis for discussion at a series of regional conferences and for a widely circulated pamphlet entitled "Legislation for Social Security."[26] To implement the recommendations made, the platform urged that (1) emergency relief administrations be consolidated "with the regular and continuing welfare activities of the state and locality"; (2) settlement laws be repealed or, if retained, be made uniform, with the federal government assuming a continuing responsibility for the care of persons who have no legal settlement within any state, and the state providing for those who meet state residence requirements but have no settlement in a particular locality; (3) federal, state, and local cooperation "in the provision of funds for relief" be continued and "extended to other welfare services, such as Mothers' Aid, Old Age Assistance and other social insurances"; and (4) statutes be enacted which would require that all welfare personnel be selected on a merit basis.[27]

In June, 1934, great hope for the establishment of a comprehensive and permanent program of public welfare was aroused when President Roosevelt sent a special message to Congress announcing his intention of formulating a program of Economic Security. This hope drew particular strength from the wording of the message:

Among our objectives I place the security of the men, women and children of the nation first. . . .
Fear and worry based on unknown dangers contribute to social unrest and economic demoralization. If as our Constitution tells us, our Federal government was established, among other things, "to promote the general welfare" it is our plain duty to provide for that security upon which welfare depends. . . .
I am looking for a sound means which I can recommend to provide at once security against several of the great disturbing factors in life . . . especially those which relate to unemployment and old age.

To implement this plan, the president appointed a Committee on Economic Security consisting of the secretary of labor (Frances

---

[25] Russell H. Kurtz, *Looking Toward a Public Welfare Plan* (New York: Russell Sage Foundation, January 2, 1935), pp. 2–3.

[26] *Ibid.*, p. 17.

[27] American Public Welfare Association, "Legislation for Social Security," in Kurtz, *op cit.*, Appendix A, pp. 26–28.

Perkins, a former social worker in New York), chairman; the secretary of the treasury; the secretary of agriculture; the attorney general; and the federal relief administrator (Harry L. Hopkins). The membership of this committee gave further impetus to the belief that a comprehensive program would be planned, but these hopes were somewhat dampened when it became evident that the committee's initial planning was focused primarily on the problem of unemployment.

In response to special requests made by the United States Children's Bureau, the United States Public Health Service, and the Office of Education, the Committee on Economic Security finally began consideration of the problems of children whose support was currently provided through mothers' aid programs in many states and of the need for more extensive programs in public health and vocational education.[28] Further hope for an expanded federal program arose in November, 1934, when the chairman of the committee appointed an Advisory Committee on Public Employment and Public Assistance, whose membership included Frank Bane, director of the APWA; Linton Swift, general director of the Family Welfare Association of America; Walter West, executive director of the AASW; Father John O'Grady, executive secretary of the National Catholic Conference of Charities; Edith Abbott, dean of the University of Chicago School of Social Service Administration; and seven other prominent leaders in social work and public welfare.[29]

The report submitted by this Advisory Committee recommended an enlarged work program for all in need of employment, federal grants to the states for the benefit of all persons in need who could not be absorbed by the work program (for example, grants "for old age pensions, mothers' aid, general home assistance, care of homeless children and adults, and other parts of the unified public welfare program"), and the establishment of a permanent Public Welfare Department in the federal government to coordinate federal, state, and local public welfare activities. The committee also recommended that grants be made on an equalization basis and the federal department empowered to require a state to consolidate its welfare functions on a state and local level as a condition of the receipt of federal funds.[30]

The fact that this report would receive little consideration was clearly indicated by the president's message to Congress on January 4,

---

[28] Josephine Brown, *op. cit.,* pp. 163–164.

[29] *Report to the President of the Committee on Economic Security* (Washington, D.C.: U.S. Government Printing Office, 1935) p. 53.

[30] Josephine Brown, *op. cit.,* pp. 304–305.

1935. In presenting his plan for a work program, the president used the figures compiled by the FERA in its classification of "employables" and "unemployables" and explained that of the five million families and single persons currently receiving relief:

About one million and a half of these belong to the group which in the past was dependent on local welfare efforts. . . . It is my thought that in the future they must be cared for as they were before. . . .
The security legislation which I shall propose to the Congress will, I am confident, be of assistance to local effort in the care of this type of cases. . . .
There are however an additional three and one-half million employable people who are on relief. . . . This group was a victim of a Nation wide depression caused by conditions which were not local but national. . . . It is a duty dictated by every intelligent consideration of national policy to ask you to make it possible for the United States to give employment to all of these three and one-half million employable people now on relief, pending their absorption in a rising tide of private employment.[31]

On January 15, 1935, the Committee on Economic Security presented its report to the president. It, too, clearly indicated a belief that responsibility for the care of the genuine unemployables—or near unemployables—should be returned to the states with provision for federal aid to the states "in giving pensions to the dependent aged and the families without breadwinners." It was also recommended that "all social welfare activities of the Federal Government be coordinated and systematized," but no mention was made of the creation of a permanent department of public welfare as recommended by the Advisory Committee and by the social work organizations.[32]

In transmitting this report to Congress two days later, the president described the report as a program of action to insure "the security of the men, women and children of the nation against certain hazards and vicissitudes of life." The Social Security Bill introduced immediately contained all of the Titles later enacted, except that of aid for the blind. The original provisions were not accepted as written, however, and many of the principles intended to protect the welfare of children were deleted from the bill as the result of the hearings held during the next seven months.

In the initial planning, "Aid to Dependent Children" was conceived as a program which would provide "general relief or assistance on a family basis to all families having children under sixteen."[33] In this

---

[31] *FERA Monthly Report*, April 1935, pp. 2–3.

[32] *Report to the President of the Committee on Economic Security*, p. 7.

[33] Josephine Brown, *op. cit.*, p. 310.

way the committee planned to remove from state and local responsibility all of the 7,400,000 children currently on the relief rolls whose needs could not be met through the public works program. With the insertion of a clause defining the reason for dependency, however, the program finally approved by Congress became in effect a Mothers' Aid program.

On August 14, 1935, the Social Security Act finally became the law of the land and nine days later, the Senate ratified the appointment of the three members of the Social Security Board (John G. Winant, chairman; Vincent N. Miles; and Arthur J. Altmeyer). In October, Frank Bane, director of the APWA, was appointed executive director and a skeleton staff assembled through the cooperation of other federal agencies. Funds for the operation of the program were not appropriated until February 11, 1936.[34]

CHANGES IN THE FEDERAL PROGRAMS

In May, 1935, the Works Progress Administration began operation and in the following month the president created the National Youth Administration (NYA) as a division of the WPA and as a successor to the Student Aid Program conducted by the FERA. In addition to assisting students in part-time employment, the new program provided a wide variety of work projects for unemployed persons between the ages of 16 and 25 who were not in school.[35]

While the Social Security Act was still pending in Congress, plans were initiated for the liquidation of the FERA. In July, the federal staff assigned to regional offices was charged with responsibility to assist the states in planning and putting into effect permanent public welfare programs. States were also advised that their last federal grants would be received in November and December, 1935. In planning for the use of their final grants, states and localities were encouraged to retain a staff sufficient to provide a nucleus for the administration of the new assistance programs included in the Social Security Act. During the period of transition, the only continuing program was that of the Federal Surplus Commodity Corporation.

---

[34] Social Security Board, *Annual Report of the Social Security Board* (Washington D.C.: Government Printing Office, March 1937), pp. 1–6.

[35] Arthur E. Burns and Edward A. Williams, *A Survey of Relief and Security Programs* (Washington, D.C.: Works Progress Administration, May 1938), pp. 49–50.

DEVELOPMENTS ON A STATE LEVEL

During 1935 the legislative as well as the administrative scene was subject to change and confusion. Every state except Virginia held one or more regular or special sessions in an effort to anticipate or implement the requirements of the Social Security Act.[36] During this period, the Committee on Economic Security provided model laws which would meet the federal requirements for unemployment compensation and old age assistance, and the United States Children's Bureau gave advice on methods of implementing the provisions for the maternal and child welfare programs. In addition, the American Public Welfare Association provided assistance to governors, legislatures, and public welfare commissions in developing plans for a comprehensive and permanent public welfare program.

As the result of these activities, an unprecedented amount of legislation was passed providing for the creation or consolidation of state and county public welfare agencies, for changes in existing poor relief laws, and for state participation in the Social Security program. Despite this fact, only seventeen states and the District of Columbia had departments of public welfare with supervisory or administrative responsibility for assistance to persons in need when the final FERA grants were made at the end of 1935. In fourteen additional states, some provision for the temporary continuation of the Emergency Relief Administration had been made, but in the remaining seventeen states no state agencies had any responsibility for the administration of general relief.[37]

Selected Bibliography

Abbott, Edith. *Public Assistance: American Principles and Policies.* Vol. I. Chicago: University of Chicago Press, 1940.

Brown, Josephine Chapin. *Public Relief, 1929–1939.* New York: Henry Holt and Company, 1940.

Children in a Depression Decade: The Annals of the American Academy of Political and Social Science. Vol. 212, November, 1940.

Clarke, Helen I. *Social Legislation.* New York: Appleton-Century-Crofts, 1957.

Williams, James M. *Human Aspects of Unemployment and Relief.* Chapel Hill: University of North Carolina Press, 1933.

---

[36] Josephine Brown, *op. cit.*, p. 322.

[37] *Ibid.*, pp. 318–319.

Chapter 9   *The Contemporary Era*

(1936—1957)

In retrospect it is evident that a new framework of social services for children developed around the services and financial benefits made available through the Social Security Act. Like all processes of evolution, this pattern did not emerge quickly or in uniform configuration. Even the impact of the Social Security Act has been a gradual process, affected not only by the changes in its provisions but by a wide variety of other factors which have served to shape the programs of individual states and localities. In subsequent chapters the services currently provided for children will be described separately. This chapter will be limited to a brief review of the historical structure within which these services developed, with some indication of the roles played by national events in shaping the resources now available to individual children and their families.

164

The Transition Years

From an overall view, the decade extending from 1936 to 1946 can be considered a period of transition in which our current services for children assumed much of their present form. When the development of a specific service is examined, however, it will be seen that its growth and characteristics have been affected by a variety of legislative, economic, and social milestones within this period. For this reason, significant developments are interrelated and cannot be described in uniform time spans.

EARLY SOCIAL SECURITY PROGRAMS

With the exception of the titles based upon an insurance principle, the provisions of the Social Security Act marked a return to the basic grant-in-aid philosophy pioneered in the field of social welfare by the Sheppard-Towner Act. In accordance with this concept, the act required that states wishing to participate in the federal program take the initative by appropriating funds and submitting a state plan for the operation of each public assistance category and for each program specified in Title V of the act. Many states, however, were not financially or administratively ready to submit plans for approval when federal funds became available on February 11, 1936. By December, only 26 states and the District of Columbia had approved plans for Aid to Dependent Children. In contrast, 40 states, Hawaii, and the District of Columbia had approved Old Age Assistance plans by that date.[1] Even by September, 1938, when every state had an Old Age Assistance program in operation, only 38 states had approved plans for Aid to Dependent Children.[2]

Delay in the development of acceptable plans for ADC was caused in part by the need for extensive change in existing state legislation. Prior to 1935, 28 of the 42 states with operating Mothers' Aid programs were not participating in their financial cost and many of these states had made no provision for state supervision of programs administered by the localities.[3] Since much of the legislation was permissive, the program was in operation in only half of the local units.[4] Basic

---

[1] *Annual Report of the Social Security Board,* 1936, p. 1.

[2] *Third Annual Report of the Federal Security Agency: Social Security Board, 1938* (Washington, D.C.: Government Printing Office, 1938), p. 135.

[3] *Annual Report of the Social Security Board,* 1936, pp. 9–10.

[4] *Ibid.,* p. 9.

changes in existing state laws were therefore necessary to meet the federal requirement that a state plan provide for state financial participation, for operation in each local unit of the state, and for the administration or supervision of the administration of the plan by a single state agency. Further legislative changes were required because the act specified that all public assistance must be given through money payments, rather than food orders or other "relief in kind," and that there must be provision for a fair hearing before a central state agency for applicants and recipients dissatisfied with denial decisions or the amounts of their grants.

Other provisions of the Social Security Act also tended to liberalize restrictive state laws. To take full advantage of the federal funds provided for ADC, previous age limits for mothers' aid (usually twelve or fourteen years) were in most instances raised to conform with the federal maximum of sixteen years. Conversely, residence requirements were reduced to comply with the federal mandate that any such restriction not exceed one year's residence in the state. In addition, many state laws which had previously limited eligibility to children living with widowed mothers were revised to make grants available to otherwise eligible children living with any of the relatives specified by the Social Security Act. Qualifying causes of dependency were also expanded to include children deprived of support because of the incapacitation or continued absence of the normal wage earner.[5]

The availability of federal funds also made it possible for many states to increase the standard of assistance on which grants were based. The fact that federal reimbursement was provided for only one-third of the total expenditures for ADC (in contrast to a 50 per cent reimbursement for Old Age Assistance and Aid to the Blind) and was not available for payments in excess of a specified amount for each child, served to counteract the adequacy of the standards established, however. As a result, the maximum grant was usually limited to the amount for which federal reimbursement could be secured, even though the act contained no prohibition against the payment of larger sums from state and local funds.

The Social Security Act specified that each state plan must be administered by a single state agency, but it did not require that all programs be administered or supervised by the same agency or prescribe the form of organization to be used. Great variation therefore occurred in the initial patterns of administration established. In some states, existing child welfare departments or local boards of child wel-

---

[5] *Ibid.*, p. 27.

fare retained responsibility for the administration of ADC, whereas other assistance programs were assigned to separate agencies. In states which already had a network of county welfare departments, these agencies usually assumed responsibility for the administration of all programs under the supervision of a state department. Other states elected a plan of state administration with local operation delegated to branch offices. In general, however, the first year of operation tended to establish a pattern of unified administration on a local level with responsibility for supervision or administration entrusted to a state department of public or social welfare.[6] This development stemmed in part from "a growing recognition of the wisdom of considering the needs of the family group in which an individual was living even though assistance was granted to him on the basis of his specific eligibility for a particular type of aid."[7] The trend in this direction received further impetus from a realization that an integrated program "provides an organizational basis for more economical and efficient administration, especially when the State agency also carries responsibility for other welfare functions such as general relief and child welfare services."[8] By June, 1938, 31 states and territories had developed administrative patterns of this type.[9]

Title V of the Social Security Act provided grants-in-aid for three types of maternal and child welfare services to be administered by the United States Children's Bureau. Unlike the public assistance sections, this title of the act did not contemplate "open-end appropriations" sufficient to meet the federal share of all payments made to eligible persons. Instead, the act specified the annual appropriation to be authorized for each program, established a basic annual amount to be paid to each state whose plan was approved, and made additional sums available to each qualifying state on the basis of prescribed formulas. The sections relating to maternal and child health services and services for crippled children stipulated that the funds be used for the extension and improvement of services "especially in rural areas and in areas suffering from severe economic distress"[10] and required that federal funds be matched by local and/or state funds. Part 3 of Title V

---

[6] *Ibid.*, p. 32.

[7] *Ibid.*

[8] *Third Annual Report of the Federal Security Agency: Social Security Board, 1938*, p. 93.

[9] *Ibid.*

[10] "Federal and State Cooperation in Maternal and Child Welfare Services Under the Social Security Act," *Maternal and Child Welfare Bulletin* 2 (Washington, D.C.: Government Printing Office, 1938), p. 94.

authorized grants "to cooperate with State public welfare agencies in establishing, extending and strengthening . . . public welfare services . . . for the protection and care of homeless, dependent and neglected children and children in danger of becoming delinquent."[11] It also required that these funds be used for paying part of the cost of "local child welfare services in areas predominantly rural and for developing State services for the encouragement and assistance of adequate methods of community child welfare organization in areas predominantly rural and other areas of special need."[12] In addition, Title V required that a state plan for maternal and child health services be administered or supervised by the state health agency and that funds for child welfare services be administered by the state public welfare department. Administration or supervision by a state agency was also a requirement for a state plan for services to crippled children but the type of state agency was not designated.

In comparison with the ADC program, the states were quick to take advantage of the grants available for the extension of services for children. By December, 1936, 49 states and territories had approved plans for maternal and child health services. By the same date, 41 plans for services for crippled children and 42 plans for child welfare services had also been approved.[13]

By June 30, 1938, approved plans for maternal and child health services were in operation in every state, the District of Columbia, Hawaii, and Alaska. More than 50 per cent of the total funds made available for these programs was used to pay the salaries of public health nurses. The remaining allocations permitted the employment of dentists, nutritionists, and health educators and the initiation or more extensive development of services similar to those previously provided under the Sheppard-Towner Act. In some states, matched funds were used to demonstrate a special type of service, such as a home delivery nursing service, special service for premature infants, service to children of migratory workers, or mobile dental units.[14]

Every state except Louisiana also had an approved plan for services to crippled children by the end of the 1938 fiscal year. In 15 states, this program was administered by the state department of public wel-

[11] *Ibid.*, p. 97.

[12] *Ibid.*, p. 98.

[13] *Annual Report of the Social Security Board*, 1936, p. 53.

[14] *Third Annual Report of the Federal Security Agency: Social Security Board, 1938*, pp. 125–126.

fare, in 24 states by the state department of health, and in other states by various departments or commissions.[15]   Regardless of the auspices of operation, the availability of these funds permitted the states to establish more effective methods for locating crippled children, to extend their diagnostic clinic services, to improve the quality of medical care through the employment of orthopedic surgeons and other specialists, and to develop more diversified services for crippled children.   With the growing awareness of the importance of meeting the social, educational, and vocational needs of crippled children, greater use was also made of convalescent homes and foster homes and of the services of social workers.[16]

When the Social Security Act became effective, eleven states had no administrative unit of government legally responsible for child welfare, and twelve additional states had no comprehensive program of preventive or protective work for children.[17]   As of June, 1938, however, state plans for child welfare services were in operation in every state except Wyoming,[18] although ten states still did not have an approved plan for ADC.

An early policy required that the limited federal funds available be used for the development of needed services for children rather than for the cost of care of children in boarding homes and institutions. State plans were therefore limited to the employment of well-qualified social workers to provide demonstration services, the provision of educational leave to permit the attendance of employed staff at schools of social work, the instruction of staff through special institutes and training units, and the development of state supervisory services.[19]

In adddition to these services for children, Title V of the original Social Security Act made permanent the grant-in-aid program for vocational rehabilitation initiated by an act of Congress in 1920.[20]   Administered by the United States Office of Education, this section also required that federal funds be matched equally by state and local money and that the program be supervised by a state board for vocational education.   Since this was not a new program, all states except

[15] *Ibid.*, p. 127.

[16] *Ibid.*, pp. 127–129.

[17] *Ibid.*, p. 129.

[18] *Ibid.*, p. 125.

[19] *Third Annual Report of the Federal Security Agency: Social Security Board, 1938*, p. 130.

[20] *Ibid.*, p. 132.

Delware, Kansas, and Vermont participated during the first year of its inclusion in the Social Security program. Although intended to prevent the permanent unemployment of vocationally handicapped adults, youth of employable age were eligible to the benefits of the program.

Title VI of the Social Security Act charged the United States Public Health Service with responsibility for the administration of grants-in-aid to the states to stimulate additional public health services and for conducting research in relation to important problems of disease and sanitation. With the assistance of federal funds, public health work was enabled to advance more rapidly during the first two years of this program than during any comparable period in the nation's history.[21] By June 30, 1938, the number of county health units under the direction of full-time public health officers (1,165 counties) had nearly doubled. In addition, federal funds were used to provide special postgraduate training in public health work and to maintain emergency short-course training centers. State health departments were also strengthened and, by the end of this period, many states had special units for the control of venereal disease, special procedures for the control of tuberculosis, programs to decrease pneumonia mortality, and cancer programs.[22]

On August 10, 1939, important changes were made in the Social Security Act.[23] For all children the most significant change probably resulted from revision of the insurance provisions to provide benefits for the widow and surviving children of a deceased insured worker and for the wife and young children of the retired worker. For children currently or potentially eligible for ADC or in need of any of the services made available through Title V of the act, other changes were of more immediate import.

The changes in Title IV were designed to increase the number of children eligible for ADC and to make more adequate grants available to them. It was also hoped that the new provisions would be of particular benefit to eligible children in the nine jurisdictions (eight states and Alaska) not yet participating in the program, by encouraging the development of programs eligible for federal reimbursement.[24] Specifically, the amendments increased from one-third to one-half the

---

[21] *Ibid.*, p. 131.

[22] *Ibid.*, pp. 131–132.

[23] Federal Security Agency, *Social Security in the United States* (Washington, D.C.: Government Printing Office, 1948), p. 15.

[24] *Fourth Annual Report of the Federal Security Agency: Social Security Board, 1939* (Washington, D.C.: Government Printing Office, 1940), pp. 178–179.

federal participation in the costs incurred for administration and assistance grants and raised the maximum age limit to eighteen years for children attending school.

Two amendments applicable to the administration of all three categories of public assistance were also important to children. As of July 1, 1941, all states receiving federal funds were required to provide legislative safeguards to restrict the use of information about applicants or recipients, to purposes directly connected with the administration of the program. This provision had the effect of protecting recipients from the humiliation which can come from publication of their names and from disclosure of confidential information about their personal affairs to persons who have no right to this information. The philosophy of the assistance programs was also clarified by a new requirement that any other income or resources of the applicant or recipient be taken into consideration in determining the amount of financial need. This provision made it evident that destitution was not a requirement for assistance if the recipient had needs in excess of the maximum grant in which the federal government would participate. In addition, it spelled out the concept that grants were to be given on the basis of need and not as a pension for all persons who met other eligibility requirements, for example, all children deprived of normal support.

Children in some states were also benefited by the amendment which, in effect, required that all state plans include, after January 1, 1940, a description of "methods relating to the establishment and maintenance of personnel standards on a merit basis."[25] Convinced that "effective administration is dependent largely upon qualified personnel,"[26] the Social Security Board had previously required that "an approved State plan must contain provisions relative to minimum objective standards of education, training and experience for State and local personnel,"[27] and had encouraged states without civil service laws to establish merit systems. The new amendment gave authority to require the use of a merit system for state and local personnel and to prescribe rules and regulations which must be met by such systems. This provision was applicable not only to programs administered by the Social Security Board (public assistance and unemployment com-

---

[25] *Ibid.*, p. 180.

[26] *Third Annual Report of the Federal Security Agency: Social Security Board, 1938*, p. 91.

[27] *Ibid.*

pensation) but to all state plans involving grants for maternal and child health services, services to crippled children, and public health services.

The final 1939 amendment affecting children increased greatly the amount of funds authorized for vocational education and for the three health services included in Titles V and VI. A slight increase ($10,-000) was also made in the amount available for child welfare services, but this was intended to cover the cost of a new program in Puerto Rico.

Although eight states were still not participating in the program of ADC and one state had not yet submitted a plan for child welfare services, the implementation of the 1939 amendment marked the end of the initial stage of development for the programs established by the Social Security Act. One additional change in that year should be noted, though it had only an indirect effect on services for children.

Under the Reorganization Act of 1939 and the subsequent President's Reorganization Plan No. 1, the Federal Security Agency was created and the Social Security Board, the Public Health Service (formerly in the Treasury Department), the Office of Education (formerly in the Department of the Interior), and several other services, made a part of that agency. The federal security administrator did not have cabinet status, but this realignment of federal administrative structure marked the first step toward the establishment of the coordinated federal department recommended by numerous professional groups at an earlier date.

Within the next five years a better coordination of responsibilities was also achieved by removing from the Social Security Act those sections not administered by the Social Security Board or the United States Children's Bureau. In 1943, the provisions for federal grants for vocational education were deleted from the act and incorporated in separate legislation to be administered by the Federal Security Administrator through a special bureau. The sections providing grants-in-aid for public health services became inoperative when the Public Health Act of 1944 consolidated in one statute all the provisions relating to public health services enacted since the inception of the United States Public Health Service in 1798.[28]

FEDERAL EMERGENCY PROGRAMS

The federal works program initiated under the Emergency Relief Appropriations Act of 1935 reached its employment goal during the

---

[28] *Social Security in the United States*, 1948, pp. 16–17.

month in which federal funds first became available under the Social Security Act (February, 1936). By this time more than three million persons were employed by the Works Progress Administration; about 450,000 by the CCC; and almost 400,000 by the NYA and other emergency works programs. By November, 1936, nearly a million families in drought areas and in rural areas of substandard productivity had also received some type of assistance from the newly created Resettlement Administration.[29] Of these programs only the distribution of surplus commodities remains a part of the current scene. It is, therefore, not pertinent to examine their history in any detail. Their effect upon the resources currently available to children, and their role in the initiation of contemporary services or philosophy require explanation, however.

The most direct benefit from these federal emergency programs can be traced to the nursery schools conducted under WPA auspices for a period of nearly seven years. The majority of these schools were established as a part of the educational program of the FERA but the operation of approximately 1,900 nursery schools was continued under the new program.[30] These projects had as their primary purpose the employment of previously unemployed teachers, nurses, nutritionists, clerical workers, cooks, and janitors, but by 1937 the nursery schools were providing for approximately 40,000 children a daily health inspection, any necessary medical care, well-balanced meals, and supervised play and rest.[31]

The significance of these schools stems from the fact that their operation represented "the first recognition by the Federal and state governments that the education and guidance of children from two to five years of age is a responsibility warranting the expenditure of public funds."[32] This caused widespread hope that nursery schools could become a permanent part of the public school system for the benefit of all preschool children,[33] but had a more immediate effect in determining government responsibility for the welfare of children in time of war.

WPA projects for the training, employment, and supervision of

---

[29] Beulah Amidon, "Resettlement," *Social Work Year Book*, 1937, p. 428.

[30] Lois Hayden Meek, "Preschool Children," *Social Work Year Book*, 1937, p. 346.

[31] *Final Report of the WPA Program, 1935–1943* (Washington, D.C.: Government Printing Office, 1946), p. 62.

[32] Meek, "Preschool Children," *loc. cit.*

[33] *Final Report of the WPA Program, 1935–1943*, p. 62.

"housekeeping aides" played an important role in the development of the homemaker service currently provided by many social agencies. The housekeeper service initiated by the Jewish Family Welfare Society of Philadelphia in 1923 is generally believed to have been the first service of this kind provided for families during the temporary absence of the mother.[34]   In November, 1924, the Jewish Home-Finding Society of Chicago[35] inaugurated a similar service and, within the next decade, a few additional family welfare agencies developed this type of program.[36]   The first projects under public auspices were initiated by the FERA, however, and the program greatly expanded after its transfer to WPA in 1935.

The WPA projects provided continuous in-service training for housekeeping aides "to improve their skills and to give them a better understanding of the problems they met in the homes to which they were assigned."[37]   At first the aides were used to give assistance in housekeeping, care of children, and home nursing when required by needy families during times of emergency. As the program developed, it became closely integrated with the work of established health and welfare agencies and served to awaken social workers to the realization that "services can be extended to needy people in their own homes in a more satisfactory and economical manner than through institutional care"[38] or care in foster homes.

Such great interest developed in the five hundred existing WPA projects that in 1937 the United States Children's Bureau invited to a conference on housekeeper services in Washington representatives of national and local agencies in the fields of social work, public health nursing, home economics, and vocational training. Its purpose was "to consider the fundamental principles of organization and satisfactory standards of service and the various means by which the future development of the service might be guided along sound lines."[39]   At the 1938 National Conference of Social Work, further interest was

---

[34] Jacob Kepecs, "Housekeeper Service in Motherless Families," *Proceedings of the National Conference of Social Work*, 1938, p. 267.

[35] *Ibid.*, p. 268.

[36] Marion Schmadel Goodwin, "Housekeeper Service in Family Welfare," *Proceedings of the National Conference of Social Work*, 1938, p. 279.

[37] *Final Report of the WPA Program, 1935–1943*, p. 69.

[38] *Ibid.*

[39] United States Children's Bureau, *Supervised Homemaker Service—A Method of Home Care*, Publication 296 (Washington, D.C.: Government Printing Office, 1946), p. 2.

stimulated by the presentation of two papers describing the experience of private agencies in providing a service of this type, and in 1939 a Committee on Supervised Homemaker Service was established to promote the standards of homemaker service and further its extension in cooperation with the United States Children's Bureau, the Child Welfare League of America, and the Family Welfare Association of America.[40]   By the time the WPA was liquidated, the service had been renamed, fundamental principles defined, and its value widely recognized as an essential tool in strengthening family life and preventing the unnecessary removal of children from their own homes.[41]

The school lunch projects conducted by the WPA also made a permanent contribution to the pattern of services currently available to children.   In some localities the provision of school lunches for undernourished children had been undertaken by Parent-Teacher Associations prior to the depression but the school lunches provided had usually included only a bowl of soup and a piece of bread.[42]   More extensive projects were initiated by the FERA and the program was greatly expanded after its transfer to the WPA.

In addition to their immediate value to malnourished children, the WPA projects proved to be of lasting benefit by demonstrating efficient methods of school lunchroom management, the importance of proper standards of sanitation in food handling, and the value of adequate nutrition in promoting progress in school work.[43]

The surplus commodities provided through the Federal Surplus Commodities Corporation and distributed by WPA work projects were widely used in the school lunch program.   Distribution of surplus foods to individual families receiving or eligible to public assistance or WPA employment and the clothing, mattresses, and household articles produced by the WPA sewing projects also served an important purpose during the transition years.   Federal funds were not available for the distribution of surplus commodities after the liquidation of the WPA in 1943, but these projects served to establish a precedent for the future use of surplus farm products.   As a result, the Agricultural Act of 1949 again made food products available for school lunches and to the Bureau of Indian Affairs, private social

---

[40] "Committee on Supervised Homemaker Service," *Social Work Year Book,* 1943, p. 623.

[41] *Final Report of the WPA Program, 1935–1943,* p. 68.

[42] *Ibid.*

[43] *Ibid.*

agencies, and public welfare departments for the use of needy persons. The National School Lunch Act of 1946 also provided a supplementary grant-in-aid program "to safeguard the health and well-being of the Nation's children," and to encourage the domestic consumption of agricultural products.[44]

The development of recreational programs under public auspices received great impetus from two types of WPA projects. Construction projects added many new buildings and special projects provided leadership and instruction in a wide variety of recreational activities for children and adults. Most importantly, perhaps, local advisory committees for these projects were organized to survey community recreational needs, secure the use of needed recreational facilities, assist in the planning of current programs, and integrate the project activities into long-range community plans for recreation.[45]

To a considerable degree, the WPA projects also contributed to the rapid extension of public health services during the early years of the Social Security program. Unemployed professional personnel (doctors, dentists, nurses, chemists, and technicians) were assigned from WPA rolls to projects sponsored by health departments, hospitals, clinics, and school health services. Nonprofessional workers were also provided with training in hospitals and institutions and later assigned to perform routine tasks to release the time of professional staff. Thousands of children benefited from the services provided by more than 1,200 WPA health projects. The permanent significance of these projects resulted, however, from their demonstration of the value of public health clinics in rural areas previously unserved by any public health service, more extensive remedial and preventive work with children, and more effective methods in the control of venereal disease. In addition, the mobile school dental clinics, staffed by a dentist, nurse, and clerk, demonstrated a practical method of providing dental services in schools that could not afford to purchase necessary equipment and employ staff for this purpose. The use of nonprofessional workers to augment available services also established a pattern which remained in use wherever its value was demonstrated.[46]

---

[44] Inter-departmental Committee on Children and Youth, *Programs of the Federal Government Affecting Children and Youth*, (Washington, D.C.: Government Printing Office, 1951), p. 12.

[45] *Final Report of the WPA Program, 1935–1943*, p. 62.

[46] *Ibid.*, pp. 69–70.

GENERAL RELIEF

Despite the achievements of the federal emergency projects, tragic conditions were produced by the abrupt termination of federal funds for direct relief in 1936. As Edith Abbott reported at the National Conference of Social Work in 1937:

The whole relief program has collapsed in many areas . . . and those people who had been our clients are now nobody's clients and nobody's responsibility.[47]

As she continued to express her conviction about the need for continued federal aid for general relief, she described "the homes without food and without fuel in bitter weather, children too hungry to go to school, whole families without warm clothing and bedding, the people without provision for medical care, and the evictions that have gone on so relentlessly."[48]

This situation resulted in part from the immediate need to use all available funds for the new Social Security programs and to reorganize or establish agencies suitable for the administration of these programs. The financial resources of some states were so limited, however, that available funds were not sufficient to provide adequate assistance to persons in need. In other states, the initiation of the federal works program was interpreted to mean that the federal government had assumed responsibility for the relief of destitution caused by national economic problems. Some legislatures, therefore, refused to appropriate funds or to permit their use for families containing employable persons even though WPA employment was not available or the so-called "employables" not physically able to work on any existing WPA project in that locality. General relief was usually provided in some degree of adequacy for those who were clearly unemployable and not eligible for any benefits under the provisions of the Social Security Act. Under most existing poor laws, however, persons who lacked legal settlement in the locality in which they currently lived were not eligible to any type of public assistance.

As unemployment continued at a high level, increasing concern developed among social workers about the plight of needy families which included an employable wage earner, particularly when these families

---

[47] Edith Abbott, "Public Assistance—Whither Bound?," *Proceedings of the National Conference of Social Work,* 1937, p. 10.

[48] *Ibid.*

had wandered from state to state in search of employment. By 1939, a general demand had developed for the "establishment of a Federal category for the care of the transients from 100% Federal funds,"[49] or for some other type of remedy. Leaders concerned about the plight of all disadvantaged persons advocated the establishment of a federal grant-in-aid program for general relief which would exercise sufficient control to eliminate existing variations in the adequacy of assistance.[50]

The latter viewpoint was reflected in a report of the Inter-Departmental Committee to Coordinate Health and Welfare Activities submitted to the president in July, 1940. After recommending immediate emergency aid to needy migrant families, the report added:

> To provide for a continuing program of aid for this and other groups, a general relief program should be established on a Federal-State basis, Federal funds being made on a "variable grants" basis under administrative provisions similar to those provided in the public assistance programs under the Social Security Act and with added safeguards to prevent discrimination against migratory workers.[51]

This recommendation was supported by the Social Security Board[52] and repeated in its *Sixth Annual Report* with the statement:

> Available funds for general relief are grossly inadequate or wholly lacking in many areas, especially in localities which are dependent upon local resources without supplementation of State funds.[53]

In the 1942 report, a similar recommendation was accompanied by a statement of the board's belief that consideration should be given to a revision of the provisions for ADC to extend the scope of the program so that federal funds would be available for "aid to any child whose family resources are insufficient to insure healthful growth and development, whatever the reason."[54]

---

[49] Ruth O. Blakeslee, "Laws and Administrative Practices as Barriers to Mobility," *Proceedings of the National Conference of Social Work* (New York: Columbia University Press, 1939), p. 240.

[50] C. M. Bookman, "Essentials of an Adequate Relief Program," *Proceedings of the National Conference of Social Work*, 1940, p. 169.

[51] *Fifth Annual Report of the Federal Security Agency: Social Security Board, 1940* (Washington, D.C.: Government Printing Office, 1941), p. 15.

[52] *Ibid.*, p. 14.

[53] *Sixth Annual Report of the Federal Security Agency: Social Security Board, 1941*, (Washington, D.C.: Government Printing Office, 1941), p. 24.

[54] *Seventh Annual Report of the Federal Security Agency: Social Security Board, 1942* (Washington, D.C.: Government Printing Office, 1942), p. 21.

Despite these recommendations, Congress took no action to liberalize the basis of eligibility for ADC or to force states participating in the program to remove their residence requirements. Pleas for the addition of a general relief category to the grant-in-aid programs included in the Social Security Act likewise received little effective support.

On a state level, the first break in the network of restrictive settlement laws was made by Rhode Island when it enacted the new General Public Assistance Act of 1942 removing all residence and citizenship requirements for eligibility for any type of public assistance.[55] This example was followed by New York in 1946 but had little effect on other states. As a result, only emergency assistance was usually available to nonresidents, and some states continued to deny any relief to those who had not lived in the state for five years.

CHILD LABOR PROVISIONS

After the National Industrial Recovery Act (NRA) was nullified by the Supreme Court in 1935, three further efforts to control child labor through federal legislation were made.

In 1936, the Walsh-Healey Public Contracts Act prohibited the employment of boys under sixteen and girls under eighteen on United States government contracts exceeding $10,000 in value. An employer was required to pay damages to the United States of $10 per day for each boy under sixteen or girl under eighteen who was knowingly employed to engage in any work specified by the act. Violation could also result in cancellation of the contract.[56]

The Sugar Act of 1937 provided for the payment of cash benefits to sugar cane and beet growers if they observed certain rules. The act also denied benefits to the grower if children under fourteen were employed or if those between the ages of fourteen and sixteen worked more than eight hours a day, but did not apply to children who were working in crops for their parents.[57]

The Fair Labor Standards Act passed in June, 1938, covered all employees engaged in interstate commerce and the production of goods involved in interstate commerce. By requiring the employer to grant

---

[55] Glen Leet, "Rhode Island Abolishes Settlement" *Proceedings of the National Conference of Social Work*, 1944, p. 335.

[56] United States Department of Labor, *Federal Labor Laws and Agencies*, Bulletin 123 (revised) (Washington, D.C.: Government Printing Office, undated), pp. 45–46.

[57] *The Sugar Act of 1936*, 50 Stat. 903.

overtime pay and to compensate employees for work in excess of the hours designated, this legislation was intended to spread employment and to control minimum wages and maximum hours of work. The act also contained child labor provisions which stipulated that "no producer, manufacturer, or dealer shall ship or deliver for shipment in commerce, any goods produced in an establishment . . . in the United States . . . in which within thirty days prior to the removal of such goods . . . any oppressive child labor has been employed."[58]

The act defined "oppressive child labor" as the employment of any-one under the age of sixteen or between the ages of sixteen and eighteen by an employer, other than a parent or guardian, "in any occupation which the Chief of the Children's Bureau . . . shall find and declare particularly hazardous for the employment of children between such ages or detrimental to their health and well-being."[59] The chief of the Children's Bureau was charged with these additional responsibilities: (1) to determine by regulation and orders that the employment of children fourteen to sixteen in other than manufacturing and mining is not oppressive when it is confined to periods which will not interfere with their schooling and to conditions which will not interfere with their health and well being;[60] (2) to establish regulations certifying that a person is above oppressive labor age;[61] (3) to make all investigations and inspections relative to records, wages, hours, and other conditions of employment of minors;[62] and (4) to institute any necessary legal action when unlawful practices exist relative to oppressive child labor.[63]

Under this law, agreements were developed whereby state departments of labor and education were usually empowered to act on behalf of the Children's Bureau in examining systems of employment certification, in providing necessary certificates of age to be filed with employers, and in carrying out the inspection and enforcement program.[64]

After the act was declared constitutional by the Supreme Court on February 3, 1941, it appeared that the long-sought goal of establishing

---

[58] *Fair Labor Standards Act*, Public Law 718, Chapter 676, Section 12(a).

[59] *Ibid.*, Section 3(1).

[60] *Ibid.*

[61] *Ibid.*

[62] *Ibid.*

[63] *Ibid.*, Section 12(b).

[64] *Four Decades of Action for Children*, p. 45.

national minimum standards for the protection of children had been achieved. With the advent of World War II, however, child labor returned in full force and the Children's Bureau found it necessary to intensify and to modify its enforcement activities. Hazardous occupation orders were issued for some jobs but, because of the need for workers, the employment of youths between the ages of sixteen and eighteen in certain occupations was not classified as hazardous.[65]

When the number of employed youths between the ages of fourteen and seventeen reached three million in 1943 (in comparison with less than one million in 1940), the War Manpower Commission issued a statement of policy declaring that youths under eighteen could best contribute to the war program by remaining in school. In addition, the Children's Bureau and the Office of Education began active campaigns to stimulate back-to-school drives. When the war ended, *Why Child Labor Laws?* and other explanatory pamphlets were issued by the Children's Bureau to encourage the enactment of better state legislation and the observance of existing laws.[66] Improvements were made in several state laws but only 32 states prohibited employment of children under fourteen outside of school hours, only 6 limited the employment of children fourteen to fifteen years of age to forty hours a week, and only 2 had adopted this standard for children sixteen to seventeen years old.[67]

PROFESSIONAL DEVELOPMENTS

During this transitional period several events significant in the development of social work as a profession had an equal impact upon the evolution of contemporary services for children.

When the Group Work Section of the National Conference of Social Work was established in 1935, this action set in motion a chain of events which soon made social group work "the most rapidly developing method in social work practice."[68] Interest in the meetings of this section also resulted in the organization of the American Asso-

---

[65] *34th Annual Report of the Chief, Children's Bureau to the Secretary of Labor, 1946* (Washington, D.C.: Government Printing Office, 1947), p. 76.

[66] *Ibid.*, pp. 93–94.

[67] Leonard W. Mayo, "The Findings of the National Commission on Children and Youth," *Proceedings of the National Conference of Social Work*, 1946, p. 375.

[68] Harleigh B. Trecker, "Social Group Work," *Social Work Year Book*, 1949, p. 487.

ciation for the Study of Group Work in 1936 and the subsequent appointment of committees to begin the study of existing courses in group work, the function of the group worker, and other areas of mutual concern.[69] In 1946, the American Association of Group Workers was formed with membership requirements which gave equal recognition to professional training and experience in education, recreation, and social work.[70]

In this decade, two groups contributed to the development of professional education for the practice of group work. In 1940, a subcommittee was established by the American Association of Schools of Social Work to consider a curriculum for group work "as one of the four basic methods of social work practice."[71] The report submitted by this committee in 1943 represented the first formulation of the content of a group work curriculum for member agencies.[72] In a separate effort, representatives of fourteen schools established the Conference of Professional Schools in Recreation and Group Work in 1943 for the purpose of building a curriculum for the training of group workers.[73] The deliberations of this conference were extensive in effect since courses in group work and recreation were being given in many colleges and universities, and some national agencies, such as the YMCA and the YWCA, maintained training schools for their own personnel or, like the Boy Scouts and similar agencies, provided short training courses for prospective employees.[74]

These diversified approaches were indicative of the widespread interest developing in this field. At an earlier date, group work had been limited primarily to character-building or youth-serving agencies and social settlements, but as social group work became an identifiable method of social work its value was recognized in new settings. As a result, demand developed for professionally trained social group workers in child guidance clinics, hospitals, summer camps, day nurseries, and institutions for children, as well as in various types of facilities for adults. By 1946, group therapy had also become a new method

---

[69] Grace L. Coyle, "Social Group Work," *Social Work Year Book* (New York: American Association of Social Workers, 1951), p. 468.

[70] *Ibid.*, p. 469.

[71] *Ibid.*

[72] *Ibid.*

[73] Ernest B. Hollis and Alice L. Taylor, *Social Work Education in the United States* (New York: Columbia University Press, 1951), p. 40.

[74] Coyle, *op. cit.*, p. 467.

of serving the emotionally disturbed and the social group worker had become a member of the traditional clinic "team" in psychiatric settings.[75]

A somewhat similar development began in 1938 when the Community Organization Section of the National Conference of Social Work was established. Discussion groups were formed in six cities, and reports on the objectives and methods of community organization were presented at the section meetings,[76] but the Association for the Study of Community Organization was not created until 1946.[77] During the intervening period, the papers presented at the National Conference, the articles appearing in the *Social Work Year Book*, and the publication of Wayne McMillen's *Community Organization* provided "a scientific orientation to the concept of community organization as a process."[78] This achievement was regarded as one of the most significant developments in social welfare in the United States during the first half of the century.[79] For children, these early beginnings were of particular importance since they indicated a growing realization that community organization is a method which can be practiced in many settings to mobilize community activity, and paved the way for the development of better community services for children.

During this period, marked progress was also made in establishing a basic curriculum in professional education for social work. As increasing agreement was reached about the fundamental principles and processes of social work, the American Association of Schools of Social Work sought to establish uniform requirements for all member schools. In 1944, this objective was achieved and a manual of accreditation was issued as a basis for the admission of new schools to the association.[80] In August, 1946, a further step was taken when the National Council on Social Work Education was formed to bring together representatives of the professional membership associations, the professional

---

[75] Gisela Konopka, "Therapy Through Social Group Work," *Proceedings of the National Conference of Social Work*, 1946, p. 228.

[76] Robert P. Lane, "The Field of Community Organization," *Proceedings of the National Conference of Social Work*, 1939, p. 495.

[77] Russell H. Kurtz, "Community Organization for Social Welfare," *Social Work Year Book*, 1949, p. 133.

[78] Leonard W. Mayo, "Community Organization in 1946," *Proceedings of the National Conference of Social Work*, 1946, p. 129.

[79] Virginia S. Ferguson, "Fifty Years of Social Work," *The Social Welfare Forum* (New York: Columbia University Press, 1950), p. vii.

[80] Hollis and Taylor, *op. cit.*, p. 47.

schools of social work, the colleges and universities, and the general field of social work. The basic research planned by the council did not affect the development of social work education until a later date, but the decision to reexamine existing content and agency needs in this field was in itself indicative of the progress made in the development of the profession.[81]

THE WHITE HOUSE CONFERENCE ON CHILDREN IN A DEMOCRACY

When President Franklin D. Roosevelt called the fourth White House Conference in mid-January of 1940, children ranging from infancy to seventeen years of age comprised nearly one-third of the population. The nation had not fully recovered from the long and tenacious economic depression which had so seriously affected the lives and welfare of millions of Americans. There were also persistent and alarming signs that the shadows of World War II were being slowly but surely cast upon this and other nations of the world. The conference could scarcely have come during more dramatic or uncertain times.

The theme of the White House Conference on Children in a Democracy grew out of the conviction that the exigencies of the moment demanded a re-evaluation and definitive analysis of the meaning of "democracy." The General Conference Report outlines these concerns:

The people of the United States have talked and lived democracy for a century and a half. We have never felt that it has reached its full stature nor that it has operated satisfactorily in every field of human endeavor. We have not always agreed as to the exact meaning of democracy, but we have never lost our belief in certain fundamental democratic principles. . . . These principles we wish to preserve for our children, and we hope so to educate them that they may improve upon and transmit this heritage to coming generations.[82]

The democratic credo of the conference emphasized the nation's growing concern for its children. There had been few times in our history when children and youth had been so helplessly victimized by a national crisis or when the consitutional guarantees of equality and

---

[81] Sue Spencer, "Education for Social Work," *Social Work Year Book,* 1949, p. 176.

[82] United States Children's Bureau, *Children in a Democracy, General Report* (Washington, D.C.: Government Printing Office, January, 1940), pp. 1–2.

protection had so little real meaning for so many. Yet much had happened since 1930 to give credence to the democratic ideal and to reinforce faith in its slowly broadening principles. In addition to the increase in tangible services, psychiatry, psychology, social work, and the social sciences were offering greater insights into human behavior and into the dynamics of men's social and environmental relations. Recognition of the progress made and of the work still to be done was evident in the conference statement:

Our standard of decent living has been raised to conform with our advancing knowledge. Our ancestors could drink polluted water, could lose a high percentage of mothers by childbed fever, could bury one baby out of three, without feeling rebellious against society, because no human being knew how to prevent those calamities. But suffering and death that we know how to prevent are an outrage against decency, not to be suffered in meek submission but to be fought with every new weapon our generation has discovered.[83]

Like the 1930 conference, the White House Conference on Children in a Democracy stressed "the common needs of all children" as they related to parents, family life, housing, health protection, education, training, and preparation for later life. Within a different framework, its recommendations reiterated some of the major emphases stressed by the first White House Conference over a quarter of a century before. The family was perceived as "the threshold of democracy" around which all other social institutions revolved. The family's responsibility to engender self-respect, self-reliance, and wholesome attitudes toward others was defined and it was generally agreed that "the welfare of children is bound up with the welfare of their families; and that a stable income sufficient to provide an 'adequate' standard of living is indispensable to family welfare."[84] In addition, it proposed measures for providing protection to migrant families moving about in search of a livelihood; for joint participation by the federal, state, and municipal governments in providing adequate housing for economically depressed families; and for expansion of unemployment compensation, Old Age and Survivor's Insurance, public assistance grants, and other financial aids. The conferees considered, too, the importance that religion plays in a child's life, as well as the educa-

---

[83] *Ibid.*, p. 13.

[84] United States Children's Bureau, *White House Conference on Children in a Democracy, Final Report*, Publication 272 (Washington, D.C.: Government Printing Office, 1942), p. 75.

tional, leisure-time, health, and social services that are so essential to his growth and well-being.

The 1940 conference is best remembered for the tenets which it held to be the convictions of the American people:

That democracy can flourish only as citizens have faith in the integrity of their fellow men and capacity to cooperate with them in advancing the ends of personal and social living.

That such faith and such capacity can best be established in childhood and within the family circle. Here the child should find affection which gives self-confidence, community of interest which induces cooperation, ethical values which influence conduct. Secure family life is the foundation of individual happiness and social well-being.

That even in infancy, and increasingly in later years, the welfare of the child depends not alone upon the care provided within the family, but also upon the safeguards and services provided by community, State and Nation.[85]

THE IMPACT OF WAR

For many children a dislocation of family living occurred long before the attack on Pearl Harbor. As the defense effort was mobilized in 1940, it became apparent that with the increased demand for employees in defense industries, children were being left home alone, locked in parked cars all day, or forced to join the increasing number of "latch-key" children left to shift for themselves. These developments caused even greater alarm when it was recognized that the relative adequacy of social services, recreational programs, and day-care facilities was being decreased by a shortage in personnel and by a greater need for these services in defense areas.

In July, 1941, the United States Children's Bureau sponsored a conference on Day-Care of Children of Working Mothers to discuss the best methods of meeting this problem. The appointment of a special Committee on Standards and Services was authorized by the conference and a comprehensive set of standards for use by community groups published in February, 1942. In addition to the specific standards established for group day care, foster family day care, and homemaker service, this document articulated the important principles that (1) mothers of preschool children should not be encouraged to work; (2) when mothers go to work, the community has an obligation to help parents plan for the care of their children; (3) infants should not be cared for in groups; (4) if necessary, care of children under two

---

[85] *Children in a Democracy, General Report*, pp. 84–85.

years of age should be provided in the child's own home through homemaker service or in supervised foster family homes; and (5) state and local governments should assume responsibility for supervising and maintaining adequate standards of day care.[86]

This statement had both an immediate and a continuing significance in the development of services for children. During the preceding month, it had been agreed that funds available under the Community Facilities Act of 1941 (commonly known as the Lanham Act) could be used for the establishment or expansion of day care centers and nursery schools and for the development or expansion of related day-care services in defense areas.[87] The United States Office of Education received responsibility for the development and extension of nursery schools to be operated in or under the auspices of local schools and for related school lunch and recreation programs. The Children's Bureau received a similar assignment with respect to day-care centers and related services sponsored by agencies not a part of the school program.[88] After July, 1942, additional funds were made available to state departments of education and public welfare for the promotion and coordination of day-care programs under their supervision.[89] These funds were used for the operation of 28 state plans administered by state departments of public welfare and 33 plans administered by state departments of education.[90] Although federal funds were not available for this purpose after June 30, 1943, many state departments retained the staff recruited for the administration of this program and incorporated as a part of their permanent function the development and supervision of day-care facilities.

On a local level the number of nursery schools operated under WPA auspices was augmented first through a Congressional appropriation of six million dollars and later through the use of Lanham Act funds. When the WPA was liquidated in 1943, Lanham Act funds were also

[86] United States Children's Bureau, *Report on Standards for Day Care of Children of Working Mothers* (Washington, D.C.: Government Printing Office, February 1942), pp. i–ii.

[87] United States Children's Bureau, "Day Care for Children of Working Mothers in Defense Areas," *Children's Bureau Commission on Children in War Time, First Meeting, March 16–18, 1942* (Washington, D.C.: Government Printing Office, 1942), p. 92.

[88] *Ibid.*

[89] Joanna Colcord, "Community Welfare Planning in Wartime," *Social Work Year Book,* 1943, p. 145.

[90] *Four Decades of Action for Children,* p. 53.

used to convert the WPA facilities to wartime projects. In July, 1945, about 1,600,000 children were receiving care in nurseries and day-care centers financed by federal funds. Before federal support was withdrawn in 1946, the Children's Bureau urged communities and states to set up planning bodies to develop long-range plans for day care,[91] and in a few states the operation of child care centers has since become a permanent part of the public school program.

A conference on the care of children under two years of age, called by the Children's Bureau in July, 1944, also had widespread influence on future services for children. Attended by representatives from the fields of child welfare, psychiatry, nursery school education, child development and child health, this group reiterated and made more specific, the recommendations of the earlier conference on day care as they related to infants. Their conclusions stressed the need to (1) "preserve for the baby his right to have care from his mother";[92] (2) provide a counseling service as a part of every program of child care; (3) limit the minimum age of admission to group care, to two and one-half to three years; and (4) develop foster family day care to meet the needs of children under two or three years of age.[93]

Despite the early recommendation that homemaker service be considered a resource for children in need of day care, no significant progress in the development of this service was made during the war period. With employment at a high level, the difficulty in securing qualified women to provide the service and the cost necessary during this period of high wages were reported to be precluding factors.[94] More fundamentally, perhaps, few social agencies were equipped with sufficient staff to undertake the development of a new service at this time.

Foster family day care homes were extensively used in some communities, but the shortage of staff in social agencies frequently meant that the service provided was limited to the licensing of homes and the direct referral of parents of these homes without benefit of any adequate service of placement and supervision.[95]

During the war years the number of delinquent children reported

---

[91] *Ibid.*, pp. 54–55.

[92] *Ibid.*, p. 45.

[93] *Ibid.*

[94] Alice T. Dashiell, "Day Care of Children," *Social Work Year Book*, 1945, p. 128.

[95] *Ibid.*, p. 127.

to the juvenile courts and the police increased rapidly. As a result, a number of studies of causative factors were made by the United States Children's Bureau, and in February, 1943, a meeting of the National Commission on Children and Youth was held at the White House. In accordance with the recommendations made, the Children's Bureau issued "Controlling Juvenile Delinquency," a pamphlet widely used by community groups in developing plans to meet the needs of troubled children. A companion bulletin, "Understanding Juvenile Delinquency," was also prepared for civic leaders and parents.[96] Because of existing staff shortages in all social agencies, little progress was made in providing more adequate services during the war, but the attention focused upon possible means of preventing juvenile delinquency served to alert the nation to the need for more adequate services for children and to establish a precedent for further activity in this field.

The Last Decade

Recent developments in the field of child welfare are reflected in the description of specialized services presented in the next chapters, and it is necessary to note here only those events which have been of general significance.

THE NATIONAL MENTAL HEALTH ACT

In 1930, the Narcotics Division of the United States Public Health Service, created in 1929, was renamed the Mental Hygiene Division and a program of consultation to states on community mental health programs and to mental hospitals was initiated. After that date, the federal government assumed an increased responsibility in the prevention, control, and treatment of mental illness. When the National Mental Health Act was passed on July 3, 1946, the Mental Hygiene Division was made responsible for its administration. In 1949, the Mental Hygiene Division became the National Institute for Mental Health, with headquarters in the research center of the Public Health Service at Bethesda, Maryland.

The National Mental Health Act was significant because it indicated a recognition of the extent of mental illness and an acceptance of fed-

---

[96] *Four Decades of Action for Children*, pp. 51–52.

eral responsibility for a serious national problem.   The act was created
at a time when over one-half of all hospital patients in the country
were suffering from mental illness and it was estimated that some
8,500,000 persons had some type of mental disorder.[97]   The provisions
of the act also reflected the lack of diagnostic and treatment services,
trained personnel, facilities for undergraduate and postgraduate training, and funds for coordinated research and public interpretation of
mental illness.

The major objective of the National Mental Health Act was to improve the mental health of the nation (1) by promoting research
through grants-in-aid to hospitals, private or public institutions, universities, laboratories, and qualified individuals; (2) by establishing a
National Institute of Mental Health for intensive clinical research in
mental illness; (3) by making grants to public and private institutions
for the training of psychiatrists, psychologists, psychiatric social
workers, and psychiatric nurses; (4) by providing grants-in-aid to
states for use in developing community mental health services; (5) by
making consultation and technical assistance available to the states; and
(6) by helping to increase public understanding of mental illness.[98]

Dr. Robert H. Felix, who became the first chief of the National
Institute of Mental Health, wrote:

To all of us who are familiar with the many obstacles that have long
impeded the progress of the mental-hygiene movement, the passage of the
National Mental Health Act is particularly encouraging.   Mistaken ideas
of what mental hygiene is and does; controversy within our own ranks;
deep-rooted prejudices against the whole subject; acute deficiencies in
personnel, facilities, knowledge, and funds—all have combined to permit
mental illness to reach grave and threatening proportions.[99]

As in all federal grant-in-aid programs, the participating state must
present to the surgeon general a plan for a mental health program to
be administered by a central state agency.   In 1946 only 24 states had
functioning mental health programs separate from those of the state
hospitals. Presently, all states have programs of this kind.   In 29 states

---

[97] Federal Security Agency, Public Health Service, *The National Mental
Health Program*, Mental Health Series, No. 4 (Washington, D.C.: Government
Printing Office, June 1948), p. 3.

[98] *Ibid.*, pp. 2–3.

[99] Robert H. Felix, "The National Mental Health Act," *Mental Hygiene*, XXXI,
No. 3 (July 1947), p. 363.   Reprinted from with permission of the National Association for Mental Health.

the programs are administered by state health departments; in 7, by departments of mental hygiene; in 5, by departments of welfare; and in 7, by other agencies.[100]

The National Mental Health Institute has devoted a substantial share of its efforts to child welfare. Grants have been made for research on various aspects of child development, the origins of mental retardation and deficiency, the effect of parental maturity on child development, and the emotional aspects of chronic physical illness.[101] The institute has also undertaken studies of mental health in relation to the child in school, and of in-patient services for emotionally disturbed children. In addition, there have been grants to the states for the study of juvenile delinquency.[102]

OTHER CHANGES IN FEDERAL STATUTES

Several important changes have been made in the laws and administrative structure through which the federal government discharges its responsibilities for children.

On July 17, 1946, the Federal Security Agency was reorganized in accordance with President Truman's Reorganization Plan No. 2. In this process, the Social Security Board was abolished, the agency previously operating under its direction renamed the Social Security Administration, and the commissioner of Social Security made the directing head of the new administration. More importantly, the United States Children's Bureau was removed from the Department of Labor, made a Bureau of the Social Security Administration, and all of its functions transferred to the Federal Security Agency except those related to the enforcement of the child labor provisions of the Fair Labor Standards Act.[103] This change brought within one agency, for the first time, all programs administered under the Social Security Act, and made possible a more complete integration of federal programs for the welfare of children.

---

[100] James V. Lowry, "Public Mental Health Agencies, State and National," *The Annals of the American Academy of Political and Social Science,* Vol. 286 (March 1953), p. 101.

[101] United States Department of Health, Education, and Welfare, *Annual Report* (Washington, D.C.: Government Printing Office, 1955), p. 101.

[102] United States Department of Health, Education, and Welfare, *Annual Report* (Washington, D.C.: Government Printing Office, 1956), p. 104.

[103] *Annual Report of the Federal Security Agency,* Section 1, Social Security Administration (Washington, D.C.: Government Printing Office, 1947), p. 2.

The long-awaited federal department headed by a secretary with Cabinet status was achieved when President Eisenhower's Reorganization Plan No. 1 was confirmed by Congress on April 10, 1953. Under this plan, the Department of Health, Education and Welfare was created to replace the Federal Security Agency. The new department included the Social Security Administration, the Office of Education, the Public Health Service, the Food and Drug Administration, and the Office of Vocational Rehabilitation. The Children's Bureau remained within the Social Security Administration but significant change occurred when the commissioner of Social Security was made a presidential appointee rather than an appointee of the agency administrator.

All of the services encompassed in the Department of Health, Education and Welfare touch in some way upon the lives of all children. In the Social Security Administration, the Bureau of Public Assistance has responsibility for the services and financial grants available through the Aid to Dependent Children program, and the Bureau of Old Age and Survivor's Insurance administers the benefits described by its title. The Children's Bureau continues to be the primary child welfare agency of the federal government.

The financial benefits and social services administered by these bureaus were significantly extended by amendments to the Social Security Act in 1950, 1954, and 1956. In each of these years, the scope of the OASI system was extended to cover additional groups of workers, and in 1956 the eligibility age for women was lowered from 65 to 62 years and a provision for disability insurance added. The latter provision was of particular value to children. It not only provided benefits for children whose parents became disabled between the the ages of 50 and 65, but made continuing benefits available to the totally disabled child of any eligible worker, if the child became disabled before the age of eighteen. All workers are now covered by OASDI except some government employees with separate retirement protection, self-employed physicians, irregularly employed farm and domestic workers, and low income persons who are self-employed.

The 1950 and 1956 amendments to the public assistance titles of the act broadened both the scope and the objectives of these programs. The 1950 amendments established a new program of aid to permanently and totally disabled persons. In addition, federal matching became available for ADC payments to meet the needs of the parent or relative caring for the child and for direct payments made by a state agency to those who supply medical care to persons receiving assistance under the provisions of the act. In 1956, each of the four public assistance titles was amended to include a new provision for federal sharing in the cost of medical care and a statement indicating that it is the objective of the program to furnish appropriate social services to strengthen family life and to help needy persons achieve more independent living. Federal grants to states for training programs were also authorized to increase the availability of skilled public assistance personnel.

In 1949, amendments to the Fair Labor Standards Act included several changes in the child labor provisions. Children under eighteen employed by their parents in hazardous occupations and children who were formerly permitted by local school law to work in agriculture during school hours were no longer exempt from the provisions of the act. Agricultural employment was also limited to hours when school is not in session. Children performing in radio and television programs and newsboys were excluded, but employment of children in commerce or in the production of goods for commerce was prohibited.

The responsibility for regulating child labor and for defining "oppressive child labor" in specific instances was given to the secretary of labor. The only change made in the definition of oppressive child labor was an increase in the age level to sixteen and eighteen years in the sections which relate to "particularly hazardous . . . employment of children . . . detrimental to their health or well-being."[104]

Despite this legislation, there is still exploitation in the employment of children. Some work at too early an age, others are employed long hours, some are in work that is too physically demanding, and others are employed under unsatisfactory conditions. Existing child labor laws also fail to cover all of the types of employment in which children are engaged.

THE MID-CENTURY WHITE HOUSE CONFERENCE

After the 1940 White House Conference, a national citizens' committee was formed with Marshall Field as its chairman. This committee had responsibility for cooperating with federal agencies in stimulating national effort to implement the 1940 conference recommendations. In 1942, the committee was succeeded by the Wartime Commission on Children and Youth, which, in turn, was replaced in 1946 by the

---

[104] *New Wage-Hour Law, Fair Labor Standards Amendments of 1949,* Sec. 116 (1) (Chicago: Commerce Clearing House, 1950), p. 47.

National Commission on Children and Youth. It was this commission which first proposed that the 1950 White House Conference be called. In April, 1948, by order of President Harry S. Truman, a Federal Interdepartmental Committee on Children and Youth was formed. This committee, whose membership included representatives of 37 agencies, departments, and bureaus within the federal government, also assumed an important role in preparing for the conference, although this was not its primary function.

The Mid-Century White House Conference was one of the most extensive national efforts ever initiated in behalf of the nation's children. Since the National Commission had the strong conviction that the 1950 Conference should reflect the nation's concern for all children throughout the country, four councils were created to coordinate the groups involved in planning for a conference to be attended by nearly 6,000 persons. The Advisory Council on State and Local Action served as a source of communication and cooperation among state committees; the Advisory Council on Participation of National Organizations coordinated the work of some 464 child and youth organizations; the Advisory Council on Federal Government Participation was concerned with federal programs directed to the physical, social, and economic well-being of children and youth; and the Advisory Council on Youth Participation directed its attention toward the many local, national, and world problems facing young people and the methods by which they might learn to assume social responsibility and leadership.

Following the appointment of a national committee, the president requested that the governor of each state designate "official White House Conferences to work with the National Committee in moving the program forward."[105] By the summer of 1950, some 100,000 persons were participating in conference projects throughout the country.[106]

The conference was opened by the chairman of the National Committee of the Conference, Oscar R. Ewing, who summarized the influences of other White House Conferences as having

. . . affected profoundly two generations of American thought. They have given us ideas, ideas that were once strange and have now achieved the high success of becoming, . . . commonplace. Ideas like these:
That all children have a right to childhood.

---

[105] *Proceedings of the Mid-Century White House Conference on Children and Youth* (Raleigh, North Carolina: Health Publications Institute, 1951), p. 17.

[106] *Ibid.*, p. 23.

That every child should have a home, and that no child should be separated from his parents save in grave and exceptional circumstances. That what is good for any child is good for all children.[107]

The Mid-Century Conference set the tone for the next decade of progress in the field of child welfare.   The needs and activities of children and youth were realistically projected into the contemporary dynamic milieu with all of its impact and demands.   In addition, there was concern about forms of mass media, the juvenile court, protective services, family income, the effects of discrimination and prejudice on healthy personality development, the plight of children of migrant workers, the influence of mobilization and war on children, and many related matters.

The platform which the conference adopted reflected the thinking of 35 work groups made up of professional and lay persons representing many regions, points of view, and proposed objectives.   There was, however, a strong commonality of purpose, as evidenced in the basic approaches to the problems of child welfare:

Believing in the primacy of spiritual values, democratic practice, and the dignity and worth of every human being, and recognizing that these are essential to individual happiness and responsible citizenship, we have come together to inquire
—How the necessary mental, emotional and spiritual qualities may be developed in children, and
—How the physical, economic, and social conditions favorable to such development may be assured.[108]

The conference platform spelled out in creative and visionary fashion the importance of "furthering healthy personality development . . . in children and youth," through the family, church, school, and other social institutions.   It also outlined the need for the expansion of professional services under private and public auspices, and for evaluating the social and economic forces which influence child development, and advocated that citizens be mobilized to improve situations affecting children and youth.

THE CHILDREN'S BUREAU IN RECENT YEARS

Interspersed with adjustments to two new administrative settings, the staff of the Children's Bureau experienced two changes in leadership within a six-year period.   Katharine F. Lenroot, the chief since

---

[107] *Ibid.*, p. 43.
[108] *Ibid.*, p. 29.

1934, completed 36 years of bureau service in 1951 and was replaced by Dr. Martha M. Eliot, who had been a member of the bureau staff for many years. In April, 1957, Katherine Brownell Oettinger became the fifth chief of the bureau after Dr. Eliot's resignation.

Despite these changes, the bureau has continued to increase the scope of its activities. Since the Clearing House for Research was created in 1948, *Research Relating to Children* has been published periodically to provide an inventory of current research projects involving the emotional, social, and physical adjustment of children. Additional research has been stimulated under a variety of auspices and consultation provided to national standard-setting agencies as well as to state and local public and private agencies.

The bureau has also continued its long-established pattern of emphasizing the needs of certain groups of children during a particular period. When Dr. Eliot became chief, she expressed the belief that attention should be focused on children in unprotected adoptions; children with congential handicaps; rural children; Negro, Indian, and Spanish-American children who often receive inferior services; children of working mothers; children of migratory families; and troubled adolescents.[109] *A Research Program for the Children's Bureau*, published in 1953, supported her recommendations. Since that time, much of the bureau's research, publication, and other activities has been focused on juvenile delinquency, children of migrants, mentally retarded children, and children placed for adoption without the protection of a social agency.

Through the grant-in-aid programs, the Children's Bureau has continued to assist the states in extending and strengthening maternal and child health services, services for crippled children, and child welfare services. With federal funds for maternal and child health services, new demonstration programs for premature infants have been developed, programs for the postgraduate training of health personnel initiated, and new emphases placed upon the mental health aspects of child development and the importance of parent-child relationships. After Congress earmarked $1,000,000 of the 1957 appropriation for special projects for the mentally retarded, 26 demonstration programs of this type were approved by the Children's Bureau in addition to those included in regular state plans.[110]

---

[109] *Four Decades of Action for Children*, p. 77.

[110] *1957 Annual Report*, United States Department of Health, Education and Welfare (Washington, D.C.: Government Printing Office, 1957), p. 59.

Services for crippled children have been extended through the development of diagnostic and treatment centers in medical schools, training courses for work with amputees, services for children with congenital heart disease, rheumatic fever, metabolic and degenerative diseases, and speech and hearing programs.

Child Welfare Services funds continue to be used primarily for professional education and the employment of qualified personnel. Because programs have been hampered by the continued shortage of professionally trained staff, a new emphasis has been placed on recruitment and in-service training. In June, 1957, the Children's Bureau and the Bureau of Public Assistance sponsored a seminar on "Group Leadership in Staff Training," attended by representatives from 26 states. The value of this conference was later increased through wide distribution of the report on its findings. A national study of the reasons for excessive staff turnover in child welfare and family service agencies was also initiated.

The bureau has given particular attention to the development of protective services, homemaker services, and other services for children in their own homes. Its research, publication, and staff consultation have also emphasized the need for increased services for unmarried mothers and for agency adoption services to curtail the independent placement of babies, the development of foster homes for emotionally disturbed and physically handicapped children, and the provision of a better quality of foster family and institutional care.

Much attention has also been given to services for the control and treatment of juvenile delinquency since 1952. In July of that year, a Special Juvenile Delinquency Project was financed by several foundations to supplement the bureau program. A National Conference on Juvenile Delinquency, held in June, 1954, was followed by other conferences on related topics, and on October 6, 1954, a Division of Juvenile Delinquency in the Children's Bureau was authorized. When the Special Project ended in June, 1955, the new division assumed responsibility for consultation to the states and localities. Its activities have centered on the care and treatment of delinquent youth in detention facilities and training schools; police, juvenile court, and probation services; work with juvenile gangs; planning and coordination of community programs; and the training of specialized personnel for this field.

In addition to its own activities, the bureau works cooperatively with the Bureau of Public Assistance in efforts to increase the quality of service available to children receiving ADC. It also assumes a prominent role in the work of the Interdepartmental Committee on Children and Youth, which meets monthly to integrate the work of 34 federal agencies and to strengthen their working relations with the states. In these other ways, the Children's Bureau continues to serve as a central coordinating agency for local, state, and national effort in behalf of children.

THE ROLE OF NATIONAL VOLUNTARY AGENCIES

Local social agencies continue to play an increasingly important role in the lives of many children and their families. Much of the impetus for raising standards in regard to professional personnel, program, and practice is stimulated by national organizations, however. Prominent among these is the Family Service Association of America, which, after five name changes, became in 1946 the modern version of The National Association of Societies for Organizing Charity.

The association continues to set standards for agency membership in terms of program, personnel, and financial support. To be accredited, an agency must now offer a family casework service, have a responsible and active board which participates with the executive and staff in agency planning, and have a paid staff of persons trained in family casework.[111] There were 264 accredited family service agencies in 1957.

The field staff maintained by the association provides consultation to member agencies and regional and national conferences are held. In addition to the monthly publication, *Social Casework*, other books and pamphlets are published from time to time and made available to any person or organization interested in professional services for troubled families.

In 1953, the Board of the FSAA approved a report of the Committee on Family Life Education which defined the functions and scope of a family agency to include the provision of a casework service, participation in community planning, group education in personality development, social adjustment and family relations, professional education, and research.

The Child Welfare League of America has continued to concern itself with the care of dependent, neglected, and delinquent children. Like the FSAA, it sets standards of practice and accredits agencies meeting these standards. In 1957, there were 229 accredited agencies

---

[111] Clark W. Blackburn, "Family Social Work," *Social Work Year Book*, 1957, p. 249.

serving children, the majority under private auspices. The league offers consultative service to member agencies, publishes *Child Welfare* monthly, compiles and distributes case record exhibits, prepares material for public interpretation, engages in community and agency studies, conducts regional conferences, and sponsors various special projects and publications.

It is estimated that some 1,250 agencies serving 75,000 children were reached by the league's program in 1955.[112] One of the league's most outstanding contributions throughout the years has been the development and publication of guides and standards for various types of services for children. A major revision of these standards was undertaken in recent years. The league has also been influential in such significant reforms as:

. . . substituting foster home for institutional care for young children; strengthening institutional programs by adding better qualified or specialized staff and improved physical plant; establishment of homemaker and day care services; and improved community planning.[113]

During the last decade, the American Public Welfare Association has devoted a substantial share of its work to public child welfare programs. In 1956, the Committee on Services to Children considered topics assigned to the subcommittees on ADC Interpretation, Medical Services in Child Welfare, Agency Relationships in Juvenile Delinquency Services, and Legislation on Interstate Placement of Children. Consideration was also given to services to unmarried mothers, casework services in ADC, and adoption resource exchanges.[114]

The Council on State Directors of Programs for Children and Youth was also established by APWA in 1956 to facilitate the exchange of ideas and information for the improvement of child welfare programs throughout the country. Increasing attention to child welfare has been evident, too, in the monthly publication, *Public Welfare*, in the technical assistance and consultation provided by the field staff, and in the agenda for the annual regional and national conferences.

There are numerous other national agencies which play an important part in setting standards and providing administrative and professional

---

[112] *Today . . . And Tomorrow*, p. 26.

[113] *Ibid*, p. 16.

[114] American Public Welfare Association, *1956—Year of Significance, Annual Report*, Chicago, 1956, pp. 4–5.

leadership for member agencies in communities throughout the country. The National Conference of Catholic Charities and the national organizations of Jewish, Lutheran, Methodist, and other religious groups maintaining institutions or social agencies have long devoted their efforts to child welfare and family life.

The National Conference of Social Welfare continues to occupy a central role in the expression of professional concerns and countless affiliated kindred groups use its meetings as an opportunity to bring together the membership of their own national organizations.

Since 1922 the National Child Welfare Division of the American Legion has been representative of another type of national organization concerned with the welfare of children. Its efforts are primarily directed toward the children of veterans, but its members have given strong support to child welfare legislation of benefit to all children. Various fraternal organizations have also contributed greatly to the solution of child welfare problems.

In addition to the national agencies whose functions are related to those of their constituent agencies or organizations, there is a group of so-called "problem centered" national agencies active in the health field. The National Society for Crippled Children and Adults, the National Foundation for Infantile Paralysis, the American Cancer Society, the American Heart Association, and the National Tuberculosis Association are perhaps the best known organizations of this type, but many others play an important role in advancing the knowledge and services necessary to meet the needs of disadvantaged children.

The National Social Work Council, established as a planning and discussion group in 1920, became the National Social Welfare Assembly in 1945. Since that date, this organization has served as a coordinating body for national organizations.

NEW PROFESSIONAL ORGANIZATIONS

The advent of two new organizations marked the beginning of a new era in the social work profession. To a considerable degree, the development of both organizations reflected a common effort to evaluate the current status of the profession, to examine its needs, and to reach agreement about its goals and future direction.

As previously indicated, the National Council on Social Work Education was formed in 1946 to undertake an extensive appraisal of current education for social work. Through a grant from the

Carnegie Foundation, a comprehensive study was made in 1948 by Ernest V. Hollis and Alice L. Taylor. The report published in 1951 caused considerable discussion and led to the formation of the Council on Social Work Education in 1952. This body replaced both the American Association of Schools of Social Work and the National Association of Schools of Social Administration, which had been organized in 1942 to assist in the development of programs on the graduate and undergraduate level. The new council includes representatives from accredited graduate schools of social work, undergraduate departments, professional associations, and employing agencies.

Another movement, which developed almost simultaneously, resulted in a merging of the seven professional membership associations into a single association. Initiated by the American Association of Social Workers in 1946, discussed with other associations in the following year, and stimulated by the American Association of Schools of Social Work, the Temporary Inter-Association Council of Social Work Membership Organizations (TIAC) was formed in 1950, and after a long process of negotiation, the National Association of Social Workers came into being on October 1, 1955.

Graduation from an accredited school of social work was made a requirement for future members of NASW, but the initial membership of the new association included all current members of the American Association of Social Workers, the American Association of Psychiatric Social Workers, the American Association of Medical Social Workers, the National Association of School Social Workers, the Social Work Research Group, and the Association for the Study of Community Organization. Provision was also made for "sections" in the national organization and in local chapters "to afford members the opportunity to participate in activities for the advancement of social work practice in a specific setting"[115] and to preserve the interest of those who had previously belonged to specialized associations.

Thus, the profession of social work is currently represented by a single membership association which gives recognition to the need for specialization in certain settings. This philosophy is perhaps most evident in the format used in *Social Work*, the quarterly journal of the NASW, and in the *NASW News*, distributed to the nearly 23,000 members of the association. In these publications, papers and items

---

[115] Melvin A. Glasser, "The Story of the Movement for a Single Professional Association," *Social Work Journal*, Vol. XXXVI, No. 3 (July 1955), p. 122.

of general interest are followed by headings for each section established (School Social Work Section, Social Work Research Section, Psychiatric Social Work Section, Medical Social Work Section, and Group Work Section).

NEXT STEPS

The preceding pages have presented the framework within which our contemporary services for children have been developed. This kaleidoscope has also indicated the point in time when effective action was taken to correct conditions detrimental to the welfare of children. Many of the problems identified in previous decades have been partially solved, but much remains to be done. In the next chapters, some of the groups of children in need of special protection will be described and the specialized services for children presented in greater detail.

Selected Bibliography

Abbott, Edith. "Public Assistance—Whither Bound?" *Proceedings of the National Conference of Social Work*, 1937.

Blackburn, Clark W. "Family Social Work," *Social Work Year Book*, 1957.

DelliQuadri, Fred. "Child Welfare," *Social Work Year Book*, 1957.

de Schweinitz, Karl. *People and Process in Social Security.* Washington, D.C.: American Council on Education, 1948.

Epstein, Abraham. *Insecurity, A Challenge to America.* New York: Random House, 1938.

Federal Security Agency. *Public Social Services to Children, A Decade of Progress.* Child Welfare Report 1. Washington, D.C.: Government Printing Office, April 1946.

Smith, A. Delafield. *The Right to Life.* Chapel Hill: University of North Carolina Press, 1955.

Part Four · Children

All children have in common certain basic needs

which must be met by their parents

or through some community resource.

Some children have additional needs

which may be caused by physical, mental, or social handicaps.

These are the children who require special protection.

in Need of Special Protection

Chapter 10   The Child

with Physical Handicaps

The terms "handicapped child," "exceptional child," "crippled child," and "child with special needs" have been used separately and interchangeably. A child is considered "handicapped" if he cannot play, learn, work, or do things in the same way as other children his age and if he is hindered in developing his full physical, mental, and social potential.[1] The "exceptional child" has also been broadly defined as one "who differs as a person to the extent that he is therefore handicapped in his relationship with others."[2] This term may

---

[1] *Services for Handicapped Children* (New York: The American Public Health Association, 1955), p. 12.

[2] Robert Coleman Longan, "The Social Group" in *The Emotional Climate of the Exceptional Child, Proceedings of the Spring Conference on Education and the Exceptional Child* (Langhorne, Pennsylvania: The Child Research Clinic of The Woods Schools, May 1949), p. 8.

relate to a child with superior intellect, to a child with limited mental capacity, to a child with a speech or reading problem, or, in fact, to any child considered "exceptional" in comparison with other children.

The 1930 White House Conference defined a "crippled child" as one who has a defect which causes a deformity or interferes with the normal functioning of the bones, muscles or joints.[3]   In another section of the same conference, a crippled child was also defined as one who "may be reasonably expected to become, deficient in the use of his body or limbs . . . including harelip, cleft palate, and some other handicaps yielding to plastic surgery."[4]   This definition, however, excluded physical handicaps affecting sight, hearing, speech, or the normal functioning of the heart.

Lesser points out that traditionally the term "crippled child" meant the orthopedically crippled, but today children are considered to be crippled in many ways.   He prefers the term "handicapped child," however, and includes in this category children having rheumatic fever, cerebral palsy, epilepsy, cleft palate and lip, eye conditions, hearing loss, speech handicaps, and orthopedic handicaps.[5]

Public programs for crippled children now include not only the services related to orthopedic defects and impairments necessitating plastic surgery, but also diabetes, congenital cataract, deafness, injuries due to burns, accidents, poisoning, epilepsy, cerebral palsy, and other conditions not generally associated with the term "crippling."

The term "child with special needs" seems to have been created by social workers in the child welfare field.   By intent it attaches significance to the child's physical, emotional, or other needs rather than his condition or problems.   It has some limitations, however, since all children have special needs unique to their own personalities, emotional satisfactions, happiness, and well-being.

The term "handicapped" appears to have won the most general acceptance and will be used here to encompass all of the defects which interfere with a child's normal growth and developmental processes.

---

[3] "Special Education," *White House Conference on Child Health and Protection* (New York: The Century Company, 1931), pp. 23–24.

[4] "The Handicapped Child," *White House Conference on Child Health and Protection* (New York: The Century Company, 1933), p. 119.

[5] Arthur J. Lesser and Eleanor P. Hunt, "The Nation's Handicapped Children," *American Journal of Public Health*, Vol. 44, No. 2 (February 1954), pp. 166–169.

The Blind and
Visually Handicapped Child

In 1955 it was estimated that there were 8,500,000 elementary school children with eye problems and 68,000 children of preschool and school age who were partially seeing. There were 5,800 preschool blind children and 6,600 school-age blind children.[6]

Identification of children with defective vision is perhaps the most important factor in the prevention of blindness. There are a variety of observable symptoms which may warrant immediate diagnosis and treatment. The child who is troubled by faulty vision often attempts to remove the blur before his eyes by excessive eye rubbing, blinking, or frowning. He may squint because of undue sensitivity to light or he may need to hold books or small objects very close to his eyes, shutting one eye or tilting his head as he does so. He may find it difficult to engage in play activities which require distant vision or he may stumble and trip over small objects which he cannot see. In addition, he may evidence his visual limitations by becoming irritable, restless, and frustrated as he attempts to do close work, or he may have such physical symptoms as dizziness, double vision, or nauseating headaches.[7] He may also show poor alignment in penmanship; have a tendency to lose the place on the page; have more difficulty in reading, the longer he reads; confuse certain letters of the alphabet, such as "o," and "a," "e" and "c," "n" and "m," or be unable to distinguish colors.[8]

Scientific measurement of visual acuity at various distances is associated with the work of Herman Snellen, a Dutch ophthalmologist. The Snellen Chart is composed of symbols, letters, or numbers drawn to an exact scale for use at twenty feet. A person who can read the twenty-foot line at a distance of twenty feet is considered to have 20/20 or normal vision. If he is able to read only the letters of the seventy-foot line, his visual acuity is 20/70 and he is adjudged to have only partial sight. If he can clearly see only the largest letter, "E,"

---

[6] The American Public Health Association, *Services for Children with Vision and Eye Problems* (New York, 1956), p. 15.

[7] Winifred Hathaway, *Education and Health of the Partially Seeing Child* (New York: Columbia University Press, 1954), pp. 192–193.

[8] *Children with Visual Problems: The Illinois Plan for Special Education of Exceptional Children*, Circular Series "D," No. 12, revised (Springfield: issued by Superintendent of Public Instruction, 1952), pp. 90–91.

his visual acuity is 20/200 and he is considered to be nearing blindness with a visual efficiency loss of 80 per cent.[9]

Causes of Blindness

Blindness in the child under seven has been attributed to infectious diseases, injuries, tumors, general diseases, and "prenatal influence." In 1951–52, "causes unknown to science" accounted for 47 per cent of blindness among preschool children.[10]   Blindness among school children in 1954–55 was due to infectious diseases, injuries, poisonings, tumors, and general diseases.   Prenatal influences accounted for the majority of eye defects in this group.[11]   Blindness due to infectious diseases is decreasing, but there is still a great deal of blindness due to unknown causes.

The Blind Preschool Child

It has been pointed out that since the blind child is born without sight, he does not know what seeing is or that he is missing anything.[12] Being unaware of his difference, he seeks the same satisfactions and makes the same demands as does any other infant.   It is during this time that he must gain his share of basic security, since he will become aware of his difference and his handicap as he emerges into childhood. His ability to live with his limitations will greatly depend upon the way he has learned to relate to those who have been closest to him during his infancy.   Like any other child, he has a deep investment in his parents and he is dependent upon them for his care and his share of love and acceptance.

The manner in which the child is helped and educated at home will be of great importance to him.   His parents will need to recognize that his lack of vision may affect his coordination and that he will be less efficient in tending to his personal needs, in eating, and in his play and learning habits.   Because he must depend largely upon touch,

---

[9] Farrell, *op. cit.*, pp. 202–203.

[10] C. Edith Kerby, "Blindness in Preschool Children," *The Sight-Saving Review*, Vol. XXIV, No. 1 (Spring 1954), Table VI, p. 23.

[11] C. Edith Kerby, "Causes of Blindness in Children of School Age," *The Sight-Saving Review*, Vol. XXVIII, No. 1 (Spring 1958), Table 3, p. 14.

[12] United States Children's Bureau, *The Pre-School Child Who is Blind*, Folder No. 39, U.S. Department of Health, Education and Welfare, Social Security Administration (Washington, D.C.: Government Printing Office, 1953), p. 3.

he will also need time to concentrate on doing things which the seeing child quickly learns by visual experience. Parents often become concerned by the blind child's apparent "dawdling" and sometimes raise question as to whether an apparent inability to learn quickly is a symptom of mental retardation. They should be helped to understand that their blind child's success in learning is not only related to the quality of his intellect but is highly correlated with the emotional climate in which he is expected to learn.

Parents and teachers are often disturbed too by the "blindisms" or gestures to which a blind child resorts when he is tired, upset, or unoccupied. The child may teeter from side to side, jiggle, become destructive, rub his eyes, or engage in other activity that appears senseless and is irritating to observe. Blindisms can often be avoided by providing the child with play outlets that are stimulating and interesting.

Education of the Blind Child

Authorities in the field of special education believe that the preschool blind child should be enrolled in a nursery school with sighted children if he is ready for a group experience. A school selected with care will give the child an opportunity for peer relationships and for doing things independent of parent or sibling guidance.

There are various kinds of education for the blind school-aged child. The traditional type is still given in a public, private, or parochial residential school for the blind. A second method is that of educating the blind with the sighted in a public, private, or parochial school with a special teacher available to the blind child during the school day. A third type is with sighted children with itinerant supervision by a special teacher. In 1956 there were 6,500 students enrolled in fifty residential schools for the blind, located in forty states, Hawaii, and Puerto Rico. Sixty-nine cities in twenty states and the District of Columbia conducted integrated classes for 1,000 blind students.

The value of residential school education for the blind child, as contrasted with an integrated public school experience, has been discussed for many years. The proponents of the residential school maintain that the child is more comfortable and able to compete more readily with his blind peers than he would be with sighted children. Since the majority of the sight-saving classes are in urban areas, the residential school is the only resource available to the blind child in rural areas.

The benefits of nonresidential education for the blind child have steadily gained support since John B. Curtis established the first Braille class in Chicago in 1900 and thus began a day school movement for the education of blind children. As similar classes were developed throughout the country, more importance was attributed to the necessity of integrating the blind into their home communities. Increasing recognition of the importance of family life also stimulated other departures from the earlier prominence of residential school education.

Home teaching has long been another means of bringing instruction to the blind and, as modern education has increased its scope, the role of the home teacher has changed in a similar manner. It is now generally accepted that the home teacher has a broader function than that of teaching the blind client to knit or to read Braille. In practice, the home teacher becomes a combination case worker and occupational therapist who offers rehabilitative services of an instructional nature to the blind. Although such instruction may be in the crafts, arts, or typewriting, the home teacher is interested in the client's total adjustment and in his emotional well-being.[13]

Aids to Teaching and Learning

The use of embossed type was one of the first educational methods employed in teaching the blind to read. Recognition of the value of embossed print came about quite by accident in a dramatic discovery by François Lesueur, a blind student. Lesueur was handling some printed sheets when he found that he could decipher, by touch, the words which had become perforated on the reverse side. Valentin Haüy, who in 1784 had been made head teacher at the first school for blind children in the world in Paris, proceeded to develop a system of raised letters and alphabets and to teach Lesueur to read and to write embossed type.[14] Louis Braille, also a Parisian and himself blinded by an accident in childhood, later created a system of reading for the blind by developing a series of raised dots representing letters of the alphabet, certain words, and combinations of letters which could be read by use of the fingertips.

Embossed books soon became a major teaching device in American schools for the blind. Each school was responsible for embossing

---

[13] Raymond M. Dickinson, "The Discipline of Home Teaching," *Proceedings of the Thirtieth Convention of the American Association of Workers for the Blind* (New York: 1956), p. 23.

[14] Farrell, *op. cit.*, p. 24.

its own books until 1879, when Congress allocated bonds of $10,000 a year for printing books for the use of children in institutions for the blind. The grant was later increased to $125,000 a year and the American Printing House for the Blind was established in Louisville, Kentucky, to administer the grant.[15] More recent congressional interest in the education of the blind was reflected in the Pratt-Smoot Law in 1931. This act authorized the appropriation of $100,000 a year to the Library of Congress for books with raised type for adults. In 1946, an annual grant of $1,125,000 was authorized, with $200,000 to be spent for embossed books and the remainder for Talking Books and Talking Book machines. It was not until 1952, however, that this legislation was amended to make the service available to children.[16]

In addition to "reading by touch" through the use of embossed materials, education of the blind now includes a newer mechanical method of "reading by ear" through Talking Books. In 1932, the American Foundation for the Blind began experimental work on methods which might be used to develop a long-playing durable record. By 1934 the first records, or Talking Books, were available. A printed book of average length can now be recorded on eighteen double-faced records with a reading time of about twelve hours. Children's Talking Books are highly significant educational equipment, since sounds can be reproduced to give the child a realistic conception of the situation dramatized.

Talking Books require a Talking Book machine to reproduce the discs. Although the machines can be purchased, they are also available on loan through agencies for the blind. These machines are the property of the Library of Congress and the applicant must have visual acuity of 20/200 or less to be eligible for use of the machine.

EMOTIONAL AND SOCIAL PROBLEMS
OF THE BLIND CHILD

Blindness or severe visual handicap places restrictions on the child's social development because his environment is circumscribed and his variety of experiences may be limited. He must depend upon others for his spatial and visual orientation and much is left to his willingness and ability to enjoy vicariously what the sighted child can readily perceive. He may be physically disfigured by surgery or have other

---

[15] *Ibid.*, p. 127.
[16] *Ibid.*, p. 128.

residuals of his blindness.   How the child approaches the adventures of growing up with these handicaps depends upon the stimulation, security, and freedom he is accorded by his family, his teachers, his peers, and his community.   Although blindness has long been dramatized as one of the most pitiful of all handicaps, the blind child does not "instinctively" feel frustrated and punished by his impairment.   He tends instead to absorb the feelings of acceptance, anxiety, or misgivings of those who have responsibility for his care.

Sommers' study of 120 residential school students, 14 to 21 years old, emphasized the influence of parental attitudes on the personality of the adolescent blind child.   The children selected were born blind or became so before the age of 6, had a sibling, and reflected an intellectual ability spread from low to superior mentality.

Parental reactions to the child's blindness reflected a wide variety of feelings, attitudes, and beliefs.   Characteristic remarks included: "What have we done that God should wish this on us?"[17]   "God has given us a cross to bear, we must make the best of it."[18]   "Perhaps it's me who's to blame . . . I resented this pregnancy."   "Whenever a child is born blind . . . people think that one of the parents have a disease."   "Our friends were sympathetic, but our family felt it was a disgrace and were ashamed."[19]   Several mothers worried that their blind child might want to marry.   One mother stated, "I am primarily concerned about marriage.   I don't see how a blind girl will ever solve this problem."   Another stated that if her son got married "it would be more than I could stand, as marriage is such a big job for sighted people."[20]

The methods of working through such feelings of shock, hostility, disappointment, and self-pity were similar to those of parents whose children suffer from other handicaps.   Although the pattern of response may not be consistent, the parent may accept the child's blindness, deny it, search endlessly for cures, camouflage feelings of rejection and guilt by overindulgence or overprotection, or simply tolerate the situation.

The study showed, too, that children were occupied with the mean-

---

[17] Vita Stein Sommers, *The Influence of Parental Attitudes and Social Environment on the Personality Development of the Adolescent Blind* (New York: American Foundation for the Blind, 1944), p. 45.

[18] *Ibid.*, p. 49.

[19] *Ibid.*, pp. 46–48.

[20] *Ibid.*, p. 39.

ing that blindness had for them. They were most aware of their handicap when people referred to their blindness or were too solicitous, when going to or eating in a strange place, when crossing streets or window shopping, and when participating in games, sports, and social gatherings. Their greatest wishes were to be independent; to be able to see movies, sports events, and nature; and, as one child said, "to see what people look like, especially my parents."[21] These children tended to worry most about school achievement, their occupational and financial future, and making a good impression on the opposite sex. Relatively few children expressed concern about or the desire for corrective eye surgery, but one child worried as to "whether I can make myself appear as sighted as possible in the seeing world."[22]

The growth, activity, and development of a blind child usually becomes the center of family life. His dependency upon his parents is greater than is that of the sighted child and consequently his expected role is somewhat different too. However, his basic needs for emancipation, for new experiences, and for love, recognition, and acceptance are like those of any child. His methods of handling his deprivations, frustrations, rejection, and unhappiness are likewise the same. He may withdraw and become depressed, or become aggressive and act out his hostilities; he may become anxious and hyperactive, or he may develop strong feelings of inferiority and reject or nurture his dependency. Sommers recognized a close relation between parental love and concern and the child's adjustment to life generally and to his handicap. The child who was spared "maudlin sentiment" and was given wholesome parental understanding was less affected by his blindness than was the child of overprotective and emotionally disturbed parents who themselves could not accept the child's handicap.[23]

THE PARTIALLY SEEING CHILD

The child with limited vision may be suffering from an eye condition that will increase his insecurity as he is faced with having to make constant adjustments to his changing vision. Sometimes there is facial disfigurement caused by strabismus, in which the eyes are crossed; nystagmus, in which there is rapid involuntary movement of the eye-

---

[21] *Ibid.*, pp. 34–35.

[22] *Ibid.*, pp. 36–37.

[23] *Ibid.*, p. 90.

ball; or enucleation of the eye.   To some children, wearing glasses or an artificial eye is also embarrassing.[24]

The child with some ability to see wants to use his eyes.   His visual activities are often curtailed, however, not only by his own limitations, but because the ophthalmologist so advises.   Aside from such extreme situations, the partially seeing child is more related to his environment because he is visually oriented to it, but he is apt to become depressed by his inability to engage in many activities that fully sighted children enjoy.   He may experience school failure due to his visual handicap and this may produce feelings of failure and frustration.

There has been considerable thought given to the wisdom of residential school education for the partially seeing child.   Children are often admitted to such facilities when the prognosis is poor and it is assumed that the child will have to live his life as a blind person. Since blindness does not always eventuate, the child is needlessly separated from his parents and expected to learn the skills of the blind while he has sight.   Children with a degree of vision want to, and should, use their eyes as long as they can unless it has been medically established that they should not do so.   If the seeing child is taught to read Braille, he will strain his eyes to do so since he will not want to learn by touch.   Partially seeing children are often sent to residential schools because it is believed that they will receive good optical care, but there is often little provision for individual treatment except on a voluntary basis or when an emergency arises.   Some institutions have no medical facilities, while others provide only for routine examinations.

Special education for partially sighted children has developed into a widely accepted concept because of the philosophy inherent in public school education.   It is now generally agreed that children should not be deprived of living in their own home and community simply because there are no special education facilities provided for them, and that it is incumbent on local school districts to educate the partially seeing child as well as the fully sighted.   This viewpoint has been reinforced by the development of special techniques by which the child may receive maximum education in terms of his own capacities and individual situation.

Typewriters have proved to be helpful to children in reducing eye-strain, and recording machines permit students to study the assign-

[24] William M. Cruickshank, *Psychology of Exceptional Children and Youth* (Englewood Cliffs, New Jersey: Prentice-Hall, 1955), pp. 276–277.

ments and transcribe them directly on the typewriter. Radios have also been used in the instruction of the partially seeing child; and magnifying devices, although not considered useful or beneficial to children with certain types of visual problems, have proved of value to others.

Copy stands, maps, globes, and other devices have been found to be excellent teaching materials. Paper which is slightly rough and unlined, pencils which are heavy and soft, pens capable of reproducing broad heavy lines, and soft chalk are a part of the classroom equipment. The distribution of light to prevent glare for study and blackboard work, as well as light-colored woodwork, are equally important as sight-saving devices.[25]

These devices are useful in the education of the partially seeing child, but the teacher, her training, her understanding of the child's handicap and its meaning to him and to his parents, and her ability to appraise his potential for learning and social growth, serve an equally important purpose. As Winifred Hathaway suggested, the effective teacher must understand the child's total pattern of behavior as it reflects his present situation and as it will affect his future.[26]

The Deaf and Hard-of-Hearing Child

The child with impaired hearing has had a strange world history. Although he has often been considered mentally deficient and without the intellect to think and speak, teachers, doctors, and other practitioners have devoted centuries of searching effort to give him the ability to think, to talk, to hear, and to learn.

A variety of terms has been developed to describe hearing handicap, but the word "deaf" is commonly used in reference to any hearing impairment. This is unfortunate, since this term does not indicate the amount of usable hearing a child has, nor the onset of his condition, although these factors are significant in relation to the acquisition of language and to the child's potential social, emotional, and educational adjustment.

The speech therapist, who is interested in the child's ability to communicate verbally, appraises the "hard-of-hearing" child as one who

---

[25] Hathaway, *op. cit.*, pp. 85–92.

[26] Winifred Hathaway, *Education and Health of the Partially-Seeing Child* (New York: National Society for the Prevention of Blindness, 1947), p. 128.

has sufficient hearing to learn to reproduce speech and to understand speech and language naturally by ear.[27] A residential school describes the hard-of-hearing child as one who cannot hear within normal distance, but whose hearing becomes usable through loud talking, amplification, or mechanical aids.[28] Although the emphasis is somewhat different, both sources agree that the hard-of-hearing child should not be considered deaf if he possesses some usable hearing.

The speech therapist describes the "deafened" child as one who has learned language and speech naturally, by ear, but who no longer has sufficient hearing to enable him to hear his own voice or that of others. The deafened child, then, is one who had normal hearing during the time that speech and language are usually learned. The term "adventitiously deaf" is also used to describe the child born with normal speech and hearing but who became deaf before or after reaching the age at which speech and language skills are acquired. Deafness is acquired after birth in about 50 per cent of all cases, and 97 per cent of all deaf children become deaf at birth or before the age of five.[29]

The "deaf" child is one who did not have sufficient hearing at the time that speech normally develops to permit the natural acquisition of language. If born deaf, this child is also referred to as being "congenitally" deaf.

Deafness has been termed a dysfunction of the ears and of the listening mind as well.[30] Since hearing, speech, and language are so interrelated in communication and socialization, they cannot be regarded separately from each other. Impaired hearing therefore represents a complex problem not only to the child, his teachers, and his parents, but to the fields of medicine, neurology, audiometry, and psychology. The problem is further complicated by age, intelligence, motivation, training,[31] and the subjective factors relating to each child's acceptance of his handicap and to his parents' understanding and willingness to help the child cope with his situation. It is estimated that there are

---

[27] Wendell Johnson, Spencer F. Brown, James F. Curtis, Clarence W. Edney, and Jacqueline Keaster, *Speech Handicapped School Children* (New York: Harper and Brothers, 1956), p. 381.

[28] *The Deaf Child and the California School for the Deaf* (Berkeley: California School for the Deaf, 1955), p. 4.

[29] *Ibid.*, pp. 7–8.

[30] William G. Hardy and John E. Bordley, "Treating Young Children for Hearing Impairment," *Children*, Vol. 2, No. 5 (September–October 1955), p. 175.

[31] Cruickshank, *op. cit.*, p. 121.

some two million children with hearing impairment in the United States.

ETIOLOGY

An examination of 2,000 children under six at the Hearing and Speech Center at Johns Hopkins Hospital indicated that 75 per cent of these children derived hearing impairment from obstetrical complications, injury to the auditory nerve or central nervous system, anemia connected with Rh incompatibility of mother and fetus, severe viral infections during the first six to eight months of life, prolonged anoxia at birth, or virus infections of the mother during the early months of pregnancy.[32]

"Conductive defect" is related to impairment of the middle ear and the hearing loss may be severe but it does not result in total deafness. It is usually acquired by measles, mumps, whooping cough, scarlet fever, allergies, middle ear infections, and diseased tonsils and adenoids. The child speaks with a soft voice, thinks other people mumble, and has slowly deteriorating speech. This type of defect leaves the child with a generally hopeful prognosis, in that it is amenable to cure or improvement; or, if the loss is severe, the child may benefit by the use of a hearing aid.

"Perceptive defect" is related to inner ear impairment and the loss may be mild or total. It is frequently congenital in nature and is often due to the mother's illness during pregnancy. Influenza, German measles (rubella), mumps, or meningitis may affect the fetus and leave a residual hearing impairment. The condition can seldom be improved by medical treatment and may be so severe that the child cannot be helped to hear speech even with a hearing aid. In contrast to the child with a conductive impairment, this child speaks loudly in order to hear himself speak. His voice may have a hollow sound and speech inflections will be limited or completely lacking.

A child may also have a mixed impairment in which both the middle and inner ear have been affected. Improvement will depend upon the treatment for the middle ear infection and a hearing aid may be used with some potential for success.[33]

---

[32] Hardy and Bordley, *op. cit.*, p. 173.

[33] *A Guide to Better Hearing*, prepared under the direction of Geraldine Garrison, Bulletin No. 52 (Hartford: Connecticut State Department of Education, Bureau of School and Community Services, 1952), pp. 20–22.

Some children may be handicapped by psychogenic hearing impairment in which there is no known pathology of the hearing organs. In some instances, too, children seemingly ignore sound. Sound penetrates the brain but brain lesions or developmental deficiencies block its relationship to meanings, thus interfering with the development of normal responses and language.[34]

Deafness-Speech: A Multiple Problem

Since deafness creates a barrier to speech, the child with a hearing handicap may have serious limitations in acquiring knowledge, stimulation, and social experiences. He will make effort to help himself, however, and he will gain some security in handling language skills if he is given understanding support by his parents and teachers.

The child with a hearing problem will begin to watch the speaker's face for lip movements, gestures, and other significant evidences of communication. He learns to read lips, first in three or four words, then phrases, and, with continued opportunity to read lips, he manages whole sentences which have meaning to him. It has been emphasized that the child expects people to talk to him and that he must be helped to become conscious of voice in order to learn vowels and consonants by sight and touch. Whereas the deafened and hard-of-hearing child can talk, the deaf child cannot learn to talk because he has never heard words and can therefore derive no meaning from them. On the other hand, a child may have good hearing acuity but become functionally deaf because he has never had the opportunity to *learn* to hear.[35] In order for any child with a hearing handicap to make full use of his hearing or learning potential, parents and teachers should understand the developmental processes of oral communication and the need to speak in clear and simple terms, repeating the same words many times until the child learns to relate to them and to use them in his speech, reading, and writing.

For many years it was assumed that the "deaf mute" did not speak because the organs of speech were linked with defective hearing. The inability of the deaf child to speak, however, is a consequence of deafness rather than a symptom of speech defect. As has been pointed out, if the ear does not customarily receive and pattern vocal speech, the organs of speech cannot reproduce these. It is now apparent that

---

[34] Hardy and Bordley, *op. cit.*, p. 174.
[35] *Ibid.*, p. 175.

the quality of the tone of the human voice and the ability to speak are dependent upon the ability to hear.[36]   It is known too, that the deaf infant who cannot hear his own voice or that of others will be deprived of a hearing vocabulary.   This is, in effect, reaffirmation that a child talks because he hears, and as he hears, and that he learns to talk by relating sounds to meanings as he develops use of language, comprehension, and verbal facility.

MEASURING HEARING POTENTIAL

In order to understand hearing losses, it is necessary to know something about the quality and measurement of speech sounds. *Frequency*, or pitch of sound, is measured by the number of cycles per second; speech is normally heard in the range of 300 to 3,000 cycles per second. The other important unit of measurement is *intensity*, or loudness, which is recorded in decibels and expresses a ratio of one sound intensity to another. The pure tone audiometer is now the standard instrument for both individual and group hearing testing. It is calibrated to produce sounds at different frequency and intensity to measure acuity and range of hearing. The subject listens and indicates by hand gesture when he hears and when he no longer hears a sound. The point at which he consistently responds correctly is considered the threshold for that frequency. Each frequency is tested separately and each ear is tested individually for each frequency.

The child with a mild hearing loss of 20 to 25 decibels (db) in the better ear can learn speech by ear, while the child with marginal loss of 30 to 40 db will have difficulty in understanding speech by ear at a distance of more than a few feet, and in following conversation in a group. Children with moderate losses of 40 to 60 db in the better ear have enough hearing to learn language and speech by ear when the sound is amplified for them and when the auditory sense is aided by the visual. Children in these three categories are considered to be hard-of-hearing.[37]

The child with severe losses of 60 to 75 db is borderline between hard-of-hearing and deaf. These children have trainable residual hearing, but their language and speech will not develop simultaneously

[36] Harry Best, *Deafness and the Deaf in the United States* (New York: The Macmillan Company, 1943), pp. 118–119.

[37] Alice Streng, Waring J. Fitch, LeRoy D. Hedgecock, James W. Phillips, and James A. Carrell, *Hearing Therapy for Children* (New York: Grune and Stratton, 1955), pp. 164–165.

and they will have to learn to communicate through use of specialized techniques. Children with profound losses of greater than 75 db cannot learn to understand language even when it is amplified by sound.[38]

Speech audiometry is a technique based on the use of speech itself as the testing stimulus in an evaluation of the child's hearing ability in relation to speech.

The speech audiometer has been described as a high quality public address system with necessary amplifiers so that speech is reproduced at a high degree of fidelity. Children may be tested with earphones by listening to material on tape, to phonographic recording, or to live voice. Younger children are tested by identifying pictures which the therapist also identifies at varying levels of intensity, thus establishing the child's ability to hear speech. Alice Streng and her associates state:

The level at which the child responds correctly 50% of the time is called the *threshold of intelligibility*. This is somewhat above the *threshold of audibility*, which is the point at which the speech is heard but not necessarily understood.[39]

METHODS OF EDUCATION

For many years the majority of deaf and hard-of-hearing children were educated in state institutions. The earlier privately financed institutions were benevolent in nature and their sponsors and administrators often described the institution's service as being a charitable enterprise. Deaf children themselves were variously regarded by the citizenry and by the institution as being scarcely more intellectually gifted than idiots, inferior creatures of God, doomed to a life of dreary desolation, and incapable of becoming self-supporting, adequate citizens.

As in the case of education for the blind, much emphasis was placed upon the vocational preparation of the child. This attitude is summarized by the British author who wrote:

The American view generally saw deaf children as members of two communities: an economic one in which they would have to try to earn their living in competition with hearing people, and a social community which only partly overlapped that of normal society.[40]

---

[38] *Ibid.*

[39] *Ibid.*, p. 105.

[40] Kenneth W. Hodgson, *The Deaf and Their Problems* (London: Watts and Company, 1953), p. 270.

The day school movement for the education of the hearing-handicapped child grew out of the conviction that children should be spared long-term institutional experience whenever possible. After the Horace Mann School of Boston was established as the first day school for deaf children in 1869, scores of others were organized, thus bringing into being an era of growing belief that a child is best cared for in his own home and that the community has a responsibility to provide special educational services for him.

Several types of teaching techniques have been employed in the education of the deaf. One of the most traditional of these in America was instruction based on a "sign language" which had originated in France. Sign language was accompanied by "finger spelling," in which several letters of the alphabet were represented on the hand. The "speaker" also used gestures and pantomimed with bodily movements to add shades of meaning to his communication. The manual alphabet method and writing were also used in instruction. The value of these was to stimulate the student to have an understanding and an ability to use written language. Manual signs are finger representations of the letters of the alphabet in which 26 hand positions are used. One of the major limitations of this method is that it is tiring to receive whole sentences letter by letter. All sign language, however, tended to isolate the child since he could only "talk" to those similarly educated. More importantly, it made deafness an obvious handicap which set the child apart from other children.[41]

Lip reading or speech reading has now replaced sign language in the schools. The child is taught to give close attention to the speaker's lip movements and to know the meaning of facial expressions, gestures, and other clues which give meaning to what is being said. A child will understand the person who speaks at a moderate rate and articulates clearly and will handle language that is familiar to him far better than words with which he has had no experience. By use of the oral method, children are taught to speak words they cannot hear. Hard-of-hearing children are also instructed by the use of hearing aids and other amplified devices.

Teachers can help to facilitate the child's ability and security in lip reading. The child should be seated in the classroom so that he can turn around to see what other children are saying. It is important to remember that the hard-of-hearing child loses a great deal of informa-

---

[41] Harry Best, *The Deaf* (New York: Thomas Y. Crowell Company, 1914), pp. 278–279.

tion about his world and should be given an opportunity to have adequate visual stimulation. The child should be encouraged to watch the speaker's lips, mouth, and face, but the speaker should talk naturally, in a moderate tone, and without exaggerated articulation. Teachers and parents will learn that the child may hear better on some days than others and that children who have defects may tire more quickly than those with normal hearing.[42] The child with a hearing defect must depend greatly upon his sensorial environment and upon the accommodations that the speaker makes for him. Lip reading is difficult in a poorly lighted room or when the speaker fails to stand in one place, puts his hands before his mouth, or otherwise makes it difficult to follow his speech.

THE USE OF HEARING AIDS

The purpose of a hearing aid is to bring sound more loudly to the listener's ear and to make speech intelligible. The electrical hearing aid is actually a miniature telephone in which the batteries, not the human voice, supply the energy by which a person hears. The receiver in the ear converts electric current back into sound. Most hearing aids have a vacuum tube amplifier to increase the weak current from the microphone from the stronger current of the receiver.[43]

Child and parental attitudes toward the use of hearing aids are reflected in a National Research Council follow-up study of 37 junior and senior high school students wearing hearing aids. The study revealed that, although these children had hearing losses from 63.9 to 98.6 per cent, the majority did not wear the aid during all of their waking hours. Some wore it only to school, one only wore it when practicing piano, and another only when listening to the radio.[44] Boys were not particularly concerned with the appearance of the aid, but girls felt it detracted from their physical appearance, made them seem different from other girls, and interfered with their social relations.

Parents were influential in the child's reaction to the use of the hearing aid. Two parents would not allow their children to wear aids

---

[42] June Miller, *The Child With a Hearing Loss* (Topeka: Kansas State Department of Education, 1952), pp. 9–10.

[43] Hallowell Davis, editor, *Hearing and Deafness* (New York: Murray Hill Books, 1947), p. 161.

[44] Arthur I. Gates and Rose E. Kushner, *Learning to Use Hearing Aids* (New York: Bureau of Publications, Teachers' College, Columbia University, 1946), pp. 4–5.

outside of school despite the child's serious hearing handicap.[45]   Parents found it easier to accept the hearing aid if deafness was not hereditary and if their attitude toward the handicap itself was not negative.[46]

The Speech Handicapped Child

Speech is considered defective when (1) it is not readily audible or intelligible; (2) it is vocally or visibly unpleasant; (3) it is labored in production or lacking in normal rhythm and stress; and (4) it is linguistically deficient or inappropriate to the individual in terms of age, sex, and physical development.   In fact, any deviation which interferes with the speaker's ability to communicate and to be understood by the normally hearing listener may be considered a speech defect.[47]

Because we have been taught to be articulate, to express our feelings about things, to verbalize freely with our fellows, and to learn by group participation and interaction, fluency and other qualities of speech become highly important to parents of small children.   Their pride in the child's "first words," the reassuring knowledge that "now he is beginning to talk," the good humor over the child's experimentation with words and phrases are all a part of the culture of childhood. It is little wonder, then, that the child feels the adults' urgency that he speak and that parents grow anxious when their child cannot do so.

It has been estimated that two million, or 5 per cent of all children five to twenty-one years of age have some speech disorder which is detrimental to school achievement or to social development. Speech pathology is often associated with other handicaps such as impaired hearing, cerebral palsy, cleft palate, and retarded speech development.   It was estimated that half of the children with a speech disorder have functional articulatory problems and that more than a quarter of a million children stutter.[48]

In 1952–53 it was reported that 307,000 speech handicapped children,

[45] *Ibid.*, p. 12.

[46] *Ibid.*, p. 65.

[47] Jon Eisenson, "The Nature of Defective Speech," in Cruickshank, *op. cit.*, pp. 184–185.

[48] Committee on the Mid-century White House Conference American Speech and Hearing Association "Speech Disorders and Speech Correction," in *The Journal of Speech and Hearing Disorders*, Vol. XVII, No. 2, June 1952, p. 130.

(twice the number of other handicapped children) were receiving special educational services in the public elementary and secondary schools.[49] It is apparent, however, that the majority of children having speech defects were not receiving special educational services.

Speech is a developmental process with identifiable elements peculiar to the individual child and his personality. Gesture and articulation accentuate and give color and meaning to speech, while tonal quality marks it as either pleasant or unpleasant to the listener. The acquisition of words, the use of language, the level of fluency, and the control of voice define the quality of speech production.

Speech defect manifests itself in terms of anatomical, physiological, and psychogenic maladjustment. Many children have some difficulty in articulation or sound production, which results in omissions, distortions, and substitution of speech sounds. Others have defects of phonation or the quality of voice production relating to loudness or variation of pitch. Stuttering has been diagnosed as a rhythm defect, and language dysfunction may result in delayed speech or aphasia. Some speech defects are related to defective hearing, cleft palate, malocclusions of the teeth, and other dental anomalies. In addition, children with normal speech mechanism may have articulation or other speech defects with functional or psychogenic causes.[50] Van Riper points out that speech is defective when it calls attention to itself and interferes with the processes of verbal communication to such an extent that the speaker is maladjusted to his environment.[51]

STUTTERING

The diagnosis and treatment of stuttering has been a concern of educators, philosophers, physicians, physiologists, and psychologists for centuries. Celsus Aurelius Cornelius, the medical encyclopedist, who began his studies before the birth of Christ, advocated that the stutterer use gargles, massage the tongue and throat, and eat pungent substances to cure the faulty articulation caused by diseases of the tongue. Johann Konrad Amman, a seventeenth century Swiss physician,

---

[49] Romaine P. Mackie and Lloyd M. Dunn, *State Certification Requirements for Teachers of Exceptional Children*, Bulletin No. 1, United States Office of Education, U.S. Department of Health, Education and Welfare (Washington, D.C.: Government Printing Office, 1954), p. 39.

[50] Eisenson, *op. cit.*, pp. 185–188.

[51] Charles Van Riper, *Speech Correction, Principles and Methods* (New York: Prentice-Hall, 1939), p. 51.

called stuttering "hesitantia" and believed it was "due to a vicious habit." Moses Mendlessohn, the logician, thought that stuttering was due to a collision between many ideas flowing simultaneously from the brain. Others wrote of the necessity of regulating the respiration of the stutterer, while some believed that stuttering was due to the coldness or the consistency of the tongue.[52]

Stuttering affected 280,000 children, or seven children per thousand, in 1950. It has been defined as a defect in rhythm accompanied by blocks of silence which may or may not be evidenced by muscular contortions, facial strain, or inappropriate bodily movements. The stuttering child may repeat a speech sound, word, or phrase in emitting the word (for example, pa-pa-pa-paper). If his speech is so blocked that it is not free, the child will strain until the muscle relaxes and he blurts out the word. Although stuttering often appears to be physical in nature, it is not related to pathology of the throat, speech mechanism, or intellectual capacity of the stutterer.[53]

Stuttering has also been defined as an "anticipatory, apprehensive, hypertonic reaction" which occurs when the speaker expects to stutter, dreads the experience, and becomes anxious and tense in anticipating or avoiding stuttering. In short, stuttering occurs because the stutterer attempts "to prevent the occurrence of something he expects, dreads, and would rather avoid."[54]

As there is no known organic condition which results in or contributes to stuttering, there is no known "cure" for this type of speech defect. Therapists, however, have observed some characteristics of children who stutter, and have contributed to an understanding of some facets of the problem.

Stuttering is a condition of childhood and is frequently related to late speech development. The stutterer is known to have slower responses of the jaw, lips, and tongue and there are metabolic differences between the stuttering and nonstuttering child. Stuttering tends to run in families and eight boys to every one girl stutter at 36 months of age. It has been observed that the stutterer lacks voice inflection and that he is more apt to stutter when he attempts to achieve natural inflection. There is also evidence that stuttering changes as conversa-

---

[52] G. M. Klingbeil, "The Historical Background of the Modern Speech Clinic," *Journal of Speech Disorders*, Vol. 4, No. 1 (March 1939), pp. 115–131.

[53] *Stuttering* (Hartford: Connecticut State Department of Education, Bureau of School and Community Services, 1952), pp. 1–2.

[54] Johnson, et. al., *op. cit.*, p. 217.

tional relationships change and there is reason to believe that stuttering is a symptom of inner conflict.[55]

The average stuttering child has difficulty with about 10 per cent of the words he speaks and, although his stuttering varies, it usually lasts two seconds or less. Stuttering begins generally at the age of three. The child has his greatest problems with words that begin sentences, that are long, and that begin with consonants rather than vowels.[56] Stuttering is not controllable and the child cannot cease to stutter on demand.

APHASIA

Aphasia is a language disability related to the central nervous system and to neurological disorder. The child is unable to associate words with experiences and he is either unable to understand what others are saying or he cannot speak.

The child who has "expressive aphasia" cannot relate the words he hears to that part of the nervous system which is used in speaking. Although he understands the word "cat" he cannot reproduce the word because of a brain deficiency. The child with "receptive aphasia" knows the spoken word but cannot associate it with a real cat. He can hear words but he cannot comprehend them since his impairment makes it impossible for him to understand what he hears.[57]

ARTICULATION PROBLEMS

The child with an articulation disorder may omit, substitute, or distort speech sounds. He may say "ra" for "rat" or "wat," thus omitting the "t" in one instance and substituting "w" for "r" in the other. Speech distortion is more likely to occur in the older child, who will attempt to approximate the proper sound but whose reproduction will be faulty.

Articulatory disorders are due to constitutional factors, such as dental irregularities, malformation of the hard palate and tongue, and mouth injuries. The child may have articulation difficulties because of faulty learning which can be traced to lack of motivation and stimula-

---

[55] Robert West, "The Pathology of Stuttering," *The Nervous Child*, Vol. II, No. 2 (January 1943), pp. 96–106.

[56] Johnson, et al., *op. cit.*, pp. 227–229.

[57] Helmer R. Myklebust, "Training Aphasic Children," *The Volta Review*, Vol. 57, No. 4 (April 1955), pp. 150–151.

tion or to imitation of poor speech.   As in all speech disorders, the functional or emotional causes of articulatory defect are an important part of the diagnostic evaluation.

Cleft Palate Speech

Cleft palate and harelip are deformities of the mouth which exist at birth.   In this condition, the soft palate, hard palate, jaw, and lip are split or cleft.   The nose and mouth have no separating wall but are one cavity.   This defect is very prevalent, but its cause is unknown.

The child has defective speech because his mouth parts are incomplete and abnormally located.   When the soft palate is split or absent, the child cannot properly regulate air or the sound needed in speech production.   The child will also develop faulty habits of muscle movement in the mouth in making the sounds of speech.   The cleft palate child may be helped by surgery, speech training, education, and vocational guidance, each carefully appraised in relation to his readiness for treatment.

The Role of the Parent and Teacher

Teachers have a responsibility to recognize and diagnose simple speech defects and to describe the child's symptoms to the speech therapist.   The teacher should observe the extent of the child's bodily coordination and recognize that the stuttering child cannot avoid swaying, squinting, grinding his teeth, or grimacing any more than he can avoid the speech defect itself.   There is need to be aware of the length of attention span, the silent reading ability, the nature and incidence of stuttering or other speech difficulties, the home situation, and the parents' attitudes toward speech.   The teacher should not ignore the child's speech handicap but should attempt to understand it as a disturbing and unpredictable involuntary activity over which the child has no control.[58]

Since the mother is the dominant person in the child's first years of life, it is important that she understand that speech expresses not only the child's relationship to her but her attitudes toward him as well. Speech is a reflection of thought and of the feelings which the child experiences; it is, in fact, a substitute or subterfuge for action.   Since

---

[58] Virginia S. Sanderson, *What Should I Know About Speech Defects?* (Columbus: The Ohio State University, Bureau of Special and Adult Education, 1946), p. 10.

the child so readily absorbs his parents' repressions, expectations, frustrations, and failures, all of these reactions may be hidden behind defective speech.

The young child may have delayed or distorted speech for a variety of reasons. His parents may be placing too much emphasis upon perfection, not only in speech but in other areas of the child's life. He may begin to stutter when a new baby arrives, when parents die or separate, or when he is placed in competition with a brother or sister. Stuttering may also begin when he is physically tired or ill or when he is under emotional stress of any kind.

Parents and teachers are advised that there are some things which they can do to help the child who has a speech difficulty. It is best to discuss the child's problem with him and to offer him support and help in effecting whatever change he can make for himself. He needs responsibilities that can culminate in success and praise so that he feels valued as a person. He should be encouraged to talk and he should not be reminded that he stutters, either in words, gestures, or embarrassed listening. The stuttering child has a right to express himself in whatever way he can manage and he should be regarded as doing the best he can under the circumstances.

The Cerebral Palsied Child

Cerebral palsy is the second greatest crippler of children. It is also one of the most serious conditions resulting from brain injury, since the child is often afflicted with multiple handicaps. Cerebral palsy is a neuromuscular condition caused by damage to some part of the brain which affects the functioning of the extremities and may also involve speech, hearing, and vision.[59] Because of the "abnormal" behavior of the cerebral palsied child, he is often regarded as being mentally retarded when in fact he may be of high, average, or superior intelligence.

The cerebral palsied child is affected by several neuromuscular disabilities. "Athetosis," which represents 40 per cent of all cerebral palsies, is characterized by uncontrolled and unpredictable involuntary motion. "Spasticity" accounts for 40 to 50 per cent of all cerebral palsies and is due to restricted movement because of contracture of

---

[59] Valerie T. Hawkins, "Educating the Brain-Injured Child," in Vol. III of *Special Education for the Exceptional*, editors, Merle E. Frampton and Elena D. Gall (Boston: F. Porter Sargent, 1956), p. 69.

the muscles. Eight to 10 per cent of the cerebral palsied suffer from "ataxia," which is characterized by disturbance of balance and direction. "Rigidity" involves lack of muscle tone and muscle resistance when the joints are flexed. "Tremor," like rigidity, is found in only a small percentage of cases.[60]

EXTENT OF CEREBRAL PALSY

Earlier studies indicated that the number of cerebral palsied per 1,000 school age children ranged from three to six. In 1952, 10 per cent, or 22,397, of all children receiving physicians' services under the crippled children's programs were cerebral palsied. A recent study in New York indicates that about 512 children per 100,000 under 21 have cerebral palsy. If applicable nation-wide, this ratio would mean that there are about 285,000 cerebral palsied children in the United States. It is estimated that with an annual birth rate of 3.8 during the present decade, the number of children who will be born with congenital cerebral palsy each year, will almost equal the number now receiving physicians' services in any one year, under the crippled children's programs throughout the country.[61]

ETIOLOGY

The prenatal causes of cerebral palsy are classified as hereditary or genetic, and congenitally acquired. Congenitally acquired cerebral palsy may be caused by anoxia, cerebral hemorrhage, infection, metabolic upset, malnutrition, or Rh incompatibility. The most common causes of cerebral palsy, however, are those which are in effect from the onset of labor to the time of immediate birth. Actually, anything happening to the brain after birth can also cause cerebral palsy.[62]

Like mental retardation, cerebral palsy has been described as a condition rather than a disease. Cerebral palsy is not progressive or contagious but it does involve neurophysical and neuropsychological symptoms which categorize it as a disease.[63]

---

[60] Arthur S. Hill, "The Cerebral Palsied Child," in Frampton and Gall, *op. cit.*, III, pp. 78–79.

[61] Lesser and Hunt, *op. cit.*, p. 167.

[62] Meyer A. Perlstein, "Medical Aspects of Cerebral Palsy," *American Journal of Occupational Therapy*, Vol. IV. No. 2 (March–April 1950), pp. 47–52.

[63] William M. Cruickshank and George M. Raus, *Cerebral Palsy, Its Individual and Community Problems* (Syracuse: Syracuse University Press, 1955), p. 3.

As in cases of mental retardation, there are many nonmedical problems which confront the cerebral palsied child and his parents. Because of the nature of the handicap, his limited and exaggerated body movements, and his general appearance, parents sometimes pretend that the child is ill and that he will recover. This belief may lead them to seek constant medical advice in the hope that their convictions will eventually be substantiated. There is also a tendency to relate the condition to "bad" heredity or to be self-blaming for the child's problems. Further concern about future pregnancies may result from a fear that any other children will be similarly afflicted. Since any of these attitudes tend to create anxiety and misgivings, the child may be burdened by parental rejection or overprotection. At any rate, he will be further handicapped by an absence of the kind of parent-child relationship needed as a basis for the many adjustments that must be made in the future.

The child suffering from cerebral palsy must come to terms with much more than his physical disability and its limitations. The involuntary activity of the athetoid child can be exhausting, whereas the spastic child may find his excess tension equally fatiguing and restraining.[64] These children want to engage in the activities of childhood and they need the help of their parents and teachers in setting realistic goals for themselves.

EARLY TRAINING

In their care of a child with cerebral palsy, parents play the role of physiotherapist and teacher. The parent who helps the child in early muscle training, eating, dressing, relaxation, and other means of comfort and survival, communicates a great deal that will also help the child accept whatever progress he may make. The mutuality of this effort will do much to give the child the security and courage needed to accomplish other things. Through the child-parent relationship the use of play equipment can also be exploited. Toys should be selected which the child can manipulate and which will encourage big grasp and long reach if the child is not too severely handicapped. Older, more active children can benefit from large outdoor play space, which encourages the use of the large thigh, shoulder, and trunk muscles used in running, jumping, and climbing.[65]

---

[64] Selma J. Glick and Catherine Donnell, "Nonmedical Problems of the Child With Cerebral Palsy," *Nursing Outlook*, Vol. 1, No. 2 (February 1953), p. 102.

[65] Ruth Hansen, *The Parents' Role in the Cerebral Palsy Problem* (Los Angeles: Orthopaedic Hospital, undated), p. 16.

The home should be furnished and arranged for the comfort of the cerebral palsied child. He should not be expected to adjust to adult-sized furniture, to rugs that are easily tripped over, or to fragile furniture that tips easily. Braces are hard on carpeting, but a highly polished floor is dangerous to the child wearing braces. Much can be accomplished through a willingness to create a home that suggests to the child an understanding of his day-by-day needs.

Activities which contribute to the mutual satisfaction of the child and his family also tend to minimize the child's feelings of difference and prevent many of the negative feelings that can develop when the child is not regarded as a functioning member of the family.

Group Counseling With Parents

Group counseling sessions have gained wide use as a means of helping parents discuss mutual concerns and problems.

A report of the Parents' League in New Jersey reveals that parents attempted to use these sessions to meet their own needs in relation to the cerebral palsied child. Many expressed a belief in old wives' tales, such as, "the child could not walk because all of her strength was going to her long hair." There was concern and embarrassment over the unfavorable attention given to the child on the street, and resentment over the derogatory and uncomplimentary comments directed to them, as parents. They talked about problems of discipline and the teaching of hygiene and cleanliness, but they were also concerned with their own personal inadequacy, with the cost of medical care, and the many problems of dealing with a cerebral palsied child. Although critical because the medical profession has not provided a cure, these parents also evidenced justifiable concern for their child's total health problems.[66]

Education for the Child

Cerebral palsied children who have only a mild motor handicap may attend and participate in school with other children. Children with additional intellectual, hearing, or visual handicaps may attend special classes within the regular school if there are special services available to meet their individual needs. Children who are handicapped by

---

[66] Harry V. Bice and Margaret G. Davitt Holden, "Group Counseling With Mothers of Children With Cerebral Palsy," *Journal of Social Casework*, Vol. XXX, No. 3 (March 1949), pp. 104–109.

more severe incoordination without other handicaps may attend classes designed for the orthopedically handicapped. Special classes have also been established for the mentally retarded cerebral palsied child whose motor activity is severely affected. Children who are too handicapped to come to school may be taught by a home teacher or receive education in an institution. These alternatives are, of course, contingent upon the type of services available in the community.[67]

Because of the multiple handicaps which the cerebral palsied child may have, the services of skilled personnel are necessary to insure proper diagnosis and the best educational placement possible. Placement follow-up is equally important and the services of the school physician, nurse, psychologist, social worker, and specially trained teachers are needed to assure the child's physical, social, and intellectual growth.

Greater emphasis is now being placed upon a nursery school experience for all children with special handicaps. Some nursery centers have demonstrated the particular value of such a facility to the preschool cerebral palsied child.

The Cardiopathic Child: Rheumatic Fever

Almost three-quarters of a million children are suffering from rheumatic fever, the disease adjudged to be responsible for 90 per cent of the chronic heart defect in childhood.[68] In 1955, over 3,000 children were diagnosed as having acute rheumatic fever, according to state reports from agencies administering crippled children's services under Title V, Part 2, of the Social Security Act.[69]

It is known that rheumatic fever is a disease which makes its first attack upon children five to ten years of age, that it is not contagious, that there is a familial tendency toward it, that it is found in the lower economic groups most frequently, and that early diagnosis is difficult. Its deeper seriousness is reflected in the knowledge that after the first attack two out of three children are left with residual heart damage and vulnerability to further attacks. Each subsequent siege tends to

---

[67] Hill, *op. cit.*, pp. 88–90.

[68] Lesser and Hunt, *op. cit.*, pp. 166–167.

[69] United States Children's Bureau, *Public Programs for Crippled Children, 1955,* Statistical Series No. 40, U.S. Department of Health, Education and Welfare (Washington, D.C.: Government Printing Office, 1955), Table 11, p. 25.

damage further the tissues and muscles of the heart, although it may affect the joints, nervous system, skin, or any other part of the body.

ETIOLOGY AND EFFECT

Although there is little knowledge of its causes, various types of infection, such as streptococcus sore throat, scarlet fever, and otitis media are known to trigger a rheumatic infection in the susceptible individual. Permanent heart damage may be evidenced by valvular dysfunction, heart muscle damage, or involvement of the pericardium, the protective membrane enclosing the heart.[70]

The earliest manifestations of rheumatic fever may be chorea, in which the child may change in personality due to organic disease within the brain. The child may seem to be misbehaving when in fact he is confused and does not understand his own behavior.[71]

The medical, psychological, and social aspects of rheumatic fever are perhaps more alarming to parents than those associated with any other illness. The child's reaction to his illness will depend upon his age, the quality of his relations with his family, their feelings about his illness and prolonged dependency, and how he is helped to understand his physical limitations and to accept medical treatment and supervision, inactivity, and long-term convalescence.

The child who has rheumatic fever is deprived of many of the normal outlets for expression, independence, social maturation, formal education, and self-assertiveness. The hospitalization of the very ill child usually necessitates long separation from his parents, siblings, and peers, and interrupts the continuity of these important relations. Returning home, he finds himself wholly dependent upon his mother at a time when he would normally seek to broaden his social horizon and move toward greater independence. He has to remain physically quiet at an age characterized by hyperactivity, adventure, and sharing of childhood experiences. The most dangerous effect stems perhaps from his physical incapacity to solve his emotional problems aggressively and to protect himself from the impact of his unresolved im-

---

[70] Lillian Rosenson and Beatrice Schenck De Regniers, "The Cardiopathic-Rheumatic Fever," in Vol. II of *Special Education for the Exceptional*, editors, Merle R. Frampton and Elena D. Gall (Boston: F. Porter Sargent, 1955), pp. 452–453.

[71] Eckka Gordon, "Medical Social Aspects of the Problem of Rheumatic Fever," *Bulletin of the St. Francis Sanatorium*, Roslyn, New York, Vol. 10, No. 1 (January 1953), p. 40.

pulses. A child normally handles his intense feelings about things in competitive play and physical activity, and works through his parental needs by developing meaningful peer relations. Dr. Irene Josselyn appraises the child's dilemma this way:

The highest frequency of initial onset of rheumatic fever is coincident with the age at which the child is either seeking or has successfully made this pragmatic transfer of his conflicting impulses. . . . Rheumatic fever and its complications make this . . . solution relatively impossible. . . . Furthermore, and more significant, aggressive behavior, expressed in the healthy pattern of the normal child through aggressive, active games, is again dangerous. Such expression of aggression carries with it the possible punishment of death![72]

Parents of the child suffering from rheumatic fever realize, justifiably, that their child has a serious disease that may cause death. Some parents, however, live in constant fear that the child will die suddenly and this anxiety is often unconsciously transmitted to the patient, regardless of his age, and to other members of the family. A long illness and convalescence tend to disturb normal family living, and constant responsibility for the child's physical care can impose physical strain upon the parents. Prolonged medical supervision and treatment are expensive and parents grow apprehensive at the sick child's demands, regression, competitive sibling relationships, and other problems connected with his illness. The parents may themselves be rheumatic and incapacitated and have strong unresolved feelings about their health, marriage, finances, and other factors.[73]

To allay these anxieties, the Grace-New Haven Community Hospital developed a series of parent meetings to help parents gain a better understanding of their rheumatic children. The group sessions were conducted by physicians and medical social workers and attended by both fathers and mothers. Parents seemed less worried at the acute bed-rest stage of the child's illness than when he was allowed to get up. They raised question as to how much excitement the child could stand and when they could feel free to discipline him. They felt they had not been carefully informed as to the nature and treatment of rheumatic fever since they were told different things by different doctors. They were concerned because there were no known cures

---

[72] Irene M. Josselyn, "Emotional Implications of Rheumatic Heart Disease in Children," in Frampton and Gall, *op. cit.*, II, p. 479.

[73] Gordon, *op. cit.*, pp. 27–28.

and there was seemingly nothing they could do about their child's medical problem.[74]

EDUCATION

Children with prolonged rheumatic fever are served educationally by home teachers. Others may enroll in regular schools or in schools with special classes. Many states provide those in hospitals or convalescent homes with instruction by especially assigned public school teachers.

The Epileptic Child

There are about 300,000 children in the United States with epilepsy. The increase in the number of epileptic children served by the crippled children's services was almost 216 per cent from 1950 to 1955.[75] The incidence of epilepsy is greater than that of polio and about that of tuberculosis and diabetes. Twenty-four states include epilepsy in the definition of a "crippling condition."[76]

There are many misconceptions about epilepsy which constitute a disservice to the child and his family. Epilepsy is not related to mental retardation, and the intelligence of the epileptic child is similar to that of children in the general population. Although generally believed to be hereditary, epilepsy is genetically transmitted no more frequently than diabetes.[77] The impression that seizures cannot be controlled is not well founded. Instead, the effective control of seizures has done much to help the epileptic to be better understood and accepted.

The person with epilepsy should be regarded as normal in all respects except during the brief periods when he suffers a loss of con-

---

[74] Jeanne K. Igersheimer, Charles H. Crothers, and Robert B. Kugel, "When Children are Convalescing From Rheumatic Fever," *The Child*, Vol. 18, No. 1 (August–September 1953), pp. 6–8.

[75] *Public Programs for Crippled Children, 1955, loc. cit.*

[76] United States Children's Bureau, *Crippled Children's Services at the Mid-Decade*, Statistical Series, No. 35, U.S. Department of Health, Education and Welfare (Washington, D.C.: Government Printing Office, 1957), Table 2, p. 9.

[77] Frederic A. Gibbs, *A Modern View of Epilepsy* (Chicago: National Epilepsy League, undated and unnumbered).

sciousness, with or without loss of motor control.[78]   The reaction of others to his physical appearance and behavior during these seizures represents perhaps the greatest problem faced by an epileptic child.

ETIOLOGY

Epilepsy is caused by injury to the brain before or during birth, encephalitis, whooping cough, head injury, glandular disturbances, and other physical and neural involvements.   Although a metabolic disorder of the brain usually becomes evident in childhood, epilepsy may be acquired at any time during life.   Seventy per cent of all persons with epilepsy show symptoms before the age of twenty, with the peak incidence in the first two years of life and during adolescence.

There are three types of epilepsy.   The "little illness," or petit mal attack, is the most common among children.   It may be manifested by a disturbance of consciousness during which time the eyelids and facial muscles may twitch.   The seizures may last from fifteen to forty seconds and may occur once a day, several hundred times a day, or several times a week.[79]

The "big illness," or grand mal attack, is also accompanied by a disturbance of consciousness but in addition there are postseizure convulsions.   The attack causes the child to black out, fall to the floor, and have muscle rigidity, followed by rapid jerking of the arms and legs.   The seizure may last from one to five minutes, after which the child goes into a coma or deep sleep, lasting sometimes for several hours.   Some children have several grand mal seizures a day, while others have one a year or fewer.[80]

Psychomotor epilepsy is not common among children, but it is one of the more disturbing of the epilepsies.   It results from attacks of the anterior portion of the temporal lobe of the brain and produces a disturbance of consciousness and peculiar, meaningless, or aggressive behavior, followed by amnesia.[81]

THE USE OF THE ELECTROENCEPHALOGRAM

The electroencephalogram (EEG) traces the electrical current of the brain and assists the physician in diagnosing epileptic symptoms

---

[78] Harry Sands, "Epilepsy," in Frampton and Gall, *op. cit.*, III, p. 207.

[79] *Ibid.*, p. 208.

[80] *Ibid.*

[81] *Ibid.*

and in prescribing a plan of treatment. The EEG is an index of electrophysiological activity of the cortex and makes available a graphic recording of the electrical activity of the brain. Fluctuating voltages coming from the brain are recorded on a moving strip of paper by a recording system of ink-writing electromagnetic pens connected with an amplifying unit.[82] The EEG informs the physician about the rapidity of the development of pathological changes in the brain, and the recency, severity, or extent of change.[83]

CHILD-PARENT-COMMUNITY RELATIONSHIPS

The epileptic child is particularly dependent upon others for recognition of his situation and acceptance as a person. As Lennox has stated:

In epilepsy, more than with most diseases, the unit of treatment is the family. An epileptic child brings psychologic and social complications for those around him which are subtle, severe, and long-lasting. Below and beyond the family is the widening sub-structure of friends, schoolteachers, acquaintances and the general public. The conception of epilepsy which resides in the public mind is most important. For centuries the pyramid of therapy has had a foundation not of masonry but of rubble and sand.[84]

From a study of over 700 epileptic children treated at the Harriet Lane Home at the Johns Hopkins Hospital in Baltimore, Bridge found that the submissive child shows fearfulness and apprehension about his seizures, becomes a hypochondriac, and regards restrictions with dependency and sulkiness. He also becomes sensitive, jealous, and solitary when segregated in group activities. When it is apparent that he is a disappointment to his family, he is filled with indecision, fear of criticism, and has a need to achieve perfection. If he is held to rigid standards of behavior by his parents, he has deep feelings of guilt and failure and is generally inefficient.

The aggressive child, on the other hand, disregards the dangers of seizures and does not follow medical instructions. He resists restriction by disobedience and temper, and rejects the idea of segregation from group activities. He handles his family's disappointment in him

---

[82] Bernard L. Pacella, "The Electroencephalogram in Behavior Disorders," in *Modern Trends in Child Psychiatry*, editors, Nolan D. C. Lewis, and Bernard L. Pacella (New York: International Universities Press, 1946), p. 103.

[83] *Ibid.*, p. 108.

[84] William G. Lennox, "The Social and Emotional Problems of the Epileptic Child and His Family," in Frampton and Gall, *op. cit.*, III, p. 227.

by belligerence and reacts to rigid adult standards by truancy and disregard for the law.[85]

Parents of epileptic children often live in dread of the child's next seizure and worry about the child's mental endowment. As the child grows older the problems increase when situations regarding dating, smoking, drinking, and marrying come to the fore. Parents who have never accepted the child's epilepsy, and who have been embarrassed, guilty, or rejecting of it, often find it difficult to encourage emancipation or socialization.

The physician, parent, teacher, and social worker need to work together in helping the epileptic child to achieve comfortable relationships. The child should be given sufficient insight into his symptoms and reassurance against fear of death. The family should be helped to appreciate the child, to establish satisfactory health habits, and to develop special interests.[86]

Responsibility for the Physically Handicapped Child

The primary responsibility for the care and well-being of a physically handicapped child is vested in his parents and family, and it is they who help to create the image that the child will have of himself. Parents often need expert guidance in understanding and accepting the child's handicap and in learning about its origins, the limitations it will place upon his activities, and the ways in which it will separate him from his siblings and peers. Parents need to be given medical information in a frank and sympathetic manner so that they are not threatened or unduly alarmed about the child's condition. Parents have a right, too, to expect that the community will provide diagnostic, therapeutic, remedial, and special educational services.

Teachers of the handicapped share in the responsibility of preparing the child to live in a world that is oriented to "normality" and to help him to have a meaningful and reassuring place in school. Regardless of any desire to believe that the handicapped or "exceptional" child is no different from other children, it would be unrealistic to expect that the child who is physically handicapped can respond in the same way

---

[85] Edward M. Bridge, *Epilepsy and Convulsive Disorders in Children* (New York: McGraw-Hill Book Company, 1949), Table 24, p. 178.

[86] *Ibid.*, p. 422.

as other children. It often takes longer for him to do things and each simple task or movement may demand more than he can readily give. Talking, walking, playing, learning, and other types of activity which give a child a sense of growth, accomplishment, and social well-being are sometimes difficult for him to achieve.

The skilled teacher is supportive in encouraging the handicapped child to make maximum adjustment to the demands of learning and socialization. She will be aware that his needs are basically the same as those of other children and yet she will be sensitive to his special needs and the ways in which these are met. She will understand and appreciate his desire to do the things that others do and she will understand the frustration that he may experience when he cannot participate in the simple activities of childhood. She will be aware, too, of her need to help him to avoid repetitive failure by encouraging him to engage in projects in which he can generally succeed and perhaps excel. The teacher's contacts with parents are especially valuable to the child when they strengthen child-teacher-parent relationships.

The community has a deep responsibility for providing the handicapped child with the same opportunities for growth, development, and social maturation available to other children. To determine the medical, social welfare, and educational services needed, however, it is necessary to know the incidence and characteristics of specific handicaps. This demands a systematic approach to case-finding, reporting, and registration.

The community should also maintain a reservoir of information about its physically handicapped children. This should include the history of the onset and development of the child's disability, his treatment and educational status, and his psychological and emotional characteristics. Adequate local and state health services should offer screening, observation, special therapies on an in-patient and out-patient basis, surgery, and other diagnostic and treatment services. Although health supervision, education, and social welfare services should be available to all children in the community, there is need for particular emphasis upon the development of cooperative community services to meet the needs of children with physical handicaps.

Selected Bibliography

Best, Harry. *Deafness and the Deaf in the United States*. New York: The Macmillan Company, 1943.

Cruickshank, William M. *Psychology of Exceptional Children and Youth.* Englewood Cliffs, New Jersey: Prentice-Hall, 1955.

Cruickshank, William M., and George M. Raus. *Cerebral Palsy, Its Individual and Community Problems.* Syracuse: Syracuse University Press, 1955.

Cutsforth, Thomas D. *The Blind in School and Society: A Psychological Study.* New York: American Foundation for the Blind, 1951.

Hathaway, Winifred. *Education and Health of the Partially Seeing Child.* New York: Columbia University Press, 1954.

Johnson, Wendell, Spencer F. Brown, James F. Curtis, Clarence W. Edney, and Jacqueline Keaster. *Speech Handicapped School Children.* New York: Harper and Brothers, 1956.

Johnson, Wendell (ed.). *Speech Problems of Children: A Guide to Care and Correction.* New York: Grune and Stratton, 1950.

Lesser, Arthur J., and Eleanor P. Hunt. "The Nation's Handicapped Children," *American Journal of Public Health,* Vol. 44, No. 2, February 1954.

Norris, Miriam, Patricia J. Spaulding, and Fern M. Brodie. *Blindness in Children.* Chicago: University of Chicago Press, 1957.

Streng, Alice, Waring J. Fitch, LeRoy D. Hedgecock, James W. Phillips, and James A. Carrell. *Hearing Therapy for Children.* New York: Grune and Stratton, 1955.

Chapter 11

The Child
with Intellectual,
Emotional, and Social Handicaps

In recent years the United States Children's Bureau has repeatedly called attention to the fact that the needs of certain groups of children are not being met by the services available to them. The groups listed customarily include children who require specialized services because of severe emotional disturbance, mental illness, and mental retardation. The children of migrant families are usually included too, since these children are severely handicapped by living conditions damaging to their physical and emotional development and are frequently denied the educational, health, and social services available to other children in the community.

In this chapter, the problems of these children will be examined with some indication of the special services needed in each state or local community.

The Mentally Retarded Child

Literature in the field of mental retardation reveals that there are various classifications and interpretations of this handicap. To clarify these variegated meanings, Cruickshank uses the term "mental retardation" in referring to individuals whose intellectual functioning is below the average of their peer groups, but whose social adequacy is such as to allow them to "function independently and adequately in the community."[1] "Mental deficiency," he believes, should be used to refer to a social inadequacy resulting from an intellectual limitation caused by incurable pathology of the central nervous system. He points out that regardless of whether this condition is hereditary, congenital, or developed soon after birth, it imposes a dependency status upon the individual in which social and vocational adequacy cannot be achieved.[2]

The World Health Organization, meeting in Geneva in April, 1954, noted the multiplicity of definitions for mental retardation and proposed another classification. "Mental subnormality" was adopted as a general term with the degree of retardation to be described by affixing the terms "mild," "moderate," or "severe."[3] This terminology was partially accepted by the Committee on Nomenclature of the American Association on Mental Deficiency when it recommended discarding the use of the terms "idiot," "imbecile," and "high grade moron," and substituting "severe" (I.Q. of 0–25), "moderate" (I.Q. of 25–50), and "mild" (I.Q. of 50–75) forms of mental retardation.[4]

A combination of the concepts expressed by these definitions produces a classification of mentally retarded children that indicates the goals which are achievable and those which are unobtainable. Use of the terms "total dependency," "trainability," and "educability" also facilitates maximum understanding of the child's personality and his potential.

The totally dependent mentally retarded child is one who is so severely handicapped that he will not be able to care wholly for his

---

[1] Cruickshank, *op. cit.*, pp. 440–441.

[2] *Ibid.*, p. 442.

[3] *The Mentally Subnormal Child*, Technical Report Series, No. 75 (Geneva: World Health Organization, April 1954), p. 7.

[4] "Progress Report of the Committee on Nomenclature of the American Association on Mental Deficiency," *American Journal of Mental Deficiency*, Vol. 59, No. 2 (October 1954), p. 348.

personal needs, to relate socially to others, or to achieve economic competence. This child will be dependent upon others for care and will need constant supervision throughout life. Because he will develop at less than one-quarter the rate of the average child, he will require assistance in all phases of living. The I.Q. range for this child will be 0–25, with a mental level of 0–4 years.

The trainable, or moderately mentally handicapped child will not profit from any sustained educational experience since he will have definite limitations in relation to academic work such as reading or arithmetic. He will have the ability, however, to learn to care independently for his personal needs and to become socially adequate and economically productive at home or in a protected environment. Although this child can develop independence in some aspects, he will probably require some supervision and economic support throughout life. The child's I.Q. will range from 25–50, with a mental level of from 3–8 years.

The educable or "mildly" mentally handicapped child, although not profiting from a regular school program, can learn to read, write, and do arithmetic at the second to fourth grade level by the age of sixteen. Academic retardation is caused by the fact that reading and number concepts are not learned until the child is between nine and twelve years of age. The whole learning process for this child is from one-half to three-fourths slower than that of other children. Although vocabulary and language may be limited, they will allow adequate communication and ultimate employment in an unskilled or semiskilled occupation. The I.Q. range for this child is 50–75, with a mental level of 6–12 years.

This terminology provides meaningful and useful criteria by which the professional practitioner and teacher may be guided. "Labels," whether they be in terms of test scores or medical and psychological diagnosis, actually tell little about the individual. They do have value, however, in permitting the proper identification of children who can live at home and benefit from special public school education, and of those whose level of educability is lower.

ETIOLOGICAL FACTORS

There are many reasons for mental retardation, despite the prevalent belief that heredity is the major cause: birth trauma; brain hemorrhage, cerebral anoxia or lack of oxygen to the brain during the period of birth; influence of the mother's contagious or infectious disease upon the fetus; the Rh factor; and mother-child incompatibility in relation to toxic conditions of the mother are well-known physiological causes of mental retardation.

Mongolism, a defect characterized by mental retardation at birth, is of unknown origin, but cretinism is caused by dysfunction of the child's thyroid gland. Other types of syndromes suggest intrauterine, congenital, or hereditary influences.

Identifying Characteristics

Although physical appearance, obvious motor coordination impairment, and other observable factors aid in identifying the mentally retarded child, his total health and social history tells much more about him.

For the younger child, delayed teething, walking, and talking may be symptoms of mental impairment. A lack of curiosity and willingness or desire to explore the world around him may be another sign of intellectual deprivation. Infantile behavior beyond the age when such behavior is appropriate may be another symptom. The older child may show very little academic progress and find it difficult to follow the most simple directions.[5]

In a recent study, 207 mentally retarded students representing a mean I.Q. of 74 were observed in eleven California secondary schools. It was found that these students had a very short attention span, little motivation, and could engage successfully only in short-range projects. Some students learned slowly and forgot quickly, so that constant review of material was necessary to assure continuity of learning. The lecture method also had to be eliminated, and "short periods of listening" alternated with periods of "doing."

In addition, these students were unable to think abstractly, to relate one idea or situation to another, to generalize, or to make critical judgments. For example, they could sometimes master the multiplication tables but were unable to use them in simple, practical problems. They also had little initiative, self-direction, or ability to engage in independent study or future planning. In fact, they lived what might be termed a day-by-day existence.[6]

---

[5] Katharine G. Ecob, *The Retarded Child in the Community* (New York: The New York State Society for Mental Health, State Charities Aid Society Association, 1955), p. 4.

[6] *Mentally Retarded Students in California Secondary Schools*, Bulletin of the California State Department of Education, Vol. XXII, No. 7, (October 1953), pp. 115–119.

THE DIAGNOSTIC EVALUATION

A re-evaluation of mental retardation resulted from the clinical knowledge that these children did not fall into a homogeneous group, but instead, like normally endowed children, they possessed individual personality and intellectual traits. As levels of educability were established, norms of learning potential were recognized, thus tending to individualize the child and to help dispel the static label, "feeble-minded."

Much of the credit for the individualization theory of mental retardation is due to Dr. Walter Fernald, director of the Massachusetts State School for the Feebleminded at Waverley for some 37 years. As director of the oldest state institution of its kind in the country, Fernald developed ten separate areas upon which to formulate a diagnostic study: physical examination, family history, school progress, examination in school work, practical knowledge and general information, social history and reactions, economic efficiency, moral reactions, and mental examination.[7]

Although individual and group psychometric examinations are the most commonly used methods of determining the level of the child's intellectual functioning, such tests do not evaluate or differentiate between the normally intelligent child with a learning disability due to emotional or social problems and the child who is mentally retarded.

METHODS OF EDUCATION

Historically, "state schools" offered custodial and educational service to the mentally retarded child, but special classes made their appearance in some of the principal cities in the United States before 1900. Providence, Rhode Island, was the first to offer special educational service in 1896, and Springfield, Massachusetts, established a special class in 1898. When Chicago, Boston, Philadelphia, and New York followed, the impetus for a wider public school educational service to the child with the low I.Q. had taken root.

Increased recognition of the importance of educational opportunity for the educable mentally retarded child is evident from the growth of such classes since World War II. Marked increases have occurred in both the number of children served and the number of school systems reporting special classes. In 1952–53 there was an enrollment of 113,565 children in special classes in 1,244 school districts, in com-

---

[7] Walter E. Fernald, "Standardized Fields of Inquiry for Clinical Studies of Borderline Defectives," *Mental Hygiene*, Vol. 1, No. 2 (April 1917), p. 212.

parison with 87,030 children in 714 districts in 1947–48.   The 1952–53 enrollment is 15,000 greater than the 1940 enrollment when 565 school districts reported special instruction.[8]

Within the last few years, parents and educators have turned their attention to the desirability of day classes for the severely mentally retarded child (I.Q. below 50) who cannot be expected to achieve academically.   There were 4,515 such students enrolled in public schools and 147 in secondary schools throughout the country in 1952–53.[9]

Educational patterns for instructing the mentally retarded showed great variation.   Ohio, whose compulsory school attendance law extends from six to eighteen years of age, provides a special class program for "slow learners" with I.Q.'s in the range of 50–75.   This category is synonymous with the "educable mentally retarded" in other states and the programs are administered and supervised by the Department of Education.   The child whose I.Q. is below 50 is regarded as being eligible for the "trainable group," educated under the auspices of the Department of Mental Hygiene.[10]

After a State Senate Interim Committee study on the care and education of mentally handicapped children, California enacted legislation in 1947 to establish special educational facilities in all school districts operating elementary schools.   The Education Code was amended in 1949 to permit high school districts to establish special classes for the mentally retarded.   The situation in California, although perhaps atypical because of the rapidly increasing population, does reflect a nationwide emphasis upon special educational services.   California enrollment in special classes for the mentally retarded minor child increased from 5,000 in 1947 to 14,000 in 1951.   In spite of the increase in special educational services, it is estimated that only 68 per cent of California's mentally handicapped school-age children are receiving needed special educational services.[11]

The California Education Code spells out the contemporary philosophy of educational service to the mentally handicapped child.   Broad provision is made for those children who cannot be educated profitably

---

[8] Office of Education, U.S. Dept. of Health, Education and Welfare, *Statistics of Special Education for Exceptional Children, 1952–53*, (Washington, D.C.: U.S. Government Printing Office, 1954), pp. 9–10.

[9] *Ibid.*, Table 3, p. 22.

[10] Amy A. Allen, *Let Us Teach Slow Learning Children* (Columbus: State Department of Education, 1955), pp. 7–8.

[11] *Mentally Retarded Students in California Secondary Schools*, p. 5.

and efficiently through ordinary classroom instruction.[12] It is mandatory that such classes be established for those children who will benefit from an educational service that will further economic and social adequacy.[13]

Additional permissive legislation provides classes for children

. . . who may be expected to benefit from special educational facilities designed to educate and train them to further their individual acceptance, social adjustment, and economic usefulness in their homes and within a sheltered environment.[14]

Mentally retarded children are educated with children of normal ability in some school districts. The advocates of this plan believe that it is academically unwise and unrealistic to isolate the mentally limited child since he must compete and live in a world with people of normal ability and intellect.

Those who advocate "special classes" do not believe that mentally handicapped children can be successfully taught in regular classes, owing to their varying needs and the lack of special teacher preparation for their instruction. Historically, special classes were an entity in themselves, but the present practice is to establish special classes as part of the regular school program. Combinations of classes or "special centers" are sometimes established as a part of the regular school to enable the mentally retarded child to have access to all of the facilities and activities available to other children. This integrated plan has won the support of many child welfare practitioners, psychologists, and educators. Heck has observed, "Such opportunities aid in building up morale in these children of low I.Q. Sometimes they need this more than academic instruction."[15]

The "special school" system is used when several school districts bring mentally retarded children together in a centrally located school. This plan has some advantages, but it isolates these children and tends to act as a deterrent to the development of special classes within a school or special center.

Many educators believe that integrating mentally handicapped with normal children is of value in the socialization of the retarded child.

---

[12] "Education of Mentally Retarded Minors," *California Education Code*, Section 9801, Division IV, Chapter 11.

[13] *Ibid.*, Section 9801.1.

[14] *Ibid.*, Section 9801.2.

[15] By permission from *The Education of Exceptional Children*, Arch C. Heck, copyright 1953. McGraw-Hill Book Company, Inc.; second edition, pp. 335–337.

It is equally important that teaching techniques be based on an understanding of the child who finds learning difficult, regardless of the etiology or his level of adequacy. Since mental retardation is considered a condition rather than a disease, home and school instruction should be directed toward modifying and strengthening those qualities which can contribute to the child's competency in all areas of his life.

Parent Groups

In recent years, parents of mentally retarded children have strongly supported their own cause by creating groups whose membership is interested in the care, treatment, and education of intellectually deficient children. Such groups have written and espoused legislation, developed educational material, given community interpretation, and, perhaps more importantly, provided for parents an opportunity to share together the feelings, attitudes, and problems they face in rearing and caring for their own mentally retarded children.

The specific concerns of parents are often caused by worry about the child's future, the embarrassment of siblings, the financial drain the child's care makes upon the family budget, the parents' own sense of inadequacy, and the problems of child-parent relationships which arise as the child grows older.[16] Such concerns are real and urgent, and when the energies of parents are redirected toward the creation of community services, the child, the parent, and the community gain immeasurably.

Since 1950, the National Association for Retarded Children has provided leadership for many parent groups. In 1957, the membership of this organization included 440 local groups and 37 state organizations.[17]

Community Services

It is now becoming clear that the dismay and taboo which formerly cloaked mental defect have deprived the child and his parents of many of the services that have been created for other children. Despite the activities of parent groups, many parents need professional counseling, and others still require out-of-home care for a mentally deficient child.

---

[16] Howard R. Kelman, "Parent Guidance in a Clinic for Mentally Retarded Children," *Social Casework*, Vol. XXXIV, No. 10 (December 1953), pp. 443–444.

[17] *Social Work Year Book*, 1957, p. 681.

The question of the value of institutional care for the mentally retarded child has been debated for many years. Although the final decision about placement necessarily rests with the child's parents, they should not be forced to bear the sole responsibility for this decision.

Parents need careful interpretation of their child's diagnosis and prognosis, as well as understanding of what residential care has to offer the child. They need help, too, in evaluating the relative merits of foster family care and institutional care, and their own stake in the choice of care they make. Perhaps they are troubled about the relationship between their mentally retarded child and other children in the family, and feel that it will be easier on everyone concerned if the child is placed in a sheltered environment with children similarly endowed. If special day school or recreational facilities are not available, parents may be anxious, too, about their ability to meet the child's needs in the home or community.

In every locality, counseling services should be available through the school, social agencies, and mental health clinics so that parents can be helped to feel comfortable in any decisions they need to make.

The Emotionally Disturbed Child

A child may be said to be emotionally disturbed when his behavior interferes with his own social acceptance, maturation, and well-being; when it adversely affects the behavior and well-being of other children; and when it comes to the attention of parents, educators, law enforcement officers, or others having responsibility for the child.

It is perhaps easier to see the emotionally disturbed child by examining the concept of the so-called "normal" child. Hyman Lippman has defined the normal child as one who has sufficient outlets for his aggressive drives but learns to control them, has the degree of emotional maturity necessary to face the issues to which he must respond, and is in harmony with his conscience. This child has the capacity to give love and to receive it in return, he can enjoy work as well as play, he has few anxieties, and he feels little hostility toward himself or others. He does not have to act out his aggressions because he is able to handle his drives in an acceptable manner.[18]

---

[18] Hyman S. Lippman, *Treatment of the Child in Emotional Conflict* (New York: McGraw-Hill Book Company, 1956), pp. 6–7.

The Institute of Child Study at the University of Toronto has conducted a research program for several years in an effort to learn more about the ingredients of mental health. The institute's clients are designated as "well children," because it has tried to learn to observe "wellness."[19] The criteria of mental health are seen as the child's ability to trust himself, others, and the world in which he lives; to accept the consequences for his own actions because he is secure enough to do so; and to learn from these experiences.[20]

In contrast to the well child, the emotionally disturbed child finds himself submerged in tension and frustration produced by his internal and external environments. He may be responding to a failure to receive love and recognition from those who have great meaning to him, or be seeking outlets of affection in an environment that rigidly withholds these basic satisfactions. Lippman describes the trauma of emotional disturbance:

A child in emotional conflict behaves in ways which produce disturbances in him or in those around him. Feelings of being disliked, or being unloved by his parents, of losing the ability to control his own behavior, of being overcome by fears, of being different from other children, unsettle him and rob him of energy that should be used in work and in play.[21]

ETIOLOGY AND
TYPES OF EMOTIONAL DISTURBANCE

It is difficult to classify the significant causal factors relating to a child's emotional difficulties because of the many variables in each situation. Some children have multiple adjustment problems which may be transient or become deep-seated. Some display symptoms at school which may have been induced by parental mismanagement, maternal deprivation, or overexpectancy, parental rejection, or rigidity on the part of their parents. Children who make a good school adjustment may have difficulty in their parent and sibling relationships, or create problems in the community. Whatever the manifestations or their causes, the child suffers from emotional turmoil when his basic needs and drives are frustrated or not met, and when the environment demands more of him than he is able to give.

---

[19] Institute of Child Study, University of Toronto, *Well Children*, Mary L. Northway, editor (Toronto: The University of Toronto Press, 1956), p. 13.

[20] *Ibid.*, p. 9.

[21] Lippman, *op. cit.*, pp. 4–5.

The St. Louis, Missouri, County Health Department has developed a classification of emotionally disturbed children for use in its child guidance clinic and school mental health service. These gradations aptly describe the children who are most often referred to the clinic for diagnosis and treatment. The first group is composed of children who are reacting symptomatically to environmental pressures but whose difficulties are not yet severe enough to interfere with personal or social maturation. The second group reflects problems of a longer duration which have now disrupted school and other relationships. The next grouping consists of children who are so aggressive, withdrawn, or disturbed that their neurotic conflicts interfere with their home, school, and community adjustment. The fourth category is made up of children whose behavior is so bizarre that it is considered prepsychotic or psychotic, and it is therefore impossible for the child to function in the community.[22]

A number of descriptive terms are used to describe emotionally disturbed children: withdrawn, aggressive, regressive, apathetic, anxious, hostile, overdependent, immature, perfectionistic, insecure, introverted, obsessional, and others. These are apt to become useless labels, however, unless there is a realistic appraisal of the meaning of the behavior and the services needed to modify it. It is often stated that the best way to solve the problems of emotional disturbance is to teach children how to become good parents. Human behavior is not that easily manipulated, however, since children must experience security, love, and recognition before they can help to develop these attributes in the next generation.

THE NEUROTIC CHILD

The neurotic child suffers from an inability to achieve what Karen Horney has described as "growth toward self-realization." Dr. Horney pointed out in a chapter aptly entitled "The Search for Glory":

Whatever the conditions under which a child grows up he will . . . develop . . . the unique alive forces of his real self: the clarity and depth of his own feelings, thoughts, wishes, interests; the ability to tap his own resources, the strength of his will power; the special capacities or gifts he

---

[22] Herbert R. Domke, and A. D. Buchmueller, "Preventive Mental Health Services in Public Health," *Children*, Vol. 3, No. 6 (November–December 1956), pp. 225–231.

may have; the faculty to express himself, and to relate himself to others with his spontaneous feelings. All this will in time enable him to find his set of values and his aims in life.[23]

She explains, however, that although only the individual can develop his own potentialities, he needs the good will and encouragement of others, as well as healthy opposition. This emotional climate will allow him to achieve the inner security and inner freedom he needs for normal growth, expression, and development.[24]

The neurotic child demonstrates that he has not had an opportunity for self-realization or the development of substantial ego-strengths. The child may be subject to acute anxiety states in which he is consumed by fear. Such episodes may be stimulated by traumatic and shocking experiences or they may be caused by the child's exaggerated apprehension. His anxiety may center around any facet of conflict, such as somatic illness, school difficulties, death of a friend or member of the family, accident, or a fear of taking responsibility for his angry feelings toward his parents, teachers, or other authoritarian persons.

The neurotic child may also develop a phobia which becomes an unreasonable, unwarranted, and persistent fear over which he has no control. He may become obsessed with ideas which persistently come to the foreground of consciousness and interfere with normal thought processes. These reactions are not voluntarily stimulated but persist against the child's will and better judgment. Compulsions are the irresistible impulses which eventuate from these obsessions. There are touching compulsions, sensory and cleanliness compulsions, compulsive and obsessive fears relating to the use of words, impending dangers, the power of his own thoughts to cause destruction, and other obsessional ideas.[25]

The withdrawn child is one who cannot risk himself in any situation for fear that the experience will call up old wounds or that the new experience itself will be disastrous. This child withdraws from others in order to feel safe and secure. The aggressive child, on the other hand, must dominate the situation and often his behavior will be destructive, cruel, and seemingly senseless.

Whatever neurotic symptoms the child exhibits, it is generally ac-

---

[23] Karen Horney, *Neurosis and Human Growth* (New York: W. W. Norton and Company, 1950), p. 17.

[24] *Ibid.*, p. 18.

[25] Harry Bakwin, and Ruth Morris Bakwin, *Clinical Management of Behavior Disorders in Children* (Philadelphia: W. B. Saunders Company, 1953), pp. 343–346.

cepted that the behavioral derivatives are lodged in faulty ego and superego structure. Redl and Wineman describe the neurotic child's ego as being "pauperized" as it attempts to deal with anxiety, fear, or feelings of insecurity, and explain that it seems to be "especially poorly equipped with those techniques which might reduce the fear or anxiety . . . and keep other ego functions and activities intact."[26]

THE NEUROTIC CHILD AND HIS PARENTAL RELATIONSHIPS

Because of the child's early dependence upon his parents, they become the persons most important to him.   As Auerbach writes:

. . . they have become the center of his universe, . . . a source of comfort when he is hurt, and they are his strength, a source of courage and confidence with which he can meet the many strange and confusing experiences that confront him in his ever-growing world.   Without them, or their acceptable substitute, he is lost.[27]

Children are born of a variety of parents and they are anticipated and received into the family in a variety of ways.   Some children are rejected at the moment of conception, others are meticulously tolerated; some are pitifully overprotected; some are overindulged with food while others are deprived of it; some are rigidly disciplined while others are taught no limits.   In the main, however, the majority of children survive and grow on to adulthood because they are in some way loved, wanted, and cared for.

For some children, parental pressures become such that the child can no longer tolerate them.   Treatment is then indicated and the parents, especially mothers, need to be brought into the treatment program.   This is necessary for two reasons.   It helps to give the mother an understanding of the treatment process and it helps her to accept a necessary role in the child's recovery.   The clinic cannot evaluate the relation between the child's unconscious emotional needs, frustrations, and conflicts if the mother does not make herself available. Durkin points out, too, that parents should not be expected to understand these unconscious conflicts, except in a setting in which they

---

[26] Fritz Redl and David Wineman, *Children Who Hate* (Glencoe, Illinois: The Free Press, 1951), p. 81.

[27] Aline B. Auerbach, "Understanding Children's Fears," *Child Study*, Vol. XXV, No. 1 (Winter 1947), p. 3.

are helped to deal with the anxieties they may provoke and, finally, to resolve these conflicts.[28]

EDUCATION AND
TREATMENT OF THE NEUROTIC CHILD

Unless the neurotic child is severely disturbed, he will attend the public school. Although the schools are extending their psychological and social services, they have quite properly placed their primary emphasis on the detection and prevention of mental illness. A recent California study of 4,400 children in the fourth, fifth, and sixth grades in 75 school districts is indicative of the current effort to identify children in need of treatment. This study showed that there were 207 emotionally disturbed children, or at least 3 children in each average-sized classroom, with the incidence increasing with each grade level.[29]

If the emotionally disturbed child must be removed from his own home, he may be referred to a residential treatment center. These facilities are usually differentiated from institutions serving less seriously disturbed children by the fact that the treatment program is under psychiatric direction. The treatment program should include individual psychotherapy, therapeutic group living, remedial education, recreation, and supervision by professionally oriented staff.

The majority of the twelve residential treatment centers studied by the Child Welfare League of America in 1952 would not admit mentally retarded or psychotic children. Some would not accept a child for treatment unless the parents had the potentiality and willingness to become involved in treatment along with the child, and at least one institution reported that acceptance for treatment depended upon the child's ability to relate to the therapist. Referrals were accepted for children two or three years old to eighteen years of age and over and from various sources, depending upon the policies of the individual facility. The majority of referrals came from physicians, social agencies, and parents.

The residential treatment center offers a great deal to the child whose ego has been damaged and to the child who needs the support

---

[28] Helen E. Durkin, *Group Therapy for Mothers of Disturbed Children* (Springfield, Illinois: Charles C Thomas, publisher, 1954), p. 8.

[29] Eli M. Bower, "A Process for Identifying Disturbed Children," *Children*, Vol. 4, No. 4 (July–August 1957), pp. 144–146.

of many professional helping hands. Few children receive such care, however. The current dearth of these badly needed facilities results primarily from the cost of the programs. Of the twelve facilities studied by the league, the highest cost per child per year was $8,079 and the lowest was $2,099. The average for the twelve institutions was $4,769 per child.[30]

The treatment of the neurotic child not requiring residential care is generally regarded as the function of a child guidance clinic. The services available in these clinics will be described in a later chapter.

THE PSYCHOTIC CHILD

There is seemingly no clear-cut medical agreement as to the etiology of schizophrenia. This mental illness is known more commonly to the layman as "split personality," and is sometimes called "dementia praecox." Schizophrenia was characterized by Bleuler as "a specific type of alteration of thinking, feeling, and relation to the external world which appears nowhere else in this particular fashion."[31]

Lauretta Bender suggested:

Childhood schizophrenia involves a maturational lag at the embryonic level characterized by a primitive plasticity in all areas from which subsequent behavior develops. It is genetically determined and activated by a physiological crisis such as birth.[32]

Dr. Bender's "maturational lag" theory, although based on twenty years of dedicated and extensive work with children in the Psychiatric Division of Bellevue Hospital in New York City, may be vulnerable to disagreement. In a group discussion at the International Institute of Child Psychiatry in Toronto in 1954, these points were made.

The theory of "maturational lag" like other theories that place the main emphasis on intrinsic hereditary or constitutional factors, not only is almost impossible to prove, but it leads to a pessimistic attitude towards the in-

---

[30] Joseph H. Reid and Helen R. Hagan, *Residential Treatment of Emotionally Disturbed Children* (New York: Child Welfare League of America, 1952), Table I, p. 306.

[31] Eugen Bleuler, *Dementia Praecox*, Monograph Series on Schizophrenia, No. 1 (New York: International Universities Press, 1950), p. 9.

[32] Lauretta Bender, "Schizophrenia in Childhood: Its Recognition, Description and Treatment," *American Journal of Orthopsychiatry*, Vol. XXVI, No. 3 (July 1956), p. 499.

vestigation and treatment of the extrinsic factors, which are, after all, the only ones we are likely to have much power to alter. This fact alone does not rule it out, but should incline us to investigate the other avenue of approach . . . There would appear to be increasing evidence . . . that there is a close association between certain types of disorders of mother-child relationship and the development of childhood psychosis.[33]

Dr. Joseph Abrahams and Edith Varon, reporting on a series of group psychotherapy sessions at St. Elizabeth's Hospital in Washington, D.C., demonstrated the influence of maternal dependency and chronic schizophrenia on adolescent and young-adult daughters. Mothers were observed to be simultaneously condescending, superior, and grossly dependent in their relationship to their daughters. The daughter, on the other hand, had conflicting feelings of inferiority and rejection of the mother.[34] Mothers also tended to relate to their daughters in a way which suggested that the mother felt she had no identity of her own. When the daughter was able to conform to the mother's image of herself, the daughter was accorded love and kindness. If the girl deviated from the mother's self-imposed image, however, the mother became disturbed and rejecting.[35] Thus the lack of security in the parental role was so threatening to the child as to cause psychosis.

Bettelheim, after some years of working with disturbed children at the Orthogenic School, University of Chicago, agreed that the psychological genesis of childhood schizophrenia is related to parental, predominantly maternal, attitudes toward the child. He believes, however, that any attempt to incorporate the mother in the treatment plan for the child is not sound since it places responsibility for help on "the very person who destroyed him in the first place."[36] In his thinking, the emotionally disturbed child must have an environment that is simple, protective, and free of persistent and damaging pressures. Since he has been deprived of a sense of identity because of conscious or unconsciously devised parental misjudgments, the child must, in fact, begin life again. The pressures which have disturbed his auton-

---

[33] Gerald Caplan, editor, *Emotional Problems of Early Childhood* (New York: Basic Books, 1955), p. 428.

[34] Joseph Abrahams, and Edith Varon, *Maternal Dependency and Schizophrenia* (New York: International Universities Press, 1953), p. 12.

[35] *Ibid.*, p. 195.

[36] Bruno Bettelheim, "Schizophrenia as a Reaction to Extreme Situations," *American Journal of Orthopsychiatry*, Vol. XXVI, No. 3 (July 1956), p. 508.

omy must be replaced with situations over which he can have some control. In addition, he must be free of a demanding mother and allowed to benefit from mothering without being required to respond to it.[37]

Dr. S. A. Szurek, in writing about more than 100 schizophrenic children seen at Langley Porter Clinic in Berkeley, California, states that very severe mental disorder in preadolescent children is wholly psychogenic and that "the psychotic disorder is due to post-natal influences which have led to generalized motivational conflict."[38]

Szurek describes childhood schizophrenia as a fierce and unpredictable battle between the child and his environment. The child is extremely unresponsive and indifferent to his parents and, although especially negative toward his mother, he is very dependent upon her. At times he is highly apathetic, wanting to do nothing for himself, but occasionally he is expert in some function of his own choice. He is phobic and fearful in some situations; in others he is inordinately heedless in dangerous activity. He is suppressed and explosive, shuns sympathy, and rarely seems to genuinely experience pleasure, happiness, eagerness, or interest. When the seriously ill psychotic child becomes angry or hurt he may laugh or manifest malicious facial grimaces. He may viciously bite his tongue or lips, punch his face and eyes, bang his head against the wall, or make cruel attacks on others. Sometimes such destructive and violent episodes alternate with withdrawal or indifference.[39]

Szurek summarizes the reasons for the parents' relationship to the psychotic child by dividing parental frustrations into two categories, namely, external frustrations or threat, based on the exigencies of war, economic pressure, or serious somatic illness of the parent; and neurotic attitudes and reactions stemming from childhood experience and aggravated by current thwarting.[40] In short: "The psychotic child manifests in his disorder the incorporation of and identification with the disorder of both of his parents' personalities."[41]

Frazee's study of 46 emotionally disturbed boys, aged five to sixteen, referred to the Institute of Juvenile Research in Chicago, presents a

---

[37] *Ibid.*, pp. 516–517.

[38] S. A. Szurek, "Psychotic Episodes and Psychotic Maldevelopment," *American Journal of Orthopsychiatry*, Vol. XXVI, No. 3 (July 1956), p. 519.

[39] *Ibid.*, pp. 524–525.

[40] *Ibid.*, p. 529.

[41] *Ibid.*, p. 535.

dramatic profile of 23 boys who were hospitalized for schizophrenia from 9 to 17 years later. The study appears to support the hypothesis that the pressures, frustrations, and demands which cause ego disintegration in childhood result in syndromes leading to schizophrenia.[42]

The study revealed that when seen at the institute, the majority of the boys were very disturbed and near the point of being psychotic; only four were diagnosed as "not especially disturbed."[43] A high truancy rate was reported and more than three-fourths of the boys were retarded or failing in school. Two-thirds of the boys had long periods of separation from their parents. Six mothers and one father were grossly neurotic, borderline or psychotic, and three mothers were institutionalized in state hospitals when the children were very young. Many mothers were overprotective or indifferent toward the child, and, in general, the boys were overtly rejected, rigidly controlled, and treated with severe cruelty by both parents.[44]

THE INCIDENCE OF PSYCHOSIS AMONG CHILDREN

There is little accurate information about the number of psychotic children in America, but it is known that there has been an increase in the incidence of mental illness among children.

Many children become schizophrenic during the first two years of life, between the ages of three and four and one-half years, and between the ages of ten and eleven and one-half years.[45] A greater number of boys have schizophrenia, but at the age of six, girls almost equal the number of boys. Girls are often seriously ill and "dramatically psychotic," but respond quickly to treatment or have a quick recovery.[46] Whereas few girls become disturbed during latency, there is a rapid increase in schizophrenia among boys during this period. All schizophrenic children tend to make their best psychological, intellectual, emotional, and social progress during puberty.[47]

---

[42] Helen Elizabeth Frazee, "Children Who Later Become Schizophrenic," *Smith College Studies in Social Work*, Vol. XXIII, No. 2 (February 1953), p. 125.

[43] *Ibid.*, Table II, p. 136.

[44] *Ibid.*, Table VI, p. 142.

[45] Lauretta Bender, "Childhood Schizophrenia," *American Journal of Orthopsychiatry*, Vol. XVII, No. 1 (January 1947), pp. 53–54.

[46] Lauretta Bender, "Schizophrenia in Childhood: Its Recognition, Description and Treatment," *op. cit.*, p. 505.

[47] *Ibid.*, p. 504.

SERVICES AVAILABLE TO THE PSYCHOTIC CHILD

The child who is severely disturbed will not be likely to find educational facilities to meet his needs in the public schools. He is ordinarily kept at home and given a home-teaching service if such service is available and if he can use this kind of learning experience. If he is so ill that he cannot remain in his own home, he may be placed in a residential treatment center or a state hospital. Unfortunately, relatively few out-patient child guidance clinics specialize in therapy with the schizophrenic child.

A national survey indicated that in 1955 about 1 per cent of the resident population in state hospitals was under the age of twenty and that little attention has been given to estimating the over-all need for hospital care.[48] The survey also revealed a rather wide variation in diagnostic and treatment services, policies, and practices. Florida reported that it had no public facilities for emotionally or mentally ill children, whereas California had ten such facilities. Five states were conducting surveys to assess the need for public institutional care; the majority of the states, however, had no reliable estimate of such need.

Although 7 states reported new facilities in progress, mentally ill children were reported housed and treated with adults in 37 states. Only 15 states had wards for children, and in 14 states mentally ill children were housed with mentally defective children. Two states were contemplating separate hospital buildings for children but only 8 states had separate facilities. Twenty-six states offered no specialized treatment program, while 14 did. More than half of the states had no special groupings by diagnosis or sex, and one-half of the jurisdictions segregated children by age.[49]

Many resources other than state hospitals were used. Alabama and Kentucky reported that they did not maintain any regional clinical services for the emotionally ill child. For the most part, states depended upon local child guidance clinics, the facilities of university clinics, and other medical facilities. One state reported the use of juvenile detention homes, state industrial schools, foster homes, or residential treatment centers for psychotic children.[50]

---

[48] *Report of Survey of State and Territorial Facilities and Programs for Mentally Ill and Emotionally Disturbed Children* (Springfield: State of Illinois, Department of Public Welfare, 1956), p. 1.

[49] *Ibid.*, tabulation of Question 3 (unnumbered page).

[50] *Ibid.*, tabulation of Question 4 (unnumbered page).

The Migrant Child

America owes much of its historical greatness to its "men on the move," for it was they who sought new frontiers and developed the natural resources which largely determined the wealth and the power of the nation. Some of these men were solely motivated by adventure, others migrated hoping to find economic opportunity, and still others sought a combination of these goals. Whatever the motivation, the saga of the hardships and glories of the pioneer has a much more respectable place in our national history than does the story of the contemporary migrant.

The plight of the migrant was made apparent in Steinbeck's dramatic and tragic description of the wandering, hungry "Okie." These and others were victims of a decade of drought, menacing grasshoppers and other insects which destroyed the crops, soil erosion caused by the misuse of the land, floods which literally carried farms away, and dust storms which made farming impossible. In 1938, six million acres of land lay useless, and tenancy and sharecropping grew when $50,000 farm investments brought $2,000 after months of relentless devastation. The Southern sharecropper, in turn, was victimized by mechanization and tenancies began slowly to dwindle.[51]

The Nature and Scope of the Problem

Contrary to general opinion, the majority of migrants are American citizens. Those who migrated from the dust bowl in 1938 were not aliens smuggled through illegal channels, but farmers whose lands had been blown away, renters whose crops did not materialize, or farm hands whose jobs had been eliminated by machinery or by the competition produced by surplus labor and lowering wages. The migrant group was reportedly made up of small merchants and businessmen, barbers, butchers, lumbermen, miners, and others who had been on relief. As the pioneers did before them, many of these people moved to the West, where the soil was fertile, the climate more amenable, and life and crops seemed easier to manage.[52]

This was perhaps the beginning of the problem which has been so dramatically stated in an appraisal of the role of the migrant child:

---

[51] James E. Sidel, *Pick For Your Supper*, Publication No. 378 (New York: National Child Labor Committee, June 1939), p. 7.

[52] *Ibid.*, pp. 10–11.

It has been pointed out that educational neglect . . . symbolizes and accentuates the attitude of indifference which the migrant farm child meets in most areas of his experience. The end product is a citizen . . . who has no social or geographical roots, has a feeling of being left out, is ill-prepared for any form of constructive citizenship and lacks the basic educational tools for satisfactory living.[53]

It is true that migrant children have the lowest educational attainment, enter school later than most children, attend fewer days, have the greatest school retardation, achieve the least progress, drop out of school earliest, and constitute the greatest source of illiteracy. These factors, however, are grossly related to their basic need for food, clothing, and shelter. They also reflect the unwillingness of the community to enforce existing child labor laws and to furnish the social welfare and health services necessary to meet the needs of migrant children and their parents.[54]

Thomas and Taylor describe four migrant communities in Colorado which appear to be typical of the areas visited by America's estimated 600,000 migrant families and one million children of school age. Their report was based on a study of 262 seasonal agricultural families composed of some 1,513 individual members. There was an average of 5.7 members per family, with children fourteen or under comprising 44 per cent of the group. Nearly all were Spanish-Americans, and 65 per cent of the children seven to sixteen years old spoke only Spanish. One-third of the parents were illiterate, with four years of schooling or less. The average job lasted four to eight weeks and the average annual income was $1,424. Eighteen per cent had been migrant laborers for a period of ten years.

More than 200 children, seven to sixteen years old, worked in the crops; the median age of those employed was 10.5 years. Eighty-eight children had begun to work before the age of ten, and 25 before the age of eight. Thirty-five per cent of the children seven to sixteen years of age had left school at the time of the study or had never been enrolled, and most of the children who had left school at the age of fourteen, fifteen, or sixteen had not gone beyond the first or second grade. Actually, the children had less command of English than had their parents.[55]

---

[53] *Report of Regional Conferences on Education of Migrant Children*, Federal Security Agency, Office of Education (Washington, D.C.: Government Printing Office, July 1952), p. 1.

[54] *Ibid.*, p. 2.

[55] Howard E. Thomas and Florence Taylor, *Migrant Farm Labor in Colorado* (New York: National Child Labor Committee 1951), pp. 3–5.

Parents were described as having a "fatalistic acceptance" of disease, poverty, lack of prenatal care, poor housing, and lack of sanitation. About one-half of the families lived in one room and the average sleeping space of 162 square feet was shared by more than four persons. Ninety-eight per cent of the families had no refrigeration and 60 per cent had no bathing facilities. Infant mortality was twice as high as that of other Colorado children.[56] Mothers took their small children to the fields with them because they had no other source of child care; eight out of ten children, however, were left alone and unsupervised, either at home or locked in cars.

The community's attitude toward this out-group was evident in the following comments:

School official: "Children of these Mexican beet workers are not the mental equals of our children. . . . Sometimes whole families are in the first grade."[57]

Restaurant manager: "I can't say they behave any different from the 'whites' who eat in here, but they (the whites) seem to think they do."[58]

Church member: "The migrants are dirty . . . they wouldn't understand our services . . . they are diseased."[59]

Grower: "I don't want my kids going to school and getting contaminated by those dirty, lousy Mexican kids . . . give 'em a little education and you ruin 'em as good farm hands. Good workers is too . . . hard to get these days."[60]

Merchant: "Everybody charges the migrants a little more if they can get it. The reason for this is that most of us lose money on the credit accounts of resident customers and in this way things are kind o' evened up."[61]

Other states attracting migrant labor have had some of the same tragic problems and consequences. In 1941, migrants found themselves far from home and involved in epidemics of diphtheria and bacillary dysentery in two Michigan counties.[62] The plight of the

---

[56] *Ibid.*, pp. 4–5.

[57] *Ibid.*, p. 90.

[58] *Ibid.*, p. 92.

[59] *Ibid.*, p. 98.

[60] *Ibid.*, p. 95.

[61] *Ibid.*, p. 94.

[62] Edgar G. Johnston, "Michigan's Stepchildren," *School of Education Bulletin, University of Michigan*, Vol. 15, No. 1 (October 1943, reprint), p. 2.

Fresno County, California, migrants came to the attention of the whole nation during the tragic, wet winter of 1949. Here there were 450 camps, each housing from 500 to 2,000 migrant laborers. As the rains continued to make a sea of mud out of the migrant communities, malnutrition and diarrhea caused the deaths of 28 infants. When a special burial fund became necessary, the community finally looked seriously into its provisions for the migrant and his family.[63]

It seems apparent that as long as there is a maldistribution of workers, nationality and racial discriminatory practices in some fields of employment, illiteracy, gross economic inequities, technological innovations, and the availability of seasonal employment, workers will continue to move with the crops. In doing so, the migrant will remain without roots and community identification and without the security accorded to citizens who have such identification. He will continue to contribute to his children's homelessness, their illiteracy, and to the risks involved in transient living. Perhaps more importantly, the migrant child will be deprived of the right to learn, to grow, and to emancipate himself from the marginality of his parents.

The greatest tragedy seems to lie in the continued embodiment of this "fatalistic acceptance" that "home" can be in a tent, a cattle car, a corn crib, or a smoke house, and that existence is all that really matters.

Because agriculture is an industry of great economic importance and short seasonal duration, the migrant and his family are needed when the work must be done. However, the migrant, the grower, and the child cannot be separated from the mores and the social, moral, and economic base of the community.

Migrant children of all ages are expected to work, not only because of their usefulness to the employer but because of the need to supplement the parents' income. Work in the fields becomes the substitute for child care, for formal education and for recreation. The migrant community becomes a subculture that is politically sterile and without the capacity to act in behalf of its own welfare and protection.

PROGRESS ON THE FEDERAL LEVEL

As indicated by earlier chapters, there has been continued concern about the migrant on a federal level. In June, 1950, President Truman

---

[63] Florence Wyckhoft, *The Citizen's Role in Community Planning for Group Work Services to Migrants* (Cleveland: The National Consumer's Committee for Research and Education, undated), unnumbered page.

established the President's Commission on Migratory Labor. Such a commission had been recommended by Congress because of the increase of illegal migration, the impact of war upon agriculture, and the serious governmental and personal problems being created by interstate transiency. After nine months of study and twelve public hearings, the commission submitted its findings and recommendations. The recommendations reflected all of the long-recognized, unmet needs of the migrant and his family and portrayed the situation as one of national gravity rather than the sole concern of individual communities.

The commission recommended the establishment of a Federal Committee on Migratory Farm Labor, to be appointed by and responsible to the president. The commitee would have authority, responsibility, and funds to coordinate the work of the various government agencies relating to migratory labor and to fulfill other responsibilities assigned by the president. To assure coordination with the various localities, it was also proposed that similar state committees be created. The commission placed emphasis upon the more effective use of our own domestic labor force, and recommended that legalization of aliens for employment purposes be forbidden and the Immigration and Naturalization Service given statutory authority to investigate illegal immigration of Mexican workers to this country.

Federal legislation was also recommended to prohibit interstate recruitment of farm labor by labor contractors or others not licensed by the United States Department of Labor. The United States Employment Service and the state employment offices were directed to protect the migrant farm laborer as to terms of employment, transportation, and housing, and to discourage interstate migration unless local help was not available.

It was also recommended that the Social Security Act be amended to include medical care on a matching grant basis for recipients of public assistance, and Old Age and Survivor's Insurance benefits for migratory farm workers. There was a further proposal that the Public Health Service Act be amended to provide matching grants to states to extend health services in the prevention, control, and treatment of tuberculosis, venereal disease, enteritis, and dysentery.

The commission also concerned itself with two of the most crucial problems relating to the welfare of children. It recommended that the 1949 child labor amendments to the Fair Labor Standards Act be rigidly enforced, that the act be amended to restrict agricultural employment of children under the age of fourteen outside of school hours, and that the child labor provisions of the Sugar Act be enforced. It also urged that the Federal Committee on Migratory Farm Labor work cooperatively with the United States Office of Education, National Education Association, American Council on Education, and state educational agencies to provide an adequate educational program for migrant children and adults. The commission also called upon the Agricultural Extension Service to broaden its scope of services so that the entire farm population, especially migrant workers, would be provided with education and instruction that would improve their farming skills and help them in the areas of homemaking, infant care, nutrition, and other aspects of day-by-day living.[64]

Although the President's Commission on Migratory Labor had only reiterated the recommendations of previous study groups, it did set some positive goals and made the President's Committee on Migratory Labor a reality. On August 26, 1954, President Eisenhower appointed a coordinating committee of cabinet members to act as the Committee on Migratory Labor. The secretary of labor is the chairman of the committee and the committee's executive secretary also represents the Department of Labor. The other cabinet members include the secretaries of agriculture; interior; health, education and welfare; and the administrator of the Housing and Home Finance Agency.

The welfare of the migrant child and his family will be greatly enhanced when the goals of the committee are realized. Emphasis is being placed not only on changing the inadequate living and working conditions of migrants, but on eliminating or reducing the need for workers to be on the move.[65] To achieve the goals established, it will be necessary that each community take responsibility for affording to migrants: employment; community health, welfare, religious, and educational services; social acceptance in spite of cultural, nationality, and racial differences, and the democratic qualities which inspire stability and a desire for civic participation.

The committee, following through on the earlier recommendations of the commission, has developed an "Action Program" for "program emphasis by its member agencies."[66] These plans involve working

---

[64] *Migratory Labor in American Agriculture*, Report of the President's Commission on Migratory Labor (Washington, D.C.: Government Printing Office, 1951), pp. 177–185.

[65] United States Department of Labor, *Report to the President on Domestic Migratory Labor*, The President's Committee on Migratory Labor (Washington, D.C.: Government Printing Office, September 1956), p. 1.

[66] *Ibid.*

with the migrant on his "home base"; selecting various localities to determine present or expected housing needs; study of income and employment opportunities in regard to the total migration problems; encouragement of the broader use of seasonal work schedules; and improvement in labor-management policies and relations. States will also be encouraged to modify their residence requirements and to extend to migrant agricultural workers, the legal rights and benefits of the residents in the communities in which they are employed. The committee hopes to secure the cooperation of national and local voluntary organizations to fulfill its recommendations and goals.[67]

COMMUNITY SERVICES

Many of the states and communities dependent upon migrant labor have begun to take a more positive view of their responsibilities to the men, women, and children whose work supports the local economy. This attitude is evident in plans for better housing, educational opportunities, health and social services, and in a desire on the part of the community to understand the migrant's culture and to learn to appreciate his social values.

State committees continue to meet throughout the nation and responsibility for migrant family life and welfare is no longer considered the prime concern of the operator. In fact, the Farm Placement Service of the United States Department of Labor lists over one hundred separate items relating to regional and national activity in behalf of migrant adults and children in its 1955–56 publication, entitled *What Some Communities Are Doing.*[68]

Selected Bibliography

Allen, Frederick H. *Psychotherapy with Children.* New York: W. W. Norton and Company, 1942.

Bakwin, Harry and Ruth Morris Bakwin. *Clinical Management and Behavior Disorders of Children.* Philadelphia: W. B. Saunders Company, 1953.

Bender, Lauretta. "Schizophrenia in Childhood—Its Recognition, Description and Treatment," *American Journal of Orthopsychiatry,* Vol. XXVI, No. 3, July 1956.

---

[67] *Ibid.,* p. 2.

[68] United States Department of Labor, Farm Placement Service, *Service to Agricultural Migrants, July 1, 1955–June 30, 1956* (second series; Washington, D.C.: Government Printing Office, 1956), pp. 1–20.

Bettelheim, Bruno, *Truants from Life*. Glencoe, Illinois: The Free Press, 1955.

Caplan, Gerald, (ed.). *Emotional Problems of Early Childhood*. New York: Basic Books, 1955.

Domke, Herbert R., and A. D. Buchmueller. "Preventive Mental Health Services in Public Health," *Children*, Vol. 3, No. 6, November–December 1956.

Horney, Karen. *Neurosis and Human Growth*. New York: W. W. Norton and Company, 1950.

Josselyn, Irene M. *The Social Psychosocial Development of Children*. New York: Family Service Association of America, 1948.

Lippman, Hyman S. *Treatment of the Child in Emotional Conflict*. New York: McGraw-Hill Book Company, 1956.

Pollock, Morris P., and Miriam Pollock. *New Hope for the Retarded: Enriching the Lives of Exceptional Children*. Boston: Porter Sargent, 1953.

Redl, Fritz, and David Wineman. *Controls from Within*. Glencoe, Illinois: The Free Press, 1952.

Sarason, Seymour B. *Psychological Problems in Mental Deficiency*. New York: Harper and Brothers, 1949.

Wallin, J. E. Wallace. *Children with Mental and Physical Handicaps*. Englewood Cliffs, New Jersey: Prentice-Hall, 1949.

Wallin, J. E. Wallace. *Education of Mentally Handicapped Children*. New York: Harper and Brothers, 1955.

Chapter 12   *The Child*

in Need of Judicial Protection

The child has more status today than at any time in American history. Even though he has lost his value as a breadwinner and his
dependency on others has increased, he is more free to make his own
decisions, to express his feelings about things, and to achieve adulthood with a minimum of parental interference. In addition, millions
of dollars are spent each year to educate, support, understand, and
help him achieve his maximum potential. Despite these facts, 2 per
cent of his twenty million peers ten to seventeen years of age are involved in juvenile delinquency and several times that number come to
the attention of the police for misconduct without referral to the
juvenile court. The number of juveniles coming before the courts
has also increased 70 per cent in the past decade, during which time
the child population, ten through seventeen years, increased only 16
per cent.[1]

---

[1] *Fact Sheet Issued in Connection with Legislative Proposals of 1957* (Washington, D.C.: United States Department of Health, Education and Welfare,
March 1957), p. 1.

268

The Delinquent Child

As the United States Children's Bureau has stated, we know that many children are "bewildered, troubled, angry, bitter or cynical about their present circumstances and future prospects."[2] We have not yet found any adequate method of preventing juvenile delinquency, however. Instead, we know that 1,500,000 children were picked up by the police in 1955 and that police arrests of juveniles under eighteen increased 11 per cent as compared to 1954. We realize, too, that juvenile delinquency court cases increased 9 per cent during the same period, an increase for the seventh consecutive year. The extent of the problem is evident in reports that one out of every thirteen children between the ages of ten and seventeen came to the attention of the police or courts in 1955.

The police arrest data of the Federal Bureau of Investigation also reveal that young people under the age of eighteen commit a great many serious offenses. In 1955, these children committed 62 per cent of the auto thefts, 52 per cent of the burglaries, and 18 per cent of the rapes.

The outlook for improvement does not appear to be encouraging. The Bureau of the Census predicts that by 1965 there will be a 50 per cent increase in the number of boys and girls in the ten to seventeen year age group as compared to the number in 1955. If the national juvenile delinquency rate remains the same, we can expect an increase in delinquency solely on the basis of the increased number of children. If the rate of delinquency continues to increase as it has in the past decade, however, the number of children involved will be far greater.

LEGAL DEFINITION OF DELINQUENT BEHAVIOR

The term "juvenile delinquency" is not self-explanatory since youthful misbehavior is what the particular community adjudges such misbehavior to be. Rubin states that "juvenile delinquency is what the law says it is,"[3] and Klein writes that "delinquency exists only by

---

[2] *Children and Youth,* United States Children's Bureau Publication 363 (Washington, D.C.: United States Department of Health, Education and Welfare, 1957), Chart 42.

[3] Sol Rubin, "The Legal Character of Juvenile Delinquency," *The Annals of the American Academy of Political and Social Science,* Vol. 261 (January 1949), p. 1.

definition."[4] Consequently, there is need to know *whose law* and *whose definition.* A simple answer to these questions is not possible since there is no uniform national pattern of juvenile court legislation and practice and, frequently, little common understanding of the legislation and judicial procedures of an individual state within its own political subdivisions.

Of some 34 offenses listed in state juvenile court laws, 48 states and the District of Columbia agree unanimously on only one common condition of delinquency, namely, that the child has violated a federal or state law or municipal ordinance. The majority of the laws indicate that a child may be adjudged a delinquent if he is: (1) habitually truant; (2) knowingly associating with thieves, vicious, or immoral persons; (3) incorrigible; (4) beyond control of parent or guardian; (5) growing up in idleness or crime; (6) absenting himself from home without just cause and without consent; (7) engaging in immoral or indecent conduct; (8) habitually using vile, obscene, or vulgar language; (9) knowingly entering or visiting a house of ill repute; or (10) deporting himself so as to injure or endanger himself or others.

Arkansas, Oklahoma, and South Dakota designate smoking cigarettes, or using tobacco in any form, as a juvenile offense. Ohio considers attempting to marry without parental consent to be in violation of the law, while Indiana, Oklahoma, and Washington legally prohibit the juvenile from habitually wandering about railroad yards or tracks. It is surprising to find that whereas the majority of the states deem habitual truancy as a juvenile offense, only two states designate loitering and vagrancy as offenses.[5]

It is obvious that such definitions as "growing up in idleness," or "absenting self from home without just cause or consent" will have a variety of interpretations as they are applied to different children, in different neighborhoods, cities, and states, under different social, racial, and economic conditions. The child who is aggressively delinquent by legal definition may also be emotionally or physically ill, dependent, or neglected. Conversely, the dependent and neglected child who comes to the attention of law enforcement authorities and the juvenile court may never have engaged in a delinquent act at all. Since delinquency is so often an extension of dependency and neglect, it is

---

[4] Philip Klein, "Next Steps in Dealing with Delinquency," *Bulletin of the New York School of Social Work,* Vol. XXXVIII, No. 4 (July 1954), p. 38.

[5] Frederick B. Sussmann, *Law of Juvenile Delinquency,* Legal Almanac, Vol. 22. (New York: Oceana Publications, 1950), pp. 20–21.

apparent that the broad arc of legal and social protection must not only meet, but transcend the common unmet needs of these children.

THEORIES OF CAUSATION

The aggressive and disturbing behavior of many children has become of increasingly deep concern to the parent, the citizen, the child welfare practitioner, the teacher, and all others with immediate responsibility for the lives of children. Deviant juvenile behavior has been of equally great concern to the behavioral and social science theorists as they continue to study and evaluate one of the most serious social problems of our times. Many comprehensive studies have proved the difficulties in measuring the reactions of a troubled child and the sum total of the many influences which have deprived him of the ability to be acceptable to himself and to others, and to have positive and meaningful relations with them.

Consequently, there has been perhaps more theorizing and postulating about the cause, prevention, and control of youthful misbehavior than any other contemporary form of personal or social disorganization. Much of the testimony given at the hearings of the Subcommittee to Investigate Juvenile Delinquency, held in a number of cities throughout the nation, reflected the conviction that delinquency can be prevented by attacking or supporting certain environmental or social institutional aspects of the culture. A cleric stated: "When parents are loyal church members, reports show a very low percentage of juvenile delinquency and practically no adult delinquency."[6] Another speaker expressed the conviction that "the greatest, one single taproot cause of juvenile delinquency in America today is liquor,"[7] while another participant, speaking on the value of sound leisure-time activities as a deterrent to delinquency, stated: "As a Scout I talked to my scoutmaster about things I didn't talk to my father about."[8] Closely associating the reading of comic books with juvenile delinquency, another speaker put it this way; "Publishers admit they are re-tooling for illiteracy,"[9] and gave this terse appraisal of the ever-available comic

---

[6] United States Congress, Senate Committee on the Judiciary, *Juvenile Delinquency*, Hearings before Subcommittee to Investigate Juvenile Delinquency, 84th Congress (Washington, D.C.: Government Printing Office, 1955), p. 17.

[7] *Ibid.*, p. 70.

[8] *Ibid.*, p. 83.

[9] *Ibid.*, p. 104.

book, ". . . old comics never die, they just trade away."[10] One of the great dangers to the child in a literary diet of comic books, the speaker warned, lies in the fact that they are psychologically unsound: "Even a mouse has to be a supermouse, to get any attention at all."[11] Educators spoke in terms of needing more classrooms, more educational facilities, and higher salaries for teachers to facilitate teacher recruitment. Representatives of the social work profession and the child development field told of the need for more staff and resources to meet the growing demands for service in the diagnosis, treatment, and prevention of juvenile delinquency.

It is easy to explain away juvenile delinquency by charging it to non-church attendance, poverty, broken homes, alcoholism, lack of adequate leisure-time activities, or other factors. However, this approach adds nothing to an understanding of the treatment needed. The tendency to see the cause of delinquency as being affixed to one source is caused, however, by what Erik H. Erikson calls our "occupation-centered" attitude toward delinquency. "We all want to say something" in terms of our own vested interests and we do not listen to what the child is telling us about ourselves, about himself, and the times in which we live.[12]

"The child's personal environment is his testing ground and his battlefield, while his relation with his parents and siblings makes up his world in this privately managed planet. Long before he reaches conscious reasoning, the child is staking out his claim to individuality and to the right to be loved for what he is and to have secure and supportive direction in what he will become." The child prepares for adolescence and adulthood in terms of his conception of himself, what he feels he means to others, what others mean to him, and what he perceives as his own role and the role of others. The psychosocial dynamics of "becoming somebody," however, are the same as "becoming delinquent."[13]

Robert K. Merton stressed the need to study the organized values and social relationships of a group since both of these phenomena exert pressures which cause some children to engage in deviant behavior.

---

[10] *Ibid.*, p. 103.

[11] *Ibid.*, p. 105.

[12] United States Children's Bureau, *New Perspectives for Research on Juvenile Delinquency*, United States Department of Health, Education and Welfare, Social Security Administration (Washington, D.C.: Government Printing Office, 1955), p. 3.

[13] *Ibid.*, p. 4.

Although the same values exist for a given group, the group does not provide equal goals for all members, and the norms which claim allegiance may also stimulate deviation from these norms.[14] More simply, society points to the goals to be achieved, but it does not tell the child nor his parents how to achieve them.[15]

Most of the earlier studies of criminality and delinquency dealt with single-factor causation theories relating to the physical, intellectual, and inborn moral degeneracy of the individual. However, by the beginning of the twentieth century, such pioneers as William Healy gave new theoretical and empirical emphasis to the multiplicity of factors influencing the child's delinquent behavior.

In his classic volume, *The Individual Delinquent*, Healy demonstrated his conviction that "the dynamic center of the whole problem of delinquency . . . will ever be the individual offender."[16]

In a five-year study of 1,000 juvenile recidivists coming to the attention of the Cook County Juvenile Court and the Psychopathic Institute, he wrote:

Just because the delinquent's character is the result of a long continued process of growth, one needs to regard him as the product of forces, as well as the sum of his present constituent parts; one must study him dynamically as well as statically; genetically as well as a finished result.[17]

In order to evaluate the individual in relation to his delinquency and total life pattern, Healy used an eleven-step analysis in which he included: (1) family history; (2) developmental history; (3) environment; (4) mental and moral development; (5) anthropometry; (6) medical examination; (7) psychological testing and analysis; (8) description and course of the delinquency; (9) diagnosis and prognostic summary; (10) follow-up records for use in further contacts; and (11) subsidiary records for statistical analysis and evaluation.[18]

In 1936, Healy collaborated with Augusta Bronner in developing a theory relating to the significance of delinquency in a study of 105 pairs of delinquent and nondelinquent siblings aged twelve to fourteen years. The project, which included children from Boston, New

---

[14] *Ibid.*, p. 29.

[15] *Ibid.*

[16] William A. Healy, *The Individual Delinquent* (Boston: Little, Brown & Company, 1915), p. 22.

[17] *Ibid.*, p. 4.

[18] *Ibid.*, p. 53.

Haven, and Detroit, was sponsored by the Human Relations Institute at Yale University and was one of the first to emphasize that nonconforming behavior has as much meaning to the offender as conformity has to the nonoffender, since each type of behavior is purposive to the individual.[19]

The study was highly significant in that it clarified delinquency as "one small part of the total stream of the individual's life activities" and indicated that, although observable behavior may itself be illegal and socially unacceptable, the mere process of categorizing the offense gives little insight into the meaningfulness of the behavior.[20]

The purposiveness of delinquency was seen as a response to internal and external pressures, an activity to compensate for frustration, failure, and the lack of affectional satisfactions, and "in common with all voluntary activities . . . one variety of self-expression."[21] This has remained one of the major contemporary theories in the analysis of the significance of juvenile delinquency.

While the delinquent child was being studied as a psychological and emotional entity, ecologists were evaluating the impact of the neighborhood upon his behavior.   Clifford R. Shaw and Henry D. McKay devoted many years to the study of delinquency in the low income areas of various large cities.   They believed that emphasis should be shifted from the study and treatment of the individual and group delinquent to the eradication of the sources of pathology which were reflected in bad housing, poverty, adult crime, contagious and mental disease, and other social problems.   In their opinion, the nature of the community must be changed since delinquency is deeply and inherently rooted in the life of the neighborhood in which the delinquent child lives and forms his associations.   This premise was well supported by the fact that in some areas of Chicago the delinquency rate remained the same throughout the years despite the changing composition of the community.[22]

The Shaw-McKay approach to causation and prevention of juvenile delinquency was also well delineated by Ernest W. Burgess, who wrote:

---

[19] William A. Healy and Augusta F. Bronner, *New Light on Delinquency and Its Treatment* (New Haven: Yale University Press, 1936), p. 2.

[20] *Ibid.*, p. 3.

[21] *Ibid.*

[22] Clifford R. Shaw and Henry D. McKay, *Juvenile Delinquency and Urban Areas* (Chicago: University of Chicago Press, 1942), p. 435.

If we wish to reduce delinquency, we must radically change our thinking about it. We must think of its causes more in terms of the community and less in terms of the individual. We must plan our programs with emphasis upon social rather than upon individual factors in delinquency. . . . We must realize that the brightest hope in reformation is in changing the neighborhood . . . in which the boy moves and lives, and has his being and to which he returns after his institutional treatment.[23]

The Illinois Institute for Juvenile Research of Chicago, the National Commission on Law Observation and Enforcement, and the Behavior Research Fund initiated the Chicago Area Project in 1932 as a private corporation. By 1942, the project, supported by funds and personnel from many agencies, had developed six "programs for community action" in areas one-half to two and one-half square miles and having populations from 10,000 to 50,000 persons. Shaw's theory of community organization as a deterrent to juvenile delinquency was tested by social action. The project was based on the premise that if the conditions, norms, and traditions were to change, this change would need to be stimulated by the citizens within the community who would ultimately develop and administer the necessary programs. Consequently, all churches, schools, industry, labor, and other individuals and groups concerned about the welfare of children were encouraged to work toward developing community centers, health programs, summer camps, and other services which could help in changing the quality of the community.[24]

The work of Shaw and McKay is a landmark in the utilization of community resources for community rehabilitation. It is also one of the pioneer projects in the use of community organization as a means of preventing and controlling juvenile delinquency. After more than three decades of work devoted to the juvenile and his community, Shaw continued to see delinquency in slum areas as a by-product of defective social relations which must be recognized and ameliorated by the organized effort of the people who live in these blighted areas. "Otherwise," Shaw asked, "how do you build strength into these; how do you give them a sense of direction? That is part of the problem, just as it is in reaching the child himself."[25]

---

[23] *Ibid.,* p. xiii.

[24] *Ibid.,* pp. 444–445.

[25] Helen L. Witmer, editor, *Parents and Delinquency,* United States Department of Health, Education and Welfare, Children's Bureau Publication 349 (Washington, D.C.: Government Printing Office, 1954), p. 31.

Frederic M. Thrasher studied the composition and activity of 1,313 Chicago gangs made up of an estimated 25,000 boys and young men. In evaluating the natural history and life of the gang in the shadows of Chicago's Loop and surrounding slum areas, Thrasher observed that the antisocial gang was a spontaneously formed, interstitial group which became integrated through conflict.

Although the gang is an informal peer group for the most part, its ultimate danger lies in the creation of cliques, clubs, and other out-group associations which isolate their members from the wider community. Defying the customs and mores of society, the gang becomes an integrated group with its own social institutional structure, tradition, "esprit de corps, solidarity, morale, group awareness and attachment to a local territory."[26]

Thrasher's study of gangs was done almost a quarter of a century ago. A more recent analysis of antisocial street club behavior in New York City indicated a glorification of violence; tension resulting from great stress placed upon racial differences; and internalized frustrations as a consequence of social, political, economic, racial, religious, and nationality discrimination, both in the city and across the nation.[27]

Thrasher supported Shaw's thesis by emphasizing the inevitability of environmental influences upon the child's life and his subsequent activities and welfare. Like Shaw, he believed that a community program would do more for delinquency prevention and control than would casework and other services offered to the individual offender. "Sociologically," Thrasher wrote, "the individual delinquent is far less important than the community influences which create him."[28]

Delinquency is in part defined by the tolerance threshold of the community; the cultural, social, and ethnic composition of the area; and the norm that is generally affixed to acceptable communal behavior. The American community is culturally heterogeneous, but the individual must be able to conform to a multiplicity of behavior expectations as he moves from neighborhood to neighborhood and from area to area. Gang grudges and fights are often the result of one group's invading the territory of another with a conscious intent

---

[26] Frederic M. Thrasher, *The Gang* (Chicago: University of Chicago Press, second revised edition, 1936), p. 57.

[27] James R. Dumpson, "An Approach to Antisocial Street Gangs," *Federal Probation*, Vol. XIII, No. 4 (December 1949), p. 22.

[28] Frederic M. Thrasher, "Reaching Crime Causes by Coordinated Action," *Yearbook of the Probation Association* (New York: National Probation Association, 1936), p. 14.

to disregard aggressively the cultural and sociolegal structure of that area. In other instances, a group may violate the mores and laws of another group through ignorance of the existing mores rather than by hostile design.

J. Thorsten Sellin espoused a theory of "culture conflict" or "conflict of culture norms" as a factor in the causation of juvenile delinquency and crime. Sellin pointed out that conflict may arise, or an offense may be committed, as a result of group differences within a cultural area or as a result of contact with different cultural systems.[29] It is necessary to know *what* violates the norm, what norms the migrant group *should* obey, and whether or not these norms are legal or nonlegal to that group.[30] This is a highly important concept since the group's definition of its cultural norms is expressed in such human associations as child-parent relationships, personal and group behavior, integrity and honesty, and in the quality of marital, legal, and governmental relations. These are the basic elements which are reflected when cultural and value systems clash.[31]

Sellin's theory appears to offer at least partial explanation for the inability of some adjudged juvenile delinquents and their parents to evaluate their responsibilities and their place in the wider community. These children might have no difficulties except for the intrusion of the universal norm. As Shaw explained: " . . . from the point of view of the delinquent's immediate social world, he is not necessarily disorganized, maladjusted or antisocial. Within the limits of his social world and in terms of its norms and expectations, he may be a highly organized and well-adjusted person."[32]

Richard C. Cabot, late Harvard professor of clinical medicine and social ethics, occupied himself with a question that had nagged child welfare practitioners for some time, namely: "Can delinquency be prevented by the treatment methods employed?" It had been Cabot's conviction that perhaps a boy cannot be prevented from becoming a delinquent, but he will learn to conform "more surely if he has had the benefit of friendly precept and example."[33]

---

[29] J. Thorsten Sellin, "Culture, Conflict and Crime," *The American Journal of Sociology*, Vol. XLIV, No. 1 (July 1938), p. 98.

[30] *Ibid.*, p. 99.

[31] *Ibid.*, p. 100.

[32] Shaw and McKay, *op. cit.*, p. 436.

[33] Edwin Powers and Helen L. Witmer, *Prevention of Delinquency, The Cambridge-Somerville Youth Study* (New York: Columbia University Press, 1951), foreword, p. xx.

Because of current emphasis upon the need for more extensive services for the predelinquent and the delinquent child, the Cabot study, which became known as "The Cambridge-Somerville Youth Study," has some pertinent implications in terms of the causation, treatment, prevention, and control of juvenile delinquency. Six hundred fifty predelinquent boys from public and parochial schools were referred for study. One-half of the group made up the "T" or "Treated Group" who would receive "sustained and directed friend-ship." The remainder made up the "C" or "Controlled Group" who would receive only the social services indicated in their particular situation and not the special services given the "T" group.[34]

The study, premised upon the value of personal relationships, good will, and interest in the boy, his home and his problems, produced what might have been foregone conclusions. Members of the "T" group were somewhat more conforming, but both groups came to the attention of authorities in the same degree. These findings indicated clearly that friendship and interest are not enough to sustain the troubled child. The key to the behavior of the members of both groups lay in the personalities of the boys themselves.

The Cambridge-Somerville Youth Study serves a solid purpose in demonstrating that, whatever service is offered, it must be appropriate to the nature of the child's difficulty. Thus, juvenile delinquency can-not be alleviated by a program which ignores contributing forces deeply embedded in a child's personality structure.

CHILD-PARENT RELATIONSHIPS
AND JUVENILE DELINQUENCY

The child receives his first preview of society within the frame-work of his immediate family. From birth, he is exposed to standards of familial behavior, to authority, to religious and racial loyalties and biases, and to most of the social attitudes with which he will grow up. The family is generally a closely knit primary group whose in-stitutional function is a biological and social one buttressed by enduring kinship ties. The family also acts as a potent means of social control, supplying the child with a sense of moral and social conscience upon which he will build his own concept of responsibility to others.

It is highly important to the child that his needs are met by accept-ing parents whose own emotional maturity is such that the child

---

[34] *Ibid.*, p. vii.

will have a deep sense of well-being, certainty that he is loved, and the satisfaction of relating to parents whom he loves. There are many ways in which parents and children lose the commonality that is so important in their relationship. When sibling relationships take on the flavor of parental favoritism, the displaced child may resort to hostile and aggressive behavior. He may compensate for his lack of ability to compete by annoying or destructive attention-getting behavior, by feigning illness, by flights of fantasy, and by whatever means he may achieve recognition. When parents are overprotective or overindulgent, the child may become so overdependent that normal personality development will be difficult to achieve. Many times a home is materially ideal, but uncongenial parents, at odds in their marital experience, cause the child to feel alone and embarrassed so that he isolates himself at home, at school, and on the playground. Lack of sensitive discipline grows out of parental apathy and, too often, punishment is mistaken for discipline. A disturbed mother may tell the court worker that she has tried hard to discipline the child by giving him his share of whippings "but nothing seems to help." It is often far easier for the hurt, sensitive child to bear physical punishment than it is for him to tolerate parental indifference. The delinquent child may feel that he has no meaning to his parents or his siblings and consequently he has no value to himself. His deviant behavior becomes understandable when he says "no one cares."

A child who is highly nonconforming in the home may be a model child in the classroom, where there is recognition of his efforts and where he is encouraged to succeed. In these cases, parents are usually limited in their knowledge of child development and understanding of symptomatic behavior. Frequently, there is little thought given to the child as an individual who is different and unique from all other members of the family. Parents are at a loss to understand why one child should be so difficult when other children in the family show no delinquent or deviating tendencies; it escapes the parents that they themselves may have unconsciously created an untenable situation for the child.

Adelaide W. Johnson and S. A. Szurek report that in a decade of clinical experience in dealing with defective child-parent relationships in so-called "normal" homes, the child's defects—stealing, truancy, and other types of misconduct—are often unknowingly sanctioned by parents who themselves receive conscious or unconscious vicarious satisfaction to compensate for their own poorly repressed impulses. Parents make an unconscious selection of the child who will be a scapegoat to live out these parental inhibitions and repressions. The child's delinquency becomes understandable when it is ultimately recognized as a clear reflection of the parents' defective conscience and faulty social integration.[35]

It should not be minimized that some problems lie in the inability of a family to compete economically and that frustrated and unsuccessful parents are often environmentally and emotionally demoralized in facing pressures they cannot overcome. Poor physical and mental health is not conducive to successful child care, and inadequate housing, overcrowding and chronic economic dependency may also hinder the child's opportunity for normal growth and development.

Parents are often unwilling to explore the source of their own deep-seated difficulties since they are convinced that the problems lie solely with the child. Or they may be ambivalent, wanting the clinic or guidance worker to assume full responsibility for the child's problem, yet resisting and rejecting improvement in the child's behavior.

An understanding of child-parent relationships, the dynamics of child growth and development, and the impact of the community upon the child and his family is highly important in any evaluation of the causes of juvenile delinquency. The child constantly expresses his many needs and he constantly reaches out for fulfillment. These needs for love, affection, acceptance, recognition, and a sense of being worth while to someone are universally present in all children, regardless of their racial, national, social, or economic heritage. When any child is so disturbed that he becomes engaged in delinquent behavior, he is telling us that something is wrong and that he is reaching out for satisfactions because of unmet needs.

Members of the community cannot be expected to have the clinician's and social scientist's understanding of child behavior and of the contributing environmental factors causing juvenile delinquency. The maladjusted, aggressive juvenile who beats and robs the aged pensioner down the street makes a bad impression on the citizens and the press, who, in turn, looking for a scapegoat, place the blame squarely on the parents. It is argued that the parents, who are recognized as the child's legal guardians and thus responsible for his behavior, should be punished because obviously they have failed in

---

[35] Adelaide M. Johnson, and S. A. Szurek, "Etiology of Antisocial Behavior in Delinquents and Psychopaths," *Journal of the American Medical Association,* Vol. 154, No. 10 (March 6, 1954), pp. 814–817.

their duty. This attitude is not new. A quarter of a century ago some of the national magazines carried articles entitled, "Home-Made Thugs," "Is the Home a Citadel of Vice?," "Sparing the Rod and Filling Jails," and "The Unspanked Generation." An examination of current periodicals discloses similar concerns.

Punishing parents may assuage an angry community, but it does not add to an understanding of juvenile delinquency nor does it tend to strengthen already disturbed child-parent relationships. The increasing emphasis upon placing blame on parents, and its consequences in terms of family disorganization, was considered so important that a conference was called by the United States Children's Bureau to discuss these problems. Questions were raised by the conferees as to the wisdom and fairness of attacking parents and whether such procedure would help or make matters worse. If parents are to blame, in *what* ways, to *what* extent, and *what* parents?[36]

Wertham points out that many parents do try to prevent their children from becoming juvenile delinquents and often the very authorities who threaten parents with punishment fail to provide the services the family may need.[37] If delinquency does begin in the home, the family should be protected against further disruption and distress. The parent can seldom be penalized without punishing the child and breaking up the family or depriving it economically.

THE SCHOOL AS A DETECTION CENTER

The school has one of the greatest influences on a child's attitudes, behavior, and interests outside of his immediate family. Here he is exposed to his first experience with formal education and to the first mandatory requirement that he conform to a secondary peer and parental group.

In order to evaluate the school as a tool or "detection center" in the prevention, treatment, and control of delinquent behavior, the school must be appraised in its proper perspective. Fundamentally, it is a tax-supported, public institution concerned with providing a learning experience for all children. Because the tax-paying community assigns to the educational system it supports a responsibility to equip its children for productive and mature adulthood and good citizen-

---

[36] Witmer, *Parents and Delinquency*, p. 1.

[37] Frederic Wertham, *The Circle of Guilt* (New York: Rinehart and Company, 1956), p. 65.

ship, services to the dependent and delinquent child have been left to the police, to the juvenile court, and to public and private social agencies. The school has done relatively little for the atypical child beyond conducting classes for children with "special needs." These needs are usually in the area of intellectual or physical handicaps, however, rather than those involving emotional disturbances.

The school receives many parental failures due to inadequacies and deprivations of various kinds. Often mothers look to the teacher, principal, and school experience to help the child to become more conforming and to behave more satisfactorily in the home and community. On the other hand, some parents are aware of their child's problems but are prone to believe that these did not begin until the child started school and that his difficulties were instigated by the teacher, the pupils, or the academic program. Some parents expect the teacher to assume a parental role in regard to discipline and punishment, while others are apathetic and care little about the program or the child's school adjustment. Parents are often understandably defensive, feeling that the teacher is being critical of them when, in fact, she is attempting to interpret the difficulties which the child is experiencing. Some parents are also critical of the teacher's interest in the child's behavior, especially when such behavior does not seem abnormal to the parents. The teacher may be regarded as an intruder and charged with concerning herself with matters outside of her sphere of authority. Consequently, under these conditions, she has little opportunity to work constructively with the parents in behalf of the child.

We are beginning to part somewhat with tradition in recognizing that the school can play a vital part in locating the child who is displaying overt symptomatic behavior. This new emphasis upon detection and treatment is highly important for the schools enroll children early in life and have responsibility for them during the critical, formative years of their childhood. The teacher usually learns to know the child and she is able to observe his behavior, his day-dreaming, his displays of temper and restlessness, his excitability, his disinterest, and his withdrawn loneliness. She is able to observe how he relates to the group and how his peer relationships stimulate aggression, hostility, rebelliousness, and irritability in himself and others. The school experience offers many opportunities for expression in which the child's strengths, weaknesses, deficiencies, and all of his personality traits become dynamically amalgamated. This wealth of excellent diagnostic data enables the well-trained teacher to make referrals to whatever service might best meet the child's needs.

Does the School Contribute to Juvenile Delinquency?

William C. Kvaraceus reports that of 616 children coming to the attention of the Passaic (New Jersey) Children's Bureau, 90 per cent of the boys had no passing grades and the girls did only slightly better.[38] Thirty-four per cent of these children left school, whereas the drop-out rate for the general school population was 6.8 per cent.[39]

A study of drop-outs from 43 secondary schools in Philadelphia revealed that there was a lack of interest in learning due "to failure of the school to stimulate because of colorless, rigid, and dehydrated curriculum," failure to individualize and to develop a curriculum to meet the wide range of student interests, lack of warmth in teacher-pupil relationships, and the tendency to allow some children just to coast along. The students' degree of frustration with the school experience was dependent upon "the attitude of the school, its flexibility and its provision for special services."[40]

Because of the differences in social and physical maturity, adolescents often find school an unsatisfying and discouraging experience. Many are highly sensitive to the indifference of their parents, to family quarrels, and to their inability to compete socially and scholastically. They find it difficult not to have the current mode of dress and to be without spending money and other symbols of belonging in the school setting. Since adolescence is a period of marginality, it produces many conflicting situations for the child from which he rebels and seeks escape.

It would be unrealistic to attempt to keep every potential drop-out in school since many who leave can have a successful work experience. However, many young people who leave school have very little idea as to what they will do or what industry has to offer them. Con-

---

[38] William C. Kvaraceus, *Juvenile Delinquency and the School* (Yonkers, New York: World Book Company, 1945), p. 142.

[39] *Ibid.*, p. 147.

[40] *Why Do Boys and Girls Drop Out of School, and What Can We Do About It?* Work Conference on Life Adjustment Education, Circular 269, reprint, 1953, United States Department of Health, Education and Welfare, Office of Education (Washington, D.C.: Government Printing Office, 1953), p. 21.

sequently, they find themselves just as unable to compete economically as they were academically. This leads to more frustration, conflict with parents, lack of money, and further feelings of rejection.

The school can play an important role in the promotion of mental health and sound personality development if its administrators accept responsibility for the detection of symptomatic maladjustments by providing guidance and social casework services and by using available community resources for those children needing additional help. Teachers should not become therapists but, with broader understanding of the child and how he behaves, they may become better teachers.[41]

The Police and the Delinquent

The Los Angeles and Seattle police departments were the first to establish separate juvenile bureaus in 1909, and in 1912 plain clothes officers were especially assigned to deal with delinquent, dependent, and neglected children. More than one-half of the communities of over 10,000 population, however, still do not have a single officer assigned to work solely with juveniles.[42] Even in cities which do assign special officers, there has been little impetus to hire police officers with special training in working with children. The majority of cities require no higher qualifications for juvenile officers than for the regular police force.

The traditional functions of the police have been to patrol, apprehend, and arrest; enforce the law; protect life and property; maintain the peace; and perform such other duties as the community might expect. Historically, the prevention and control of crime and juvenile delinquency were rooted in the arrest and prosecution of the offender and not in services and programs directed toward his rehabilitation.

The juvenile division, youth guidance bureau, juvenile aid bureau, or juvenile control bureau, as it is variously named in different localities, has four major functions. (1) It has responsibility for locating juvenile delinquents and children who are in danger of becoming delinquent and for evaluating the conditions and circumstances which have contributed to the child's problems. This involves a study of information gathered from reliable sources such as the school, the child's parents

---

[41] Frederick H. Allen, *Psychotherapy With Children* (New York: W. W. Norton and Company, 1942), p. 9.

[42] *Fact Sheet Issued in Connection with Legislative Proposals of 1957*, p. 2.

and companions, social agencies, the juvenile court and probation office, and other community contacts the child may have had. (2) It must promptly investigate the nature of the child's offense or condition and make a full report to the juvenile court or to the probation office. (3) It assumes responsibility for referring the child to the probation office or juvenile court, for detaining him in detention, or releasing him to his parents or guardian. (4) Finally, it has responsibility to protect the child by removing him from a detrimental environment and by apprehending and prosecuting adults who willfully contribute to the child's delinquency. The bureau also protects the child by practicing sound child welfare methods as these relate to apprehension, custody, care, intelligent referral, and treatment of children in trouble.[43]

It is unfortunate that memories of the old Keystone cops still linger and that they are being revived by the showing of old movies in which the officer is portrayed as an amusing comedy figure. The nature of police work with juveniles demands that the community insist upon trained men and women to do this important job of working with troubled children and their parents. At the critical time of apprehension and during all of his contacts, the officer's approach should be nonjudgmental, reassuring, and helpful. Much care and thought should be given to the disposition of cases and a child should be detained only if his welfare or that of others is in jeopardy.

The juvenile bureau should not be converted into a social agency, but it has the same responsibilities for community action in behalf of children as do other agencies. Fundamentally these are the broadening and strengthening of child welfare services needed by all children, the protection of delinquent children needing special care, the eradication and control of detrimental community influences, and support for professional training and higher standards of service.

JUVENILE DELINQUENCY PREVENTION
BY COORDINATION

In any consideration of possible methods of combating the increasing incidence of juvenile delinquency, the most important factor is *what is the community willing to do about juvenile delinquency?* Whatever the community is willing or able to do can often be best

---

[43] John P. Kenney and Dan G. Pursuit, *Police Work With Juveniles* (Springfield, Illinois: Charles C Thomas, 1954), pp. 19–23.

accomplished through a coordinating council designed to bring together lay persons, representatives of public and private health and welfare agencies, schools, churches, civic and fraternal organizations, parent-teacher groups, and others.

The progress of the New York Youth Board, which began to function in 1949, is an excellent example of a delinquency prevention and community organization program in action. Confined to New York's eleven highest delinquency areas, containing over 600,000 children over 5 and under 21 years of age, the program serves 36 per cent of the city's children. Delinquency in these areas is 76 per cent greater than in the rest of the city. The Youth Board maintains nine "referral units" which function through contact with the Board of Education.

The staff of the Youth Board locates children with personality and behavior problems that may lead to delinquency and takes the initiative in going to the child and his family, offering whatever services are needed. This approach, sometimes called "aggressive casework," reaches many families who would not voluntarily seek help with their difficulties. To meet the needs of these children and their parents the Youth Bureau maintains close contact with group work, psychiatric, child guidance, court clinic, and vocational counseling services. Recreation programs, such as the Police Athletic League, the Council of Social and Athletic Clubs, and community centers, have been organized throughout the areas, and special demonstration, research, and field projects put into operation.

Almost half of the 11,232 children seen by the Youth Board from 1949 to 1955 were referred to agencies; slightly more than a quarter were served by caseworkers in the referral units; and less than a seventh of the families refused service. The process of going into the community to offer unsolicited services has proved to be a "pattern of prevention." This is evident in the fact that during this period, juvenile delinquency declined 12.5 per cent in Youth Board areas, while it declined only 5.9 per cent in other areas.[44]

The United States Children's Bureau in May, 1957, called a historic national conference devoted to "Youth Groups in Conflict." The bureau, in cooperation with the National Association of Social Workers, the National Social Welfare Assembly, and the United Community Funds and Councils of America, planned this conference "to

---

[44] See *Pattern for Prevention*, New York City Youth Board Publication, New York, 1955.

study programs designed to serve hard-to-reach youth groups in conflict with the culture in their communities." Two hundred conferees attended, representing schools of social work, the police, the clergy, medicine, welfare planning, social work, housing personnel, court personnel, and others serving hard-to-reach youth groups.[45]

In this conference, the hard-to-reach delinquent was identified as a member of the institutionalized street-corner group, who would not voluntarily ask for the services of a group worker. It was also recognized that the ultimate aim of "street-corner programs" is to bring about a new system of values for the child, so that gang fights, group vandalism, group theft, illegal behavior, and truancy will be reduced and eventually become unnecessary as problem-solving devices.[46]

Juvenile delinquency is now receiving extensive public attention, focused on the prevention and control of juvenile delinquency as a national concern. Since 1953, a Senate Subcommittee on Juvenile Delinquency has been studying the matter of juvenile delinquency reduction. In early 1957, legislation was introduced in both houses of Congress proposing a five-year program of federal grants to the states to coordinate health, welfare, and educational services; to improve, strengthen and develop state and local juvenile delinquency programs; to develop demonstration projects; and to make training grants available for professional study, institutes, or in-service training. To receive federal funds appropriated on the basis of child population, states would be required to match funds and to make provision for administration of the program by a single state agency. The Children's Bureau would have responsibility for administering the federal aspects of the program, and a Federal Advisory Council on Juvenile Delinquency would be established in the Department of Health, Education and Welfare to advise the secretary in matters relating to the administration of this act.[47]

SUMMARY

Juvenile delinquency has been studied empirically, but there has been little research upon which to build a theoretical framework of causation based on the relationship between sociocultural and psy-

---

[45] "Highlights of National Conference on Hard-to-Reach Youth Groups," *Social Legislation Information Service*, Issue 20 (Washington, D.C.: Social Legislation Information Service, May 27, 1957), p. 137.

[46] *Ibid.*, p. 141.

[47] *Fact Sheet Issued in Connection with Legislative Proposals of 1957*, pp. 3–5.

chological influences as they affect the individual. Prediction tables, morphologic measurements, the spatial distribution of delinquents, and other academic approaches have brought progressively greater understanding of the delinquent and his problems, however.

Although there is a great deal of statistical data about the juvenile delinquent, he is as stigmatized and isolated in the community as he ever was. Harris B. Peck and Virginia Bellsmith have compared the stigma resulting from moral judgments about delinquency with that of mental illness, stating:

Unfortunately, such irrelevant moralizing tends to hinder the development of public understanding of both psychotic and delinquent behavior and thereby to postpone the establishment of services to meet their needs.[48]

Quite aside from the consequences involved, any attempt to interpret a child's delinquent behavior in terms of morality is usually based on an inaccurate and false appraisal of his behavior. In most instances, the child will be showing symptoms of disturbance "that may range anywhere from the most severe organic or psychotic illness to a transient reflection of an acute situational crisis."[49]

The American child lives for the most part in a small, individualistic, competitive, mobile, and quasi-independent family. His larger cultural sphere, however, is highly heterogeneous and he is expected to conform to its multitudinous standards of behavior, expectations, and inconsistent demands while retaining all of the characteristics his forefathers would have required of him. Like the Lady Bountiful of previous eras, we have expected gratitude for our investment in him, or at least fulfillment of our ambitions for him.

It is strangely paradoxical that, although society has legally provided for the child's physical and intellectual survival, it has not learned to come to terms with its own ambivalent expectations of him. Although we have devoted a half century to an effort to understand the juvenile delinquent and his lack of personal and social fulfillment, we have not yet recognized that the inability to implement the little we understand is a reflection of our own immaturity and our failure to appraise fully, the puzzling and competitive social system which we ourselves have created.

---

[48] Harris B. Peck and Virginia Bellsmith, *Treatment of the Delinquent Adolescent* (New York: Family Service Association of America, 1954), p. 6.
[49] *Ibid.*

Albert K. Cohen, speaking on youth subcultures, evaluated the situation this way.

. . . Society has not yet made up its mind which kinds of behavior are acceptable and which are not. Youth therefore is led to setting its own standards in terms of its own reference groups.[50]

The Juvenile Court

As earlier chapters indicated, the American children's court had its antecedents in England, where the king became the protector of all incompetent persons, including minors. The king, as *parens patriae*, father of his country, gave assurance that children would receive equitable treatment. This power was later assumed by the king's secretary or "chancellor," who became, in effect, the judge of the court of equity. Authority to protect the welfare of minors was subsequently vested in the English courts of equity or chancery.

In this country, the principle of chancery and equity also protected the interests of dependent and neglected children. As in England, however, this benevolent concept of the state as protector and guardian of the child did not extend to situations involving law violations. Early records indicate that delinquent children were treated in much the same manner as adults who appeared before the courts, and that they were routinely sentenced to long prison terms and hard labor. As we have seen, the juvenile court movement was stimulated by public reaction to the demoralizing experiences of children who were placed in public lockups, jails, penitentiaries, and mixed almshouses, and, as public sentiment grew, there was an increasing insistence upon removing children from the jurisdiction of the criminal courts which sentenced them to these facilities.

In 1921, the Children's Bureau appointed a committee to prepare a set of juvenile court standards concomitant with the philosophy, practices, and procedures of that era. The recommendations of this committee were adopted by a conference held by the Children's Bureau and the National Probation Association, and published in 1923 as *Juvenile Court Standards*. To reflect the growing body of knowledge in the child welfare field developed during the past thirty years, the Children's Bureau prepared a new set of standards in 1954 in co-

---

[50] "Highlights of National Conference on Hard-to-Reach Youth Groups," *op. cit.*, p. 139.

operation with the National Probation and Parole Association (formerly the National Probation Association) and the National Council of Juvenile Court Judges.[51]

In May, 1923, a committee was authorized by the National Probation Association to prepare a juvenile court act which would be in conformity with the original *Juvenile Court Standards. A Standard Juvenile Court Act,* adopted in 1925, subsequently had great influence on the philosophy, practice, and procedures of juvenile courts throughout the country.[52]   Several revisions of the original act were issued prior to the current edition in 1949.

The contemporary approach to the treatment of the juvenile delinquent is based on the theory of multiple causation and not on the principle of punitive justice or the avenging of a wronged society. Under this concept, the juvenile court is legally obligated to explore all of the facets of a child's life in order to assure his safety and well-being.   The assumption that all behavior is problem solving and goal-directed forms the premise upon which the juvenile court must function if it is to be an effective sociolegal agency.   The modern juvenile court therefore operates on the principle that its function can only be fulfilled through an understanding of etiology and the provision of adequate treatment facilities to supplement the due process of law.

The juvenile court usually has exclusive jurisdiction over cases involving dependent, neglected, and delinquent children, and over those adults who are alleged to be contributing to the conditions which bring these children before the court.   The juvenile court may also have original jurisdiction in the case of an adult charged with the paternity of a child born out of wedlock.   In addition, the court customarily has power to terminate parental rights if it is deemed necessary to the well-being of a child.

The court is usually a unit of county government, but several state legislatures have created children's courts with city jurisdiction only. Utah, Connecticut, and Rhode Island have state-administered and state-financed juvenile courts which operate in large districts.[53]

---

[51] United States Children's Bureau, *Standards for Specialized Courts Dealing with Children,* Publication 346, United States Department of Health, Education and Welfare (Washington, D.C.: Government Printing Office, 1954), foreword, p. v.

[52] Sussmann, *op. cit.,* p. 16.

[53] *Ibid.,* p. 24.

The juvenile court, although functioning as a legal entity, may be a completely separate court or an adjunct to another branch of the judiciary. In California and Arizona, the superior court serving the county functions as the juvenile court, and in Maine the municipal courts function as children's courts. Maryland has a polyglot system in which three counties and the city of Baltimore have special magistrates for juvenile causes, one county has a separate juvenile court with Circuit Court status, and in the remaining counties the Circuit Court judge hears juvenile cases. In Michigan and Idaho, juvenile courts are divisions of the probate courts. New Jersey has a juvenile and domestic relations court in each county. Wisconsin juvenile courts are administered by a judge of the court of records, and in Alaska the justice court functions as a juvenile court.[54]

New York City has a rather extensive judiciary for handling children's cases. In this system, Special Magistrate's Courts or "social courts" include the Adolescent Court, Youth Term, Girls' Term, Home Term, and Narcotics Term. The Court of Special Sessions and the county courts also hear cases involving children. There are, in fact, over 300 children's courts in New York State.[55]

The Standard Juvenile Court Act defines a "child" as a person less than 18 years of age, but laws vary as to the age of jurisdiction and the offenses over which juvenile courts have exclusive jurisdiction. The majority of the states and the District of Columbia have exclusive and original jurisdiction over children under 18; several of the states have a 17 and 18 year differential for boys and girls. Five states have original and exclusive jurisdiction over children under 16, and eight hear cases of children under 17. Arkansas, California, Colorado, and Montana extend juvenile court jurisdiction to children under the age of 21.

DEPENDENCY AND NEGLECT

Definitions vary in different states, but *dependent* and *neglected* children usually include the child who is without proper care and guardianship; who has been abandoned; whose parent or guardian is unfit either physically, mentally, or morally to care properly for him; or who is being denied food, clothing, shelter, or medical care.

---

[54] *Ibid.*, pp. 67–79.

[55] Bureau of Public Affairs, *Justice for Youth* (New York: Community Service Society of New York, 1955), p. 7.

When the parent cannot or will not properly safeguard the child's health and welfare, the juvenile court judge may act to make the child a ward of the court, or, more properly, a ward of the state. In cases of wilful neglect, the court has the authority to try the offending parent or guardian. The court may give custody of the child to another person or agency if this is deemed best.

JUVENILE COURT PROCEEDINGS

A court experience, even in the case of a minor traffic offense, may be unpleasant, embarrassing, and unwelcome to any of us. To the child, it can be a very threatening and fearful experience in which he feels rejected, not only by his parents but by the community as well. Some children who appear before the court have broken no laws and have little understanding of why they are being involved in a court procedure.

To emphasize the treatment aspects of the juvenile court the children's court is devoid of criminal court procedures. When a person informs the court that a child is delinquent, dependent, or neglected, a preliminary study is made to determine what further action is necessary. Informal action may be taken and an unofficial disposition made by offering casework services to the child and his family. In these cases, no petition is filed, no court record is made, and there is no court hearing upon which to base adjudication. Formal action is required when a *petition* is filed in the child's behalf by any person having knowledge of the child's situation. This may be a probation officer, the police, the child's parents, a school or agency social worker, or an interested citizen. The petition contains the child's name and address, the names and addresses of his parents or legal guardians, and any other pertinent facts about his situation. Subsequently, a *summons* is served, ordering the parent or guardian to appear in court at a given time. If the summoned parties fail to appear without cause, a *warrant* may be issued for contempt of court.

When a child is found violating a law, he may be *taken into custody* by the police or juvenile probation department, but in most instances he is not *arrested*. If it is necessary to detain a child, he should be immediately released to his parents whenever possible. If he cannot be released, he should be taken to the probation office, or to a properly designated detention facility. The apprehending officer has an immediate responsibility to officially notify the probation office about the necessity of detention and the details of the situation. The child should be held only when this is necessary for his own protection or for that of others. He should not be detained as a form of punishment.

Most juvenile courts require a *prehearing study* of each child. This study is made by a probation officer and is one of the most significant characteristics of juvenile court procedure. Its purpose is to help the judge understand the child in terms of his behavior and general welfare, so that he can order an appropriate program of treatment for him. For the delinquent child, the prehearing study is consistent with the premise that the juvenile court is interested in the child's basic motivations and that it does not *convict* him for an offense but *adjudicates* in his behalf. For all children, the study includes an evaluation of the child's developmental history; familial environment; status in the family; school experience; mental, emotional, and physical health; attitude toward his present difficulties; and whatever contacts he or his family may have had with other agencies.

The child is not *arraigned* and he does not have a *trial*. When a *hearing* is held, it is usually conducted informally and privately in the judge's office. The press is excluded and only those who are immediately related to the case are allowed to be present. The child's case record, likewise, is a confidential document which is not made available to other sources. In most counties, the names of juvenile delinquents are not published in the newspapers. Although this high degree of professional secrecy has been attacked from time to time, it protects the child and his family from unfavorable publicity and helps in making them more amenable to treatment.

DISPOSITION OF CASES

The judge may dismiss a petition or otherwise dispose of a case in a variety of ways. Since the child is not *sentenced*, the judge is free to *issue an order* based upon a plan which can meet the needs of the child. Such plans are usually effective *pending further order of the court.*

There are a number of variables which influence the judge's decision about the disposition of a case. The most important of these are the treatment facilities available, the size and training of the probation staff, the quality and quantity of available foster care, the number of collateral agencies, the adequacy of the parents, the age and sex of the child, and his capacity to benefit from a specific treatment plan.

Placing a child on probation and commitment for care in a foster home or institution are the most frequent methods of disposition when a child is made a ward of the court.

PROBATION

Probation has been defined as a form of "community treatment" involving the use of protective casework services to children who are living in or out of their own homes. The function of the probation department is to study and supervise those juvenile delinquents who have been made wards of the court and to protect children who are abused, neglected, or mistreated by parents, guardians, or other adults. The probation department also determines the need for court action and may give informal supervision to children who need casework service but are not court wards.[56]

However, probation has been variously interpreted and administered. Children have been known to receive a court edict ordering them to keep a diary of their activities and to report to the probation office "without fail every two weeks." Recently the newspapers carried the story of a judge who allowed a youngster to be placed on probation providing that the "girl keep her room neat and clean, return to high school and get B plus in all of her work." These are examples of a kind of "personalized probation" which may have value for some children but does not reflect the use of probation as a professional service to the child and his family.

When a child is placed on probation, the juvenile court strives to relieve him of the pressures and the impact of those things which have caused his difficulties. The judge may place the child on probation, allowing him to live at home, in a foster home, or with a relative, under the jurisdiction of the court. During the period of probation, the child is supervised by a probation officer on a casework basis.

The granting of probation is the most frequently used method of disposition. It is assumed that the child should remain in his own home if this is at all possible, since the child and his family should be rehabilitated as a unit. Separation often leads to more family disruption, stigma, and strained child-parent relations and may add to the widening breach already existing between the child, his family, and the community. Juvenile courts are sometimes criticized for using probation too freely because "nothing is accomplished by sending the

---

[56] Department of the Youth Authority, State of California, *Standards for the Performance of Probation Duties* (Sacramento: State Printing Office, 1954), p. 5.

child home to his parents." Both the child and his parents have the right to succeed in their relationship, however, and to establish a more orderly and secure place for themselves within the community. They can be helped to achieve these ends together. Another practical problem that escapes the critics is that foster care is expensive and few communities could bear the financial cost of removing every juvenile delinquent from his own home.

COMMITMENT FOR FOSTER FAMILY CARE

The court may decide that a child's needs will be best met by foster home placement. When this decision is made, the child should be given reassurance that he is not being punished for his "badness," and helped to understand that he will be away from home only until he and his family are better able to manage things together. The child also needs reassurance that he and his parents will be given help in achieving the necessary changes and that he will have contact with his parents.

Separating a child from his parents and siblings is seldom without trauma and heartache, regardless of how brave or sophisticated the child or how sensitive the placement worker. When separation comes as a result of a court hearing, there is often increased anxiety, fear, or belligerence which makes the selection of the foster home more crucial and often more difficult. If the child is to benefit from the foster home experience, he must be provided with foster parents who can accept his nonconforming behavior and can meet his needs so that he can become more secure and better adjusted.

Juvenile courts generally call upon the placement services of the county or city welfare department or a licensed private child-placing agency to select and place children in foster homes. Some courts, however, have a home-finding and placement unit attached to the probation department.

COMMITMENT TO AN INSTITUTION

Care in an institution is indicated when a child cannot make an adequate adjustment while on probation in his own home and cannot benefit from a foster home placement. Traditionally, institutional commitment was considered to be punishment for not succeeding elsewhere, but judges are tending to view probation, foster care, and institutional care as three distinct services to children, to be used in accordance with individual needs. Children may be committed to a private child caring institution or to a training school for delinquent children. About 40,000 delinquent children are committed to training schools each year.[57]

In the fall of 1953, the Children's Bureau initiated a study of the policies and operations of all 129 public state training schools. On the basis of the information received from the 109 schools reporting, it was estimated that there were 45,000 children in these institutions from October 1, 1952, to September 30, 1953. The average age of the children was sixteen years. Seventy-two per cent were boys and 69 per cent were Caucasian.

Four out of ten schools had a capacity of over 200 children and two of the schools had an occupancy of 91 per cent to 100 per cent. Boys stayed an average of 10.8 months, whereas girls stayed 15.5 months. The annual per capita cost of care per child ranged from $439 to $4,399, with an average cost of $1,985.[58]

The Children's Bureau study also indicates the type of service and care available to children in these institutions. Since the training school is a treatment facility, the staffing pattern is important in rehabilitation. Nearly all of the schools reported full-time day cottage personnel and teachers, but only eight out of every ten schools had full-time vocational education teachers. Part-time physicians, dentists, chaplains, and psychologists were employed in many schools. Three out of ten schools had a part-time psychiatrist and six out of ten had full-time social workers or recreation workers on the staff.[59]

Forty-five per cent of the vocational education teachers had not gone beyond high school. It is generally recognized that cottage parents have a great influence on the children supervised, but these employees had the least formal education and received the lowest annual salaries. Sixty-three per cent of the day cottage staff and 81 per cent of the night cottage staff did not go beyond high school. Seventy-six per cent of the superintendents and 79 per cent of the social workers had some graduate education.[60]

Prior to or shortly after admission, the various schools secured data about medical, dental, and social background, and required educational

---

[57] *Fact Sheet issued in Connection with Legislative Proposals of 1957*, p. 2.

[58] United States Children's Bureau, *Some Facts About Public State Training Schools for Juvenile Delinquents*, Statistical Series, No. 33, U.S. Department of Health, Education and Welfare (Washington, D.C.: Government Printing Office, 1956), pp. 1–2.

[59] *Ibid.*, p. 19.

[60] *Ibid.*, p. 21.

achievement, intelligence, aptitude, personality, and psychiatric examinations. Three schools required no examinations and only 21 required all pertinent examinations.[61]

AFTER-CARE

When a child is released from an institution or permitted to leave his foster home, he is not considered to be on *parole* but to be returned to his parents under supervision. Such supervision is called *after-care* and may be provided by a social agency, the training school, a private institution, a state agency, the probation department of the committing court, the State Parole Authority, or by other designated agencies.

Only one school in the bureau's study of training schools reported that no after-care services were available to the child.[62] After-care following foster home placement may be provided by the placing agency or the probation department. No figures are available regarding the frequency of this type of supervision.

THE JUVENILE COURT STAFF

The judge assumes a major role in the operation of the juvenile court. He is not only responsible for adjudication of petitions, but he must, in effect, administer and give direction to one of the community's most important child protection services. To make appropriate judicial decisions, he must have not only a knowledge of law but an understanding of the dynamics of human behavior, since he must reconcile the concepts of constitutional rights with a need for rehabilitation of the child. In fact, many things are expected of the juvenile court judge that are not expected of other jurists. It has been pointed out that at no time in our civilization has a judge ever been expected to reform, supervise, or treat the adult criminal.[63] There has been a tendency to feel, however, that the rising delinquency rate, chronic recidivism, and apparent disregard for law reflect the inability of juvenile court judges to evaluate and deal properly with delinquency.

Few juvenile court judges are recruited from the child welfare field. Consequently they are obliged to acquire knowledge of another pro-

---

[61] *Ibid.*, p. 34.

[62] *Ibid.*, p. 38.

[63] Klein, *op. cit.*, p. 19.

fession and to adapt their legal training to the methods of another discipline. The judge of the children's court cannot adjudicate in the traditional manner by studying, analyzing, and interpreting legal procedure based on written law and precedents. Instead, he has the unusual task of protecting the offender from further difficulty and stigma while keeping the juvenile court identified with the community's law enforcement structure.

Judge Paul W. Alexander has pointed out that the judge is "both foundation and keystone of the court" and that the best of legislation, buildings, and staff "will not make a good court if the judge is not qualified for his particular job."[64] In outlining desirable qualifications for judges, the *Standards for Specialized Courts* explains that, in addition to his legal training and experience, the judge should be eager to learn all aspects of juvenile court practice, administration, and procedures. He should be interested in the rights of people and the problems of children and their families, and should have the ability to evaluate evidence and situations objectively, uninfluenced by his own personal concepts of child care. He should be sufficiently aware of modern psychological, psychiatric, and social work concepts and processes to give due weight to the findings of these sciences and professions. He should also be able to conduct hearings in a kindly manner and to talk to children and adults sympathetically and at their own level of understanding without loss of the essential dignity of the court.[65]

The breadth and scope of the responsibilities assigned to the juvenile court judge were summarized by Louisiana's chief justice, John B. Fournet. In addressing the New Orleans meeting of the National Council of Juvenile Court Judges, he stated:

Your court lies closer to those questions that involve human rights and human privileges than any other in the land, and its influence is felt in every section of the Country . . . in all places where men read and think . . . The privilege that is yours of having a part in the moulding of the lives of children in the full impressibility and receptiveness of their youth is a proud and enviable one. It is no wonder that your work and your responsibility have put you in a class that is unique in the judicial family.[66]

---

[64] Paul W. Alexander, "Redirecting the Delinquent," *1947 Yearbook*, editor, Marjorie Bell (New York: National Probation and Parole Association, 1947), p. 198.

[65] *Standards for Specialized Courts Dealing with Children*, p. 83.

[66] *The Significance of the Juvenile Court*, New Orleans Conference (Pittsburgh: National Council of Juvenile Court Judges, National Juvenile Court Foundation, 1953), p. 35.

REFEREES

In some states, the judge may delegate certain functions to referees empowered to adjudicate juvenile court petitions, subject to the approval of the judge. The chief probation officer or supervising probation officer is usually designated to act in this capacity. When this procedure is followed, the referee's decision may be appealed to the judge.

It is recommended that the referee be directly responsible to the judge, that he be a member of the bar in the state in which he serves, and that he be experienced in the practice of law.[67]

PROBATION STAFF

Because probation officers must have an understanding of human behavior and motivation and diagnostic skill in the evaluation of personal and social maladjustment, they are now being recruited from the field of social work in increasing numbers. As a result, methods of social casework, group work, and community organization are now utilized in the probation process.

The probation officer has many responsibilities, which include learning to know the child before the hearing, making the prehearing study, preparing the court report, and representing the child in court. He also adjusts cases unofficially, prepares case records, develops social histories for collateral agencies and institutions, provides casework and other services to the child and his family, and participates in community education and planning. In some communities, the probation officer administers and supervises the detention facility, acts as referee, and has other required duties. However, only one out of ten probation officers has full graduate social work training and four out of ten do not have a college degree.

The juvenile court judge depends heavily on his probation staff, since it is his liaison with the child, the family, and the community, and his primary resource in treatment and rehabilitation. Probation officers should therefore be selected on the basis of an impartial civil service examination with careful evaluation of the candidate's education, personal qualifications, and experience.

Many counties are too small to employ a probation staff or to have more than one probation officer. In these counties, the court may

---

[67] *Standards for Specialized Courts Dealing with Children*, p. 85.

delegate probation duties to other law enforcement bodies, to school attendance officers, to private or public social agencies, to church representatives, or to citizens who volunteer their services.

The Youth Authority

The Youth Correction Authority Act is considered one of the most visionary, potentially sound, and controversial proposals in the treatment of youth 16 to 21 years old. A book and an unpublished manuscript played significant roles in its creation. The book, *Youth in the Toils,* was an expose of the methods of handling juvenile offenders in New York City. The authors, Leonard V. Harrison and Pryor M. Grant, made the study under the auspices of the Community Service Society and recommended that there be created a Delinquent Minor Court with responsibility for determining the offender's guilt or innocence and his treatment, if found guilty. They also recommended that decisions relating to the disposition of offenders be based on a diagnosis by experts who would comprise a special board. Minors would be under the supervision and control of this board until discharged or until another decision is made.[68]

The Youth Correction Authority Act was further stimulated by Sellin's extensive research, later published in *The Criminality of Youth.* In early 1938, the Council of the American Law Institute adopted the recommendation of its Advisory Committee on Criminal Justice and authorized the committee to draft a model act dealing with the offenses, detention, trial, sentencing, and treatment of youths 16 to 21 years of age.

It was hoped that the Youth Correction Act, adopted by the Institute on May 21, 1940,[69] would become a blueprint for service to the delinquent child throughout the United States. Only five states (California, Minnesota, Wisconsin, Massachusetts, and Texas) have followed the pattern established, however. The name or stated purpose of each youth authority indicates that its objective is that of a child welfare program. Minnesota calls its authority the Youth Conservation Commission; Massachusetts uses the name, Youth Service

[68] Leonard B. Harrison and Pryor McNeil Grant, *Youth in the Toils* (New York: The Macmillan Company, 1938), p. 131.

[69] Thorsten Sellin, *The Criminality of Youth* (Philadelphia: The American Law Institute, 1940), p. 9.

Board; and Texas, the title of Youth Development Council. Wisconsin has created the Division of Child Welfare and Youth Service in the Department of Public Welfare.

The California Youth Correction Authority Act was established by legislation enacted in 1941. The Youth Authority began to function a year later, patterning its program and objectives on recommendations of the American Law Institute. Prior to this date, the administration of treatment programs in California had been dispersed among several state departments. When the act was amended in 1943 to eliminate the term "Correction" from the title of the Authority, this legislation also removed responsibility for the operation of the state correctional schools from the Department of Institutions and responsibility for the supervision of probation from the State Department of Social Welfare, and assigned both functions to the Youth Authority.[70]

The major objectives of the California Youth Authority are the treatment and rehabilitation of children committed to the agency and the prevention of delinquency. The agency accepts commitment of children whose behavior is so disturbed that they cannot be cared for in the community. When the court decides that commitment to the Youth Authority is indicated, the Authority makes a careful study of the child's case history. The Youth Authority may accept the case or reject it, depending upon the child's needs and the availability of services to meet those needs.[71]

Rehabilitation is accomplished through (1) clinical diagnosis and discovery of factors which influence deviant behavior; (2) classification of children on the basis of age, mental ability, emotional stability, and treatment required; (3) treatment, retraining, and reeducation to fit the child's needs and abilities as they are reflected in diagnosis and study; and (4) adequate parole supervision.[72]

The five members of the California Youth Authority serve as an administrative board and have sole responsibility for the acceptance, classification, placement, parole, and discharge of youths committed to it. Members of the Authority board are appointed by the governor with the approval of the Senate and serve four-year terms. The chairman also serves as director of the agency.

---

[70] Vandyce Hamren, *Organization of the Youth Authority and An Outline of Its Program* (Sacramento: California Youth Authority, 1951), introduction (mimeographed).

[71] *Ibid.*, p. 2.

[72] *Ibid.*

Any youth authority will only be as effective as the services at its disposal. It will have little meaning if its own treatment resources are meager or if it does not stimulate child welfare services on the local level. In 1955–56, 85 per cent of California's delinquent children were treated in their home communities, with the most disturbed and maladjusted children becoming the responsibility of the Youth Authority.[73]

The California Youth Authority maintains two reception centers to which committed children are sent for study, diagnosis, and treatment. Evaluation of each child is made by a professional team of psychiatrists, psychologists, social workers, physicians, dentists, teachers, and counselors. On the basis of such study and recommendations, the Youth Authority determines the most appropriate treatment plan for the child. This may be a return to his own home under supervision, placement in a foster home or wage home, placement in an appropriate institution operated by the Youth Authority, or, for older youths, assignment to a CYA Forestry Camp.

Selected Bibliography

Aichhorn, August. *Wayward Youth*. New York: The Viking Press, 1951.

Beck, Bertram M. *Youth Within Walls*. New York: Community Service Society of New York, 1950.

Bloch, Herbert A., and Frank T. Flynn. *Delinquency—The Juvenile Offender in America Today*. New York: Random House, 1956.

Bowlby, John. *Maternal Care and Mental Health*. Geneva: World Health Organization, 1952.

Cohen, Frank, J. *Children in Trouble: An Experiment in Institutional Care*. New York: W. W. Norton and Company, 1952.

Deutsch, Albert. *Our Rejected Children*. Boston: Little, Brown and Company, 1950.

Eissler, K. R. (ed.). *Searchlights on Delinquency*. New York: International Universities Press, 1949.

Glueck, Sheldon, and Eleanor Glueck. *Unraveling Juvenile Delinquency*. New York: The Commonwealth Fund, 1950.

Healy, William A., and Augusta F. Bronner. *New Light on Delinquency and Its Treatment*. New Haven: Yale University Press, 1936.

Kenney, John P., and Dan G. Pursuit. *Police Work With Juveniles*. Springfield, Illinois: Charles C Thomas, 1954.

Kvaraceus, William C. *Juvenile Delinquency and the School*. Yonkers, New York: World Book Company, 1945.

McCorkle, Lloyd W., Albert Elias, and F. Lovell Bixby. *The Highlands Story*. New York: Henry Holt and Company, 1958.

---

[73] California Youth Authority, *Biennial Report 1955–56*.

Mulford, Robert M., Victor B. Wylegala, and Elwood F. Melson. *Caseworker and Judge in Neglect Cases.* New York: Child Welfare League of America, 1956.

Sellin, J. Thorsten. *The Criminality of Youth.* Philadelphia: The American Law Institute, 1940.

Shaw, Clifford R., and Henry D. McKay. *Juvenile Delinquency and Urban Areas.* Chicago: University of Chicago Press, 1942.

Sussmann, Frederick B. *Law of Juvenile Delinquency.* New York: Oceana Publications, 1950.

United States Children's Bureau. *New Perspectives for Research on Juvenile Delinquency.* United States Department of Health, Education and Welfare, Social Security Administration. Washington, D.C.: Government Printing Office, 1955.

United States Children's Bureau. *Standards for Specialized Courts Dealing with Children.* Publication 346. United States Department of Health, Education and Welfare. Washington, D.C.: Government Printing Office, 1954.

Part Five · Services for

*There are many children
whose lives are incomplete and insecure
because of economic, emotional, or social handicaps.
Situational developments may also create problems
with which the family cannot cope
and it becomes necessary for them to seek special health,
education, and social welfare resources within the community.*

Children with Special Needs

Chapter 13

Services for All

Children with Special Needs

As we have seen in previous chapters, the history of child welfare since the first White House Conference in 1909 has accented a growing realization that the needs of a child are best met when he can live with his own family in his own home. This conviction was originally based upon a general knowledge of the damage suffered by children in the type of mass care provided by almshouses and large institutions for children. During the last two decades, however, there has been scientific documentation of the emotional, physical, and social effects of any separation of a child from his own family.

Lauretta Bender, combining her research with that of Margaret A. Ribble, Lawson O. Lowrey, David M. Levy, and others, pointed to the serious consequences of separating the young child from his parents. Their findings showed that the child who is deprived of continuous mothering will remain infantile in behavior and be retarded in personality growth and development. His language development will

305

be defective and his behavior will be impulsive and tend to imitate that of other children. He will also be unable to identify with others because he has not had an opportunity to develop a feeling of his own identity through emotional experiences with meaningful persons. As a result, his defective personality structure cannot be modified through later experience or treatment.[1]

John Bowlby's work, *Maternal Care and Mental Health*, published in 1951, gave new emphasis to the harmful effects of depriving children of a continuing relationship with a mother person in early childhood. His scholarly review of all previous studies in this field amassed overwhelming evidence that mental health and personality development are seriously impaired by maternal deprivation. His specific indictment of child care agencies which fail to give skilled service to parents in helping them to provide a happy family life for their children caused many agencies to reexamine their placement practices.

Specialized Services for Children in Their Own Homes

HOMEMAKER SERVICE

In all families there are times when crises upset the ordinary routines of living. This is especially true when the mother becomes ill or incapacitated or is temporarily out of the home for other reasons. The father is then faced with the responsibility of feeding, dressing, and supervising the children, in addition to maintaining his role as breadwinner. In these situations, a homemaker service can often prevent the necessity of breaking up the family for brief or prolonged periods of time. This service also has value when a family is permanently disrupted by the death or desertion of the mother. Under these circumstances a homemaker service often permits the children to remain in their own home until the father can arrange for a relative or another person to assume the role of mother-substitute.

Homemaker service can also be used to supplement the services of a mother in caring for a sick child or for children who have special handicaps. For a large family of young children, it has further value when it becomes necessary for the mother to work or to be absent

---

[1] Lauretta Bender, "There Is No Substitute for Family Life," *Child Study*, Vol. XXIII, No. 3 (Spring 1946), p. 76.

during the day for other reasons.[2] It can also serve as an important resource when a child of a working mother becomes ill and therefore unable to use the care customarily provided by a day care facility.

Although the need for this service is receiving increasing recognition, it has been aptly pointed out:

Homemaker service cannot create a home. It can help to sustain what is already there and supplement what families are able to do for themselves. It is a service that tides over without taking over.[3]

Mildred Arnold of the Children's Bureau extends this concept by reflecting:

When I think of homemaker service I think of it first as a service to families—a service that safeguards, protects, stabilizes and unifies families. Next I think of homemaker service as growing out of a community's conscience and concern for the well-being of all people.[4]

By definition, a "homemaker service" is a process through which a public or private social agency makes available the services of a woman who can assume the role of homemaker. The agency caseworker plays a significant part in the parents' understanding and use of the homemaker and in helping to meet the family's needs. The caseworker has the initial contact with the family, learns about the crisis the family is facing, and helps to explore other alternatives in handling the problem. The caseworker's early contacts with the parents are very important since the service can prove helpful only when parents understand the role that the homemaker will play and can decide that this is a service they really want. Learning to know the members of the family also assists the caseworker in selecting the homemaker who will best meet their needs in terms of personality and training.

There are basic differences between a "homemaker" and a housekeeper, as the latter usually takes responsibility only for "running the house" and is employed independently without agency affiliation or supervision. Maud Morlock, long identified with homemaker service

[2] United States Children's Bureau, *Homemaker Service: A Method of Child Care,* Publication 296 (Washington, D.C.: Government Printing Office, 1946), p. 4.

[3] Leon H. Richman, Mrs. Tracy C. Clough, and Mrs. Eleanor B. Dornenburg, *Homemaker Service: A Preventive to Placement of Children in Foster Care,* U.S. Children's Bureau, 1952, p. 1.

[4] Mildred Arnold, *Meeting Family Need Through Homemaker Service,* U.S. Children's Bureau, 1957, p. 1.

as a method of child welfare, describes the triangular relationship between agency and family this way:

In a good homemaking service the caseworker, the homemaker, and the parents can comprise a team working together in the children's behalf. And casework is the cornerstone of the service.[5]

The family that is disrupted by sudden tragedy, illness, or other serious problem often needs more than help with the physical care and supervision of the children. It needs the combination of professional services given by the homemaker and the caseworker. When the mother is absent from the home, the children become upset, evidence need for the missing mother, and worry about her well-being. A distraught father is often little comfort to his children nor can he avoid sharing some of his anxiety, worry, and weariness with the rest of his family. The homemaker is aware of these problems and is prepared to help the family with its emotional crises through the skill and supervision of the caseworker, with whom she works closely.

Child welfare workers know the value of a homemaker service and the demand for it, yet it is one of the least available of all child welfare services. Only 89 localities in 31 states, Washington, D.C., and Puerto Rico benefit from the homemaker service offered by 103 voluntary agencies and 25 public agencies.[6] In many communities there is an increasing realization that foster home care is economically expensive and does not meet the child's need for affectional ties with his own family. Social agencies have found it difficult to initiate homemaker services, however, because the time required to recruit, train, and supervise homemakers cannot be made available when staff shortages are already limiting the provision of existing services.

PROTECTIVE SERVICES

Protective services to children are specialized casework services in behalf of children who are abused, neglected, or receiving inadequate care and supervision. Protective service has also been described as "a service to parents, guardians or custodians who are unable or unwilling to ask for and use help from other resources and who are failing to meet the basic needs of their children."[7]

---

[5] Maud Morlock, "Homemaker Services—Major Defense for Children," *Children,* Vol. 4, No. 3 (May–June 1957), p. 103.

[6] *Ibid.,* p. 102.

[7] "Statement of Standards," *Standards for Child Protective Agencies,* (Albany, New York: The American Humane Association, undated), unnumbered pages.

Children and their parents come to the attention of an agency offering a protective service through a complaint by the juvenile court, another social agency, a public health nurse, the police, the school, relatives, or some other citizen. The agency may be operated under public or private auspices, but the parents it serves are involuntary clients who are reported to be contributing to the neglect of their child. When an agency has a working relationship with the juvenile court, it will accept court referrals for protective service. In any event, the agency will be obliged to report to the court those situations in which casework methods have failed because the parents are unwilling or unable to effect any change in their own behavior.

In a protective service, the child is considered to be the primary client, but the parents are the focus of treatment. Esther Lazarus has written:

Nothing helpful or even fundamentally protective can happen to a neglected child unless his parents take some responsibility for making this possible.[8]

Claire Hancock evaluates the neglectful parent in the following manner:

The parent who finds so little satisfaction in one of the most deeply personal relationships that living involves, has surely suffered a long series of emotional mishaps that make him the fearful, immature, unstable person that he now is. The individual who seems not to care about his own child . . . is painfully different from his fellow man.[9]

Parents are legally and culturally charged with responsibility for the care, protection, and supervision of their children. When parents are not fulfilling these responsibilities, they usually want to effect change in their relationships with each other, with their children, and with the community. Frequently, however, they lack motivation, have no knowledge of existing services, or are insensitive to the part that they are playing in their child's welfare. The protective agency offers the parents an opportunity to become more responsible, to resolve some of the problems which interfere with family relations and proper child care, and to re-evaluate the child's situation in terms of the total environment in which he lives.

---

[8] Esther Lazarus, "The Positive Approach to Protective Service," *Child Welfare*, Vol. XXVIII, No. 9 (November 1949), p. 9.

[9] Claire R. Hancock, "Protective Service for Children," *Child Welfare*, Vol. XXVIII, No. 3 (March 1949), p. 4.

Claire Hancock reviewed the importance of protective service this way:

I am convinced that persons, court orders, in fact all the means of control that society exerts to stop the wrongdoer, both for his sake and his child's protection, will not unaided, achieve its whole purpose. I believe there needs also to be an opportunity for the parent to have an individualized professional relationship to help him connect his present dilemma with his own destructive way of operating and correct this if it is possible for him to do so.[10]

Protective services have been offered in some American communities for almost a century, but there are still many localities which have no resources of this kind. Parents who are adjudged to be contributing to the abuse or neglect of their children are often admonished, fined, or jailed, without any help in solving the problems which caused the lack of care. Services are sometimes made available after court action, but the parent who has been sentenced to jail or prison for child neglect, or fined after he has received newspaper publicity, may not feel inclined to plan constructively in behalf of the family. For this reason, protective service is most effective when it is offered to parents before the situation becomes so serious that a court is involved. Parents do not have the right to exploit or mistreat their children but, whenever possible, the causes of neglect should be explored and ameliorated to prevent the need for adjudication and separation.

A recent study made by the Children's Division of the American Humane Association indicated that thirteen states have no legal provision for child protective services. Thirty-five states and the District of Columbia impose legislative responsibility on the public welfare agency for provision of protective services. Three states—Connecticut, Massachusetts, and Maryland—impose no legal obligation on the state department of public welfare for providing protective services, but delegate this responsibility to state-wide private agencies.[11] Under the leadership of the Child Welfare League and the Children's Bureau, increasing emphasis is now being placed on the development of protective services so that children will be spared separation from their parents and families will be helped to solve the problems which result in inadequate care.

---

[10] *Ibid.*, p. 9.

[11] Vincent DeFrancis, *Child Protective Services in the United States* (Denver: Children's Division, The American Humane Association, 1956), pp. 40–41.

OTHER CASEWORK SERVICES

A third type of specialized service for children living in their own homes is known by a variety of names, dependent upon the auspices under which the service is given, the defined function of the agency providing the service, and perhaps upon the "working titles" of the staff assigned to this service. For some considerations, these services are loosely classified as "preventive services," since their availability may obviate the need for out-of-home care, referral to a child guidance clinic or juvenile court, the harming of the child from neglect or abuse, or the disruption of family living. More frequently, however, they are known as "services to parents in behalf of children," "family social work," or "child welfare services."

In general, these services are designed to

. . . enable parents and children to live more happily with themselves; with each other, with other family members and with their neighbors; to have useful, productive and satisfying lives; and to deal successfully with the situations and conditions with which they are confronted.[12]

Services of this kind may be provided by a public welfare department or a private family and/or children's agency, but they are usually given at the request of a parent when some problem arises in family living, in the development or behavior of a child, or in parent-child relations.

In some instances the primary service required may be the provision of information about other resources available in the community, help in accepting and using these resources, or reassurance that a child's development or behavior is within normal limits. In others, intensive casework treatment may be necessary to help the parent understand the child's problem, recognize his own part in creating the problem, and assume some responsibility for effecting a change in his own feelings and behavior. Direct work with the child may also be indicated in some situations, and the casework service may need to be accompanied by auxiliary services, such as financial assistance, homemaker service, or day care.

This type of service forms an important part of the program of every private family service agency and is usually provided to some extent by each private children's agency. When both types of agencies exist in a given community, however, the children's agency may

---

[12] Annie Lee Davis, *Children Living in Their Own Homes*, Federal Security Agency, Children's Bureau (Washington, D.C.: Government Printing Office, 1953), p. 7.

provide a service for children living in their own homes only (1) when it is necessary to determine whether out-of-home care is the only practical method of meeting the needs of the child and his family, and (2) when such service is needed to help a child adjust in his own home after a period of foster care.

In public agencies, this service may be given as a part of the child welfare service program initiated with funds made available under the Social Security Act. If the service is available in the community through a private agency, however, the shortage of professionally trained staff in the county welfare department may result in a policy that the public agency will make the service available only to those families which receive financial assistance or are eligible to some other service provided by the agency, for example, foster care or placement for adoption.

Financial Benefits for Children

Since the first White House Conference in 1909, it has been generally agreed that no child should be compelled to live apart from his parents because of economic deprivation alone. In the intervening decades there has also been an increasing recognition that the physical and emotional welfare of children is affected in many ways by the adequacy of income in their homes. Rapid strides have been made in the extension of financial resources for the support of children since the Social Security Act became effective in 1936. Unfortunately, the resources available to meet the needs of a particular child are still dependent upon the cause of his deprivation, the locality in which he lives, and the length of time he or his parents have lived in a particular community. Under prescribed conditions, certain benefits are usually available to children whose need is caused by the death, incapacitation, or prolonged absence of a parent. Even for these children, however, the source of payment and the adequacy of the amount received may be determined not by the child's need but by factors related to the laws of the state in which he lives or by the military service or prior employment of his parents.

Aid to Dependent Children

A milestone was reached in July, 1955, when Nevada (the only jurisdiction since 1945 which had not provided ADC under the provisions of the Social Security Act) initiated its program.[13]   In June, 1957, grants were paid by 53 jurisdictions to 647,200 families containing 1,831,900 children.[14]   The average family on ADC was composed of 3.7 persons in June 1957[15] and the average payment was $96.52 per family ($26.04 per person), with average grants ranging from $28.18 per family in Mississippi to $150.12 in Wisconsin.[16]

As currently set forth in Title IV of the Social Security Act, this program is designed for:

... the purpose of encouraging the care of dependent children in their own homes or in the homes of relatives by enabling each State to furnish financial assistance and other services, as far as practicable under the conditions in such State, to needy dependent children and the parents or relatives with whom they are living to help maintain and strengthen family life and to help such parents or relatives to attain the maximum self-support and personal independence consistent with the maintenance of continuing parental care and protection. . . . [17]

A "dependent child" is defined as a needy child under the age of eighteen, who is without parental support or care because of the death, continued absence from the home, physical or mental incapacitation of a parent, and "who is living with his father, mother, grandfather, grandmother, brother, sister, stepfather, stepmother, stepsister, uncle, aunt, first cousin, nephew, or niece in a place of residence maintained by one or more of such relatives as his or their own home."[18] Any of the relatives named may apply for ADC in the child's behalf; eligibility, however, is based upon need as determined by standards created on a state level.

The welfare department is obligated to process all applications for ADC with "reasonable promptness" and to report to law enforcement

---

[13] *Annual Report*, United States Department of Health, Education and Welfare (Washington, D.C.: Government Printing Office, 1956), p. 19.

[14] *Annual Report*, United States Department of Health, Education and Welfare, 1957, p. 40.

[15] *Trend Report*, United States Department of Health, Education and Welfare, Social Security Administration, Bureau of Public Assistance (Washington, D.C.: Government Printing Office, October 1957), p. 29.

[16] *Annual Report*, U.S. Department of Health, Education and Welfare, 1957 p. 40.

[17] *Compilation of the Social Security Laws*, Doc. 156, (Washington, D.C.: Government Printing Office, 1957), Section 401, p. 102.

[18] *Ibid.*, Section 406(a), p. 106.

officials when assistance is being given to a child who has been abandoned or deserted by his parent or parents.[19] An allowance for the relative caring for the child may be included in the grant and the caretaker may also receive medical or remedial care, providing the payee has a definable need and is not receiving Old Age Assistance. A child cannot be denied assistance if he has resided in the state one year immediately preceding application, or was born within that year, and the parent or relative with whom he lives has resided in the state for one year immediately preceding the child's birth.[20]

Although the ADC program has generally received strong support from state and federal legislators, it has become the most controversial public assistance program. Several factors have contributed to this development. As the death rate decreased because of advances made in medicine, the availability of medical care, and the improvement of working conditions, the number of fatherless children in the nation dropped from 2.8 million in 1934 to 1.9 million in 1954[21] despite the great increase in the total number of children. By 1954, more than 1,000,000 fatherless children were receiving OASI, while only 240,000 received ADC.[22] As a result, the percentage of children receiving ADC because of the death of their fathers dropped from 37 per cent in 1942 to approximately 15 per cent in 1954.[23]

During this period, too, the total number of employed mothers with children under eighteen years of age increased from one out of every ten mothers in the general population in 1940 to one out of every four mothers in 1955.[24] This change in the cultural pattern was reflected in the attitudes of the community toward ADC recipients. As a greater proportion of the nation's mothers entered the labor force, there was less acceptance of the need to utilize public funds to make it possible for mothers to remain at home to care for their children, despite increasing evidence of the personality damage suffered by children deprived of maternal care.

The critical attitudes of the community toward recipients of ADC

---

[19] *Ibid.*, Section 402 (*a*), p. 102.

[20] *Ibid.*, Section 402 (*b*), p. 103.

[21] *Annual Report*, United States Department of Health, Education and Welfare (Washington, D.C.: Government Printing Office, 1955), p. 22.

[22] *Ibid.*

[23] *Ibid.*

[24] *Annual Report*, United States Department of Health, Education and Welfare, 1956, p. 58.

have also been augmented by a frequent lack of any visible evidence of the disability of a father whose children receive assistance because of his incapacitation. More importantly, perhaps, the great increase in the proportion of children receiving ADC because of the separation or desertion of parents has led to a prevalent resentment against the use of funds to compensate for an evasion of parental responsibility. This has been most evident, perhaps, in the feelings engendered by the use of tax funds for the care of children born out of wedlock. There has been no evidence that the proportion of illegitimate children receiving ADC exceeds the ratio of children born out of wedlock in the general population, but it has been frequently alleged that the availability of ADC is responsible for the national increase in the rate of illegitimacy. (In 1940, 7.1 of every thousand unmarried women between the ages of 15 and 44 years gave birth to a child out of wedlock, and by 1955 this rate had increased to 18.3 per thousand unmarried women in this age range.) However unwarranted these charges may be, the fact remains that more than half of the children now receiving ADC are deprived of normal support because of the separation, divorce, desertion, or unwed status of their parents.

Public attitudes toward the ADC program, coupled with professional recognition of the need for a variety of services to assist parents to achieve a more independent and satisfying way of life, have had three important results. In addition to the 1952 requirement that law enforcement officials be informed of the aid provided for a child whose parent has deserted, a new emphasis has been placed on the discovery of the causes of dependency and on the development of the social services needed to strengthen family ties and encourage self-support. Effective July, 1957, Congress authorized $5,000,000 for research and the use of federal funds in the training of personnel for the public assistance programs. As a result, it is hoped that an additional 5,000 professionally trained social workers will become available and that many of the children currently receiving ADC can then be assured of a home life more conducive to their physical and emotional well-being.

GENERAL RELIEF

Despite the fact that this is the only type of aid available to families who lack legal residence and to those who fail to meet eligibility requirements for other categories of public assistance, the number of recipients of general relief has declined by approximately 80 per cent

since 1936.[25] In December, 1956, 305,000[26] general relief cases received $17,133,000 from state and local public funds.[27] The narrow
scope of these programs is evident in comparison with the ADC program, in which 616,226 families[28] were reported to have received
$58,571,167 in December, 1956.[29]

OLD AGE SURVIVOR'S
AND DISABILITY INSURANCE

In June, 1957, benefits under the OASDI program were paid to 1.4
million children in 797,800 families. Approximately 400,000 mothers
also received benefits.[30] In February of that year nearly 32,000 of
these families also received a supplementary ADC grant.[31] In 1956,
about 80 per cent of the latter group was receiving insurance benefits
based on the work record of a deceased father, while the benefits of
17 per cent were derived from the work record of an aged retired
father and an additional 3 per cent from the work record of a deceased mother.[32]

Under all circumstances, a legitimate child of a parent entitled to
OASDI benefits or a parent currently insured at the time of his death
is eligible to receive benefits if the child is (1) unmarried, (2) under
the age of eighteen or disabled before reaching this age, and (3) dependent upon the insured parent on the date the application is filed
or at the time of the parent's death.[33] An adopted child who meets
these conditions is also eligible except that he is required to have the
status of an adopted child for a period of three years if his parent is
living at the time of application. (If adoption has occurred, a prior
status as a stepchild can be counted in fulfilling this requirement.)
The rights of a stepchild are the same as those of an adopted child,

---

[25] *Trend Report*, p. 13.

[26] *Ibid.*, p. 54.

[27] *Ibid.*, p. 67.

[28] *Ibid.*, p. 54.

[29] *Ibid.*, p. 67.

[30] *Annual Report*, 1957, p. 24.

[31] *Ibid.*, p. 41.

[32] *Annual Report*, 1956, p. 46.

[33] *Compilation of the Social Security Laws*, United States Department of Health,
Education and Welfare (Washington, D.C.: Government Printing Office, 1957),
pp. 15–16.

except that a stepchild of a deceased worker must have had this status for a period of one year prior to the death of his stepparent.[34]

If other conditions are met, a natural or adopted child who was not receiving support from his father at the time specified, may receive benefits if he was living with his father at that time. A legitimate or adopted child who fulfills neither of these requirements is also eligible if he was not (1) living with and receiving more than half of his support from a stepfather, or (2) adopted by some other individual.[35]

An otherwise eligible child whose natural or adopting mother was currently insured at the time specified is not required to have been dependent upon her support unless other factors are involved. Eligibility to benefits based on her earnings would be present if the child were (1) living with his mother at the required time, (2) living with his father or adopting father but receiving at least one-half of his support from his mother, or (3) living elsewhere and receiving some support from his mother but not from his father or adopting father. A stepchild who meets the conditions listed would also be eligible to benefits based on his stepmother's earnings.[36]

OTHER BENEFITS ESTABLISHED BY LAW

A network of other financial benefits is available to certain children under prescribed conditions. Some are paid in uniform amounts in similar situations but others reflect the laws of individual states.

In general, these benefits are based on the concept of compensation for a foreseeable risk involved for an individual and his family. When a program is financed through "a plan whereby funds are built up out of contributions made by or on behalf of an individual,"[37] it is properly classified as a system of social insurance. Benefits not financed in this way usually represent (1) a public acceptance of responsibility for the risk incurred by the individual (for example, veterans' benefits); or (2) a realization of the danger to the public interest or economy if large groups are permitted to suffer the natural consequence of the potential risk involved (for example, the indirect benefits which a child might receive through the payment of government crop subsidies to farmers).

---

[34] *Ibid.*, p. 76.

[35] *Ibid.*, p. 16.

[36] *Ibid.*

[37] Wilbur J. Cohen, "Social Insurance," *Social Work Year Book*, 1957, p. 537.

It is not appropriate to review here the conditions under which these benefits might be available to an individual child or his family. It is important, however, that all persons in a helping profession or preparing to enter such professions, have an awareness that the following benefits exist and may be available to meet the needs of a child deprived of normal parental support.

1. *Workmen's Compensation.* In all states, legislation has been enacted to provide compensation for employees[38] suffering injury or disease as a result of their employment. The occupations covered, the conditions under which the employer is liable, and the amount of benefits required by law show wide variations.

2. *Unemployment Insurance.* The federal-state system of unemployment compensation established by the Social Security Act in 1935 constitutes a temporary financial resource for children whose unemployed parents previously worked in a "covered employment," and the laws of some states make provision for additional allowances for dependents.

The federal system established for the railroad industry in 1938 represents a somewhat more adequate resource for the children of unemployed railway workers than do the programs established in most states under the Social Security Act.[39]

3. *Railroad Social Insurance.* This plan, administered by the Railroad Retirement Board, provides "the most comprehensive and most adequate social insurance program in the United States."[40] Since it is wholly administered by the federal government, its benefits are uniform throughout the nation. Direct benefits are available for children of deceased workers and the total program protects railroad employees and their families from six types of wage loss.

4. *Disability Insurance.* In addition to the OASDI benefits made available to eligible insured workers who become permanently and totally disabled after 1957, four states (California, New Jersey, New York, and Rhode Island) provide temporary disability benefits similar to unemployment compensation.[41]

5. *Veterans' Benefits.* The most extensive benefits are those administered by the Veterans' Administration as compensation for a

---

[38] *Ibid.,* p. 538.

[39] *Ibid.,* p. 543.

[40] *Ibid.,* p. 546.

[41] *Ibid.*

service-connected disability which results in a loss of earning power, or as a pension for veterans with a total and permanent disability, not service-connected.[42] Veterans whose disability is 50 per cent or more and has been adjudged to be service-connected receive additional allowances for their children and other dependents. Children of deceased veterans are eligible to death compensation or death pension payments under certain conditions.[43] Monetary assistance is also available for the education of children whose parents died as a result of war service.[44]

6. *Others.* Under certain conditions, survivors' benefits are available under various retirement systems established for the employees of federal, state, county, and city agencies.

Grants available under the Social Security Act to eligible blind, aged, and permanently and totally disabled persons also constitute an indirect resource for children when their parents would otherwise find it necessary to assume responsibility for the support of their needy relatives. In some instances, the needs of parents can also be met through a public assistance grant of this type (for example, parents who are over 65 years of age, blind, or totally and permanently disabled).

Services Authorized by the Social Security Act

The amounts authorized for the maternal and child welfare programs established by Title V of the Social Security Act have consistently increased since 1936. As a result, these programs have played important roles in gradually expanding the services available to children.

CHILD WELFARE SERVICES

Although the actual amounts appropriated by Congress for this program have frequently been less than the sums named in the act,

---

[42] Virginia C. Karl, "Veterans' Benefits and Services," *Social Work Year Book,* 1957, p. 578.

[43] *Ibid.,* p. 581.

[44] *Ibid.,* p. 580.

the legal maximum specified has gradually risen from $1,500,000 in 1936 to $17,000,000 in 1958.

During this period, other provisions of Part 3 of the act have remained comparatively unchanged. The 1950 amendment, however, added an authorization for (1) the expenditure of federal funds for the cost of returning a runaway child less than sixteen years of age to his own community in another state when "such return is in the interest of the child and the cost thereof cannot otherwise be met," and (2) the use of "the facilities and experience of voluntary agencies" in developing services for children when authorized by the state. In 1958, the requirement that funds be expended "in areas predominantly rural or other areas of special need" was deleted.

In 1947, the increased funds available for the program resulted in a change in the policy which originally prohibited the use of federal funds for care in foster family homes and institutions. Since that date, several states have elected to include in the plans submitted to the Children's Bureau for approval amounts to be used in the expansion of foster care programs.[45] Funds have also been used to demonstrate the value of homemaker service, to recruit additional foster homes, to conduct a wide variety of community studies, and to initiate other needed services. Throughout the years, however, the grants made to states have been used primarily for the employment and training of staff equipped to provide the skilled services needed by troubled children and their families.

In June, 1956, there were 5,628 persons employed in state and local public child welfare programs in America.[46] Eight states, however, had less than 25 such workers, eight states had from 25 to 49, and only six states had 200 or more child welfare workers.[47] The three states with the largest number of workers (New York, California, and Ohio) together employed almost one-third of the nation's total, although only one-fifth of the country's child population under 21 lived in these states. Perhaps the lack of child welfare staff is better revealed by the fact that one-half of the nation's counties did not have the services of any full-time public child welfare worker, and one-fourth of the child population lived in these counties. In counties which had child welfare workers, the rate of coverage was only one worker per 10,000

---

[45] *Four Decades of Action for Children*, p. 76.

[46] United States Children's Bureau, *Staff in Public Child Welfare Programs, 1956*, Statistical Series No. 41 (Washington, D.C.: Government Printing Office, 1957), p. 1.

[47] *Ibid.*, Figure 2, p. 5.

children under 21, and in the entire nation there were only .7 workers per 10,000 children.[48]

To increase the preventive, protective, and rehabilitative services available to children, federal grants-in-aid for the training of child welfare personnel were used for educational leave by all states except Indiana, Nebraska, Nevada, and Vermont in 1956. Such funds were also unavailable in Alaska and in the District of Columbia.[49]

MATERNAL AND CHILD HEALTH SERVICES

The grants made to 53 states and territories have continued to promote the health and welfare of mothers and children by making it possible to extend the services available to them.

In 1956, health supervision at prenatal clinics was given to about 224,000 expectant mothers, public health nurses served more than 430,000 mothers before and after delivery, and more than 2,000,000 children of preschool age received health supervision through well-child clinics. Nursing service was also provided for more than 2,500,-000 preschool children, almost the same number received smallpox inoculations or diphtheria immunizations, and polio shots were given to 10,500,000 children.[50]

Institutes, conferences, and research projects have also been conducted with special attention to the emotional problems of ill children, mental retardation, and the need to bring an interdisciplinary approach to these problems. New demonstration projects were conducted in 26 states in 1957 to develop patterns of service for mentally retarded children, particularly those of preschool age.

Since 1936, Title V of the Social Security Act has been repeatedly amended to increase the federal funds available for this program. Though Congress has frequently failed to appropriate the maximum amount permitted by the act, the specified sums authorized have increased from $3,800,000 in 1936[51] to $21,500,000 in 1958.

CRIPPLED CHILDREN'S SERVICES

With the exception of Arizona, all states and territories have continued to participate in this program. Despite the variation of aus-

---

[48] *Ibid.*, p. 4.

[49] *Ibid.*, Table H, p. 15.

[50] *Annual Report*, 1957, p. 58.

[51] *Four Decades of Action for Children*, p. 90.

pices under which the program is conducted in the different states, the services provided have a uniform objective: "to locate children who require care, and to provide the means of physical restoration through diagnosis, medical and surgical treatment, and alleviation of unfavorable social and psychological influences which adversely affect the degree and duration of the disability."[52]

In 1956 this program served more than 290,000 children through clinics, hospitals, convalescent home care, and physicians' visits.

The appropriations authorized for this program have been increased from $2,850,000 in 1936[53] to $20,000,000 in 1958.

Social Services in the School

The importance of the school social worker, or visiting teacher, cannot be stressed too greatly because of the setting in which he works. The relations between the child's school experience, his reaction to control, competition, conformity, learning, and cooperation are significantly reflected in his academic and social achievements.

The public school has been charged with a variety of responsibilities reaching into many facets of the child's present and future welfare. It is expected to provide an environment in which all children can acquire adequate mental, emotional, and physical health, oral and written communication skills, and an ability to obtain a job and earn a living. The school is charged with responsibility for helping children to develop desirable attitudes toward others; to think and to utilize pertinent material effectively; and to appreciate their homes, churches, schools, and "the ideals of the American way of life." The school is also expected to help the child to distinguish between "propaganda and fact," and to emphasize democracy in the classroom.[54]

Biber points out that the school has a responsibility to give the child a "sense of trust," and that child growth and development often get caught in the thorny snare of the teacher's demand for behavioral conformity.

---

[52] *Annual Report,* 1956, p. 65.

[53] *Four Decades of Action for Children,* p. 90.

[54] R. E. Robinson, *Some Basic Needs for the Education of Teachers and Personnel for Special Education* (Vol. I of *Special Education for the Exceptional,* editors, Merle E. Frampton and Elena D. Gall; Boston: F. Porter Sargent, 1955), p. 274.

The traditional school is typified by the dignified, modulated tones of adjusted, maybe over-adjusted middle age. . . . The pressure most schools exert upon a child to be as grown up as possible at all times and on all occasions but mirrors social, maybe middle-class, sanctions against excitement, disorder, emotionality, and impulsiveness.[55]

The child, however, may not be able to respond to adult expectations because wholesome and healthful maturation is based on a strong desire to be independent and grown-up during a period in which there is also a need to maintain some of the dependency of childhood. Consequently, what may appear to be nonconformity may be the very process of growth itself, with its gradual, uneven, wavering, regressive, and inconsistent behavior.[56]

The school is also seen as a mental health resource:

. . . The schools are organized social experiences for children which set a pattern for personal relations outside of the family and thus exert a powerful influence on the direction personality development follows. Educators vary in the degree to which they are conscious of this total effect—but the effect of schools on personality development is great whether or not educators intend it to be so.[57]

The importance of the school as a mental health agency has emerged from a definition of community mental health services. The activities which tend to enhance the mental health of a community are (1) services to persons who are presently involved in a crisis and need immediate treatment and care, and (2) services which meet the needs of persons not struggling with an immediate crisis but who need preventive service. The schools fall into the latter category.[58]

There has been a preponderance of literature supporting the view that the school has responsibility for the development of the child's personality, for detecting symptomatic behavior, and for treating it. Despite this fact, many questions have been raised regarding the wisdom of offering mental hygiene or social services in the schools. Educational philosophy has concerned itself justifiably with "the whole child," but there has been a tendency to overlook the reality that dependency, indigency, and delinquency are also a part of this "whole-

---

[55] Barbara Biber, "Schooling as an Influence in Developing Health Personality" (in *Community Programs for Mental Health*, editors, Ruth Kotinsky and Helen L. Witmer; Cambridge: Harvard University Press, 1955), p. 160.

[56] *Ibid.*

[57] *The Elements of a Community Mental Health Program* (New York: Milbank Memorial Fund, 1956), p. 13.

[58] *Ibid.*, p. 12.

ness," and that these conditions inevitably affect the child's reactions in the classroom.

In some school systems, this problem continues to exist because of deeply entrenched definitions of function. The National Education Association of the United States and the American Association of School Administrators defined the purpose of the school as the intellectual, physical, and social development of the individual and added that the clientele of the public school is made up of "minors and some adults." The purpose of "public welfare" was properly given as "the amelioration of circumstances of individuals," but the clientele of public welfare departments was listed as "defectives, delinquents, dependents, indigent, and the maladjusted."[59]

There can be little doubt that the clientele of the school and that of the public welfare department, child guidance clinic, juvenile court, and other social agencies overlaps and that there can be no arbitrary division of function and clientele. Likewise there can be no doubt that the school must offer an educational service to the child who is indigent, delinquent, defective, or maladjusted. It has been this unfortunate dichotomy, however, that has tended to raise questions as to whether schools should assume functions considered to be in the mental health or social welfare field, in addition to their traditional educational function. For this reason, it was not until school performance and behavior were evaluated in terms of the child's total adjustment that public school administrators sought to strengthen their staffs with psychiatric consultants, clinical psychologists, and school social workers.

Altmeyer points out that there is no cleavage between education and therapy since they are different aspects of the same problem. Education is, in itself, a therapeutic process which effects change in the learner by giving him knowledge, skills, and experiences with which to cope with his environment.[60] Psychotherapy, on the other hand, is an educational process in which the individual gains knowledge and understanding of his own behavior that will help him in discovering ways to come to terms with his personal environment.[61]

---

[59] *Social Services in the Schools* (Washington, D.C.: Educational Policies Commission, National Education Association of the United States and the American Association of School Administrators, 1939), Table I, p. 8.

[60] John R. Altmeyer, "Public School Services for the Child with Emotional Problems," *Social Work*, Vol. 1, No. 2 (April 1956), p. 97.

[61] *Ibid.*

Teachers should not do therapy, not only because they are not trained in this highly specialized field but because the teacher must remain oriented to the group, and therapy demands a one-to-one relationship.[62] The teacher does have a special function in relation to the mental health of the children in her class, however, since she must have adequate knowledge of normal child behavior and an ability to identify children in need of referral to other resources. Altmeyer, in stressing the teacher's need to understand "what is considered to be normal behavior," points out:

There is much glib talk by all people dealing with children about normal and abnormal behavior, but too frequently basic knowledge is lacking about what is normal and how to achieve it. In evaluating behavior, teachers and other professional people must be constantly on the alert not to label behavior abnormal purely because it offends personally . . . or does not fit in with an individual code of ethics or behavior.[63]

The school has lost few of the many responsibilities described by Patey and Stevenson almost a quarter of a century ago. Developing what might be called "the dynamism of public school function," the authors recognized that in helping a child to develop and achieve his highest potential, the school must often act *in loco parentis* and this role, in turn, places many responsibilities on the school.[64] Among these are the development of special classes for children with intellectual, emotional, or physical handicaps; testing, counseling, and social work service; extracurricular activities; the maintenance of sound interdepartmental relations; "humanized curriculum content"; and other aspects of administrative function, determined by the needs of the child in school.[65]

THE SCHOOL SOCIAL WORKER

The school social worker or visiting teacher is a member of the "team" and, as such, she works cooperatively with the teacher, parent, principal, superintendent, nurse, physician, psychologist, counselor, and collateral agencies. Specifically, she extends casework service to

---

[62] *Ibid.*, p. 98.

[63] *Ibid.*, p. 99.

[64] Henry C. Patey and George S. Stevenson, *The Mental Health Emphasis in Education* (New York: National Committee for Mental Hygiene, 1935), p. 17.

[65] *Ibid.*, p. 13.

children and their parents when the child's problems interfere with school achievement and adjustment. Schools employing social workers are therefore fulfilling their dual responsibilities, namely the education and socialization of the child.[66]

School social work involves application of the knowledge and skills of social work to the solution of educational problems. It is premised on the social worker's concern for the individual, his social environment, and his emotional experiences.[67] The child in school often has a network of tenuous relationships with parents, teacher, principal, siblings, and peers with which he needs help when they interfere with school adjustment. Indeed, some children are unable to profit from their school experience without individual help in resolving these problems.[68]

Grace W. Mitchell describes the goals of the process somewhat more fully:

The school social worker helps the child face and claim his own patterns of feeling and acting, how he responds to life and people. He does this so that the child can begin to weigh where his patterns do and do not further the purposes which his heart values most.[69]

The child achieves a different kind of relationship with the social worker than he has with the teacher; he does not have to share the worker with the group, and he does not have to put his best foot forward, since he will learn to know that it is all right to have some difficulties. Mitchell stresses a "working together" as the social worker helps the child to acquire "a new and different image of adults" as she

. . . opens to the child new and different avenues of interacting thought, interacting feeling, and interacting experience through which he can arrive at more harmonious relations with all adults and with all people.[70]

---

[66] Florence Poole, "The Social Worker's Contribution to the Problems of the Classroom Teacher," *Journal of Exceptional Children*, Vol. 17, No. 3 (December 1950), p. 74.

[67] Kermit T. Wiltse, "Education and Social Welfare," *The Annals of the American Academy of Political and Social Science*, Vol. 302 (November 1955), p. 51.

[68] Opal Boston, "School Social Work in Modern Education," *Understanding the Child*, Vol. XIX, No. 1 (January 1950), p. 2.

[69] Grace W. Mitchell, "Casework with the School Child," *Social Work*, Vol. 2, No. 3 (July 1957), p. 79.

[70] *Ibid.*, p. 80.

While the child is helped to take responsibility for resolving his problems, the social worker also works closely with his parents by carefully explaining the service she has to offer, interpreting the child's difficulties, giving casework support, and making referrals to other agencies, if that is indicated. The same pattern of cooperation and identification of function and role must be extended to the teacher and to other school personnel having some responsibility for the child. Florence Poole points to the need of the school social worker to accept and understand the function of the school and the pertinence of developing a casework service that will be compatible with the school's structure and organization. The social worker must, in fact, "define the service and her contribution in such a way that the school personnel can accept it as a service which contributes to the major purpose of the school."[71]

The concept of the school social worker has changed as education itself has changed—as public school function became more clearly defined and as compulsory school attendance laws were enacted in the various states. Children of varied nationality and race brought a myriad of diverse ethnic, cultural, social, and economic backgrounds to the schools. In this era, the emphasis was upon democratizing public education and making it a fundamental right of all children. However, there was little thought given to the child's personality or to the intrinsic and extrinsic environmental influences which molded his personality. Later, when the schools were influenced by the mental hygiene movement, social work services were extended only to children in serious difficulty. Like the public health nurse, the earlier "visiting teacher" frequently visited the homes and reported symptoms and conditions to school officials. Education has been given a new dimension by the current emphasis upon emotional readiness to learn, the influence of parental attitudes on child development, the relation between personality structure and patterns of behavior, the importance of interpersonal relationships, and the child's right to develop according to his own capacities and potentialities. This development has indeed made the emotional adjustment of children the key approach to the educational process.[72]

The school social worker now receives the majority of her referrals from the teachers, school nurse, psychologist, counselor, or principal

---

[71] Florence Poole, "An Analysis of the Characteristics of School Social Work," *The Social Service Review*, Vol. XXIII, No. 4 (December 1949), pp. 455–457.

[72] Biber, *op. cit.*, pp. 173–174.

and has frequent conferences with them about the children referred. Although child guidance has been described as "the responsibility of every member of the school staff and the sole responsibility of no one person,"[73] the school social worker assumes major responsibility for the school's casework services and for the school's relation with other health and welfare agencies in the community.

Consultation Services

In some school districts, the school social worker has major responsibility for work with disturbed children and families, for arranging case conferences, for staff consultation, and for collateral duties connected with the professional casework function. Other schools employ, in addition, psychiatrists who give consultation to the school staff. Such consultation is in effect "in service training" in which the teaching staff is helped to gain greater knowledge of the emotional needs of children. Through "case-centered and problem-centered consultation"[74] the psychiatrist participates in working out plans for treatment with the teacher and other staff. The psychiatric consultant also helps the educator to use his own personality more adequately by recognizing strengths which may be mobilized for more effective activity.[75]

The consulting psychiatrist sometimes finds that his function in the school is appraised with some question and misgivings by teachers and administrators since the process of consultation itself is often not clearly understood. The consulting psychiatrist ordinarily does not see children or parents and does not directly engage in treatment. The consultant has no ready remedies nor is it his function to assume responsibility for solving problems relating to individual children.[76] Instead, he holds case conferences in which members of the staff bring information regarding the behavior or symptoms of specific children. The consultant will orient the group to the dynamics of the problem,

---

[73] Gertrude P. Driscoll, *Child Guidance in the Classroom* (New York: Bureau of Publications, Teachers' College, Columbia University, 1955), p. 86.

[74] Gerald Caplan, "Mental Health Consultation in Schools," in *The Elements of a Community Mental Health Program* (New York: Milbank Memorial Fund), p. 78.

[75] *Ibid.*, p. 79.

[76] For an interesting account of a psychiatric consultant to two school systems, see: I. N. Berlin, "Some Learning Experiences as Psychiatric Consultant in the Schools," *Mental Hygiene*, Vol. XI, No. 2 (April 1956), pp. 215–236.

feasible treatment plans, and probable prognosis. Although the psychiatrist is available for diagnostic evaluation, interpretation of behavioral problems and treatment planning, therapy must be given by the school staff or referral made to an appropriate social agency.

The Child Guidance Clinic

It is difficult to evaluate the importance of the contemporary child guidance clinic without an appraisal of dynamic psychiatry as it relates to the whole field of mental health.

Mental health has been called "a social goal and cultural value"[77] and there is ample evidence that mental hygiene and child guidance clinic programs are steadily gaining legislative and community support. Nevertheless, the concept of mental health continues to be impressively elusive, primarily because it is a generic term infused with a variety of meanings.

The psychiatric clinician and other psychotherapists tend to associate mental health with mental illness, whereas the sociomoral idealist perceives the person as having mental health if he possesses such virtues as doing more than is expected of him, thinking of others before himself, and always keeping his emotions under control. Another stereotyped criterion of mental health is the individual's ability to adjust to society regardless of the demands or inconsistencies of that society. Mental health has also been associated with normality or the manifestation of such behavior as tends toward the "average."[78]

Although psychiatry is generally defined as a branch of medicine dealing with the study, diagnosis, evaluation, and treatment of the neuroses and psychoses, it is perhaps more adequately identified with its specific concerns about people. Willian Menninger points out that the practice of psychiatry is related to the way people behave, feel, and think. It raises questions as to why the person does what he does, why he becomes what he is, and whether his pattern of behavior is normal or not.[79] All of these basic concerns are applicable to the practice of child psychiatry.

---

[77] Sol W. Ginsburg, "The Mental Health Movement: Its Theoretical Assumptions," in Kotinsky and Witmer, *op. cit.*, p. 3.

[78] *Well Children*, pp. 5–7.

[79] William C. Menninger, *Psychiatry* (Ithaca: Cornell University Press, 1948), p. 20.

The Clinic Team

The professional service offered by the child guidance clinic is usually given by a team, made up of the psychiatrist, the clinical psychologist, and the psychiatric social worker. The psychiatrist generally has major responsibility for the administration and supervision of the clinic and for the treatment program, the clinical psychologist administers and interprets intelligence and personality tests and other diagnostic materials, and the psychiatric social worker has the initial interview with the child's parents and works with them throughout the child's contact with the clinic. The psychologist and social worker may also engage in therapy with the child or parents, depending upon the assignment of cases, special skills and interests of the therapists, and the policy of the clinic.

Functions and Structure of Child Guidance Clinics

The major functions of the child guidance clinic are (1) to screen cases for diagnostic and treatment service and (2) to offer individual therapy to the child and his parents. Other important functions of the clinic include the provision of training for students preparing for the medical, psychological, and social work aspects of child psychiatry. All community clinics assume responsibility for acting as an educational and consultant resource for parents, teachers, juvenile probation departments, social agencies, community groups, and others requesting information relating to child behavior, clinic policy, referral procedures, and other phases of the clinic's relationship with the wider community. The clinic may also serve a research purpose, not only in terms of studying and evaluating its own practice, but in making a contribution to the knowledge and literature in the field.

Child guidance clinics operate under various patterns of sponsorship, financial support, structure, policy, and governmental relationship. The community child guidance clinic is frequently a part of a statewide mental hygiene program and may be supported by state or local public funds or by public funds supplemented by financial support from the Community Chest or United Crusade. In some communities, however, a community clinic may be, in effect, a private social agency wholly supported by voluntary contributions which may or may not be received through a community chest. In any event, this type of clinic serves children referred by the juvenile court, schools, social agencies, parents, health agencies, and other sources on a city, county, or regional basis. It usually accepts referrals of children who are emotionally disturbed, rather than those who are psychotic or mentally retarded. Other types of child guidance clinics are specialized in function and appended to another medical, educational, or social service. Some juvenile courts and schools maintain child guidance facilities for their own clientele and clinics are also operated by universities for training in research and teaching in the behavioral sciences. Gardner points out that some general hospitals have established psychiatric services for children "because of the recent emphasis on the importance of psychiatry in adult medicine" and "as a response to the expressed needs of pediatricians who had been dealing with such children for many years."[80] The general hospital clinic also provides training for interns and medical students "in the care and treatment of this large segment of child pediatric practice."[81]

The Dilemma of the Children's Clinics

The child guidance clinic has a place of great importance in the community because of the changing emphasis from the treatment of mental illness in adults to a preventive process designed for the early detection of emotional disturbance in children. The clinic tends to enjoy professional prestige, to have an expensive program, to have great demand for its services, to have long waiting lists, and to experience difficulty in recruiting staff. As a result, the clinic may be accused of being a disappointment and of being aloof, because the community expects more of it than it can realistically give. These reactions often result from confusion as to what and how much the clinic can accomplish. This is borne out by the fact that it is not uncommon for a clinic staff of five or six to be expected to serve a community with several hundred thousand population which requires 25 public schools, and to give, in addition, diagnostic treatment and consultation service to several contiguous counties or localities.

The purpose and function of the children's clinic and its relation to other social agencies, the juvenile court, the schools, and other sources of referral greatly influence the time that is left for individual therapy. Many children referred are screened out at intake because they are not in need of clinic service and many parents do not follow through after the initial interview, neglect to cancel appointments, or

---

[80] George E. Gardner, "American Child Psychiatric Clinics," *The Annals of the American Academy of Political and Social Science*, Vol. 286 (March 1953), pp. 129–132.

[81] *Ibid.*

stop bringing the child to the clinic.   These are understandable factors in therapy, but they result in loss of staff time which might be used in seeing greater numbers of children.

To test the readiness of parents to support the child in therapy and to participate in the treatment process, the Child Guidance Clinic of the Buffalo Children's Hospital inaugurated a "short-term" clinical service which was something of a departure from the time-consuming traditional method.   In this service, the psychiatric social worker interviews the parents at intake and has a second interview in which the child is prepared for future clinic contacts.   The child is then seen by the psychiatrist for three sessions at weekly intervals.   Next, three concurrent appointments are arranged with the social worker, two with the mother and one with the father.   This is followed by a conference of parents, psychiatrist, and social worker.   This process is accomplished in five to six weeks and readily tests the validity of the referral and the parents' readiness to evaluate the problem and to work cooperatively with the child and clinic in resolving it.[82]

In a recent study of five hundred children, one to seventeen years of age, seen at the Los Angeles Child Guidance Clinic, question was raised as to "whom shall the clinic serve?"   The senior investigator observed that in his judgment four-fifths of these children could have been referred to private physicians or other counseling resources in the community and that only one-fifth required the services of the child guidance clinic.[83]

There is ample reason to believe that the services of some child guidance clinics are misused, not only because their function is not clearly understood but because the whole concept of child behavior and emotional disturbance has been poorly interpreted, if not over-dramatized.

The Los Angeles study revealed that slightly more than 42 per cent of the children were referred by their parents, relatives, friends, or neighbors.   (One quarter of the children were referred by their own families.[84])   This means, in effect, that over two hundred cases came

---

[82] Evelyn Alpern, "Short Clinical Services for Children in a Child Guidance Clinic," *American Journal of Orthopsychiatry*, Vol. XXVI, No. 2 (April 1956), pp. 314–315.

[83] Forrest N. Anderson, and Helen C. Dean, "Some Aspects of Child Guidance Clinic Intake Policy and Practices," *Public Health Monograph* 42, Public Health Service, United States Department of Health, Education and Welfare (Washington, D.C.: Government Printing Office, March 1956), p. 13.

[84] *Ibid.*, Table 3, p. 3.

from nonprofessional sources in which neither the child nor his parents had any preparation for the clinic experience. The loss of staff time and the consequent misuse of the clinic are evident in the fact that 31 per cent of the cases referred by parents, relatives, or friends were self-terminated.

The investigators state that this high rate of client loss suggests

. . . "shopping around" and a lack of understanding on the part of the applicants as to what is involved when the clinic accepts a child for study.[85]

Group Activities for Children and Youth

Recreation is no longer looked upon as a frivolous substitute for work but rather as a primary source of personality growth and development. Play and recreation provide the essential group experiences by which the child learns to express his interests, his need for status and achievement, and his striving for self-assertion, recognition, and independence. Participation in group play tends to develop a sense of social responsibility, and an ability to accept cultural, nationality, and ethnic differences. The activity itself is incidental to its value as a creative socializing force and to the democratic participation it allows.

Current interest in recreation has broadened to the extent that it is estimated some $456,000,000 will be spent on recreation by local, state, and federal government in 1960.[86] Millions more will be spent by private youth-serving organizations and a great deal of time, effort, and money will be devoted to defining the need for leisure-time activities and for determining which areas are most in need of such services. These expenditures will reflect both a recognition of the importance of meeting the recreational needs of children and youth and a growing concern regarding juvenile delinquency, emotional illness, and other social problems believed to be associated with a lack of acceptable group activities.

The practice of arbitrarily associating unmet recreational needs with various types of social pathology tends to defeat a careful evaluation

---

[85] *Ibid.*, p. 14.

[86] J. Frederic Dewhurst and Associates, *America's Needs and Resources: A New Survey* (New York: The Twentieth Century Fund, 1947), Table 105, p. 377.

of the problem and to create unrealistic expectations with respect to those who administer group work programs and those for whom these services are made available. If recreation and play are to contribute to the child's self-realization, social and emotional maturation, and self-direction, they must reflect a community understanding of this important relationship. Recreation is not the mere development, financing, and operation of a facility or program, but a partial reflection of the citizens' concern for all phases of the child's physical, social, intellectual, and emotional well-being. It is also an expression of the adult community's cultural values, its social orientation and structure, and its institutionalized roles and criteria of social behavior.

There is little doubt that public and private youth-serving organizations have received much support from the community because their "character building" objectives are designed to facilitate democratically inspired social relationships and to constitute a preparation for adulthood. Although these goals are reassuring, there is need to examine some of the reasons why recreational services for children and youth often do not fulfill some of the major expectations established for them.

Nathan Cohen, in discussing the relation between mental health, the social processes, and social institutions, raises several significant questions about the practice of social group work which are equally applicable to the function of youth-serving organizations and the goals of recreation generally:

1. Do we have a sufficient understanding of the youth and adult cultures in our society to help youth in the preparation of their future roles?
2. Have we accentuated a conflict for youth by emphasizing the humanistic values in the youth culture without acquainting them sufficiently with the gaps in such values in the adult culture?
3. Can we achieve our goals by emphasizing humanistic values for youth without taking greater responsibility for working with the adult culture to change their attitudes and values? . . .
4. . . .
5. Are our agencies and groups overprotective, with greater concern for conformity than for stimulating creativity and adventure in new ideas? . . .
6. Do we emphasize loyalty to the group to the extent that youth find it difficult to find identification with more than one group?
7. . . . have we lost sight of the value of different types of group experiences at different age levels? . . . have we gone too far in discouraging the special purpose groups?[87]

---

[87] Nathan E. Cohen, "Implications of the Present Scene for Social Group Work Practice," *National Conference of Social Work Proceedings, 1955* (New York: Columbia University Press, 1955), pp. 55–56.

These questions also identify some of the fundamentals so often disregarded in the persistent struggle between youth and adult culture. The processes of socialization, social adjustment, and preparation for adulthood do not occur in a vacuum but, rather, are fused by the continual transmission of cultural identifications, values, and attitudes from one generation to another. The child's ability to live securely in contemporary society will not depend solely on opportunities to learn and to adjust but also on his capacity to relate to a world that does not resist the reality and the inevitability of change.

Meyer and Brightbill appraise the status of youth in America in this way:

The community has always been concerned about its youth. As potential citizens, builders of families, industrial and agrarian workers, educational or religious leaders, they are a rich community asset. As potential defectives, they challenge the community. As members of the family, school, church, and club, they are a vital part of society's organizations. . . . The force and influence of youth in action is immeasurable.[88]

Children and youth find recreational outlets in the family, with their peer groups, and within school and church programs, but the services of public and private youth-serving agencies are also used extensively.

The Role of the Community Welfare Council

MacRae states that "the community welfare council . . . sees itself as a vehicle for citizen action in the promotion of human welfare."[89] It is one of the functions of the council to mobilize the interests and efforts of representatives of public and private agencies and of other professional and lay persons to identify and study social problems and to work toward resolving unmet community needs. The council also engages in social planning, a process which "aims to bring about a more effective adjustment between social welfare needs and resources"[90] and to "provide the medium for representatives

---

[88] Harold D. Meyer and Charles K. Brightbill, *Community Recreation* (Englewood Cliffs, New Jersey: Prentice-Hall, 2nd edition, 1956), p. 261.

[89] Robert H. MacRae, "Community Welfare Councils," *Social Work Year Book*, 1957, p. 186.

[90] *Ibid.*, p. 186.

of operating agencies with common interests to come together for sharing problems and the development of effective working relationships."[91] In addition the council has responsibility for interpreting social welfare function and philosophy, and for research, community education, and consultation.

The majority of the councils engage in the study of community problems by use of committees on family and child welfare, health, recreation and group work, and perhaps other designated subjects. The committees are composed of representatives of private and public social welfare, health, and recreation agencies, other professional persons, and interested lay citizens, all of whom serve on a volunteer basis. This plan affords an amalgamation of professional leadership and citizen participation on behalf of the community.

In considering the best method of solving identified community problems or meeting recognized gaps in service, council committees (or divisions) frequently come to the conclusion that an intensive study of existing services by a professional person or group is needed. When the services required by children are involved, such studies may be conducted by a staff member of the Child Welfare League of America, the National Probation and Parole Association, the Family Service Association, or a team representing any or all of these national organizations. In many instances, too, a "self-study" may be made by a community group or conducted under the direction of an "outside expert." In any event, the sponsorship of a representative local committee will be essential to interpret the problems identified before and after a community study and to implement the recommendations made.

Through this process, many communities have reexamined their structure of child welfare services, embarked upon plans for the realignment of functions among long-established agencies and institutions, initiated the development of the new services needed, and ultimately evolved a comprehensive pattern of services for children.

Another dramatic aspect of community organization is that which takes place in the neighborhood councils which are "citizens' organizations composed of people living or working in a neighborhood or district and concerned with improving conditions in the area."[92] A member of the professional staff of the council is ordinarily assigned

---

[91] *Ibid.*, p. 187.

[92] *Ibid.*, p. 189.

to establish or supervise the work of a neighborhood council, or the council may have staff which devotes full time to this function.

To evaluate the dynamic and significant influence of coordinated council-community action, it is important to understand how the need for service is generally determined. In establishing "areas of need," the Welfare Council of Metropolitan Los Angeles selected the following criteria; the prevalence of juvenile delinquency, the presence or absence of minority groups, population movement and mobility, lack of home ownership, density of population, family income, and level of education.[93]

The Welfare Federation of Cleveland established "criteria of community characteristics which affect need for community-sponsored leisure-time activities." The factors selected included population of the areas by age, sex, and race; ethnic, cultural, and religious groupings; number of children, adolescents, and young adults; educational level; percentage of people subjected to discriminatory practices; socio-economic level; health practices; availability of leadership; stability of population; physical characteristics of the area; and the degree of social organization.[94]

The process of matching community need and community resources involves many facets of joint participation by agencies and citizens. This is true, not only in regard to the determination of needed services but in the financing of these services, either by voluntary contributions to the Community Chest or United Crusade or by taxation in the case of public services.

Employment Service for Youth

There is deep concern about the great numbers of children dropping out of school each year. Although some succeed in finding satisfying employment, thousands remain involuntarily idle because of a lack of personal adequacy or vocational preparation, job scarcity, or other factors.

---

[93] *Youth Project Yardstick*, Special Report Series No. 36 (Los Angeles: Research Department, Welfare Council of Metropolitan Los Angeles, undated), pp. 35–37.

[94] *Measuring Leisure-Time Needs* (Cleveland: Group Work Council, Welfare Federation of Cleveland, 1955), pp. 37–42.

Sol Markoff has pointed out that there is a difference between "child labor" and "youth employment"[95] and it is apparent that the two have been confused. "Child labor" involves the basic concepts of protection, while "youth employment" is concerned with the provision of job opportunities for children from fourteen to seventeen years of age. Youth generally find it difficult to obtain jobs not because of child labor laws but because there is little demand for their services.

The rationale for child labor legislation is rooted in the belief that the child should have sufficient time for physical, emotional, social, and intellectual development. He should have an opportunity to go to school, to be trained to earn a living, to develop attitudes toward work, and to participate in the life of the community.[96]

Legislators have thoughtfully instituted provisions for child protection in industrial and other occupations, but youth is faced with the crucial problem of finding employment in a technological age when academic and vocational preparation and professional training are demanded. It is estimated that some 1,800,000 boys and girls leave high school each year to seek employment. Half of this number graduate, but the remainder are dropping out before completion of their high school education.[97]

The young potential worker, whether he is a high school graduate or not, will benefit from vocational guidance service while he is still in school. The United States Department of Labor explains:

Vocational guidance and job placement services contribute directly to the development of healthy personality in youth. Professional help in achieving satisfying work adjustment is a factor in the prevention of maladjustment and can be a contributing factor in modifying the correction of personality deviation. In turn, youth's ability to plan constructively and to utilize effectively vocational services is related directly to the degree of personality development achieved from birth to maturity.[98]

Because many young people who leave school have never been seriously helped to evaluate job opportunities in terms of their own capacities and interests, they tend to move from job to job and to

---

[95] Sol Markoff, "Youth and Work," *Children*, Vol. 4, No. 2 (March–April 1957), p. 61.

[96] "Why Child-Labor Laws?," *Bulletin* 185, United States Department of Labor (Washington, D.C.: Government Printing Office, September 1956), p. 2.

[97] *Counseling and Employment Service for Youth*, United States Department of Labor (Washington, D.C.: Government Printing Office, December 1954), p. 17.

[98] *Ibid.*, p. 49.

find dissatisfactions in each one. This experience creates the habit of "drifting," of being without direction, and having little inclination to plan for a career. Because the young person who has little formal education must seek a job with meager educational requirements, he may tend to depress his opportunities for doing more stimulating and creative work. If he has had no helpful vocational guidance, the matter of job selection may be difficult for him since he has little knowledge of the various occupational fields, the availability of jobs, the qualifications for employment, working conditions, or opportunities for advancement. Job counseling is an educational service which helps the young worker to plan for the future and to develop meaningful and useful occupational and professional objectives. Because the teen-ager seeking employment will be in competition with experienced adults and will sense his own immaturity and lack of skills, he will benefit greatly from guidance in job selection and placement.

School Employment Service

The school should not only provide vocational guidance by trained and well-informed counselors, but courses which will prepare the student for employment when he leaves school. It has responsibility for aptitude and interest testing; for keeping adequate cumulative records which include personal data, completed courses and grades, physical condition, vocational interests, and test results; for employment screening and for follow-up when students are placed in jobs. The school also has responsibility for developing a cooperative working relationship with the employment service and for planning "career talks" for students by representatives of industry and other potential employment resources.[99]

The employment service plays an important part in the young worker's future by acting as liaison between the school and the community. It has many functions, which include interpreting its services, registering applicants for positions, administering group aptitude and interest tests, exploring availability of jobs, holding case conferences with the school counselor or teacher, conducting individual interviews with the applicant, and developing cooperative programs with the school to interpret vocational guidance objectives to the community.[100]

---

[99] *Ibid.*, pp. 21–22.
[100] *Ibid.*

FEDERAL PROGRAMS

The federal government has been active in evaluating the relation between early school drop-outs, vocational counseling, and the employment of youth. In April, 1957, the President's Committee on Government Contracts, which is charged with the elimination of racial, nationality, and religious discrimination in work done under federal government auspices, held a Youth-Training Incentives Conference in Washington, D.C. The conference was held in cooperation with the American Personnel and Guidance Association and was attended by representatives of labor, industry, and schools from sixteen major cities having a large minority group population. The emphasis of the meeting was upon expanding job opportunities for minority youth and preparing these young people to train for skilled employment.[101] The United States Department of Labor also has taken leadership in other phases of teen-age employment and given guidance to the states and localities.

The Bureau of Apprenticeship and Training is concerned with the National Apprenticeship Program authorized in August, 1937. The program is directed by the Federal Committee on Apprenticeship, which is made up of employer, labor, and government representatives.

The Federal Committee on Apprenticeship has made the following recommendations: (1) the starting age of an apprentice should be not less than sixteen; (2) the apprentice should be given "a schedule of work processes" which will assure organized instruction, proper supervision, training, and experience on the job; (3) a progressively increasing schedule of wages should be provided; and (4) there should be a periodic evaluation of the apprentice's work. A state may achieve recognition of its apprenticeship agencies by the Bureau of Apprenticeship and Training.[102]

The Vocational Division of the United States Office of Education allots money to the states each year "to develop programs of vocational education in trades and industries, distributive occupations, home economics, and agriculture."[103] Such funds, authorized by the Smith-

---

[101] *Youth Training-Incentive Conference Proceedings,* United States Department of Labor, the President's Committee on Government Contracts (Washington, D.C.: Government Printing Office, April 1956), p. 1.

[102] "Federal Labor Laws and Agencies," *Bulletin* 123 (revised), United States Department of Labor, Bureau of Labor Standards (Washington, D.C.: Government Printing Office, undated), pp. 93–94.

[103] *Ibid.,* p. 94.

Hughes and George-Barden acts, are distributed on a federal-state-local matching basis in accordance with the population of a given state. Funds are provided for the salaries of vocational teachers, counselors, teacher training, research, and instructional supplies and equipment. Programs are carried out and directed by state boards and must be approved by the U.S. Department of Education. Courses must be given in public schools, must "be of less than college grade," and must equip the student for gainful employment. Courses made possible under Vocational Division grants are all-day classes which offer "pre-employment training for young people of high school age and part-time and evening classes for apprentices and others over sixteen."[104]

Selected Bibliography

Arnold, Mildred. *Meeting Family Need Through Homemaker Service*. Washington, D.C.: United States Children's Bureau, 1957.

Bowlby, John. *Maternal Care and Mental Health*. World Health Organization, 1952.

DeFrancis, Vincent. *Child Protective Services in the United States*. Denver: Children's Division, The American Humane Association, 1956.

Kaufman, Irving. "The Contribution of Protective Services," *Child Welfare*, Vol. XXXVI, No. 2, February 1957.

Wiltse, Kermit T. "Social Casework Services in the Aid to Dependent Children Program," *Social Service Review*, Vol. 29, No. 2, June 1954.

Witte, Ernest F. "Who Speaks Now for the Child on Public Assistance?," *Child Welfare*, Vol. 33, No. 3, March 1954.

---

[104] *Ibid.*

Chapter 14   *Services for Children*

Who Require Out-of-Home Care

*T*he growing conviction that a child should be helped to remain in his own home with his own family has not displaced the need for out-of-home care. Instead, the same studies which support the belief that the child is best nurtured physically, socially, and emotionally by his own parents have led to new recognition of the values of the various types of out-of-home care developed during previous decades, and to a more purposive use of these values.

Care outside of the child's own home is now believed to fulfill four essential purposes: (1) to supplement the care available in the family home; (2) to provide a temporary substitute for the child's own home during periods of family crisis or disorganization; (3) to facilitate the treatment of a child seriously damaged by his prior life experience; and (4) to insure for a child, whose own parents cannot meet his needs, a permanent place in another family. In some instances, two or more of these purposes may be served by a single placement, but some chil-

342

dren may require placement in different types of facilities in sequence or at different periods in their lives.

The new emphasis in this decade is upon the careful diagnosis of a child's needs and the selection of the placement facility best equipped to meet these needs. To make this possible, skilled professional services are necessary to assist parents in determining the needs of a child and in developing a plan to meet these needs. When out-of-home care is necessary, many parents will also require professional help in finding a resource where the child's needs can be met, in helping their child to accept care outside of his own home, in maintaining and strengthening their relationship with the child during the period in which he receives care elsewhere, and perhaps in creating, re-creating, or maintaining the kind of family life which he should have when return to his own home is possible. When it is apparent that his own parents have no capacity to assume the responsibilities of parenthood, skilled help is also required to assist parents in freeing the child for permanent placement in another family home.

These services to parents on behalf of a child may be given by a social agency or group care facility which will also accept responsibility for the placement, supervision, or treatment of the child. Under other circumstances, some or all of these services may be provided by a county welfare department or a family agency, while the child's care and treatment is entrusted to a separate children's agency or group care facility. This chapter will describe the services provided to meet the differing needs of children who require out-of-home care.

Group Day Care

Group day care has been defined as an organized program for children "not of common parentage and apart from their parents during any part of the twenty-four hour day, with or without stated educational purpose."[1] It may be provided under a variety of names (for example, day nurseries, child care centers, nursery schools) and for a number of purposes:

Programs may be set up for the education of the child, to meet the needs of the child in relation to his family, for parent education, for research, for

---

[1] *A Guide for the Development of Day Care Programs* (New York: Child Welfare League of America, May 1951), p. 1.

teacher training, for the training of other professionals such as pediatricians, psychiatrists, psychologists, nurses, and home economists.[2]

Facilities designed to meet the needs of the child and his family may be operated under private or public auspices. In most instances, those financed from public funds function under the direction of a local school district. Facilities operated under private auspices may be conducted by individuals for profit, by parent-cooperative groups organized for this purpose, or by nonprofit organizations, for example, churches, social agencies, settlement houses, and fraternal organizations.

The day care facility "supplements the home by sharing daytime responsibility with parents, whether for economic, social, health or educational reasons . . . "[3] and "assists the parent in fulfilling his responsibilities for protecting the child and for providing opportunities for his development."[4] Specifically, group day care is an essential service to a child (1) when the father is absent from the home and the mother's employment may serve the best interests of the child and family by relieving tensions or preserving a sense of self-support; (2) when the mother is absent or ill and the father hopes to avoid the necessity of placing his children in foster homes; (3) when the father is ill and the mother is compelled to seek employment outside of the home; (4) when the child needs a supervised group experience because of behavior problems; (5) when the child lacks companionship with his peer group; or (6) when the family is being troubled by marital problems.[5]

Group day care is most appropriate for children between the ages of three to twelve years; it is recommended that children below the age of three be placed in foster family homes where they will receive individual care and attention. Regardless of the age served, however, an adequate program should assure the care and supervision which the mother would give if she were with the child, provide for activities that will enhance the child's growth and development, and sustain a relationship with the parents that will encourage their participation in carrying out plans in the child's behalf.[6]

The day care facility should not offer mere custodial care which

---

[2] *Ibid.*

[3] *Ibid.*, p. 2.

[4] *Ibid.*, p. 1.

[5] Alfreda Yeomans, "The Day Nursery," *Child Welfare*, Vol. XXVIII, No. 4 (April 1949), pp. 13–14.

[6] United States Department of Labor, *Report on Standards for Day Care of Children of Working Mothers*, Preliminary Report to the Children's Bureau (Washington, D.C.: Government Printing Office, February 1942), p. 1.

assures the child's safety and supervision; in addition, it should provide services which promote the child's health, welfare, and education, and share with the parent a responsibility for helping the child develop capacities to use these services. It is recognized that these services are not available in all facilities, but it seems important to describe the type of program needed by children who receive out-of-home care during the day.

EDUCATIONAL SERVICES IN GROUP DAY CARE

The teacher plays a highly significant and meaningful role inasmuch as she assumes major responsibility for the child's care while he attends the group day care facility. The teacher has responsibility, too, for helping each child to benefit from his group experience and for creating an environment that makes this possible. These responsibilities demand an understanding of child development, knowledge of emotional needs and the ability to translate these needs in terms of the child's total living experiences. She must be able to provide an adequate learning experience so that the "child's skill, judgment and understanding will develop" and he will be encouraged to increase his "independence, responsibility and self-expression."[7] It is expected that the teacher will "provide experience for individual growth and well-being" by "allowing for each child's individuality through a varied and flexible approach," and that she will help the child to attain "optimum health, physical, mental and emotional."[8]

The teacher also shares with other members of the staff, a responsibility for the child's general welfare and achieves many of these objectives by being a part of the team which works cooperatively in behalf of the child and his family.

If the day care facility does not have the services of a social caseworker, one of the teacher's most helpful attributes will be an ability to have a useful and supportive relationship with the child's parents.

A good teacher . . . respects parents and knows that life does not offer a harder, a more perplexing, or a more stimulating job than that of attempting to be a good parent.
She knows that if she is to understand and to be successful with children, she must understand and work with parents.[9]

---

[7] *Daytime Care: A Partnership of Three Professions* (New York: Child Welfare League of America, March 1945), p. 14.

[8] *Ibid.*

[9] "Some Qualities of a Good Teacher," *Program Guides for Day Care Centers,* Series C (Springfield, Illinois: Department of Public Welfare, July 1954), p. 3.

CASEWORK SERVICES
IN THE DAY CARE FACILITY

Whenever possible, each day care facility should secure the services of a social caseworker, either through employment as a member of the staff team or through some arrangement with a social agency.

The social caseworker has a responsibility to help parents understand what group day care is, to evaluate its ability to meet the needs of the child and his parents, and to explore and understand the parents' motivation in seeking the service. As the person responsible for receiving applications, she should discuss the program, eligibility factors, policies, and fees and orient the parent to the contacts the child and parent will have with the pediatrician and teacher. In these initial interviews, the parent should also be helped to consider other plans if it appears that the child is not ready for group day care and that it will not serve his needs. The caseworker should also take responsibility for directing the parent to other community resources if this is indicated.[10] If the child is accepted for care at the day care facility, the caseworker should act as liaison between the parent, the child, the teacher, the pediatrician, and other social agencies as long as the child remains in care.

The caseworker's contact with the parents is most significant in terms of its influence upon the child during the hours he is at home. The child does not ordinarily respond to placement in a group day care facility without feelings of separation, loneliness, and some question as to why all of this is happening to him. One of the most important contributions that the caseworker makes to the child is that of helping his parent to prepare him for separation and for the group care experience. In referring to the use of group day care, Eleanor Hosley writes:

. . . Not only do the parents have to realize so far as possible what they are taking on, but the child must know too. A slow and painstaking introduction for him may save everyone much anguish later. It will, of course, save him the most. It is not natural for him to be away from his mama all day long; remember how long a day is at three or four years old. He is an organic part of this family from which he is being separated; this is a major experience in the life of the young child.[11]

The caseworker is sensitive to the adjustment that the child makes to the group, to his relationships to the rest of the staff, and to the

---

[10] *Daytime Care: A Partnership of Three Professions*, p. 22.

[11] Eleanor Hosley, "Casework in Day Care Centers," *Child Welfare*, Vol. XXX, No. 7 (July 1951), p. 13.

school, if he is old enough to attend. These reactions are shared and interpreted to the parent who, in turn, is encouraged to describe and evaluate the child's behavior and adjustment at home. Thus, the group day care facility places emphasis upon the child's total sense of well-being as he functions in the facility, the family, the school, and in the community.

HEALTH SERVICES

Because the child's health and physical needs are as important to his development as the fulfillment of his emotional and intellectual needs, the pediatrician, nurse, nutritionist, and psychiatrist will have an important place on the group day care team.

The health services should include parent education regarding the health and nutritional needs of the child, health supervision, and maximum protection of the child's health and safety while he receives care in the facility.   Among other health services, there should be daily inspections to detect the sick child before he associates with the group, and adequate measures for the prevention and control of infectious and communicable diseases.   The health service available to the child should also include ear, eye, nose, and throat examinations and treatment, dental prophylaxis and repair, orthopedic care, and psychiatric and other special services.   If these are not provided by the facility, parents should be encouraged, or required as a condition of continued care, to obtain needed diagnosis and treatment.

Health services should also include the maintenance of the child's cumulative health record and "evaluation of the adequacy of the total program from the health point of view."[12]

THE GROUP DAY CARE FACILITY
AS A COMMUNITY SERVICE

The child who is placed in a group day care facility is less likely to be regarded as an "eight-hour orphan," a "latchkey child," or a "dayshift orphan," than he was several decades ago.   The "emergency" day care programs which became prominent during World II are now regarded as a part of the community's basic child welfare services. Lundberg observes:

Community planning for day care should approach the problem from the point of view of the child as a member of a family group whose integrity

---

[12] *Ibid.*, pp. 16–17.

must be maintained and whose rights and obligations must be safeguarded. The physical, emotional and developmental needs of the individual child cannot be ignored without harm to child and community.[13]

Group day care services should be available to children from the age of three and for the older child in school. After-school care is especially important since the older child needs to have a place to go where he will be welcomed and where he will have the opportunity to engage in play and other activities until his mother is available to him. Facilities should be near the child's home and near the mother's place of work. To make this possible, the community must be willing to finance needed services through public funds. Some facilities are usually provided under private auspices or subsidized by community chest funds, but there is a growing tendency to regard group day care as a public child welfare service.

The California child care centers enroll some 28,000 children a year. From 1946 to 1955, children from more than 250,000 families were given service in day care centers administered by the governing boards of the school districts under standards established by the state superintendent of public instruction.[14] A child is eligible for care in these centers if (1) both parents are employed or one parent is employed and the other is unable to care for the child, and the total family income does not exceed a certain amount; (2) one parent both supports and cares for the child; (3) either parent is a veteran attending school and the other parent is gainfully employed; (4) the parent responsible for the care of the child is attending school or receiving instruction under the State Vocational Rehabilitation Program; or (5) the parent responsible for the care of the child is employed as a teacher in a California public school or a child care center, a registered nurse, a worker in industry essential to the mobilization effort, or a worker in the harvesting or processing of crops.[15]

Group day care will continue to be in demand as a child welfare service because of the increasing number of mothers who find it necessary to work. Although women having very young children are generally not encouraged to work outside of the home, other employed

---

[13] Emma O. Lundberg, "A Community Program of Day Care for Children of Mothers Employed in Defense Areas," *The Child*, Vol. 6, No. 7 (January 1942), p. 155.

[14] California State Department of Education, *Professional Preparation for Work in Child Care Centers* (Sacramento: California State Printing Office, 1956), pp. 1–2.

[15] *Ibid.*, pp. 2–3.

mothers would not be able to accept employment if they were compelled to use the more expensive private facilities. Public and nonprofit agencies offering group day care tend to alleviate financial dependency and assure the working mother that her children are receiving adequate supervision.

Foster Care

Foster care is a term used with a variety of meanings. There is general agreement among social workers that "foster care" is a generic term properly applied to several types of out-of-home care. When used in this sense, the term customarily includes care in foster family homes and in child caring institutions, whether provided on a continuing basis or as a day care service available to children who continue to live in their own homes.

Some definitions of foster care include care provided when "the child and the adoptive parents will acquire all of the responsibilities and privileges of the natural child-parent relationship through legal adoption."[16] There has been some reluctance to accept this usage, however, since it seems to deny the fact that in adoption a child acquires a new set of parental relationships and tends to obscure the temporary characteristic now considered to be an essential factor in foster care.

The term "foster care" is also used with a more restrictive connotation. In most instances, the term includes only the care provided for the child whose primary need is that of care outside of his own home. This usage excludes from consideration, care provided by institutions which have as their primary purpose the provision of special education, training, or treatment of the child with special needs. It usually excludes, too, private "boarding schools" or "military schools" whose purpose is primarily educational, even though some students who require substitute parental care may be admitted. (Facilities of this type are frequently used as a child care resource by divorced parents, and by some courts which believe that a controlled environment would prevent further antisocial behavior.) Day nurseries or nursery schools whose programs are designed solely for education and socialization may also be excluded by this definition if they are in operation only part of the day.

---

[16] Helen R. Hagan, "Foster Care for Children," *Social Work Year Book*, 1957, p. 269.

Even more frequently, the term "foster care" is used as an abbreviation for "foster family care." Some agencies which accept no responsibility for the placement and supervision of children in institutions may designate as a "foster care program" a service which relies solely upon the use of foster family homes. Agencies and individuals may also exclude foster family day care in their usual reference to "foster care."

Further problems in semantics arise from the synonyms used. By definition, foster family care includes all care provided by unrelated persons in a family setting, regardless of whether the persons providing such care receive compensation for their services or for the cost of the child's care. In some states, licensing laws differentiate between "boarding homes" wherein the foster family is paid for the child's care, "free homes" in which there is no compensation, "work homes" in which compensation is received in the form of services performed by the child, and "wage homes" in which the child receives payment for his services in addition to his maintenance.

Statutory interpretation of the term "boarding home" also leads to further confusion in some programs. When state laws refer to "boarding homes and other places for the care and reception of children" or to "boarding homes and institutions," the term "boarding home care" may become in common parlance, a synonym for all foster family care and thus include the care provided in free and wage homes.

Other terminology is also used to indicate the auspices under which a child is placed in foster family care. Foster homes which accept responsibility for the care of children directly from their parents, or other persons acting in lieu of parents, without the services of a child-placing agency are sometimes known as "independent boarding homes," and those which accept children only from a child placing agency, as "agency foster homes" or "agency boarding homes."

THE PHILOSOPHY OF FOSTER FAMILY CARE

Foster home placement is designed to meet the needs of children who require the security of family living during a temporary period in which it is not possible for them to live with their natural parents. Regardless of the quality of care available in a foster family home, it is generally recognized that every possible alternative should be explored before a child is removed from his own home. This point of view is very different from the previous misconceptions about the use of foster family care:

That is the mistaken idea that one has only to remove a child from a bad environment and place him in a good one where he is surrounded by character-building influences to make him into a respectable citizen. This concept of the child's being an impressionable, pliable piece of material which could be molded into a desirable finished product by proper training and environment is part of the historical development of child-care programs. . . . [17]

Although it is often imperative that a child be removed from his own home to prevent continued neglect or mistreatment, foster home placement should be regarded as only one step in helping the child. It is equally important to help his family to effect change during the child's stay in foster care so that he can return to more secure and satisfying relationships with his family.

Foster care should not be regarded as a permanent or long-time separation of the child from his family, but as a means of preventing his continued exposure to whatever pressures his family is experiencing. Foster home placement without the casework services of an agency interested in the rehabilitation of the family may produce long separation or numerous separations, if he is placed and returned again and again to the same distressing and unaltered familial environment. It may mean, too, numerous replacements from one foster home to another, since the child may become so upset by his parents' inability to make things different that he will manifest his feelings of loneliness and discouragement by such deviant behavior that no foster parent can tolerate his presence for any prolonged period.

The Growing Need for Placement Services

Although foster care does not meet the needs of every child or provide a panacea to cure all of the child's social and emotional ills, it has tended to influence child welfare practice in several ways. Because foster home programs are developing in more communities, there is less need to place infants and preschool children in institutions or to use the institution for the long-time custodial care for any child. There is also a growing tendency for institutions to offer foster family care as part of their service to a child. [18]

---

[17] Almeda R. Jolowicz, *The Hidden Parent* (Washington, D.C.: United States Children's Bureau, July 1948; reprint), pp. 2–3.

[18] Spencer H. Crookes, "For the Child Who Must Live Away From His Own Home," *The Child*, Vol. 16, No. 6 (February 1952), p. 84.

The Children's Bureau recently surveyed the availability of foster care services and the unmet need for such services by directing a questionnaire to all of the state public welfare agencies. Fifty-one states and territories responded, giving information about the influences which caused existing foster care services to be inadequate to meet the current need for such services. Among these were: (1) "the tremendous growth of the child population of the Nation has not been matched by a parallel growth of child welfare services";[19] (2) disruption of family life due to mobility; (3) increasing spread of industrialization and urbanization involving the employment of women; (4) population movement to the suburbs where child welfare services must be developed; (5) poor housing which contributes to family disruption and the subsequent need for foster care; and (6) "the stranded community" which becomes depressed when industry moves out and thus presents many family and child welfare problems.[20]

Forty-nine of the responding states and territories reported that existing foster home placement services were not adequate to meet the needs of the following categories of children:

	NUMBER OF STATES
Emotionally disturbed children	47
Older children	39
Mentally retarded children	38
Children of minority groups; most frequently mentioned were Negro children (16 states) and Indian children (11 states) with many states not specifying the minority groups concerned	33
Children with behavior problems (commonly aggressive, predelinquent and delinquent children)	28
Physically handicapped children[21]	25

There was also an expressed recognition that children should be removed from various types of substitute parental care because the current placement was considered detrimental to their growth and development:

---

[19] United States Children's Bureau, *Foster Care, 1956*, Child Welfare Report 8 (Washington, D.C.: Government Printing Office, 1957), p. 3.

[20] *Ibid.*

[21] *Ibid.*, p. 5.

	NUMBER OF STATES
Children now in institutions who could profit from foster family care	38
Children now in foster family care or in institutions who could be adopted	36
Children, generally adolescents, now in foster family care or in institutions who could profit from living in small group homes	25
Emotionally disturbed children now in foster family care or in institutions who should be under treatment in a residential treatment center	24
Children now in state training schools for whom foster family care or group care is needed	22
Children now in detention care or in jails who should be placed in foster family care or group care[22]	14

Careful study of these appraisals indicates the need for every type of foster care service, including foster family homes, residential treatment centers for emotionally disturbed children, small group homes for the adolescent, and adequate temporary shelter care.

The states charged the "outstanding limitations or problems" in regard to foster care programs to (1) shortage of professionally trained personnel; (2) inadequate financing of foster care programs; (3) excessive case loads; (4) inadequate board rates for care of children; (5) inadequate social services for families; and (6) inadequate medical care for foster children.[23]

THE FOSTER PARENTS, THE CHILD, AND THE COMMUNITY

A foster home is licensed for placement of an unrelated child when the licensing agency feels that the foster parents have the qualities and capacities to deal with a lonely, unhappy child who needs the warmth, acceptance, and understanding of two substitute parents. Licensing is a casework process through which a legally authorized agency attempts to protect the welfare of children who require care outside of their own home. Indeed, the licensing process itself remains one of

---

[22] *Ibid.,* p. 6.
[23] *Ibid.,* p. 17.

the most important means of assurance that the child will receive the type of care he needs when he is required to live apart from his parents.

Foster parents are motivated to accept children for foster care for a variety of reasons. Some are of the opinion that they can supplement the family income by child care fees, others no longer having small children in the family fill this void by making their home available to an agency, and some are childless and hope that they may eventually be able to adopt legally a foster child placed with them. Sometimes foster home applicants are seeking a companion for their own child or for themselves. Applicants for a foster home license may also be looking for free labor on the farm, in other home-connected enterprise, or as a maid or houseboy. However, the majority of persons seeking foster home licenses are sincerely interested in providing an environment for a child where his needs can be adequately met and in which they can give him a secure and meaningful experience in family living.

Foster parents, however, need considerably more than good intentions to understand a child's upset behavior and the fear and anxiety that a child experiences when he is forced to leave his home, his family, and all that he feels is really his. The caseworker will help the foster parents to understand that a child's loyalty to his own family is ordinarily deep and full, and the pain of separation often intolerable. Many children have little understanding as to why they must live away from home, because their parents have had difficulty in facing the situation squarely or because a family emergency allowed little or no time to prepare the child. In some instances, too, a child who has been well prepared for placement by his parents and caseworker may be so traumatized by his experiences that he cannot accept the reality of placement.

Responsibility for a child's adjustment in foster care is jointly shared by the child, his parents, the agency, the foster parents, the school, and the wider community. To help a child benefit from foster care, it is well to remember the reasons for which he may have come into foster care and to evaluate what that experience means to him as he forms new relationships among persons who are strangers to him. If a child has been temporarily separated from his family because of parental neglect and inadequacy, this may cause him to be embarrassed, yet wholly loyal to those he loves. A similar conflict will be created if the need for placement resulted from a parent's alcoholism, mental illness, or mental retardation, all of which are, unfortunately, highly stigmatizing in our culture. The same reactions will probably be present when the parent is morally illiterate, with little capacity to teach, guide, or supervise the child. In other instances a child is help-lessly caught in an impending marital breakup which leaves him torn with conflict as he weighs his relationship with both of his parents. Many times a parent who sincerely recognizes his obligations to his children cannot change the family situation because of chronic illness, injury, or the need for surgery and hospitalization. The child's feel-ings about these things may be compounded if the circumstances warranted a juvenile court hearing, regardless of the sensitivity with which the hearing may have been conducted. Unless the child is or becomes a full orphan, he will probably be returning to his own home as soon as the agency and the child's parents can develop plans for him to do so. It is, therefore, highly important that his foster home expe-rience give him support and reassurance and help him to retain or to build a sustaining relation with his parents and siblings.

Although his foster parents have an over-all responsibility for the child while he lives in their home, others have an equally important stake in his welfare. The school has responsibility for allowing the child to enroll without needlessly questioning him about his family or other personal matters and for regarding information that it receives about him, as highly confidential. Too often, children in foster homes find themselves quickly labeled as "welfare kids," "state wards," or "juvenile court cases." The school cannot protect the child from all of the stigma he may face, but it should take responsibility for help-ing him to make an adequate school adjustment and to feel secure with his peers, teachers, and principal.

The agency has responsibility for selecting the foster home and placing the child. It also has responsibility for visiting him in his foster home and learning about his adjustment, for encouraging parents to visit, and for helping foster parents to understand the child's need for contact with his own family. Parents, in turn, have a responsi-bility to help the child to understand the circumstances which made foster home placement necessary, to assure the child that he will be returning home as soon as possible, to keep in contact with him, and to arrange pleasant home visits whenever this is feasible. The foster parents should be helped to understand that they will not be taking the place of the child's own parents on a permanent basis and that they should not encourage the child's emotional dependency upon them so that he will be in conflict about his relationships with them and with his own parents. They should encourage him to think and to talk about his parents, and should understand that their substitute parental role should be sensitively correlated with his feelings and attitudes toward his own family.   As Almeda Jolowicz has stated:

The more we recognize the importance of the parent in the life of the placed child, the more we come to know and to like the parent, the more we come to respect him as a human being, the fewer will be the children who are placed too hastily and without every effort and skill being made to preserve for them their own niche in this universe, which is purely and simply their place in their own home.[24]

INSTITUTIONAL CARE

The concept of institutional care has greatly changed from the traditional function of the facility which offered long-term congregate care to dependent children, many of whom were full or half orphans. There are presently few "orphanages" as such, since parents live longer and there has been a diminution of the crippling or otherwise handicapping diseases which previously caused permanent dependency. Modern public assistance and social insurance programs also assure the child of an opportunity to remain in his own home when loss of income results from the illness, death, or desertion of the breadwinner.

The attitudes, policies, and philosophy formerly held by many institutions are described by Eva Burmeister in her review of the early intake procedures of the Lakeside Children's Center in Milwaukee. The decision to admit a child for care centered around three questions: Is there a bed available?   Is this a conforming child who will give us no trouble?   Is the family deserving of our services?[25]   In contrast, the primary purpose of the contemporary institution is now seen as treatment directed to all of the child's needs.   Gisela Konopka defines group living itself as treatment and states: "The most important part of treatment in any institutional setting is the mental hygiene climate of the whole living situation."[26]

It is generally recognized that children who must live in institutions share the common needs of all children and that they need help with the situations and problems which have made institutional care necessary.[27]   This implies that the institution must offer professional serv-

---

[24] Jolowicz, *op. cit.*, p. 11.

[25] Eva Burmeister, *Forty-five in the Family* (New York: Columbia University Press, 1949), p. 210.

[26] Gisela Konopka, *Group Work in the Institution* (New York: Whiteside, *and* Wm. Morrow and Company, 1954), p. 11.

[27] Mary Lois Pyles, *Institutions for Child Care and Treatment* (New York: Child Welfare League of America, February 1947), p. 12.

ices including casework, social group work, psychiatric treatment and consultation, medical care, and any other service that will be helpful in the child's adjustment. Children who can best use institutional care have a special need for the support and guidance of a skilled case-worker and a social group worker to preserve parental ties, to help in resolving conflicts and hurt relating to separation, and to find new strength and support in the group. This is especially true of the child who has had a satisfactory relationship with his own parents but whose home has been broken by death, divorce, or abandonment. However, as Susanne Schulze points out:

These children come from homes less often broken by death than made undesirable by a variety of family problems. . . . Their problem is no longer lack of a roof over their heads, food in their stomachs, and clothes on their backs. Rather, too little love, too much or too little discipline or indulgence, or combinations of these factors have led to the youngsters' variously expressed problematic behavior.[28]

It has also been asserted that " . . . the outdated institution provided mass care. The modern institution provides group care which is built upon the individualization of every child in the group."[29]

The child who comes into institutional care is compelled to leave home because of some family situation generally beyond his control. Like the child who lives in a foster home, he is a victim of circumstances which he may find difficult to accept or to understand. Because of the child's reaction to the problems he faces, the choice of institutional or foster home care is highly important to his adjustment and treatment. The choice does not revolve around the ancient debate as to which is the best type of care, but rather which can best meet the needs of the individual child.

The institution and the foster home are no longer regarded as competitive services but rather as being complementary to each other with each having a specialized function. Samuel Lerner has identified certain aspects of institutional care which cannot be given to the child as appropriately in a foster home. These include supplying the child with (1) a controlled environment, (2) experience in group living and interaction, (3) the opportunity for "diluted emotional relationships," and (4) opportunity for greater permissiveness "for acting out or withdrawing in a group setting."[30]

---

[28] Susanne Schulze, editor, *Creative Group Living in a Children's Institution* (New York: Association Press, 1951), p. 6.

[29] *Institutions for Child Care and Treatment*, p. 13.

[30] Samuel Lerner, "The Diagnostic Basis of Institutional Care for Children," *Social Casework*, Vol. XXXIII, No. 3 (March 1952), pp. 106–107.

The institutional community provides the child with opportunities to work through many problems and to manifest various kinds of behavior that would not be permissible in most foster homes. Since these are children who have been damaged by emotional deprivation and rejection, they have need for warm but often casual relationships with a variety of adults in whom they can find continuous acceptance. The hostile, lonely child may have need to punish the adults about him by being aggressive, destructive, or cruel. This kind of behavior can be more readily absorbed, evaluated, and treated by the institution's professional staff than by foster parents. The institution also offers a child the opportunity of working his problems through at his own pace and spares him the pain of having to form substitute parental relationships for which he may have neither the need, the desire, nor the capacity. There can also be security in a known daily routine where the child begins to know that he can count on some things being the same for him. The institution also offers the child a variety of activities which will help him to grow and to become mature and independent.

It is generally agreed that institutional care is best for (1) children who cannot sustain the primacy of foster family living because of their experiences with their own parents, (2) children whose own parents have difficulty in accepting foster parents, (3) those who have been socially retarded or have no training in family living, and (4) those who require "special facilities for diagnostic observation and study and consistent coordinated treatment."[31]

Institutional placement is not recommended for children from birth to school age because of their need for attention and individualized care. Children who are orphans and free for adoption should be placed with permanent parents, and institutional care is not indicated for the child who cannot use or benefit from a group experience.[32]

The Institution as a Child Welfare Service

It has been pointed out that the child should not remain in an institution for too long a period of time since extended institutional care can be more damaging than long-term foster home placement because the institution provides a "more unnatural setting."[33] How, then, is the

[31] *Institutions for Child Care and Treatment*, pp. 15–16.

[32] *Ibid.*, p. 17.

[33] New York Jewish Child Care Council, *Who Does What in a Children's Institution?* (New York: Child Welfare League of America, 1955), p. 7.

institutional setting used to meet the needs of the child and what are the criteria by which there is assurance that these needs are being met?

THE INSTITUTION STAFF

The institutional team is composed of child, parent, administrator, physician, dentist, nurse, teacher, caseworker, group worker, nutritionist, psychiatrist, and house parents. Each plays an important part in the child's institutional experience although it is generally conceded that the house parent is one of the most important staff members in the daily life of the child.

THE CHILD CARE STAFF

The house parent is responsible for the supervision of a group of ten to twelve children in a cottage or a living unit. The house parent's rooms (or apartment) usually adjoin the children's living quarters and he or she fulfills a parental role in terms of counseling, supervision, and general care of these children. Some institutions endeavor to hire married couples as house parents, with each couple assigned to a cottage, thus simulating a family constellation and giving the child the benefit of a homelike environment. This practice has virtue, but it is often difficult to recruit couples who have equal knowledge of child behavior and similar skill in working with deprived and disturbed children. Some institutions employ house parents of both sexes, while others use men only. Except in institutions serving adolescent boys only, the house parent is most frequently a "housemother," assisted by a relief housemother in off-duty hours.

The house parent may be considered the "group leader" rather than a "parent" person, since the function assigned is that of creating a group living situation which, together with casework, education, medical, and psychiatric care, "represents a therapeutic channel through which the child develops into a stronger personality."[34] More specifically, the house parent has responsibility for creating "a purposeful organization of every day living" and for developing the cohesiveness identified with the "we" feeling of the group. There is further responsibility for the development of a relationship with the individual

---

[34] Morris F. Mayer, "The Houseparents and the Group Living Process," *Creative Group Living in a Children's Institution,* p. 97.

child and for integrating the job of house parent with the over-all function of the total institution.[35]

Susanne Schulze describes house parents as "the hub of the wheel in the institutional life."[36]   In writing of the scope of their responsibility, she explains that the house parent should have knowledge of health, child growth and development, the educational processes, housekeeping, food preparation, and leisure-time activities.   She must also possess knowledge of the dynamics of human behavior and group living and have capacity to relate well to children.   She should have leadership and personal qualities which children seek to emulate and have knowledge and acceptance of individual, cultural, and religious differences.

In a group living situation the most important responsibility is that of helping the child to retain a sense of identity as an individual.   As David Hallowitz writes:

The individualized relationship is an important force in the treatment program for the emotionally disturbed child.   In addition, it contains elements that all children require in order to achieve greater emotional security and to become more mature.   The cottage parent can be a substitute mother or father figure for some children whose lives are lacking in those respects. . . . [37]

The ability to create a feeling of self-worth and security is paramount in the child's rehabilitation and in improving his relationship with others.   There is, in fact, no area of the child's institutional experience that is not directed toward this goal, although there are often limitations in the achievement of these goals.   For this reason, the house parent must flexibly play many roles, have more than ordinary knowledge and wisdom about child care, growth, and development, and be motivated to work with children who have many problems.

Many institutions have recognized that the house parent is truly "the hub" of the institution, but they have seemingly not been able to provide either the salary or status concomitant with the required skills and responsibilities.   This situation is changing in many parts of the country, as it is being more clearly recognized that institutional care is predicated on treatment and rehabilitation and that this approach

---

[35] New York Jewish Child Care Council, *op. cit.*, p. 8.

[36] Susanne Schulze and Morris Fritz Mayer, *Training House Parents*, United States Children's Bureau (Washington, D.C.: Government Printing Office, undated), p. 7.

[37] David Hallowitz, "Experiment in the Supervision of Cottage Parents," *The Jewish Social Service Quarterly*, Vol. XXV, No. 2 (December 1948), p. 194.

demands a significantly different kind of personnel than that needed for the outmoded mass congregate care formerly provided.

THE SOCIAL GROUP WORKER

Gisela Konopka colorfully portrays the inevitability of man's dependency on others and the value of the group to each individual member:

Human beings cannot stand all alone. The group is not just one other aspect of human life, but it is life blood itself because it represents the belonging to humanity. . . . I am speaking about group life that gives the individual security and nourishment so that he can fulfill his greatest promise while helping others to fulfill theirs too.[38]

While the living group in the institution most nearly resembles the family, children often need help in learning to adjust and to be happy in a group in which they have been placed with no volition of their own. It is therefore important that there be activity or interest groups which allow the child to participate in a variety of functions on a voluntary basis, both inside and outside the institution.

The group worker is the member of the institution's staff responsible for helping each child to achieve desirable social goals and to find his place as an acceptable member of the group. Gertrude Wilson emphasizes that:

Diagnosis is the core of practice. This involves a study of each individual to secure as much understanding of the meaning of his manifest behavior as the combination of accessible facts of his life experience and theory can provide.[39]

This knowledge enables the social group worker to provide activities that will contribute to the child's growth and adjustment to other persons, other groups, and to society. In most institutions, the group worker will also use this knowledge to assist other members of the staff to understand the child's behavior in groups and to help him benefit from a group living experience.

THE SOCIAL CASEWORKER

The caseworker concerns herself with the child and his family, working with them from placement to the time the child returns to his

---

[38] Konopka, *op. cit.*, p. 22.

[39] Gertrude Wilson, "Social Group Work—Trends and Developments," *Social Work*, Vol. 1, No. 4 (October 1956), p. 74.

own home. The caseworker's first task is to evaluate the child's need for placement. It has been pointed out that "it is not enough to know that the child does not have good care at home. The social worker must consider whether he will be helped by the removal."[40] If it is believed that the child will benefit from care in an institution, the social worker will help the parents to prepare the child for placement and will help him to understand why he is being placed, what the institution will be like, and that she will retain a day-by-day interest in him. The worker will also encourage the parents to visit and help them to use other community resources in resolving their difficulties. In addition, she will act as the liaison between the child and his family and will provide a continuing service to the child in helping him work through the problems which have brought him to the institution.

Although the social caseworker is recognized as a significant member of the institutional team, only 500 out of some 1,900 institutions are known to have a casework staff. This would seem to indicate that the boards of many institutions have not yet fully incorporated into practice the concept of the institution as a treatment facility.

The Institution and the Community

Since the institution is one of our oldest forms of child care, the community has long been aware of its orphanage, or children's home. There has been considerable progress in incorporating the principles of child development, human behavior, and other scientific and professional concepts into institutional practice, but a high level of child welfare services is needed to support, supplement, and complement institutional service.

Each community should recognize that a large, overpopulated institution is evidence of unresolved family conflict and deprivation and that children may be needlessly removed from their own homes because of a lack of social services. Esther P. Hill offered a challenge to each community when she stated:

Public assistance has underwritten maintenance across the board. Child welfare has underwritten foster care across the board. But there is a large group of families which need something beyond maintenance and foster care, and this is a sound sustaining casework service. . . .

---

[40] Sarabelle McCleery, "Institutions and Child Placement," *Child Welfare*, Vol. XXXVI, No. 4 (April 1957), p. 18.

We say the family is the basis of our society . . . but do we really believe it?[41]

Out-of-Home Care
for Unmarried Mothers

Both foster family care and institutional care are used to meet the needs of unmarried pregnant girls who are unable or unwilling to remain in their own homes before and after confinement.

Illegitimacy is a social problem in which traditional conventions have been broken. Today there is considerably more acceptance of the child born out of wedlock, or born socially illegitimate (a child of a married woman whose legal husband is not the natural father of the child), than in earlier years. Parenthood outside of sanctioned channels still remains one of the most deeply entrenched taboos, however. Because this is true, the illegitimately pregnant girl or woman is not only denied family and community support in many cases but is exploited and often forced to behave and to make decisions contrary to her own convictions and welfare, and the well-being of her child.

It is estimated that each year 150,000 mothers give birth to children born out of wedlock and that 62,000 of these mothers are under the age of twenty.[42] These girls represent a cross-section of society in terms of nationality, race, religion, socioeconomic status, level of intelligence, education, and other factors. Leontine R. Young points out, however, that illegitimacy is a response to emotional need and conflict:

The psychology of the unmarried mother—what she is like and why she becomes an unmarried mother—is an infinitely complex question. Its roots are deeply embedded in those powerful emotions of early childhood which form the basic pattern and structure for the individual's life. Far more than most, this specific problem represents a direct expression of early fantasies and emotional conflicts. Clearly, she is a human being who like all other human beings responds dynamically to her particular life situation, but, also clearly, she chooses one common and specific response, having a child out of wedlock.[43]

---

[41] Esther P. Hill, "Is Foster Care the Answer?," *Public Welfare*, Vol. 15, No. 2 (April 1957), p. 72.

[42] Margeret A. Thornhill, "Unprotected Adoptions," *Children*, Vol. 2, No. 5 (September–October 1955), p. 181.

[43] Leontine R. Young, "Personality Patterns in Unmarried Mothers," *The Family*, Vol. XXVI, No. 8 (December 1945), p. 296.

There are many patterns of behavior and many different ways of reaching out, but essentially the unmarried mother is seeking to fulfill unmet dependency needs which are related to her earliest identifications with her father and mother.   Every child needs and seeks parental love and, if it is withheld, it will be sought elsewhere in the form of fantasy, submission or aggression, juvenile delinquency or unmarried parenthood.

Illegitimacy is a many-pronged phenomenon.   It involves questions of morality, community mores and child welfare, and it threatens the bulwark of the Judeo-Christian ethic.   There has been a tendency to regard the unmarried mother with more compassion and charity through public interpretation and education, through broadening child welfare services and by improved legislation.   Although there has also been a gradual disuse of such terms as "baseborn" and "bastard," the unmarried mother is not adequately protected in many American communities, as she faces the overwhelming questions of how she will maintain herself during pregnancy, how she will get proper medical care, and what she will do with her baby.[44]

MATERNITY HOMES

The history of the maternity home movement has been described quite fully in an earlier chapter.   It will be recalled that unmarried mothers were cared for by compassionate persons who provided shelter, care, and an opportunity for spiritual salvation and reformation. There was little understanding of the psychological implications of illegitimacy and girls were expected to repent and mend their ways. Maternity homes were sanctuaries and were only incidentally regarded as sources of treatment and rehabilitation.

The contemporary maternity home must meet certain standards set up by a state licensing authority.   Its program should be designed to meet the girls' needs during pregnancy and confinement and should provide a basis for reeducation and more constructive motivation. Some maternity homes offer a foster home placement service to older pregnant unmarried mothers but others operate only a residential program.

The goals and objectives of a maternity home should reflect positive attitudes toward treatment and rehabilitation.   An examination of a

---

[44] Thornhill, *loc. cit.*

portion of *Standards for Maternity Homes in California* reveals a succinct description of the objectives of a residential program:

1. To provide a setting which will facilitate the provision and constructive use of professional services designed (*a*) to meet emotional, medical, spiritual, educational, and recreational needs during pregnancy; (*b*) to prepare the girls served for a more mature, emotionally satisfying, and socially acceptable way of living; and (*c*) to the extent possible, to insure for their babies, a life of normal health and happiness.

2. To provide an experience of living with other girls with similar problems, which can alleviate guilt, decrease hostility against others, increase self-esteem and self-understanding, and provide an opportunity for companionship, and for participation and self-expression in group activities.

3. To make possible a process of daily association with staff members which can provide a personification of qualities for emulation, an opportunity to develop satisfying relationships with adults who are well-adjusted in their own lives, and a means by which daily living experiences can be used to foster the personality growth of individual girls.

4. To provide an environment which will insure comfortable shelter, appropriate food, privacy, security, relaxation and freedom from pressures, with simultaneous opportunity for optimum self-direction, self-responsibility and self-determination.[45]

To achieve these objectives there is need for trained professional staff and supporting collateral agencies in the community.

Adoption

Like other phases of child welfare, adoption practice has greatly changed in emphasis, philosophy, and acceptance by the community. Traditionally, the orphan or child born out of wedlock was considered fortunate indeed if he were given a home with some benevolent couple and there were few questions asked. Adoption was approached cautiously since it was considered risky to adopt a child born out of wedlock who might inherit the immoral tendencies of his natural parents. In addition, adopting parents were not anxious to assume the responsibilities of caring for handicapped children or those having speculative health or social background. For these reasons, the practice of child placing agencies was frequently focused on the needs, desires, and inclinations of the adopting couple rather than on the needs of the child.

---

[45] *Standards for Maternity Homes in California* (Sacramento: California State Department of Social Welfare, September 23, 1954), p. 118 (mimeographed).

Perhaps no area of child welfare practice has been as greatly influenced by the social and medical sciences as adoption. Psychiatrists, psychologists, and social workers first joined professional forces to emphasize the emotional damage and deprivation suffered by infants cared for in mass congregate institutions and the equally damaging results of long-term institutional care for children of any age. Later, when foster family care was used as indiscriminately, psychiatrists and social workers documented the permanent personality damage caused by repeated replacement and the lack of any sense of belonging to a family group.

As children began to have more status in the American community and as the behavioral sciences became more secure in their findings, these developments began to be reflected in the adoption process. Adopting parents could be reliably assured that parental morality or immorality was not genetically transmitted, that the adopted child would reflect their behavior and attitudes rather than those of his natural parents, and that the child's illegitimate birth status was not tantamount to his becoming a criminal, a sexual psychopath, or some other type of deviate. With the security of this knowledge, the demand for children free for adoption greatly increased and the agencies soon found it possible to be more selective in their attempts to find the home best suited to the needs of a particular child.

Adoption as a Legal Process

There is no uniform adoption law in the United States; each state has its own statutes and although there are variations in legislation, many of the fundamental objectives and procedures are similar. All of the laws reflect society's concern for the well-being of the child and are directed to his protection. Adoption is rooted in civil law and is defined as "the legal process by which the relationship of parent and child is established between persons not so related by nature."[46] Adoption has been more broadly defined as "the process, legal and social, by which a child is transplanted from his own family into a new family. It involves severing the blood ties with his own parents and establishing a similar relationship with adopting parents."[47] It en-

---

[46] United States Children's Bureau, *Adoption of Children, 1951*, Children's Bureau Statistical Series, No. 14 (Washington, D.C.: Government Printing Office, 1953), unnumbered page.

[47] California State Department of Social Welfare, *Adopting A Child in California* (Sacramento: State Printing Office, November 1953), p. 3.

tails the same rights, responsibilities and permanent child-parent relationships as those effected between the natural child and his parents.

There are two distinct types of adoptive placements and each has its own sociolegal bases, policies, philosophy, and procedures. An "independent placement" is one "where a child is placed in the adoptive home by parents, friends, relatives, physicians, lawyers or others, without the aid of a recognized child-placing agency."[48] An "agency placement" is one in which a child is relinquished by his own parent or parents to a licensed child placing agency with the agency assuming responsibility for the selection of the child's new and permanent family.

Welfare departments in 39 states reported that about 93,000 children were named in adoption petitions filed in the courts of the United States and its territories in 1955.[49] Forty-eight per cent of these children were adopted by relatives, primarily by stepparents (36 per cent), and 52 per cent were adopted by nonrelatives. Of the latter, 56 per cent were placed by social agencies and 44 per cent were placed independently.[50]

In evaluating the effectiveness of legislation intended to assure protection to the child and his parent, it is apparent that social, economic, and cultural pressures often interfere with the objectives of the legal adoptive process. There are several reasons why legislators, child welfare practitioners, citizens' committees, and board members have been unable to eliminate or effectively control the black market and the illegal procurement and sale of infants. Most significant among these is the fact that unlawful practices are encouraged by the unavailability of child welfare services, financial assistance, and medical care for the unmarried mother, and by the unrealistic adoption practices of some child placing agencies. These are vitally important community issues if there is a genuine belief that adoption should be a "child-centered" process.

The unmarried mother very often finds herself rejected by her own family and by the father of her child. She may receive little financial help from either, and consequently she turns to a social agency, a doctor, lawyer, clergyman, or other professional source. If she brings

---

[48] *Ibid.*

[49] United States Children's Bureau, *Adoption in the United States and Its Territories, 1955*, Children's Bureau Statistical Series, No. 39 (Washington, D.C.: Government Printing Office, 1957), p. 1.

[50] *Ibid.*, p. 3.

her problem to a social agency, she will be told that she may apply for public assistance under the Aid to Dependent Children program, but she is likely to be required to go to the district attorney or another law enforcement official who will attempt to hold the alleged father financially responsible for the girl's care. Because many girls are unwilling to involve the alleged father, they do not proceed with their application for assistance. Another barrier exists when girls leave small home towns and go elsewhere until their baby is born. Some counties have reciprocity arrangements whereby a nonresident unmarried mother may receive assistance, with her own county reimbursing for her care. The girl who has left her home for the purposes of anonymity is not likely to accept assistance when told that it will be necessary to inform the public welfare department in her own community. Counties without reciprocity agreements often deny assistance to the nonresident girl and some private agencies cannot help any client who does not live within a designated community chest area. Some sectarian agencies will give service only to girls of a particular religious faith, and other agencies accept children for adoptive placement only when they are free of physical or mental defects, are of a certain race, or fulfill other eligibility requirements.[51]

The black market activities encouraged by these practices and by the great demand for babies often create deep tragedy for children, since many couples who are rejected by recognized adoption agencies as being unsuitable to assume the responsibilities of parenthood find children available to them through illegal channels. State laws prohibiting the placement of a child by anyone other than a parent or licensed child placing agency are sound in principle. Unless the community implements this legislation by providing the kinds and quality of care needed by the unmarried mother, however, she will have no choice about relinquishing her child and terminating all rights to him in order to receive the help she needs.

ADOPTION AS A SOCIAL PROCESS

One of the major purposes of marriage in Western culture is the procreation, nurture, and socialization of the offspring. Childless couples consequently reach out to fulfill their unmet maternal and paternal needs by caring for, loving, and rearing an adopted child.

---

[51] Michael Schapiro, *A Study of Adoption Practice*, Vol. I (New York: Child Welfare League of America, 1954), pp. 53–54.

The process of adoption then tends to complete the cultural image of the most sanctified and revered of our social institutions—marriage and the family. For this reason, adoption seems so "right" to the adopting parents that they hasten to reinforce the image by delightfully exclaiming how much the child resembles his new daddy, grandpa, or Uncle Bill. The child not only acquires a new set of parents, but he inherits a constellation of people and becomes a part of a unique familial structure that will have a lasting and significant influence on him.

Choosing permanent parents for a child is one of the most exacting and demanding tasks in the child welfare field. The social worker is aware that she is establishing a lifetime relationship between the child and the new parents and that hurried judgment, the desire to do something "nice" for a childless couple, or capitulation to community or agency pressure may bring hardship and unhappiness to all persons involved.

The Adoption Unit of the Sacramento County Department of Social Welfare interprets the worker's responsibility in an informative brochure that is made available to all adoptive applicants:

The agency recognizes that the baby, in his helplessness, cannot act as his own agent, and therefore his wishes cannot be known or respected. The agency, then, acts for him and is his representative in this relationship which will so profoundly affect his entire future. As his agent, the agency seeks to assure him a happy, secure stable home, complete with parents who will love him for himself, who will accept him as he is, who will understand him and his needs, and will expect no more from him than he can do. This . . . is the function of the adoption agency.[52]

The social worker's responsibilities to the child are of particular importance in relation to the implicit and explicit motivation for parenthood expressed by the adoptive applicant. Most applicants have a sincere desire to adopt because they feel that they have the capacity to love and care properly for a child, but others may express less healthy motivation. On one occasion a male adoptive applicant came to an adoption agency asking if he might "borrow" one of the infants for a few months to help his wife get over a nervous breakdown! Not all of the unsuitable applicants are this frank, and in many instances they are not aware of their real reasons for wanting a child. The agency, in safeguarding the child's future, must take responsi-

---

[52] Adoption Unit, Sacramento Department of Social Welfare, *The Child, the Agency and You!* (Sacramento: The Inland Press, 1955), pp. 3–4.

bility for knowing the couple as well as it can in terms of marital relationship, health, employment, stability, infertility and sterility,
family relations, attitudes toward illegitimacy and adoption, willingness to tell the child of his adoptive status, and other factors which will
prove to be important to the child and to his new family.

The agency also makes a careful study of the unmarried mother,
her family, her background, secures all possible information about the
natural father, and helps the mother to move toward relinquishment
of the child if that is her choice. The agency is therefore able to
assure the adopting couple that the child is legally free for adoption,
and that it will share pertinent information about the natural parents.
These aspects of the adoptive process are often missing in "independent placements," especially when intermediaries are involved.

THE ADOPTED CHILD

In 1955, the welfare departments reporting to the Children's Bureau
indicated that 73 per cent of the children involved in adoption petitions filed by unrelated petitioners were born out of wedlock, either
to an unmarried or married woman. Twenty-seven per cent of the
petitions involved children born in wedlock whose parent or parents
were dead, divorced, living together, or whose parents' whereabouts
were unknown.[53]

Adoption affects the natural parents, the adoptive parents, and
society, but its greatest influence is upon the child. Consequently,
"adoption agencies exist to find the best opportunity for a child; not
necessarily to find children for adults."[54] As Joseph Reid of the
Child Welfare League of America states:

Social agencies are placing children in order to find permanent family
homes for them. We are not placing children to save an unhappy
marriage, to try to prevent a woman from having a psychosis, or for
any of the other reasons concerned with fulfilling an adult's desire to
have children. Rather, we are attempting to fulfill the child's right to have
parents.[55]

Because the agency and society have placed the major emphasis
upon the child's welfare, the whole concept of adoption has changed

---

[53] *Adoptions in the United States and Its Territories, 1955*, p. 2.

[54] United States Children's Bureau, *Protecting Children in Adoption*, Publication 345 (Washington, D.C.: Government Printing Office, 1955), p. 26.

[55] *Ibid.*

in regard to the permanent placement of children. Children now regarded as adoptable would have spent their lives in institutions and foster homes only a few decades ago. Schapiro has pointed out that:

The upward adoption trend is . . . encouraged by a growing realization that adoption is appropriate for any child without family ties who is in need of a family and for whom a family can be found to meet his need.[56]

Because of this "child-centered" approach, adoption is now being considered for older children, handicapped, and children of minority groups. Fewer children are now considered to be "unadoptable" and many adoptive applicants are no longer seeking the "perfect child."

The adopted child is protected in the majority of states from any stigmatizing identification on his birth certificate. Such protection is usually less adequate for the child who is born out of wedlock but not placed for adoption. One state issues a white birth certificate for a child born in wedlock and a colored one for children registered as illegitimate. Another segregates birth records of children born out of wedlock and makes them available only after an interview with a designated clerk. In some states, however, birth certificates indicate the child's birth status and other personal information which could prove embarrassing and troublesome throughout the child's life.

The birth certificate issued for an adopted child usually does not reveal his original antecedents or any other personal information. In California, for example, after the state registrar has received a certificate of the adoption decree, a birth certificate is issued bearing the name of the child as shown on the adoption decree, the names of the adopting parents, their age, and the child's sex, date, and place of birth, but there is no mention of the adoption of the child.[57] This birth certificate supplants any other previously issued for the child and is the only one open for public inspection. The child's original birth certificate is filed with the state registrar or sealed by the local registrar or county recorder.[58]

Selected Bibliography

Allen, Winifred Y., and Doris Campbell. *The Creative Nursery Center.* New York: Family Service Association of America, 1953.

---

[56] Schapiro, *op. cit.*, p. 9.

[57] *Health and Safety Code*, Chapter 3, Article 5, 10252.

[58] *Ibid.*, 10253.5.

Bender, Lauretta. "There Is No Substitute for Family Life," *Child Study*, Vol. XXIII, No. 3, Spring 1946.

Burmeister, Eva. *Forty-Five in the Family*. New York: Columbia University Press, 1949.

Charnley, Jean. *The Art of Child Placement*. Minneapolis: University of Minnesota Press, 1955.

Crookes, Spencer H. "For the Child Who Must Live Away From His Own Home," *The Child*, Vol. 16, No. 6, February 1952.

Gordon, Henrietta L. *Casework Services for Children*. Boston: Houghton-Mifflin Company, 1956.

Hagan, Helen R. "Foster Care for Children," *Social Work Year Book, 1957*.

Hill, Esther P. "Is Foster Care the Answer?" *Public Welfare*, Vol. 15, No. 2, April 1957.

Hutchinson, Dorothy. *In Quest of Foster Parents*. New York: Columbia University Press, 1943.

Konopka, Gisela. *Group Work in the Institution*. New York: Whiteside, *and* Wm. Morrow and Company, 1954.

Kornitzer, Margaret. *Child Adoption in the Modern World*. New York: Philosophical Library, 1952.

Program Guides for Day Care Centers. Series C, *Some Qualities of a Good Teacher*. Springfield, Illinois: Department of Public Welfare, July 1954.

Schapiro, Michael. *A Study of Adoption Practice*, Vols. I and II (New York: National Child Labor Committee 1951), pp. 3–5.

Schulze, Susanne (ed.). *Creative Group Living in a Children's Institution*. New York: Association Press, 1951.

"Social Work in the Public Schools," *Social Work Papers*, Vol. 4. Los Angeles: The School of Social Work, University of Southern California, December 1956.

Thornhill, Margeret A. "Unprotected Adoptions," *Children*, Vol. 2, No. 5, September–October 1955.

United States Children's Bureau. *Foster Care, 1956*. Child Welfare Report, No. 8. Washington, D.C.: Government Printing Office, 1957.

Wrieden, Jane E. "To Strengthen Maternity Home Services for Unmarried Mothers," *The Child*, Vol. 16, No. 1, August–September 1951.

Young, Leontine R. "Personality Patterns in Unmarried Mothers," *The Family*, Vol. XXVI, No. 8, December 1945.

Name Index

Subject Index